The Spratly Islands and International Law

Queen Mary Studies in International Law

Edited by

Malgosia Fitzmaurice

VOLUME 46

The titles published in this series are listed at *brill.com/qmil*

The Spratly Islands and International Law

Legal Solutions to Coexistence and Cooperation in Disputed Areas

By

Xuechan Ma

BRILL
NIJHOFF

LEIDEN | BOSTON

The views in this book are those of the author and do not represent the position of the author's institution or affiliation.

The Library of Congress Cataloging-in-Publication Data is available online at https://catalog.loc.gov
LC record available at https://lccn.loc.gov/2021050524

Typeface for the Latin, Greek, and Cyrillic scripts: "Brill". See and download: brill.com/brill-typeface.

ISSN 1877-4822
ISBN 978-90-04-50432-5 (hardback)
ISBN 978-90-04-50433-2 (e-book)

This book is printed on acid-free paper and produced in a sustainable manner.

Contents

Acknowledgements

This book is a revised and updated version of the thesis that I defended on 19 May 2020 at Leiden University in fulfillment of my Ph.D. degree. The thesis would not have been completed without the generous help from my supervisors prof. dr. Nico Schrijver and dr. Cecily Rose. While I researched on how to bridge 'troubled waters' in the Spratly Islands through international law, prof. dr. Nico Schrijver was truly a bridge that guided me through 'troubles waters' during my Ph.D. journey not only with his extensive knowledge, rich experience and great passion on international law but also with his warm heart, kindness and compassion. I would also like to extend my deep gratitude to dr. Cecily Rose for her constructive discussions and countless inspiring comments and suggestions.

Special thanks also go to the members of my Ph.D. thesis reading committee for their valuable inputs and comments: prof. dr. Eric De Brabandere, prof. dr. Malgosia Fitzmaurice, prof. dr. Marcelo Kohen and prof. dr. Seline Trevisanut. I would further like to express my sincere appreciation to Ingeborg van der Laan, Brill's Associate Editor, to prof. dr. Malgosia Fitzmaurice, Editor of the Queen Mary Studies in International Law series, and to the anonymous reviewer, for their precious help in the process of preparing the manuscript for publication.

Notwithstanding the above contributions, the full and sole responsibility for the content of this book rests with the author, and the views in this book are those of the author and do not represent the position of the author's institution or affiliation. I would also like to thank Springer for the permission to use my previously published work as part of chapter 2 in this book.

I am much indebted to my dear friends and family, especially dr. Nicolás Bastidas, for support of various kinds during my Ph.D. journey. This book is dedicated to my parents, Yinggen Lin and Yawu Ma, with my deepest gratitude for their unconditional support and confidence in me.

Maps, Tables and Figures

Maps

Tables

Figures

Abbreviations

AFS	International Convention on the Control of Harmful Anti-fouling Systems on Ships
AJIL	American Journal of International Law
AMM	ASEAN Ministerial Meeting
ASEAN	Association of Southeast Asian Nations
APFIC	Asia-Pacific Fishery Commission
BIICL	British Institute of International and Comparative Law
BWM	International Convention for the Control and Management of Ships' Ballast Water and Sediments
BYIL	British Yearbook of International Law
CBD	Convention on Biological Diversity
CCRF	Code of Conduct for Responsible Fisheries
CITES	Convention on International Trade in Endangered Species of Wild Fauna and Flora
CJIL	Chinese Journal of International Law
CLCS	Commission on the Limits of the Continental Shelf
CMATS	Treaty between Australia and the Democratic Republic of Timor-Leste on Certain Maritime Arrangements in the Timor Sea
CNOOC	China National Offshore Oil Corporation
COC	Code of Conduct of Parties in the South China Sea
CODES	Code of Safety for Nuclear Merchant Ships
CSIS	Center for Strategic and International Studies
CTS	Convention on the Territorial Sea and Contiguous Zone
CUP	Cambridge University Press
DDT	Dichloro-Diphenyl-Trichloroethane
DOALOS	Division for Ocean Affairs and the Law of the Sea Office of Legal Affairs
DOC	Declaration on the Conduct of Parties in the South China Sea
EIA	Environmental Impact Assessment
EJIL	European Journal of International Law
FAO	Food and Agriculture Organization of the United Nations
FONOPS	Freedom of Navigation Programs

Friendly Relations Declaration	Declaration on Principles of International Law concerning Friendly Relations and Co-operation among State
GDP	Gross Domestic Product
GEF	Global Environment Facility
GHG	Greenhouse Gas
IBRU	International Boundaries Research Unit
ICLQ	International & Comparative Law Quarterly
ICJ	International Court of Justice
ICSID	International Centre for Settlement of Investment Disputes
IJMCL	International Journal of Marine and Coastal Law
ILC	International Law Commission
ISEAS	Institute of Southeast Asian Studies
ISNT	Informal Single Negotiating Text
ITLOS	International Tribunal for the Law of the Sea
IUU Fishing	Illegal, Unreported and Unregulated Fishing
JMSU	Joint Marine Seismic Undertaking
JOC	Joint Operating Committee
JPDA	Joint Petroleum Development Area
LJIL	Leiden Journal of International Law
London Convention	Convention on the Prevention of Marine Pollution by Dumping of Wastes and Other Matter
London Protocol	Protocol to the Convention on the Prevention of Marine Pollution by Dumping of Wastes and Other Matter
M	Nautical Mile(s)
MARPOL	International Convention for the Prevention of Pollution from Ships
MEPC	Marine Environment Protection Committee
MJIL	Melbourne Journal of International Law
MoU	Memorandum of Understanding
MPEPIL	Max Planck Encyclopedia of Public International Law
MSY	Maximum Sustainable Yield
MUP	Manchester University Press
NIAS	Nordic Institute of Asian Studies
North Vietnam	Democratic Republic of Vietnam
OCM	Ocean & Coastal Management
OCLJ	Ocean and Coastal Law Journal
ODA	Official Development Assistance

ODIL	Ocean Development & International Law
OES	Unite States Department of State Bureau of Oceans and International Environmental and Scientific Affairs
OPRC	International Convention on Oil Pollution Preparedness, Response and Co-operation
OUP	Oxford University Press
PCA	Permanent Court of Arbitration
PCIJ	Permanent Court of International Justice
PNOC	Philippine National Oil Company
PRC	People's Republic of China
PSSAs	Particularly Sensitive Sea Areas
RFMO	Regional Fisheries Management Organization
RIAA	Reports of International Arbitral Awards
ROC	Republic of China
SBT	Southern Bluefin Tuna
SDG	Sustainable Development Goal
SEAFDEC	Southeast Asian Fisheries Development Center
SOLAS	International Convention for the Safety of Life at Sea
SPLOS	Meeting of States Parties on UNCLOS
South Vietnam	Republic of Vietnam
Stan. J. Int'l L	Stanford Journal of International Law
SYBIL	Singapore Year Book of International Law
TAC	Total Allowable Catch
TPP	Trans-Pacific Partnership
UK	United Kingdom
UN	United Nations
UNCLOS	United Nations Convention on the Law of the Sea
UNCLOS I	The First United Nations Conference on the Law of the Sea
UNCLOS III	The Third United Nations Conference on the Law of the Sea
UNEP	United Nations Environment Programme
UNFSA	Agreement for the Implementation of the Provisions of the United Nations Convention on the Law of the Sea of 10 December 1982 relating to the Conservation and Management of Straddling Fish Stocks and Highly Migratory Fish Stocks
US	United States of America
USSR	Union of Soviet Socialist Republics
UNTS	United Nations Treaty Series
WTO	World Trade Organization
WWII	World War II

Table of Cases

PCIJ

Electricity Company of Sofia and Bulgaria (*Belgium v. Bulgaria*), Interim Measures of Protection, Order of 5 December 1939, PCIJ Series A/B, No. 79.

German Settlers in Poland, Advisory Opinion of 10 September 1923, PCIJ Series B No. 6.

Legal Status of Eastern Greenland (*Denmark v. Norway*), Judgment of 5 April 1933, PCIJ Series A/B No. 53.

Mavrommatis Palestine Concessions (*Greece v. Britain*), Judgment of 30 August 1924, PCIJ Series A No. 2.

ICJ

Aegean Sea Continental Shelf (*Greece v. Turkey*), Request for the Indication of Interim Measures of Protection, Order of 11 September 1976.

Application of the International Convention on the Elimination of All Forms of Racial Discrimination (*Georgia v. Russian Federation*), Preliminary Objections, Judgment of 1 April 2011.

Armed Activities on the Territory of the Congo (*New Application: 2002*) (*Democratic Republic of the Congo v. Rwanda*), Jurisdiction of the Court and Admissibility of the Application, Judgment of 3 February 2006.

Asylum (*Colombia v. Peru*), Dissenting Opinion by Judge Alvarez of 20 November 1950.

Certain Activities carried out by Nicaragua in the Border Area (*Costa Rica v. Nicaragua*), Provisional Measures Order of 8 March 2011; Separate opinion of Judge Koroma of 8 March 2011; and Separate opinion of Judge Sepúlveda-Amor of 8 March 2011.

Continental Shelf (*Libyan Arab Jamahiriya/Malta*), Judgment of 3 June 1985.

Delimitation of the Maritime Boundary in the Gulf of Maine Area (*Canada/United States of America*), Judgment of 12 October 1984.

East Timor (*Portugal v. Australia*), Judgment of 30 June 1995.

Fisheries (*United Kingdom v. Norway*), Judgment of 18 December 1951.

Fisheries Jurisdiction (*Spain v. Canada*), Judgment of 4 December 1998.

Fisheries Jurisdiction (*United Kingdom of Great Britain and Northern Ireland v. Iceland*), Provisional Measures, Order of 17 August 1972.

Frontier Dispute (*Burkina Faso/Republic of Mali*), Judgment of 22 December 1986.
Gabčíkovo-Nagymaros Project (*Hungary/Slovakia*), Judgment of 25 September 1997.
Land and Maritime Boundary between Cameroon and Nigeria (*Cameroon v. Nigeria: Equatorial Guinea intervening*), Preliminary Objections Judgment of 11 June 1998; and Judgment of 10 October 2002.
Land, Island and Maritime Frontier Dispute (*El Salvador/Honduras: Nicaragua intervening*), Judgment of 11 September 1992.
Legality of the Threat or Use of Nuclear Weapons, Advisory Opinion of 8 July 1996.
Maritime Delimitation and Territorial Questions between Qatar and Bahrain (*Qatar v. Bahrain*), Judgment of 16 March 2001.
Military and Paramilitary Activities in and against Nicaragua (*Nicaragua v. United States of America*), Judgment of 27 June 1986.
Minquiers and Ecrehos Case (*France v. United Kingdom*), Judgment of 17 November 1953; and Individual Opinion of Judge Basdevant of 17 November 1953.
North Sea Continental Shelf Cases (*Federal Republic of Germany/Denmark or Netherlands*), Judgment of 20 February 1969; and Dissenting Opinion of Judge Sørensen of 20 February 1969.
Passage through the Great Belt (*Finland v. Denmark*), Request for the Indication of Provisional Measures, Separate Opinion of Judge Shahabuddeen attached to Order of 29 July 1991.
Pulp Mills on the River Uruguay (*Argentina v. Uruguay*), Judgment of 20 April 2010.
Questions relating to the Obligation to Prosecute or Extradite (*Belgium v. Senegal*), Request for the Indication of Provisional Measures, Order of 28 May 2009.
Request for Interpretation of the Judgment of 15 June 1962 in the Case concerning the Temple of Preah Vihear (*Cambodia v. Thailand*), Request for the Indication of Provisional Measures, Order of 18 July 2011.
South West Africa (*Ethiopia/Liberia v. South Africa*), Judgment of 21 December 1962.
Sovereignty over Pedra Branca/Pulau Batu Puteh, Middle Rocks and South Ledge (*Malaysia/Singapore*), Judgment of 23 May 2008.
Sovereignty over Pulau Ligitan and Pulau Sipadan (*Indonesia/Malaysia*), Judgment of 17 December 2002.
Territorial and Maritime Dispute (*Nicaragua v. Colombia*), Judgment of 19 November 2012.
Territorial and Maritime Dispute between Nicaragua and Honduras in the Caribbean Sea (*Nicaragua v. Honduras*), Judgment of 8 October 2007.

ITLOS

Case concerning Land Reclamation by Singapore in and around the Straits of Johor (*Malaysia v. Singapore*), Provisional Measures, Order of 8 October 2003.

Dispute Concerning Delimitation of the Maritime Boundary between Ghana and Côte d'Ivoire in the Atlantic Ocean (*Ghana/Côte d'Ivoire*), Provisional Measures Order of 25 April 2015; Judgment of 23 September 2017; and Separate opinion of Judge Paik of 23 September 2017.

MOX Plant Case (*Ireland v. United Kingdom*), Provisional Measures, Order of 3 December 2001.

Responsibilities and obligations of States sponsoring persons and entities with respect to activities in the Area (*Request for Advisory Opinion submitted to the Seabed Disputes Chamber*), Advisory Opinion of 1 February 2011.

Southern Bluefin Tuna Cases (*New Zealand v. Japan; Australia v. Japan*), Provisional Measures Order of 27 August 1999; and Separate opinion of Judge Treves of 27 August 1999.

Arbitral Awards

Arbitration between the Republic of Croatia and the Republic of Slovenia, Final Award of 29 June 2017.

Arbitration on Territorial Sovereignty and Scope of the Dispute (*Eritrea/Yemen*), Award on the First Stage of 9 October 1998, RIAA, Vol. XXII.

Arctic Sunrise Arbitration (*Netherlands v. Russia*), Award on the Merits of 14 August 2015.

Award between the United States and the United Kingdom relating to the Rights of Jurisdiction of United States in the Bering's Sea and the Preservation of Fur Seals, Decision of 15 August 1893.

Award in the Arbitration regarding the Delimitation of the Abyei Area between the Government of Sudan and the Sudan People's Liberation Movement/Army, Award of 22 June 2009.

Claims Arising Out of Decisions of the Mixed Graeco-German Arbitral Tribunal set up under Article 304 in Part X of the Treaty of Versailles (*Between Greece and the Federal Republic of Germany*), Decision of 26 January 1972, RIAA, Vol. XIX.

Clipperton Island (*France v. Mexico*), Decision of 28 January 1931.

Guyana v. Suriname, Award of 17 September 2007.

Island of Palmas (*The United States of America v. The Netherlands*), Award of 4 April 1928.

Land Reclamation by Singapore in and around the Straits of Johor (*Malaysia/Singapore*), Award on Agreed Terms of 1 September 2005.

Meerauge (*Austria/Hungary*), Arbitral Award of 13 September 1902, RIAA Vol. XXVIII.

MOX Plant Case (*Ireland v. United Kingdom*), Order No. 6 (Termination of Proceedings) of 6 June 2008.

S. S. 'I'm Alone' (*Canada, United States*), Awards of 30 June 1930, 5 January 1935, RIAA, Vol. III.

Second stage of the proceedings between Eritrea/Yemen (*Maritime Delimitation*), Decision of 17 December 1999.

The Chamizal Case (*Mexico/United States*), Arbitral Award of 15 June 1911, RIAA Vol. XI.

The South China Sea Arbitration (*The Philippines v. China*), Award on Jurisdiction and Admissibility of 29 October 2015; and Award of 12 July 2016.

Others

Conciliation between The Democratic Republic of Timor-Leste and The Commonwealth of Australia, Decision on Competence of 19 September 2016.

Eritrea-Ethiopia Claims Commission – Partial Award: Jus Ad Bellum – Ethiopia's Claims 1-8, 19 December 2005, RIAA, Vol. XXVI.

Investigation of Certain Incidents Affecting the British Trawler Red Crusader (*UK/Denmark*), Report of 23 March 1962 (Commission of Enquiry), RIAA, Vol. XXIX.

Report and Recommendations of the Compulsory Conciliation Commission between Timor-Leste and Australia on the Timor Sea, 9 May 2018.

US-Import Prohibition of Certain Shrimp and Shrimp Products, WT/DS58/AB/R, Appellate Body Report of 12 October 1998 (WTO).

List of Treaties

Agreement between Norway and Iceland on the Continental Shelf between Iceland and Jan Mayen, adopted 22 October 1981, entered into force 2 June 1982, 2124 *UNTS* 247.
Agreement between Saudi Arabia and Sudan relating to Joint Exploration and Exploitation of Red Sea Seabed and Subsoil Resources, adopted 16 May 1974, entered into force 26 August 1974, 952 *UNTS* 193.
Agreement between the Government of the Kingdom of Sweden and the Government of the Russian Federation in the Fields of Fisheries, adopted 11 December 1992, entered into force 10 August 1993, 1823 *UNTS* 103.
Agreement between the Kingdom of Saudi Arabia and the State of Kuwait on the Partition of the Neutral Zone, adopted 7 July 1965, entered into force 10 July 1963, 1750 *UNTS* 39.
Agreement between the Libyan Arab Socialist People's Jamahiriya and the Republic of Tunisia to Implement the Judgment of the International Court of Justice in the Tunisia/Libya Continental Shelf Case, adopted 8 August 1988.
Agreement between the USSR and Sweden on Mutual Relations in the Field of Fisheries, adopted 22 December 1977, entered into force 24 January 1980, 1260 *UNTS* 220.
Agreement concerning Joint Development of the Southern Part of the Continental Shelf Adjacent to Japan and South Korea (with map, appendix, agreed minutes and exchanges of notes), adopted 30 January 1974, entered into force 22 June 1978, 1225 *UNTS* 113.
Agreement concerning Settlement of Offshore Boundaries and Ownership of Islands between Qatar and the United Arab Emirates, adopted and entered into force 20 March 1969, 2402 *UNTS* 49.
Agreement Establishing the Southeast Asian Fisheries Development Center, adopted and entered into force 28 December 1967, 651 *UNTS* 20.
Agreement for Cooperation in dealing with Pollution of the North Sea by Oil and Other Harmful Substances, adopted 13 September 1983, entered into force 1 September 1989, 1605 *UNTS* 34.
Agreement for the Establishment of the Indo-Pacific Fisheries Council (later became the Asia-Pacific Fishery Commission), adopted 15–29 November 1948, entered into force 9 November 1948, 120 *UNTS* 59.
Agreement on Port State Measures to Prevent, Deter and Eliminate Illegal, Unreported and Unregulated Fishing, adopted 22 November 2009, entered into force 5 June 2016, *UNTS* Registration No. 54133.

Agreement on the Constitution and Other Matters Relating to the Establishment of the Malaysia-Thailand Joint Authority, adopted 30 May 1990.

Agreement relating to the Exploitation of the Frigg Field Reservoir and the Transmission of Gas therefrom to the United Kingdom (with annexes), adopted 10 May 1976, entered into force 22 July 1977, 1098 *UNTS* 3.

Agreement to Promote Compliance with International Conservation and Management Measures by Fishing Vessels on the High Seas, adopted 24 November 1993, entered into force 24 April 2003, 2221 *UNTS* 91.

Bahrain-Saudi Arabia Frontier Agreement, adopted and entered into force 22 February 1958, 1733 *UNTS* 3.

Convention between the Government of the French Republic and the Government of the Spanish State on the Delimitation of the Continental Shelves of the two States in the Bay of Biscay, adopted 29 January 1974, entered into force 5 April 1975, 996 *UNTS* 344.

Convention on Biological Diversity, adopted 5 June 1992, entered into force 29 December 1993, 1760 *UNTS* 79.

Convention on International Trade in Endangered Species of Wild Fauna and Flora, adopted 3 March 1973, entered into force 1 July 1975, 993 *UNTS* 243.

Convention on the Control of Transboundary Movements of Hazardous Wastes and their Disposal, adopted 22 March 1989, entered into force 5 May 1992, 1673 *UNTS* 57.

Convention on the High Seas, adopted 29 April 1958, entered into force 30 September 1962, 450 *UNTS* 11.

Convention on the Prevention of Marine Pollution by Dumping of Wastes and Other Matter, adopted 29 December 1972, entered into force 30 August 1975, 1046 *UNTS* 120.

Convention on the Territorial Sea and the Contiguous Zone, adopted 29 April 1958, entered into force 10 September 1964, 516 *UNTS* 205.

Exclusive Economic Zone Co-operation Treaty between the State of Barbados and the Republic of Guyana concerning the exercise of jurisdiction in their exclusive economic zones in the area of bilateral overlap within each of their outer limits and beyond the outer limits of the exclusive economic zones of other States (with annex and figure), adopted 2 December 2003, entered into force 5 May 2004, 2277 *UNTS* 201.

Management and Cooperation Agreement between the Government of the Republic of Senegal and the Government of the Republic of Guinea-Bissau, adopted 14 October 1993, entered into force 21 December 1995, 1903 *UNTS* 3.

Maritime Delimitation Treaty between Jamaica and the Republic of Colombia (with chart), adopted 12 November 1993, entered into force 14 March 1994, 1776 *UNTS* 17.

Montevideo Convention on the Rights and Duties of States, adopted 26 December 1933, entered into force 26 December 1934.

International Convention on the Control of Harmful Anti-fouling Systems on Ships, adopted 5 October 2001, entered into force 17 September 2008.

International Convention for the Prevention of Pollution from Ships, adopted 2 November 1973, 1340 *UNTS* 184; Amended by Protocol of 1978 Relating to the International Convention for the Prevention of Pollution from Ships, adopted 17 February 1978, entered into force 2 October 1983, 1340 *UNTS* 61.

International Convention for the Safety of Life at Sea, adopted 1 November 1974, entered into force 25 May 1980, 1184 *UNTS* 277.

Protocol to the Agreement of 14 October 1993, concerning the Organization and Operation of the Management and Cooperation Agency, adopted 12 June 1995, entered into force 21 December 1995, 1903 *UNTS* 7.

Protocol to the Convention on the Prevention of Marine Pollution by Dumping of Wastes and Other Matter 1972, adopted 11 July 1996, entered into force 24 March 2006.

Sino-Japanese Peace Treaty (also known as the Treaty of Taipei), adopted 28 April 1952, entered into force 5 August 1952.

Timor Sea Treaty between East Timor and Australia, adopted 20 May 2002, entered into force 2 April 2003, 2258 *UNTS* 3.

Treaty between Australia and the Democratic Republic of Timor-Leste on Certain Maritime Arrangements in the Timor Sea, adopted 12 January 2006, entered into force 23 February 2007, 2483 *UNTS* 359.

Treaty between Australia and the Democratic Republic of Timor-Leste Establishing their Maritime Boundaries in the Timor Sea, adopted on 6 March 2018, entered into force 30 August 2019.

Treaty between Australia and the Republic of Indonesia on the Zone of Cooperation in an Area between the Indonesian Province of East Timor and Northern Australia, adopted 11 December 1989, entered into force 9 February 1991, 1654 *UNTS* 105.

Treaty between the Federal Republic of Nigeria and the Democratic Republic of Sao Tome and Principe on the Joint Development of Petroleum and other Resources, in respect of Areas of the Exclusive Economic Zone of the Two States, adopted 21 February 2001, entered into force 16 January 2003.

Treaty concerning the Archipelago of Spitsbergen, adopted 9 February 1920, entered into force 14 August 1925, 2 *UNTS* 7.

Treaty of Peace with Japan, adopted 8 September 1951, entered into force 28 April 1951, 136 *UNTS* 45.

Treaty on Principles Governing the Activities of States in the Exploration and Use of Outer Space, Including the Moon and other Celestial Bodies, adopted 27 January 1967, entered into force 10 October 1967, 610 *UNTS* 205.

United Nations Agreement for the Implementation of the Provisions of the United Nations Convention on the Law of the Sea of 10 December 1982 relating to the Conservation and Management of Straddling Fish Stocks and Highly Migratory Fish Stocks, adopted 4 August 1995, entered into force 11 December 2001, 2167 *UNTS* 3.

United Nations Charter, adopted 26 June 1945, entered into force 24 October 1945.

United Nations Convention on the Law of the Sea, adopted 10 December 1982, entered into force 16 November 1994, 1833 *UNTS* 396.

Vienna Convention on the Law of Treaties, adopted 23 May 1969, entered into force 27 January 1980, 1155 *UNTS* 331.

CHAPTER 1

Introduction

The modern development of the law of the sea in the twentieth century has enabled coastal States to claim a vast area of the seas to be under their jurisdiction, thus significantly increasing overlapping claims and generating or exacerbating maritime disputes between States.[1] As a result of the proliferation of sovereign rights at sea, the maritime dispute in the Spratly Islands area profoundly affects the international relations between the disputant States, which consist of China, Vietnam, the Philippines, Malaysia and Brunei.[2] Considering that the delimitation of maritime boundaries can be time-consuming and sometimes even politically impossible,[3] it is essential for the disputant States to think about how to handle their international relations when no maritime boundary is in place. Hence, this book focuses on the legal problems arising from the absence of maritime boundaries in the Spratly Islands area and tentatively provides legal solutions to these problems.

1.1 Historical Background of the Spratly Islands Dispute

The Spratly Islands area is located between 11°30' to 4° N and 109°30' to 117°50' E (Map 1),[4] and it spreads out over a vast area of ocean measuring 240,000 km^2, roughly equivalent to the size of the United Kingdom (UK).[5] It is clustered in a semi-enclosed sea,[6] namely the South China Sea, in the shape of

1 R.R. Churchill and V. Lowe, *The Law of the Sea* (MUP 3rd ed. 1999), 13–22. T. Treves, Historical Development of the Law of the Sea, in D.R. Rothwell *et al.* (eds.), *The Oxford Handbook of the Law of the Sea* (OUP. 2015), 1–2.

2 B. Womack, The Spratlys: From Dangerous Ground to Apple of Discord, 33 *Contemporary Southeast Asia: A Journal of International and Strategic Affairs* (2011), 370.

3 S.P. Kim, *Maritime Delimitation and Interim Arrangements in North East Asia* (Martinus Nijhoff Publishers. 2004), 1, 315.

4 D. Heinzig, *Disputed Islands in the South China Sea: Paracels, Spratlys, Pratas, Macclesfield Bank* (Otto Harrassowitz. 1976), 17. L. Odgaard, *Maritime Security Between China and Southeast Asia: Conflict and Cooperation in the Making of Regional Order* (Ashgate. 2002), 61. M. Samuels, *Contest for the South China Sea* (Taylor & Francis. 1982), 188.

5 D.J. Dzurek, *The Spratly Islands Dispute: Who's On First?* (IBRU. 1996), 1.

6 The South China Sea Arbitration (The Philippines v. China), Award of 12 July 2016 (PCA), para.3. According to Article 122 of UNCLOS, an 'enclosed or semi-closed sea' refers to 'a gulf, basin or sea surrounded by two or more State and connected to another sea or the

 | DOI:10.1163/9789004504332_002

a parallelogram between the Philippine island of Palawan and the southeast coast of Vietnam.[7] This area, known as a navigational hazard in the South China Sea, had been known to navigators at least since 225–230 A.D.[8]

The territorial dispute over the islands emerged nearly ninety years ago between China and France when France, as a colonial power in Asia, proclaimed the occupation of some islands in this region by virtue of a decree in 1933.[9] The occupation met diplomatic protests from the Chinese government, asserting that only Chinese fishers lived on these islands and that the islands belonged to the territory of China.[10] The French occupation did not last long. Japan occupied this area by the end of 1939, which constituted part of the Asian beginnings of what would become the Second World War (WWII).[11] In the post-war era, under French sponsorship, a delegation sent by the Republic of Vietnam (South Vietnam) participated in the 1951 San Francisco Peace Conference and declared the Vietnamese sovereignty over the Spratly Islands.[12] By contrast, the Democratic Republic of Vietnam (North Vietnam) held a different position, supporting China's authority over the Spratly Islands.[13] Subsequently, the Philippines and Malaysia entered into this territorial dispute in the 1970s when their troops started to visit and control some maritime features in the Spratly Islands.[14] Moreover, since North Vietnam and South Vietnam were officially reunited as the Socialist Republic of Vietnam (Vietnam) in 1976, Vietnam has been following South Vietnam's positions regarding this region.[15]

In contrast to the territorial dispute, the maritime dispute has a shorter history. In the early 1970s, coastal States bordering the South China Sea were

---

ocean by a narrow outlet or consisting entirely or primarily of the territorial seas and exclusive economic zones of two or more coastal States'. See United Nations Convention on the Law of the Sea, adopted 10 December 1982, entered into force 16 November 1994, 1833 *UNTS* 396, Article 122.

7 D. Denoon and S.J. Brams, Fair Division: A New Approach to the Spratly Islands Controversy, 2 *International Negotiation* (1997), 304.

8 Heinzig, n 4, 22. B.K. Murphy, Dangerous Ground: The Spratly Islands and International Law, 1 *OCLJ* (1995), 188.

9 Journal officiel de la Republique Francaise, No. 172 (25 July 1933), 7794, available at <https://gallica.bnf.fr/ark:/12148/bpt6k6546978f/f46.image>.

10 Z. Han, *The Collection of the Historical Materials of the Islands in South China Sea* (*Wo Guo Nan Hai Zhu Dao Shi Liao Hui Bian* (Eastern Publishing House. 1988), 261. Dzurek, n 5, 10. Murphy, n 8, 191.

11 Dzurek, n 5, 11. Murphy, n 8, 191.

12 M.M. Whiteman, *Digest of International Law*, Vol. 3 (Department of State publications. 1964), 595. Dzurek, n 5, 15–16.

13 Heinzig, n 4, 37.

14 Dzurek, n 5, 21–22.

15 Dzurek, n 5, 19.

stimulated by the prospect of finding rich hydrocarbon resources in this region.[16] Meanwhile, legal developments in the law of the sea, notably the third UN Conference on the Law of the Sea (UNCLOS III, 1973–1982), provided these States with an opportunity to claim sovereign rights to resources in vast maritime areas beyond their immediate coasts.[17] This historical background also explained why the Philippines, Malaysia and North Vietnam all began to assert titles to the islands of this area in the 1970s.

Owing to the geographical setting of the Spratly Islands area,[18] once Vietnam, the Philippines, Malaysia and Brunei claimed 200-nautical-mile (M) exclusive economic zones (EEZs) and continental shelves generated respectively from their mainland or archipelagic territories, these claimed areas would inevitably extend over the Spratly Islands area. China also claims an EEZ and continental shelf generated from the islands.[19] Therefore, in theory, once these disputant States adopted the regimes of the 200-M EEZ and continental shelf, their maritime claims would undoubtedly overlap with one another in the Spratly Islands area. In reality, a disputed marine area came into existence in the 1970s. Though the Philippines and Malaysia had passed domestic laws to claim sovereign rights over the continental shelf in the 1960s, such legislation did not set out precise outer limits.[20] It was not until the 1970s when the disputant States started to adopt national legislation to formally claim an EEZ and/or continental shelf with a breadth of 200 M that overlapping maritime claims occurred in this region (Table 1).[21]

16 Y.-H. Song and S. Tonnesson, The Impact of the Law of the Sea Convention on Conflict and Conflict Management in the South China Sea, 44 *ODIL* (2013), 238. Murphy, n 8, 188. Dzurek, n 5, 18.

17 Song and Tonnesson, n 16, 238–239.

18 The Shortest distances from the coastal States to the center of the Spratly Islands are measured as about 540 M from Hainan Island of China, 860 M from Taiwan, 330 M from the Cam Ranh Bay of Vietnam, 247 M from Kota Kinabalu of Malaysia, and 200 M from Brooke's Point of the Philippines. It is also about 405 M from the center of Paracel Islands. See C. Lin, Taiwan's South China Sea Policy, 37 *Asian Survey* (1997), 328. Heinzig, n 4, 18.

19 China claimed in a note *verbale* that 'China's Nansha Islands [the Spratly Islands] is fully entitled to Territorial Sea, Exclusive Economic Zone (EEZ) and Continental Shelf'. See China, Note Verbale No. CML/8/2011 (14 April 2011).

20 The Philippines, Presidential Proclamation No. 370 'Declaring as Subject to the Jurisdiction and Control of the Republic of the Philippines all Mineral and other Natural Resources in the Continental Shelf' (1968), para.4. Malaysia, Continental Shelf Act 1966 (28 July 1966), Article 2.

21 UNCLOS explicitly stipulates that the rights enjoyed by a coastal State over the continental shelf are inherent and do not depend on any express proclamation. It follows that when UNCLOS became binding on the disputant States in the 1990s, or even at an earlier time when the regime of the continental shelf, with its rule on entitlement by reason of

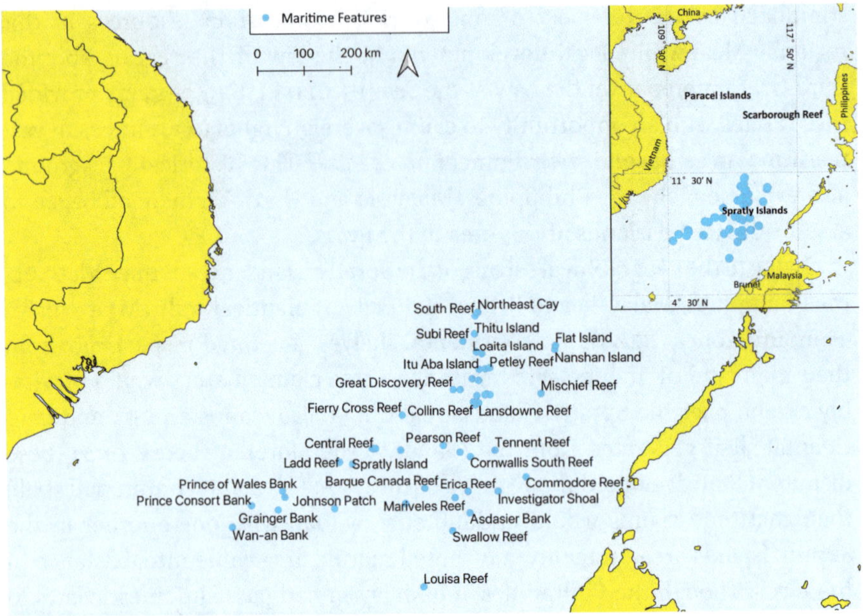

MAP 1 The geographical setting of the Spratly Islands area
Notes: The author produced this illustrative map using the QGIS software. The coordinates of the maritime features are obtained from GoogleEarth.

1.2 Unilateralism, Cooperation and Request for Legal Responses

States tend to undertake diverse activities in disputed marine areas preceding delimitation, including offshore hydrocarbon activities, fisheries and land reclamation.[22] The Spratly Islands area is not exceptional. Sporadic oil exploration activities, especially seismic surveys, are reported to have occurred in this region.[23] Some disputant States, including China, Vietnam and the

---

distance, was recognized to become a rule of customary international law in the 1980s, the disputant States were automatically entitled to claim maritime entitlements over a continental shelf out to a distance of at least 200 M for their land territories, thus resulting in contested areas of overlapping claims. See UNCLOS, Article 77(3). Continental Shelf (Libyan Arab Jamahiriya/Malta), Judgment of 3 June 1985 (ICJ), para.32-34. R.R. Churchill, The Greenland-Jan Mayen Case and its Significance for the International Law of Maritime Boundary Delimitation, 9 *IJMCL* (1994), 1, 13.

22 N. Schrijver, Law of the Sea, in W.J.M. van Genugten, *et al.* (eds.), *Discover International Law: With Special Attention for the Hague, City of Peace and Justice* (Wolf Legal Publishers. 2017), 197.

23 J. Laude, China gunboats harass RP vessel (4 March 2011), available at <http://www.philstar.com/headlines/662502/china-gunboats-harass-rp-vessel>. C. Buckley, China accuses

TABLE 1 National legislation on EEZ and/or continental shelf and ratification of UNCLOS by the disputant States

Disputant states	National legislation on EEZ and continental shelf	Ratification of UNCLOS (in force since 16 November 1994)
Brunei	– 1993 Declaration on the Exclusive Economic Zone	5 November 1996
China	– 1998 Law on the Exclusive Economic Zone and the Continental Shelf	7 June 1996
Malaysia	– 1966 Continental Shelf Act – 1978 Proclamation of the Economic Zone – 1984 Exclusive Economic Zone Act	14 October 1996
Philippines	– 1968 Presidential Proclamation No. 370 Declaring as Subject to the Jurisdiction and Control of the Republic of the Philippines all Mineral and other Natural Resources in the Continental Shelf – 1978 Presidential Decree No. 1599 Establishing an Exclusive Economic Zone and for Other Purposes	8 May 1984
Vietnam	– 1977 Statement on the Territorial Sea, the Contiguous Zone, the Exclusive Economic Zone and the Continental Shelf	25 July 1994

Notes: The author made this table based on the deposits on national legislation submitted by these States to the UN Secretary-General. For the status of UNCLOS in relation to the disputant States, see Chronological lists of ratifications of, accessions and successions to UNCLOS and the related Agreements, available at <http://www.un.org/depts/los/reference_files/chronological_lists_of_ratifications.htm>.

Vietnam in escalating sea tensions (10 June 2011), available at <https://www.reuters.com/article/us-china-vietnam/china-accuses-vietnam-in-escalating-sea-tensions-idUSTRE75904N20110610>.

Philippines, have declared or issued oil lease blocks over part of the disputed waters.[24] As regards fisheries, all the disputant States have been licensing or authorizing fishing in this region.[25] Moreover, China, Malaysia, the Philippines and Vietnam have all undertaken land reclamation projects on their controlled islands.[26] Notably, such conduct is of a unilateral nature owing to the absence of any binding provisional arrangement at the moment and might act as a catalyst for international conflicts.[27]

Apart from unilateral conduct, the disputant States have expressed their willingness to negotiate and undertake cooperative arrangements concerning 'less sensitive issues' than natural resources exploitation, such as marine environmental protection.[28] For instance, under the Declaration on the Conduct of Parties in the South China Sea (DOC) of 2002, China and ASEAN, to which Vietnam, the Philippines, Malaysia and Brunei are member States, recognized the possibility of exploring or undertaking cooperative activities in fields including marine environmental protection pending a comprehensive and durable settlement of the disputes in the South China Sea.[29] Subsequently, in 2017, China and ASEAN endorsed a framework of the Code of Conduct of Parties in the South China Sea (COC), reaffirming these States' commitments to explore and undertake cooperative arrangements.[30]

24 The South China Sea Arbitration, n 6, para.652. OES, China: Maritime Claims in the South China Sea, *Limits in the Seas* (5 December 2014), 16. Crisis Group, Stirring up the South China Sea (IV): Oil in Troubled Waters (27 January 2016), available at <https://medium.com/@CrisisGroup/stirring-up-the-south-china-sea-iv-oil-in-troubled-waters-7d4b7286aaco>.

25 A. Greer, The South China Sea Is Really a Fishery Dispute (20 July 2016), available at <https://thediplomat.com/2016/07/the-south-china-sea-is-really-a-fishery-dispute/>.

26 For more information regarding land reclamation projects in the Spratly Islands area, see Center for Strategic and International Studies (CSIS), Asia Maritime Transparency Initiative, available at <https://amti.csis.org/>.

27 Unilateral State conduct is not a rare phenomenon in the international arena. From the perspective of international law, a distinction can be made between unilateral acts and bilateral/multilateral acts in terms of State conduct. The former is the result of the will of one sovereign State alone while the will of two or more States participate in the latter. See Asylum (Colombia v. Peru), Dissenting Opinion by Judge Alvarez (ICJ), 290. BIICL, *Report on the Use of Force in relation to Sovereignty Disputes over Land Territory* (2018), para.25.

28 China and Vietnam, Agreement to Guide Settlement of Maritime Issues (11 October 2011), available at <http://www.gov.cn/jrzg/2011-10/12/content_1966682.htm>.

29 ASEAN and China, Declaration on the Conduct of Parties in the South China Sea (2002), para.6(a).

30 P. Parameswaran, Will a China-ASEAN South China Sea Code of Conduct Really Matter? (5 August 2017), available at <https://thediplomat.com/2017/08/will-a-china-asean-south-china-sea-code-of-conduct-really-matter/>.

The duality of the unilateralism and cooperation in international relations corresponds to the duality of international law. International law has been primarily divided between the law of coexistence and the law of cooperation since the end of WWII.[31] The law of coexistence grows out of the need for survival or avoidance of armed conflicts due to conflicting interests of States and mainly consists of a collection of 'don'ts', or said differently, prohibitive rules that restrain sovereign States from conducting specific activities that could aggravate the dispute and finally lead to armed conflicts.[32] By contrast, the law of cooperation seeks to pursue the realization of common interests shared by sovereign States through cooperation[33] and essentially contains incentive rules that endow States with particular rights or obligations to take active measures necessary for promoting positive cooperation and common interests.[34] These incentive rules are usually established and implemented by way of treaties and, in some cases, permanent international organizations.[35]

On the one hand, the prevalence of unilateralism in the Spratly Islands area reflects the proliferation of sovereign rights and the consequent multiplication of clashing national interests, which express the need for the law of coexistence. The prohibitive rules contained in the law of coexistence are based on the mutual respect for each other's sovereignty and sovereign rights, denoting the principle of mutual restraint and serving as an instrument for preserving the *status quo*.[36] Admitting the existence of the deep-seated conflicts of national interests between the disputant States, the law of coexistence requires these States to deal with each other in continuous attempts to adjust their respective national interests in order to avoid armed conflicts or wars.[37] Wars were no longer a lawful means to settle disputes after the 1928 Kellogg Pact and,

31 W. Friedmann, *The Changing Structure of International Law* (Columbia University Press. 1964), 297. P.M. Dupuy, International Law: Torn between Coexistence, Cooperation and Globalization. General Conclusions, 9 *EJIL* (1998), 285–286.

32 Friedmann, n 31, 89.

33 Friedmann, n 31, 58–59.

34 For example, the Outer Space Treaty provides that State parties are obliged to co-operate with each other in exchanging information and in developing the knowledge and research capabilities of all States. See Treaty on Principles Governing the Activities of States in the Exploration and Use of Outer Space, Including the Moon and other Celestial Bodies, adopted 27 January 1967, entered into force 10 October 1967, 610 *UNTS* 205.

35 Friedmann, n 31, 61–62. For the discussion about the forms of international cooperation, see R. Wolfrum, Cooperation, International Law of, *MPEPIL* (2010), para.39.

36 Wolfrum opined that perhaps the most crucial prohibitive rule in the entire traditional law of coexistence is the rule of prohibition of the threat or use of force as set out by way of general treaties. See Wolfrum, n 35, para.7.

37 Friedmann, n 31, 16.

subsequently, the United Nations (UN) came into operation.[38] Rather, peaceful settlement of international disputes has become a key principle in contemporary international law.[39] Tailored to the Spratly Islands area, it is reasonable to anticipate that the law of coexistence does not aim to preclude all kinds of unilateral activities and turn this region into a 'forbidden zone'.[40] Therefore, a question that presents itself is what are the legal parameters to determine what sort of unilateral conduct should be prohibited and what should be permissible.

The disputant States' desire for cooperation, on the other hand, represents their pursuit of common interests in specific areas of inter-State relations, which falls within the scope of the law of cooperation. The term 'cooperation' can be defined as 'the voluntary co-ordinated action of two or more States which takes place under a legal regime and serves a specific objective'.[41] Conceived as the opposite of acting unilaterally, cooperation requires collaboration between States in different forms, intensities and stages, which implies 'a sharing of certain authority, competence, or power'.[42] In the context of the Spratly Islands area, a relevant question is to what extent international law can contribute to the promotion of cooperation between or among the disputant States in resource and pollution management respecting this region.

1.3 Purpose, Scope and Structure of the Book

The purpose of this book is to examine how international law addresses unilateralism and cooperation in the Spratly Islands area. It seeks to answer the question of to what extent international law provides a normative framework for the management of the Spratly Islands area in the absence of agreed maritime delimitation, with the aim of maintaining peaceful coexistence of the disputant States and promoting international cooperation in this region. This book focuses on the roles of international law as regards the Spratly Islands area in four key respects: (1) addressing the underlying territorial dispute,

38 G. Schwarzenberger, Title to Territory: Response to a Challenge, 51 *AJIL* (1957), 322.

39 United Nations Charter, adopted 26 June 1945, entered into force 24 October 1945, Article 2(3).

40 Guyana v. Suriname, Arbitral Award dated 17 September 2007 (PCA), para.465. M.H. Nordquist, *et al.* (eds.), *United Nations Convention on the Law of the Sea, 1982: A Commentary. Vol. 2: Articles 1 to 85, Annexes I and II, Final Act, Annex II* (Nijhoff. 1993), 815.

41 Wolfrum, n 35, para.2.

42 F.X. Perrez, The Efficiency of Cooperation: A Functional Analysis of Sovereignty, 15 *Arizona Journal of International and Comparative Law* (1998), 521.

(2) identifying the disputed marine areas, (3) regulating unilateral State conduct, and (4) promoting cooperation in resource and pollution management. These four aspects are selected because a legally predictable territorial order and a set of restraints upon unilateral behaviours within a clearly defined spatial area are essential to maintaining peaceful coexistence of the disputant States as well as for enabling proactive cooperative arrangements on resource and pollution management which can be beneficial to prosperous development of the region.

The scope of this book is defined by four dimensions, including the spatial extent, the temporal sphere, the scope of actors, and the range of subject matters. First, the spatial ambit of this book is the Spratly Islands area. Compared with other disputed areas in the South China Sea, namely the Paracel Islands and the Scarborough Shoal, the territorial and maritime disputes in the Spratly Islands area are the most complicated ones since they involve multiple States parties including China, Malaysia, the Philippines, Vietnam, and Brunei. The analysis respecting the Spratly Islands area might have analogical implications for disputes in other areas of the South China Sea. Second, with respect to the temporal sphere, this book mainly deals with the 'transitional period' in the absence of maritime delimitation,[43] and does not address issues about the procedures to reach maritime delimitation and how the maritime boundaries should be delimited. Third, as to the scope of actors, this book analyses the interaction between States that are parties to the Spratly Islands dispute, and to a lesser extent, the role of international organizations such as ASEAN in facilitating cooperation in resource and pollution management in this region. Besides, it should be noted that the Taiwan authority or the Republic of China (ROC) occupies the largest maritime feature – Itu Aba – in the Spratly Islands area, and it also has territorial and maritime claims therein. However, owing to the one-China policy as well as the fact that claims advanced by the ROC are largely identical with those of the People's Republic of China (PRC),[44] for simplicity, this book treats the PRC and the ROC as one claimant, namely China.

43 The term 'transitional period' is used in Articles 74(3) and 83(3) of UNCLOS, referring to a period before the final delimitation takes place either by a maritime delimitation agreement or binding judicial decisions. See UNCLOS, Articles 74(3) and 83(3).

44 F.-K. Liu, Mainland China-Taiwan Interplay in the South China Sea, in K. Zou (ed.), *Routledge Handbook of the South China Sea* (Routledge. 2021), 376. H. Tseng, *Rethinking South China Sea Disputes: The Untold Dimensions and Great Expectations* (Routledge. 2016), 3. G. Xue, The South China Sea: Competing Claims and Conflict Situations, in C. Schofield, *et al.* (eds.), *The Limits of Maritime Jurisdiction* (Brill. 2014), 228. K.-H. Wang, The ROC's Maritime Claims and Practices with Special Reference to the South China Sea, 41 *ODIL* (2010), 237.

Nevertheless, this treatment should not be interpreted as negating the chance of Taiwan to participate in the future development and management of the Spratly Islands area. For example, since 1991, government officials and scholars from PRC and ROC together with other claimant States have continuously participated in their private capacities in the annual Workshop on Managing Potential Conflicts in the South China Sea, an informal regional forum hosted by the government of Indonesia.[45] Fourth, in terms of the analysis of potential cooperative arrangements, the range of subject matter is limited to three sectors of the uses of the ocean, namely the management of hydrocarbon resources, fisheries and pollution. The main underlying reason is that the disputant States have shown willingness to negotiate and facilitate collaboration in these three sectors.[46] These three sectors also represent an urgent need for cooperation, largely because of the disputant States' increasing demand for hydrocarbon resources owing to rapid economic growth, as well as the depletion, overfishing and pollution issues caused by mismanagement.[47]

As to the structure, this book is divided into two parts, including nine chapters. In addition to the introductory and concluding chapters (chapters 1 and 9), chapters 2–8 analyse the existing legal regulatory frameworks under international law and their potential for providing an adequate normative

45 V.H. Dang, Biodiversity and Conservation, in K. Zou (ed.), *Routledge Handbook of the South China Sea* (Routledge. 2021), 287–288. Y.-H. Song, The South China Sea Workshop Process and Taiwan's Participation, 41 *ODIL* (2010), 262.

46 For cooperative willingness in relation to hydrocarbon resources, see *e.g.*, China and Philippines, Memorandum of Understanding on Cooperation on Oil and Gas Development (20 November 2018), available at <https://www.fmprc.gov.cn/mfa_eng/wjdt_665385/2649_665393/t1616644.shtml>. For cooperative willingness in relation to fisheries, see *e.g.*, the peaceful coexistence of Chinese, Philippine and Vietnamese fishing boats in the South China Sea, which, according to some scholars, amount to 'some sort of provisional fishery agreement appeared to be reached among' these three parties. Supporting literature includes: H. Zhang, Fisheries Cooperation in the South China Sea: Evaluating the Options, 89 *Marine Policy* (2018), 67; M. Petty, Exclusive: At strategic shoal, China asserts power through control, and concessions (10 April 2017), available at <https://www.reuters.com/article/us-southchinasea-china-philippines-exclu-idUSKBN17B124>. For cooperative willingness regarding pollution abatement, see *e.g.*, ASEAN and China, n 29, para.6(a).

47 World Bank, Energy Imports Statistics (2017), available at <http://data.worldbank.org/indicator/EG.IMP.CONS.ZS>. FAO Asia-Pacific Fishery Commission, *Regional Overview of Fisheries and Aquaculture in Asia and the Pacific* (2012), RAP Publication 2012/26, 17–18. R. Jennings, South China Sea Succumbing to Pollution Due to Political Impasse (12 September 2017), available at <https://www.voanews.com/a/south-china-sea-pollution/4025014.html>.

framework for the disputant States on their coexistence and cooperation in the Spratly Islands area.

Part 1, comprising chapters 2–4, seeks to set out a predictable territorial order and permissible scope of unilateral behaviors to ensure peaceful coexistence of the disputant States in the region. Chapter 2 deals with the underlying territorial dispute in the Spratly Islands. According to the legal principle of '*la terre domine la mer*' or 'the land dominates the sea', a State can only claim maritime entitlements over specific marine areas when it enjoys territorial sovereignty over certain land territories.[48] The disputant States base their territorial claims on multiple legal bases including historic title, *effectivités*, treaty title, cession, and discovery of *terra nullius*.[49] Thus, this chapter employs the titles/*effectivités* dichotomy as the analytical framework to evaluate whether the legal arguments advanced by the disputant States are substantiated under international law.[50] Chapter 3 identifies the spatial extent of disputed marine areas within the Spratly Islands area. The identification process is difficult, particularly because of ambiguous claims put forward by the disputant States and the situation that other disputant parties view a claim as being excessive.[51] Two competing approaches are: (1) the areas of overlapping claims approach taking into account all claims, and (2) an alternative approach excluding unreasonable claims. The analysis requires an examination of three questions: What are the categories of maritime claims that must be taken into account under each approach? What are unreasonable claims? And what is the impact of the *South China Sea Arbitration* award on the categorization of disputed marine areas?[52] Chapter 4 clarifies the permissible scope under international law for unilateralism in the Spratly Islands setting. For this purpose, this chapter takes into account Articles 74(3) and 83(3) and Part XII of UNCLOS as well as general principles in customary international law (the principles of no-harm, peaceful settlement of disputes, the prohibition of the threat or use of force, and good faith) and relevant international jurisprudence.[53] Three types of

48 North Sea Continental Shelf (Federal Republic of Germany/Denmark), Judgment of 20 February 1969 (ICJ), para.96. C. van Bijnkershoek, *De Dominio Maris Dissertatio* (OUP 2nd ed. 1744) (translated by R. Van Deman Magoffin), 43.

49 See chapter 2, section 2.3.

50 M.G. Kohen, Titles and Effectivités in Territorial Disputes, in M.G. Kohen and M. Hébié (eds.), *Research Handbook on Territorial Disputes in International Law* (Edward Elgar Publishing. 2018), 146.

51 The South China Sea Arbitration (The Philippines v. China), Award on Jurisdiction and Admissibility of 29 October 2015 (PCA), para.167.

52 The South China Sea Arbitration, n 6 & n 51.

53 UNCLOS, Articles 74(3) and 83(3) and Part XII. For relevant international jurisprudence, see *e.g.*, Aegean Sea Continental Shelf (Greece v. Turkey), Order of 11 September 1976,

unilateral conduct are examined, respectively: (1) offshore hydrocarbon activities, (2) fisheries-related conduct including those concerning traditional or artisanal fishing, and (3) law enforcement measures as a response to other States' unilateral resource-related conduct.

Part 2, consisting of chapters 5–8, outlines the international legal frameworks for inter-State cooperation in resource and pollution management concerning the Spratly Islands area. Chapters 5–8 answer the question of to what extent international law can promote cooperation between or among the disputant States in the management of hydrocarbon resources, fishery resources and pollution in the Spratly Islands area. In particular, chapter 5 mainly focuses on two questions: to what extent the disputant States are obliged to cooperate in resource and pollution management in the Spratly Islands area? And whether momentum has been generated at this stage for cooperation in the region? On the basis of the answers to these questions, Chapter 5 further maps out a theoretical framework on institutionalized cooperation, which calls for a paradigm shift from the balance of power to more organized international collaboration. Chapters 6–8 then turn to the implementation of institutionalized cooperation in the Spratly Islands setting concerning the management of hydrocarbon resources, fishery resources, and pollution, respectively. Institutionalized cooperation consists of two dimensions, namely the substantive element and the procedural element. The substantive element refers to substantive norms according to which resources and the marine environment should be utilized and conserved, whereas the procedural element refers to cooperative institutions for maintaining order, resolving disputes and considering, applying or otherwise revisiting substantive norms.[54]

Finally, chapter 9 provides summary responses to the questions posed in this chapter 1. It then reflects on the functions and limitations of international law in managing the Spratly Islands area.

Request for the Indication of Interim Measures of Protection (ICJ); Guyana v. Suriname, n 40; Dispute Concerning Delimitation of the Maritime Boundary between Ghana and Côte d'Ivoire in the Atlantic Ocean (Ghana/Côte d'Ivoire), Order of 25 April 2015, Request for the prescription of provisional measures, and Judgment of 23 September 2017 (ITLOS); Fisheries Jurisdiction (United Kingdom of Great Britain and Northern Ireland v. Iceland), Order of 17 August 1972, Provisional Measures (ICJ); Fisheries Jurisdiction (Federal Republic of Germany v. Iceland) – Provisional Measures, Order of 17 August 1972 (ICJ); Southern Bluefin Tuna Cases (New Zealand v. Japan; Australia v. Japan), Order of 27 August 1999, Provisional Measures (ITLOS); Arctic Sunrise Arbitration (Netherlands v. Russia), Award on the Merits of 14 August 2015 (PCA); The South China Sea Arbitration, n 6.

54 S. Huntington, *Political Order in Changing Societies* (Yale University Press. 1973), 8–9.

PART 1

Coexistence: Setting out Predictable Territorial Order and Permissible Scope for Unilateralism

CHAPTER 2

The Underlying Territorial Dispute

2.1 Introduction[1]

Territory remains an indispensable component of statehood in this contemporary world even after over 370 years of the Peace of Westphalia since the emergence of modern sovereign States.[2] The influence of territorial disputes cannot be overstated because these disputes fundamentally shape and sometimes shake the foreign relations between relevant States. This is due to various factors such as pressures of national sentiment and the strategic significance of areas in question.[3] The territorial dispute in the Spratly Islands is one illustrative example, which has caused tensions in diplomatic relations between the disputant States consisting of China, Vietnam, the Philippines and Malaysia.[4] Moreover, the territorial dispute is an underlying cause of the maritime dispute in this region, as according to the legal principle of '*la terre domine la mer*', a State can only claim maritime entitlements over specific marine areas when it enjoys territorial sovereignty over certain land territories.[5] Resolving

1 Part of this chapter includes some texts that the author has published previously, and the author would like to thank the publisher Springer for the permission to use her previous work: adapted by permission from Springer Nature: Springer, Global Encyclopedia of Territorial Rights, The Spratly Islands and Territorial Rights, by Xuechan Ma. © 2020. Available at <https://doi.org/10.1007/978-3-319-68846-6_44-1>.

2 The Peace of Westphalia, adopted 24 October 1648, Article 8(1): 'Constitutional Position of Imperial Estates/ Confirmation of Rights'. Montevideo Convention on the Rights and Duties of States, adopted 26 December 1933, entered into force 26 December 1934, Article 1. N. Schrijver, The Changing Nature of State Sovereignty, 70 *BYIL* (1999), 65–66. M.G. Kohen and M. Hébié, Introduction to the Research Handbook on Territorial Disputes in International Law, in M.G. Kohen and M. Hébié (eds.), *Research Handbook on Territorial Disputes in International Law* (Edward Elgar Publishing. 2018), 1.

3 For instance, territorial disputes may increase States' chances of military conflicts. See S.F. Abramson and D.B. Carter, The Historical Origins of Territorial Disputes, 110 *American Political Science Review* (2016), 675. J. Crawford, *Brownlie's Principles of Public International Law* (OUP 9th ed. 2019), 203.

4 Brunei is not a party to the territorial dispute discussed here. Albeit Brunei claims sovereign rights over Louisa Reef, it claims Louisa Reef to be a submerged feature located on its continental shelf. See B.K. Murphy, Dangerous Ground: The Spratly Islands and International Law, 1 *OCLJ* (1995), 208.

5 North Sea Continental Shelf (Federal Republic of Germany/Denmark), Judgment of 20 February 1969 (ICJ), para.96. C. van Bijnkershoek, *De Dominio Maris Dissertatio* (OUP 2nd ed. 1744) (translated by R. Van Deman Magoffin), 43.

 | DOI:10.1163/9789004504332_003

the underlying territorial dispute would alleviate tensions and serve as a prerequisite for the ultimate settlement of the maritime dispute, thereby creating a relatively peaceful environment for the sustainable use and management of the Spratly Islands area. Hence, the legal analysis of the territorial dispute is necessary if the role of international law in the management of the Spratly Islands area is to be discussed. In light of this, this chapter mainly addresses the question of whether the legal arguments put forward by the disputant States for claiming territorial sovereignty over the Spratly Islands are substantiated under international law.

Despite the numerous discussions which this territorial dispute has attracted,[6] scholarly opinions vary a lot on this issue. Some claim that none of the territorial claims of the disputant States is legally strong under international law,[7] while others argue that one of these States has the strongest legal argument.[8] The discrepancy between these opinions is understandable considering that this territorial dispute, involving multiple States and various maritime features, relates to a complicated web of factual and legal issues. Moreover, some arguments invoked by the disputant States are based on 'ancient oriental concepts of ownership' and 'imaginative interpretations of contemporary international law' and thus are difficult to be evaluated under contemporary international law, which therefore also contribute to the discrepancy.[9]

To overcome these difficulties, this chapter employs the dichotomy of titles and *effectivités* as the analytical framework, which is perhaps the first attempt of this kind in the literature on the Spratly Islands disputes. The titles/*effectivités* dichotomy is built upon the special nexuses between these

---

6 See *e.g.*, H. Chiu and C.H. Park, Legal Status of the Paracel and Spratly Islands, 3(1) ODIL (1975); R. Haller-Trost, *The Spratly Islands: A Study on the Limitations of International Law* (Canterbury: Centre of South-East Asian Studies. 1990); G. Valero, Spratly Archipelago Dispute: Is the Question of Sovereignty Still Relevant?, 18 *Marine Policy* (1994); Murphy, n 4; D.J. Dzurek, *The Spratly Islands Dispute: Who's On First?* (IBRU. 1996); M. Koo, *Scramble for the Rocks: The Disputes over the Dokdo /Takeshima, Senkaku /Diaoyu, and Paracel and Spratly Islands* (ProQuest Dissertations Publishing. 2005); H. Chen, Territorial Disputes in the South China Sea under the San Francisco Peace Treaty, 50(3) *Issues & Studies* (2014); M. Hasan and H. Jian, Spratly Islands Dispute in the South China Sea: Potential Solutions, 12(1) *Journal of East Asia and International Law* (2019).

7 M.J. Valenicia, The Spratly Islands Dispute, 166 *Far Eastern Economic Review* (2003), 21.

8 For literature supporting that China has the strongest legal argument under international law, see *e.g.*, Dzurek, n 6, 54. For literature supporting Vietnam, see *e.g.*, M. Chemillier-Gendreau, *Sovereignty over the Paracel and Spratley Islands* (Springer. 2000), 137–138. For literature supporting the Philippines and Malaysia, see *e.g.*, Murphy, n 4, 200–208.

9 L.G. Cordner, The Spratly Islands Dispute and the Law of the Sea, 25 ODIL (1994), 62.

two concepts and is a well-accepted pattern of analysis in cases involving territorial disputes (section 2.2).[10] This chapter then sorts out the legal arguments advanced by the disputant States in chronological sequence against the historical background of the territorial dispute involving the Spratly Islands (section 2.3). These legal arguments are restated according to the law of territory. This chapter further appraises whether the disputant States' territorial claims based on the titles of territorial sovereignty and *effectivités* (sections 2.4–2.8) are substantiated in contemporary international law. Based on the appraisal results, the titles/*effectivités* analytical framework is applied to reach a conclusion about the territorial situation of the Spratly Islands as it is today (section 2.9).

Two caveats are worth mentioning. First, although this study has been careful not to overlook any available and relevant official documents and secondary literature, the conclusion made in this chapter may still be subject to the risk of not depicting a complete picture of this territorial dispute, provided that evidence of significant importance might not be available to the public owing to confidentiality or other reasons. Second, the scope of this chapter is limited to the territorial dispute over the nearly twenty islands in the Spratly Islands area.[11]

10 M.G. Kohen, Titles and Effectivités in Territorial Disputes, in M.G. Kohen and M. Hébié (eds.), *Research Handbook on Territorial Disputes in International Law* (Edward Elgar Publishing. 2018), 146.

11 There are at least 19 islands in the Spratly Islands area: Itu Aba Island, Thitu Island, West York Island, Spratly Island, North-East Cay, South-West Cay, Sin Cowe Island, Nanshan Island, Sand Cay, Loaita Island, Swallow Reef, Namyit Island, Amboyna Cay, Flat Island, Fiery Cross Reef, McKennan Reef, Gaven Reef (North), Cuarteron Reef, and Johnson Reef. This list is based on the *South China Sea Arbitration* award: first, the tribunal has conducted a detailed examination on the status of eleven (11) maritime features identified in the Philippines' submissions and concluding that Scarborough Shoal (not a part of the Spratly Islands), Fiery Cross Reef, McKennan Reef, Gaven Reef (North), Cuarteron Reef and Johnson Reef are high-tide elevations; and second, by passage, the tribunal has confirmed that Itu Aba Island, Thitu Island, West York Island, Spratly Island, North-East Cay, South-West Cay, Sin Cowe Island, Nanshan Island, Sand Cay, Loaita Island, Swallow Reef, Namyit Island, Amboyna Cay and Flat Island are high-tide elevations. See The South China Sea Arbitration (The Philippines v. China), Award of 12 July 2016 (PCA), paras.382 (regarding Fiery Cross Reef, McKennan Reef, Gaven Reef (North), Cuarteron Reef and Johnson Reef), 401 (regarding Itu Aba Island), 402 (regarding Thitu Island), 403 (regarding West York Island), 404 (regarding Spratly Island), 405 (regarding North-East Cay), 406 (regarding South-West Cay), 407 (regarding Amboyna Cay, Flat Island, Loaita Island, Namyit Island, Nanshan Island, Sandy Cay, Sin Cowe Island, and Swallow Reef).

2.2 Analytical Framework: Titles/Effectivités Dichotomy

In international law, the notion of 'title' is used to denote the source or root of a right over territory.[12] A French term '*effectivité*' is employed to refer to the act of exercise of State authority over territory.[13] A title arises not simply by physical occupation or *effectivités* but through acquisition in accordance with international law.[14] Several international cases have shown that the possessor who exercises State authority over a disputed territory is not necessarily the title-holder.[15] As rightly pointed out by Kohen, '[i]nternational law is indeed richer than the simplistic idea that actual possession is tantamount to sovereignty'.[16]

The ICJ has described four types of relationship between these two concepts – 'title' and '*effectivité*' – in *Burkina Faso/Republic of Mali*.[17] First, in circumstances where the exercise of State authority corresponds to the right to territory, *effectivités* confirms the territorial title. Second, in the event of incompatibility between *effectivités* and a legal title, the preference is given to the title, and *effectivités* are deemed unlawful. Third, in the absence of any legal title to the territory, *effectivités* may itself be constitutive of a territorial title. In this instance, effective occupation of *terra nullius* is itself one kind of the sources or roots of territorial sovereignty. Fourth, if a legal title is obscure, *effectivités* can play a critical role in clarifying and interpreting the extent of that title.

Apart from the above four types, Kohen has added a fifth type of the titles/ *effectivités* relationship. That is, when a legal title is not duplicated by any *effectivité*, the absence of *effectivités* does not prevent this title from taking effect.[18] This fifth type can be read as a normal corollary to the second type, according to which the legal effect of a title is not adversely impacted by the presence of incongruous *effectivités*, not to mention the absence of *effectivités*. Table 2 summarizes five types of the titles/*effectivités* relationship.

---

12 Frontier Dispute (Burkina Faso/Republic of Mali), Judgment of 22 December 1986 (ICJ), para.18.

13 Kohen, n 10, 145. M.N. Shaw, *International Law* (CUP. 8th ed. 2017), 379.

14 Crawford, n 3, 204.

15 See *e.g.*, Clipperton Island (France v. Mexico), Decision of 28 January 1931; Legal Status of Eastern Greenland (Denmark v. Norway), Judgment of 5 April 1933, PCIJ Series A/B No. 53; Territorial Dispute (Libyan Arab Jamahiriya/Chad), Judgment of 3 February 1994 (ICJ); Land and Maritime Boundary between Cameroon and Nigeria (Cameroon v. Nigeria: Equatorial Guinea intervening), Judgment of 10 October 2002 (ICJ).

16 Kohen, n 10, 148.

17 Frontier Dispute, n 12, para.63.

18 Kohen, n 10, 164.

TABLE 2 Five types of the titles/effectivités relationship

Type no.	Existence of title	Existence of effectivité	Compatibility between title and effectivité	Preference or consideration given to	The role played by effectivité
1.	Yes	Yes	Yes	Title	Confirmatory
2.	Yes	Yes	No	Title	N/A
3.	No	Yes	N/A	Effectivité	Constitutive
4.	Obscure	Yes	N/A	Effectivité	Interpretative
5.	Yes	No	N/A	Title	N/A

Notes: 'N/A' means non-applicable.

This table allows several remarks. First, a legal title always prevails over *effectivités*. Where *effectivités* corresponds to the title to territory, *effectivités* are confirmatory of that title. In contrast, *effectivités* contradictory to an existing title are unlawful, which have been called '*effectivités* contra legem' in the *Cameroon/Nigeria* judgment.[19] Second, in the absence of a title, the role of *effectivités* becomes significant and can be constitutive of a title. In this circumstance, *effectivités* become a 'law-establishing mechanism'.[20] Third, where a legal title, or more precisely, the evidence of a legal title, is obscure or equivocal, *effectivités* can play a probative or interpretative role in clarifying the extent of that title.[21] These remarks accord with the general statement made by the most recent arbitral award on territorial disputes – the 2017 *Croatia/Slovenia* award – that 'legal title takes precedence over *effectivités*. Where no legal title can be established, or where legal title is established but not with sufficient precision to establish the exact location of the boundary, the *effectivités* play a crucial role'.[22]

Furthermore, as showcased in *Malaysia/Singapore*, a legal title previously established may lapse due to a common understanding or tacit agreement developed between the disputant States, and in this circumstance, *effectivités* can come into play. In *Malaysia/Singapore*, the ICJ first concluded that the predecessor of Malaysia – the Sultan of Johor – obtained an original or ancient title to the disputed island (Pedra Branca/Pulau Batu Puteh), but Malaysia lost this title later since it failed to protest against Singapore's *effectivités* over the island.[23] In particular, Malaysia's official statement in 1953 indicated that it did not claim ownership of the disputed island.[24] The ICJ considered that the lack of protest and the 1953 statement constituted an 'evolving understanding shared by the Parties'[25] or 'a convergent evolution of the positions of the Parties'.[26] In the ICJ's view, territorial sovereignty may 'pass' as a result of a State's failure to respond to conduct *à titre de souverain* of the other State,[27] as

19 Land and Maritime Boundary between Cameroon and Nigeria, n 15, para.223.
20 Shaw, n 13, 382.
21 In Kohen's opinion, the obscurity of a legal title refers to the obscurity of evidence. See Kohen, n 10, 164.
22 Arbitration between the Republic of Croatia and the Republic of Slovenia, Final Award of 29 June 2017 (PCA), para.340.
23 Sovereignty over Pedra Branca/Pulau Batu Puteh, Middle Rocks and South Ledge (Malaysia/Singapore), Judgment of 23 May 2008 (ICJ), para.276.
24 *Ibid.*, para.275.
25 *Ibid.*, para.224.
26 *Ibid.*, para.276.
27 *Ibid.*, para.121.

the absence of reaction 'may well amount to acquiescence' and the concept of acquiescence 'is equivalent to tacit recognition manifested by unilateral conduct which the other party may interpret as consent'.[28] As a result, the ICJ concluded that the territorial sovereignty over the disputed island had 'passed' from Malaysia to Singapore.[29] When Malaysia's original title had lapsed, the situation of the case transformed into the third type of the titles/*effectivités* relationship, where in the absence of any legal title, *effectivités* could be constitutive of a territorial title.

Based on the five types of relationships described in Table 2, the dichotomy of titles and *effectivités* is a well-accepted pattern of analysis in cases involving territorial disputes.[30] The only case that has departed from this analytical framework is the 2002 *Eritrea/Ethiopia* arbitral award,[31] but this award has not been followed by any further judicial decision.[32] This chapter will use the titles/*effectivités* dichotomy as the framework to analyze the territorial dispute in the Spratly Islands area. One point is worth mentioning before the analysis. Under contemporary international law, the list of titles of territorial sovereignty has grown beyond the orthodox five modes of acquisition reflecting Roman law (namely effective occupation of *terra nullius*, acquisitive prescription, cession, accretion and subjugation or conquest).[33] Tailored to the Spratly Islands setting, the arguments advanced by the disputant States also go beyond

---

28 *Ibid.* Delimitation of the Maritime Boundary in the Gulf of Maine Area (Canada/United States of America), Judgment of 12 October 1984 (ICJ), para.130.

29 Sovereignty over Pedra Branca/Pulau Batu Puteh, Middle Rocks and South Ledge, n 23, para.276.

30 See *e.g.*, Frontier Dispute, n 12, para.63; Territorial Dispute, n 15, paras.75-76; Land and Maritime Boundary between Cameroon and Nigeria, n 15, para.68; Sovereignty over Pulau Ligitan and Pulau Sipadan (Indonesia/Malaysia), Judgment of 17 December 2002 (ICJ), para.126; Frontier Dispute (Benin/Niger), Judgment of 12 July 2005 (ICJ), para.77; Territorial and Maritime Dispute between Nicaragua and Honduras in the Caribbean Sea (Nicaragua v. Honduras), Judgment of 8 October 2007 (ICJ), para.152; Territorial and Maritime Dispute (Nicaragua v. Colombia), Judgment of 19 November 2012 (ICJ), para.66; Arbitration between the Republic of Croatia and the Republic of Slovenia, n 22, para.340.

31 Decision regarding delimitation of the border between Eritrea and Ethiopia, 13 April 2002, Vol. XXV, para.3.14. (holding that subsequent conduct mainly *effectivités* might supersede a title prescribed by the relevant treaty provisions) M.G. Kohen, The Decision on The Delimitation of The Eritrea/Ethiopia Boundary of 13 April 2002: A Singular Approach to International Law Applicable to International Law Applicable to Territorial Disputes, in M.G. Kohen (ed.), *Promoting Justice, Human Rights and Conflict Resolution Through International Law: Liber Amicorum Lucius Caflisch* (Brill. 2006), 770.

32 Kohen, n 10, 167.

33 For an account of the types of titles of territorial sovereignty, see Kohen, n 10, 146–157; Shaw, n 13, 367–387; Crawford, n 3, 203–230.

the orthodox five modes of acquisition and concern historic title, *effectivités* of *terra nullius*, boundary treaties, cession, and discovery of *terra nullius*. A more elaborate analysis of the applicable law of these titles and their application to the Spratly Islands setting is provided in sections 2.4–2.8.

2.3 Legal Arguments of the Disputant States

To better understand the legal arguments advanced by the disputed States, this section presents and analyses them in chronological sequence against the historical background of the territorial dispute involving the Spratly Islands. It then gives a summary of these legal arguments.

Among the four disputant States, China claimed to be the first one to discover the Spratly Islands.[34] There is little dispute that ocean activities especially navigation conducted by the Chinese people in the South China Sea date back to at least 225–230 A.D.[35] Several Chinese official records mentioned the islands therein to be located in an area called 'Zhang Hai' ('rising sea'), and at least since Song Dynasty (960–1279), geographic names had been given to the Spratly Islands ('Qian Li Chang Sha', or 'Thousands of Miles of Long Sand').[36]

During the seventeenth century, the Spratly Islands became known to the European navigators.[37] However, it was not until the nineteenth century that the UK became the first European power to conduct official hydrographical surveys in the Spratly Islands which it called 'Dangerous Ground' due to the presence of countless reefs and shoals.[38] During surveys in the 1860s, the crew

34 China, White Paper: China Adheres to the Position of Settling Through Negotiation the Relevant Disputes Between China and the Philippines in the South China Sea (13 July 2016), para.3.

35 D. Heinzig, *Disputed Islands in the South China Sea: Paracels, Spratlys, Pratas, Macclesfield Bank* (Otto Harrassowitz. 1976), 22.

36 M. Samuels, *Contest for the South China Sea* (Taylor & Francis. 1982), 10–13. Guangdong Province Geographic Names Committee, *The Collection of the Geographic Names of the Islands in South China Sea* (*Nan Hai Zhu Dao Di Ming Zi Liao Hui Bian*) (Guangdong Province Map Publishing House. 1987), 400.

37 The maritime features in this area were called 'Archipelago of Reefs' by Western navigators. See D. Hancox, *Secret Hydrographic Surveys in the Spratly Islands* (ASEAN Academic Press. 1999), 'Foreword', 4.

38 The first systematic attempt to chart the Spratly Islands was in 1812 under the instructions of Caption James Horsburgh, a hydrographer to the British East India Company. The chart resulting from this survey was published in 1821, which became the basis for other charts which were published later by the hydrographic offices all around the world. The UK published a chart comprehensively showing the main reefs in this area in 1888. Until

of British surveying ships encountered Chinese fishers from Hainan on some islands thereof.[39]

In 1883, the German government sent a military detachment to the Spratly Islands to carry out survey work, which triggered protests from the Chinese government.[40] In the end, Germany discontinued its survey work under pressure from the Chinese government.[41]

In 1887, as a result of the Tokin War for deciding whether France would supplant China's control of northern Vietnam, China and France concluded a treaty to delimit the frontier between China and northern Vietnam. The third clause of this treaty used the Paris meridian 105°43'E as the demarcation line and allocated the islands east of this line to China.[42] This treaty has only specified the starting point of the demarcation line, namely 'the eastern point of the island of Tcha's Kou, or Ouan Chan (Tra Co)', but not the ending point.[43] The Spratly Islands area lies east of the demarcation line if it could extend southwards to reach into the South China Sea.[44]

The first military occupation of the islands happened in the 1930s when France, as a colonial power in Asia, proclaimed the occupation of several islands in the Spratly Islands by the French Navy under a decree of 26 July 1933.[45] The French government based its territorial claim over the rule of discovery of *terra nullius*.[46] Nevertheless, France admitted that when it occupied

---

1936, British surveys were the sources of most of the publicly available hydrographical information concerning the Spratly Islands. See Hancox, n 37, 30, 161.

39 Hancox, n 37, 10. Heinzig, n 35, 23. China, n 34, para.15. Moreover, some historians claim that a Chinese fisherman, named Zaide Fu, was the first person from Hainan to fish in the Spratly Islands in 1286. See W. Zhou and L. Tang, *Hainan Tianshu-Hainan Fishermen's Cultural Explanation of 'Geng Lu Bu'* (Kunlun Publisher. 2015), 4, 227.

40 Heinzig, n 35, 25–26. D. Whiting, The Spratly Islands Dispute and the Law of the Sea, 26 *Denver Journal of International Law and Policy* (1998), 897, 900–901.

41 Heinzig, n 35, 25–26, 72. Samuels, n 36, 52.

42 Clause 3 of the China-France Treaty on the Delimitation the Frontier between China and Northern Vietnam (26 June 1887). Chemillier-Gendreau, n 8, 36.

43 Chemillier-Gendreau, n 8, 36.

44 C.H. Park, The South China Sea Disputes: Who Owns the Islands and the Natural Resources?, 5 *ODIL* (1978), 33 ('China also relies in part on an important boundary pact it signed with Vietnam in 1887. This agreement stipulated that all islands situated east of a specified line-as the Paracels and the Spratlies were belonged to China'.). Dzurek, n 6, 9 ('The 1887 treaty has been cited as evidence against French and Vietnamese claims to the Paracel and Spratly Islands'.).

45 Journal officiel de la Republique Francaise, No. 172 (25 July 1933), 7794.

46 Note dated 26 November 1928 addressed to the Under-Directorate for Asia and Oceania regarding the Spratly Island or Strom Island, reproduced in: Chemillier-Gendreau, n 8, Annex 19.

the islands, it found Chinese people living on some of those islands.[47] China protested against France's occupation, claiming that only Chinese fishers lived on these islands and that they belonged to China.[48] France offered to settle this dispute with China by submitting the case to arbitration.[49] However, no record of any reply from the Chinese government has been found.

The French occupation did not last long. Japan occupied the Spratly Islands area by the end of 1939 and renamed it the 'Shinnan Gunto' archipelago, which constituted part of the Asian beginnings of what would become WWII.[50] Following the surrender of Japan at the conclusion of the war in 1945, the Japanese forces withdrew from the Spratly Islands.[51] In 1946, China sent military fleets to occupy the Spratly Islands by erecting the steles, measuring and scouting the islands.[52] According to the statement of the commissioner carrying out this assignment, Yunyu Mai, the Chinese government controlled the main islands (including Itu Aba) in this area and claimed that the control of the main islands should be regarded as the control of the whole archipelago.[53]

In 1947, China formally incorporated the Spratly Islands into Guangdong Province.[54] Moreover, in the same year, China published the first U-shaped line map with the title of 'Map of the Locations of the South China Sea Islands' ('Nan Hai Zhu Dao Wei Zhi Tu'), using the U-shaped line to enclose a vast area of the South China Sea, including the whole of the Spratly Islands.[55] This map would play a prominent role in the discussion on the South China Sea in the 21st century. Yet, China has never published the geographic coordinates specifying the precise location of the U-shaped line.[56]

47 Heinzig, n 35, 28.

48 The protest from China was made through its ambassador WeiJune Gu. See Z. Han, *The Collection of the Historical Materials of the Islands in South China Sea* (*Wo Guo Nan Hai Zhu Dao Shi Liao Hui Bian*) (in Chinese) (Eastern Publishing House. 1988), 261. Chen, n 6, 176–177.

49 Heinzig, n 35, 29. France's suggestion to settle the dispute with China was also confirmed in the 1975 Vietnamese White Paper. See Republic of Vietnam, White Paper (1975), Chapter III.

50 Dzurek, n 6, 11. Murphy, n 4, 191–192.

51 Hancox, n 37, 151. Murphy, n 4, 192.

52 Chen, n 6, 178. Heinzig, n 35, 31.

53 Heinzig, n 35, 31–32.

54 Samuels, n 36, 76.

55 The U-shaped line published in the 1947 map consisted of eleven dashes. Two dashes originally depicted inside the Gulf of Tonkin were removed later around 2000 in the Chinese maps, probably owing to the adoption of the delimitation agreement relating to the Gulf of Tonkin between China and Vietnam in 2000. The U-shaped line was also attached to China's 2009 Note Verbale addressed to the UN Secretary-General. See China, Note Verbale No. CML/17/2009 (7 May 2009).

56 OES, China: Maritime Claims in the South China Sea, *Limits in the Seas* (5 December 2014).

As a result of the 1951 San Francisco Peace Conference, which was convened to solve territorial issues that remained in Asia in the wake of WWII, Japan formally renounced its territorial claims over the Spratly Islands by signing the Peace Treaty.[57] Nevertheless, this Peace Treaty did not mention who received the territorial sovereignty over the Spratly Islands after Japan's renouncement.[58] France was a participant in this conference, but it did not use this opportunity to reassert its territorial claims.[59] Rather, France sponsored South Vietnam to send a delegate to participate in this conference, and the latter used this chance to declare the Vietnamese sovereignty over the whole of the Spratly Islands.[60] Though China did not attend this Conference,[61] the Chinese government made an official statement to reiterate its territorial claims to all islands of the Spratly Islands.[62] The Philippines was a participant in this conference and thus would have been aware of the Spratly Islands since the territorial disposition of this island group was one of the most debated topics during the conference,[63] but it did not protest against the territorial claims of either South Vietnam or China, which indicated its lack of interest at that time.[64]

In 1956, through perhaps one of the most novel approaches to claim the Spratly Islands, a Philippine citizen, Tomas Cloma, without any authorization from the Philippine government, claimed his ownership over some islands in this area based on the rule of discovery of *terra nullius* and attempted to create

57 Treaty of Peace with Japan, adopted 8 September 1951, entered into force 28 April 1951, 136 *UNTS* 45, Article 2(f).

58 The Peace Treaty was signed by 49 out of the 52 participating States on 8 September 1951. The then Soviet Union, Poland, and the then Czechoslovakia refused to sign because the provision concerning the South China Sea islands did not indicate that the sovereignty of these islands belonged to China. See Heinzig, n 35, 39–40; M.M. Whiteman, *Digest of International Law, Vol. 3* (Department of State publications. 1964), 595; Chen, n 6, 173, 180.

59 Murphy, n 4, 192. M. Bennett, The People's Republic of China and the Use of International Law in the Spratly Islands Dispute, 28 *Stan. J. Int'l L.* (1991), 425, 432.

60 South Vietnam did not specify the legal arguments for its territorial claim. Whiteman, n 58, 595. Dzurek, n 6, 15–16.

61 The underlying reason was that the US and the UK had different opinions as to which one of the Chinese governments was the legitimate one: Beijing or Taiwan. See Chen, n 6, 180.

62 China, Statement on the joint US/UK draft for the Peace Treaty with Japan, dated 15 August 1951.

63 M.H. Loja, The Spratly Islands as a Single Unit Under International Law: A Commentary on the Final Award in Philippines/China Arbitration, 47 *ODIL* (2016), 313.

64 Murphy, n 4, 193.

a new country on these islands, called 'Kalayaan' or 'Freedomland'.[65] His claim stimulated official protests from China and South Vietnam.[66] North Vietnam published public statements to support the Chinese government's authority over the Spratly Islands.[67] In response to Cloma's claim and protests from other States, the Philippine government declared that it had no official claim in relation to the area concerned.[68]

In the 1960s when the Vietnam War took place, States paid less attention to the issue of the remote islands in the Spratly Islands, and relevant territorial claims remained latent.[69] In 1975, with the Vietnam War approaching the end, South Vietnam reasserted its territorial claims to the Spratly Islands by publishing a White Paper, in which it gave a detailed account of the alleged legal basis for its territorial claims.[70] In this White Paper, while admitting the lack of sufficient historical contacts with the Spratly Islands,[71] South Vietnam claimed that France incorporated the Spratly Islands into Vietnamese territory on behalf of Vietnam in 1933, stating that:

> the French, who occupied the Southern part of Vietnam known as Cochinchina, took all those measures necessary for the establishment of the legal basis for possession of the Spratly Islands. In 1933, the Spratlys were incorporated into the French colony of Cochinchina and from that year forward have had an adequate administrative structure. It is true that French jurisdiction was disrupted by the Japanese invasion of 1941. However, shortly after the Japanese defeat in 1945, France returned Cochinchina to Vietnam, which then recovered all the rights attached to the former French colony.[72]

This statement showed that South Vietnam claimed to succeed the French claim of territorial sovereignty over the islands in the Spratly Islands established in the 1930s.[73] In 1976, North Vietnam defeated South Vietnam and established a reunited country, namely the Socialist Republic of Vietnam

---

65 *Ibid.* Samuels, n 36, 82. Republic of Vietnam, n 49, Chapter III.
66 Murphy, n 4, 193. China, n 34, para.58.
67 China, Note Verbale No. CML/42/2020 (17 April 2020). Haller-Trost, n 6, 60.
68 Samuels, n 36, 84. China, n 34, para.58.
69 Murphy, n 4, 194.
70 Republic of Vietnam, n 49.
71 *Ibid.*, Chapter III.
72 *Ibid.*
73 Murphy, n 4, 203.

(Vietnam). Vietnam has been following South Vietnam's positions regarding the Spratly Islands since then.[74]

In 1974, Tomas Cloma formally relinquished his territorial claim over some islands in the Spratly Islands to the Philippine government by the 'Deed of Assignment Waiver of Rights'.[75] Furthermore, by the 1978 Presidential Decree No. 1596, the Philippine government clarified the scope of its territorial claim to be the islands within an area called 'Kalayaan Island Group'.[76] The Philippines articulated the legal bases for its territorial claim over these islands as below:

> by reason of their *proximity* the cluster of islands and islets in the South China Sea situated within ... Kalayaan Island Group ... these areas *do not legally belong to any state or nation* but, by reason of history, indispensable need, and *effective occupation and control* established in accordance with international law, such areas must now be deemed to belong and subject to the sovereignty of the Philippines.[77] [emphasis added]

From this statement, the Philippines advances two legal arguments to support its territorial claim, namely discovery of *terra nullius* and effective control.[78]

In 1979, Malaysia published a map of its territorial waters and continental shelf and claimed territorial sovereignty over some insular features in the southeastern portion of the Spratly Islands.[79] Furthermore, the 1970s, 1980s and the 1990s witnessed a number of occupations by military forces in the Spratly Islands (Table 3).

The Philippines began to take up military control over islands in this area since the early 1970s.[80] For instance, the Philippines controlled Nanshan Island and Flat Island in 1970, Loaita Island, Thitu Island, West York Island and North-East Cay in 1971.[81] Malaysia also sent military troops to occupy several features between 1977 and 1999, including Swallow Reef, Asdasier Bank, Mariveles Reef, Louisa Reef, Erica Reef and Investigator Shoal.[82] Turning to Vietnam, in 1973,

74 Dzurek, n 6, 19.

75 Haller-Trost, n 6, 54.

76 The Philippines, Presidential Decree No. 1596 (11 June 1978).

77 *Ibid.*

78 Murphy, n 4, 206–207.

79 Heinzig, n 35, 65. R. Haller-Trost, *The Brunei-Malaysia Dispute over Territorial and Maritime Claims in International Law* (IBRU. 1994), 48–49.

80 Heinzig, n 35, 36.

81 China, n 34, para.59.

82 C. Schofield, Untangling A Complex Web: Understanding Competing Maritime Claims in the South China Sea, in I. Storey and C.Y. Lin (eds.), *The South China Sea Dispute: Navigating Diplomatic and Strategic Tensions* (Singapore: ISEAS Yusof Ishak Institute. 2016), 209.

TABLE 3 Islands controlled by the disputant States in the Spratly Islands[a]

Controlling state	Island	The year when control began
China (6)	Itu Aba Island	1946
	Fiery Cross Reef	1988
	McKennan Reef	1988
	Gaven Reef (North)	1988
	Cuarteron Reef	1988
	Johnson Reef	1988
Malaysia (1)	Swallow Reef	1977
Philippines (6)	Flat Island	1970
	Nanshan Island	1970
	Thitu Island	1971
	West York Island	1971
	North-East Cay	1971
	Loaita Island	1971
Vietnam (6)	Spratly Island	1975
	South-West Cay	1975
	Sin Cowe Island	1975
	Sand Cay	1975
	Namyit Island	1975
	Amboyna Cay	1975

a The author compiled this table mainly based on the following literature: Chemillier-Gendreau, n 8, 178; Y. Zhang, *China Politics and Geography Study on Oceans* (Science Publishing House. 2004) (in Chinese), 129.

South Vietnam sent military troops to occupy Namyit Island.[83] In 1975, North Vietnam occupied Namyit Island, Sand Cay, Spratly Island, Sin Cowe Island and Amboyna Cay.[84] The tension reached a peak in 1988 when both China and Vietnam started campaigns to occupy remaining islands in this region.[85] Finally, in March 1988, armed conflicts took place between the Chinese and Vietnamese forces over Johnson South Reef.[86] Within this year, China occupied

83 Heinzig, n 35, 36.
84 *Ibid.*, 37.
85 Murphy, n 4, 195.
86 *Ibid.*

and took over six maritime features, and Vietnam occupied twelve features. After taking control of the islands, all the disputant States have been conducting a variety of activities thereon, based on which they claim *effectivités*. Section 2.5.3.1 will provide a detailed description of such activities subsequent to the military control.

In summary, all four disputant States put forward multiple legal bases for their territorial claims. First, China may claim a historic title to the Spratly Islands based on its alleged prolonged historical contacts with the region.[87] Second, all the disputant States resort to *effectivités* for their territorial claims to this region. Third, China and Vietnam claim themselves to be the rightful recipients when Japan renounced its titles and rights to the Spratly Islands according to Article 2(f) of the 1951 Treaty of Peace with Japan. China also refers to the 1887 treaty as evidence of its territorial title to the Spratly Islands.[88] Fourth, Vietnam bases its territorial claim on cession through which it succeeded the French territorial title to the Spratly Islands established in 1933. Fifth, both China and the Philippines claim a title established by discovery of *terra nullius*. China alleges itself to be the first State to have discovered the Spratly Islands, while the Philippines bases its claim on the discovery of certain features thereof by its citizen, Tomas Cloma, in 1956. Table 4 summarizes the legal arguments of these four States. Against the applicable law, sections 2.4–2.8 will examine whether the territorial claims based on historic title, *effectivités*, treaty title, cession, and discovery of *terra nullius* are respectively substantiated under international law.

2.4 Historic Title

This section discusses the concept of historic title as a legal argument for territorial claims. This concept, compared with other well-established titles

---

87 Some scholars argue that Vietnam also bases its territorial claim over the islands in the South China Sea including those in the Spratly Islands on the rule of historic title. However, this argument is inconsistent with the practice of Vietnam. In its 1975 White Paper, South Vietnam claimed 'early historical rights' over the Paracel Islands but not the Spratly Islands. In fact, South Vietnam explicitly admitted that '[u]nlike the case of the Hoang Sa (Paracel) Islands, the former emperors of Vietnam did not have the time to strengthen [the intermittent] contacts [with the Spratly Islands] through the organization of an administrative jurisdiction'. See J.D. Fry and M.H. Loja, The Roots of Historic Title: Non-Western Pre-Colonial Normative Systems and Legal Resolution of Territorial Disputes, 27 *LJIL* (2014), 728. Republic of Vietnam, n 49, 'The Early Historical Rights of Vietnam' and Chapter III.

88 Park, n 44, 33. Dzurek, n 6, 9.

of territorial sovereignty, is complicated and sometimes controversial. Thus, this section takes the opportunity to analyze issues including the terminology, validity and operation of this concept.

2.4.1 *Terminology*

It is not uncommon in the ICJ cases that States base their territorial claims on historic titles.[89] In those cases, occasionally, terms including 'original title', 'ancient title' or 'ancient or original title' are used interchangeably to refer to a 'historic title'.[90] Take *Malaysia/Singapore* for example. Malaysia claimed an 'original title' to Pulau Batu Puteh,[91] and Singapore referred to Malaysia's above claim as 'historic title'.[92] The ICJ endorsed the 'ancient original title' of Malaysia's predecessor (the Sultanate of Johor) to Pulau Batu Puteh.[93] Similarly, in *Minquiers and Ecrehos*, both the UK and France based their territorial claims to the disputed Minquiers and Ecrehos on an 'ancient title' or 'original title' dating back to the Middle Ages.[94] Despite the lack of support for the 'ancient or original title' alleged by the parties in the majority opinion,[95] Judge Alvarez referred to such allegations as 'historic titles' in his declaration.[96] Likewise, in the *El Salvador/Honduras* judgment, the ICJ, when citing the *Minquiers and Ecrehos* judgment, referred to these arguments advanced by the UK and France as 'ancient historical titles'.[97] Similar uses have occurred in *Cameroon v. Nigeria*.[98] Apart from the ICJ cases, the *Eritrea/Yemen* arbitral

89 The focus of this sub-section is on the rule of historic title over land territory instead of the rule of historic title over maritime territory. In another separate paper, the author has argued that the concept of historic title has developed separately under the frameworks of land and sea. For further discussions on this point, see X. Ma, Historic Title over Land and Maritime Territory, 4 *Journal of Territorial and Maritime Studies* (2017), 31–46. A. Gioia, Historic Titles, *MPEPIL* (2013), paras.1-29.

90 For a mention of the interchangeable use of 'ancient, original, or historic title', see Crawford, n 3, 209.

91 Sovereignty over Pedra Branca/Pulau Batu Puteh, Middle Rocks and South Ledge, n 23, para.37.

92 *Ibid.*, paras.123-124.

93 *Ibid.*, para.75.

94 Minquiers and Ecrehos Case (France v. United Kingdom), Judgment of 17 November 1953 (ICJ), 50.

95 *Ibid.*, 53.

96 *Ibid.*, 73 (Judge Alvarez's Declaration).

97 Land, Island and Maritime Frontier Dispute (El Salvador/Honduras: Nicaragua intervening), Judgment of 11 September 1992 (ICJ), para.343.

98 Nigeria claimed 'historical consolidation of title' with respect to the Lake Chad region and an 'ancient title' or 'original title' with respect to the Bakassi Peninsula. See Land and Maritime Boundary between Cameroon and Nigeria, n 15, paras.47, 65, 218, 220.

TABLE 4 Summary of the legal arguments advanced by the disputant states

Titles/ Effectivités dichotomy	Historic title	Effectivités	Treaty title	Cession	Discovery of terra nullius
China	√	√	√	--	√
Vietnam	--	√	√	√	--
Philippines	--	√	--	--	√
Malaysia	--	√	--	--	--

Notes: The symbol '√' means that the State concerned advances the legal argument and the symbol '--' indicates the opposite.

tribunal has explicitly endorsed the linkage between 'historic title' and 'ancient title' by holding that historic titles can manifest in diverse forms, one of which can be termed 'ancient title', which this tribunal referred to as 'a title that has so long been established by common repute that this common knowledge is itself a sufficient title'.[99]

Furthermore, the notions of 'historical consolidation of title' and 'possession immemorial' are both linked to the concept of historic title. In *Eritrea/Yemen*, Eritrea claimed a 'historic consolidation of title' to the disputed islands.[100] The tribunal regarded this 'historic consolidation of title' as another form of historic title distinct from the kind of 'ancient title'.[101] According to the tribunal, 'historic consolidation of title' is a title that 'has been created, or consolidated, by a process of prescription, or acquiescence, or by possession so long continued as to have become accepted by the law as a title'.[102] Similarly, in *Cameroon v. Nigeria*, Nigeria claimed territorial sovereignty over certain areas of Lake Chad as a consequence of 'historical consolidation of a title'.[103] With respect to 'possession immemorial' or 'immemorial

99 Arbitration on Territorial Sovereignty and Scope of the Dispute (Eritrea/Yemen), Award on the First Stage (PCA), para.106.
100 *Ibid.*, para.115.
101 *Ibid.*, para.106.
102 *Ibid.*
103 Land and Maritime Boundary between Cameroon and Nigeria, n 15, paras.62, 65.

possession', Malaysia claimed an ancient or original title to Pedra Branca/Pulau Batu Puteh based on possession since time immemorial, 'which has lasted for such a long time that it is impossible to provide evidence of a different situation and of which anybody recalls having heard talk'.[104] In *Eritrea/Yemen*, Yemen also relied on a claim of historic title stemming from 'time immemorial'.[105]

2.4.2 *Validity*

The successful application of the concept of historic title has been rare in international jurisprudence. The *Eritrea/Yemen* tribunal, though considering the concept of historic title to be well recognized in international law, did not uphold the parties' arguments based on this concept owing to the specific circumstances of the case where the alleged historic titles, if any, would be necessarily interrupted and adversely impacted by the Ottoman sovereignty over the regions as well as by the subsequent 1923 Treaty of Lausanne.[106] The ICJ has upheld territorial claims based on historic title in only one case, namely *Malaysia/Singapore*, where Malaysia claimed an ancient or original title to Pedra Branca/Pulau Batu Puteh based on immemorial possession.[107] The ICJ concluded that the Sultan of Johor – Malaysia's predecessor – enjoyed an original title to the disputed islands (Pedra Branca/Pulau Batu Puteh and Middle Rocks).[108]

The ICJ, nevertheless, has been cautious and never explicitly denied the validity of the concept of historic title. In those cases where the ICJ has rejected the application of this concept, the rejection has never been based on the invalidity of this concept but rather on its inapplicability in concrete circumstances. Occasionally, the ICJ, though not giving full support for historic titles alleged by parties, does take these alleged titles into account for the ultimate determination of territorial sovereignty. An illustrative example is the *Minquiers and Ecrehos* case where the ICJ did not simply disregard historic titles asserted by the UK and France but instead took these alleged titles

104 Sovereignty over Pedra Branca/Pulau Batu Puteh, Middle Rocks and South Ledge, n 23, para.48. (citing Meerauge (Austria/Hungary), Arbitral Award of 13 September 1902, RIAA Vol. XXVIII, 391.).

105 Arbitration on Territorial Sovereignty and Scope of the Dispute, n 99, para.246.

106 *Ibid.*, para.125.

107 Sovereignty over Pedra Branca/Pulau Batu Puteh, Middle Rocks and South Ledge, n 23, para.48.

108 *Ibid.*, para.69.

into account, and thus did not assimilate the disputed islands (Minquiers and Ecrehos) to *terra nullius*.[109]

The rejection of applying this concept is usually based on one of the following four reasons. First, in *Minquiers and Ecrehos* where the alleged historic-title holders were European States, the ICJ rejected the application of historic title to Minquiers and Ecrehos mainly because of the historical controversies surrounding the evidence dating back to the Middle Age.[110] Second, in cases involving Latin American and African countries such as *El Salvador/Honduras* and *Cameroon v. Nigeria*, the ICJ rejected the application of historic title on the ground that the predecessors of the countries concerned, being either local tribes or internal administrative subdivisions established by colonial powers, were incapable of holding a historic title to territory as a sovereign.[111] Third, when appreciating historic titles of an Asian kingdom, the ICJ tends to have no reservations in regarding such a kingdom as a sovereign to hold a particular territorial domain under its authority.[112] Hence, in *Indonesia/Malaysia*, the ICJ's rejection has been based on a rather different ground than the sovereign issue that the ties of allegiance or loyalty between the Sultan of Sulu and the Bajau Laut who frequently used the two disputed islands (Pulau Ligitan and Pulau Sipadan) did not suffice to prove that the Sultan of Sulu had a title to these two islands.[113] Fourth, the ICJ would not consider the application of historic title at all in the presence of an established territorial title based on binding boundary treaties or decisions. In *Qatar v. Bahrain*, the ICJ felt it unnecessary to entertain Qatar's alleged 'original title' to the Hawar Islands because the binding British decision of 1939 had attributed these islands to Bahrain.[114]

---

109 This observation is given by the ICJ in *Land, Island and Maritime Frontier Dispute* when citing the *Minquiers and Ecrehos* judgment. See Land, Island and Maritime Frontier Dispute, n 97, para.344.

110 Minquiers and Ecrehos Case, n 94, 56.

111 See Land, Island and Maritime Frontier Dispute, n 97, para.345 (holding that the 'original title' or 'historic title' belonged to the Spanish Crown rather than the internal administrative subdivisions established by it); Land and Maritime Boundary between Cameroon and Nigeria, n 15, paras.207, 212 (rejecting Nigeria's contention that the Bakassi Peninsula had remained under the sovereignty of the Kings and Chiefs of Old Calabar on the ground that Old Calabar could not be regarded as States and were without any international personality).

112 N. Schrijver and V. Prislan, Cases Concerning Sovereignty over Islands before the International Court of Justice and the Dokdo/Takeshima Issue, 46 *ODIL* (2015), 285.

113 Sovereignty over Pulau Ligitan and Pulau Sipadan, n 30, para.110.

114 Maritime Delimitation and Territorial Questions between Qatar and Bahrain (Qatar v. Bahrain), Judgment of 16 March 2001 (ICJ), para.148.

Only in one case – *Cameroon v. Nigeria* – where Nigeria claimed territorial sovereignty over the Lake Chad region as a consequence of 'historical consolidation of a title', the ICJ has simply stated, without further explanations, that the notion of 'historical consolidation' was highly controversial.[115] The ICJ did not go further to give an absolute denial of this notion, possibly because it did not need to do so since in the circumstances of this case, the presence of an established treaty title to the disputed territory at stake had already provided it with a strong and sufficient reason to disregard the alleged 'historical consolidation of a title'.[116] However, this finding did not win unanimous support from inside the court. Judges Koroma and Ajibola, in their dissenting opinions, disagreed with the majority opinion, and instead, supported Nigeria's claim based on the concept of historical consolidation.[117]

The opinions of scholars are also divided when it comes to the notion of 'historical consolidation of a title'. De Visscher introduced the notion of 'consolidation' to substitute 'acquisitive prescription' with an attempt to avoid the difficulties and controversies that had developed around the latter.[118] Acquisitive prescription properly so called, referred to as acquisition through adverse possession, is an alleged mode of establishing title to territory, which has a previous holder and thus not *terra nullius*, through the possession *à titre de souverain* over a prolonged lapse of time.[119] The difficulties confronting acquisitive prescription, which give rise to controversies,[120] are that its application requires not only 'the efflux of a fixed period of time'[121] or a fixed deadline for prescription, but also the authority of an adjudicator to declare the transfer of title from its legitimate owner to the possessor.[122] Attempted to avoid the difficulties and controversies in relation to the concept of acquisitive prescription, De Visscher introduced the notion of 'consolidation' to substitute 'acquisitive

115 Land and Maritime Boundary between Cameroon and Nigeria, n 15, para.65.

116 *Ibid.*

117 *Ibid.*, Dissenting Opinion of Judge Koroma, 476, para.8; Dissenting Opinion of Judge Ad Hoc Ajibola, 562, para.64.

118 C. De Visscher, *Theory and Reality in Public International Law* (Princeton University Press. 1957) (Translated from the French by P.E. Corbett), 199 (fn 68), 200. The first edition of this book was first published in French in 1953. Johnson's comments in 1955 were based on that edition.

119 Kohen, n 10, 154. Shaw, n 13, 374.

120 For an account of these controversies, see the bibliographies established by: D.H.N. Johnson, Acquisitive Prescription in International Law, 27 *BYIL* (1950), 334–340; Y.Z. Blum, *Historic Titles in International Law* (The Hague: Nijhoff. 1965), 8–12.

121 Blum, n 120, 59.

122 Kohen, n 10, 155.

prescription' based on the 1951 *Anglo-Norwegian Fisheries* judgment where he served as a member of the court.[123] In De Visscher's view, the foundation of the 'consolidation' of a title to a certain portion of land or sea is the 'proven long use', which represents 'a complex of interests and relations', rather than 'the passage of a fixed term, unknown in any event to international law' as required by the notion of 'acquisitive prescription'.[124] De Visscher further stated that the notion of 'consolidation' differed from 'acquisitive prescription' in the sense that it could also apply to 'territories that could not be proved to have belonged formerly to another State', whereas 'acquisitive prescription' only applied to territories previously owned by others.[125]

Johnson, Schwarzenberger and Udombana supported De Visscher's concept of historical consolidation of title.[126] Johnson perceived the approach of De Visscher as embracing the notion of 'acquisitive prescription' properly so called or 'adverse possession' on the one hand and the notion of 'immemorial possession' on the other hand under a single heading of 'consolidation'.[127] Johnson further commented with endorsement that the notion of 'consolidation' not only removed certain confusion and ambiguity surrounding the notion of prescription but also emphasized the close relationship between the acquisition and maintenance of titles.[128] Schwarzenberger also supported the concept of historical consolidation of title, stating that this concept transformed relative titles into absolute title through a gradual process in time and underlined the interplay between fundamental principles of sovereignty, recognition, consent and good faith governing titles to territory.[129] Udombana argued that historical consolidation, when coupled with *effectivités* and supported by the requisite evidence, could be a sound and valid means of creating title.[130] However, Kohen held the opposite opinion, arguing that the so-called 'historical consolidation of titles' doctrine constructed by scholars had not been successfully

123 De Visscher, n 118, 199 (fn 68), 200.

124 *Ibid.*, 200.

125 *Ibid.*

126 D.H.N. Johnson, Consolidation as a Root of Title in International Law, 13 *Cambridge Law Journal* (1955), 223–225. G. Schwarzenberger, Title to Territory: Response to a Challenge, 51(2) *AJIL* (1957), 311, 324. N.J. Udombana, The Ghost of Berlin Still Haunts Africa! The ICJ Judgment on the Land and Maritime Boundary Dispute between Cameroon and Nigeria, 10 *African Yearbook of International Law* (2002), 35.

127 Johnson, n 126, 223.

128 *Ibid.*, 223–225.

129 Schwarzenberger, n 126, 311, 324.

130 Udombana, n 126, 35.

established in international law.[131] In his view, this doctrine fails to 'find any echo in case law' and rather, was set aside by the ICJ in *Cameroon v. Nigeria* for being controversial.[132]

In contrast, a historic title informed by the notion of immemorial possession is less disputed among scholars. After examining opinions of different writers towards prescription and 'immemorial possession', Johnson reached a conclusion that 'even those writers who deny the existence of prescription as such in international law admit the existence of ..."immemorial possession" '.[133] Johnson's conclusion, albeit based on opinions of legal writers expressed decades ago, is still tenable today. For instance, Kohen, though rejecting the legal significance of the notion of 'historical consolidation of titles' under international law, was of the view that immemorial possession, where 'the origin of that possession is unknown and no one can advance a better title', was not problematic from a legal perspective.[134] In a similar vein, Schrijver and Prislan also observed that at least the ICJ had no problem applying the concept of original title based on immemorial possession to a territory claimed by European States or even Asian kingdoms.[135] The wider acceptation of the concept of immemorial possession than the concept of historical consolidation of title might result from the fact that the former applies to territory without a previous holder, whereas the latter also applies to territories previously owned by others and is thus more likely to trigger disputes.

2.4.3 *Operation*

Malaysia/Singapore, being the only case that has upheld a territorial claim to a disputed island (Pedra Branca/Pulau Batu Puteh) based on a historic title informed by the notion of immemorial possession, offers unique and useful hints for the application of this concept in concrete circumstances.[136] Malaysia claimed that Pedra Branca/Pulau Batu Puteh was under the sovereignty of the Sultan of Johor based on possession since time immemorial.[137] To decide whether Malaysia's territorial claim was sound in international law, the ICJ has

---

131 Kohen, n 10, 146, 154, 156–157; M.G. Kohen and M. Hébié, Conclusion, in M.G. Kohen and M. Hébié (eds.), *Research Handbook on Territorial Disputes in International Law* (Edward Elgar Publishing. 2018), 437.

132 Kohen, n 10, 146.

133 Johnson, n 126, 219. Johnson, n 120, 334–340.

134 Kohen, n 10, 154.

135 Schrijver and Prislan, n 112, 283, 285.

136 Sovereignty over Pedra Branca/Pulau Batu Puteh, Middle Rocks and South Ledge, n 23, para.69.

137 *Ibid.*, para.48.

examined three elements: (1) the possession element, (2) the time element, and (3) the ties of allegiance or loyalty.

2.4.3.1 The Possession Element

First, the possession should be completed by a sovereign. The ICJ admitted without any difficulty that the Sultan of Johor was a sovereign that could hold a particular territorial domain under its sovereignty since it came into existence in 1512.[138] Second, concerning the required degree of possession, given that Pedra Branca/Pulau Batu Puteh was a small and uninhabited island,[139] the ICJ was satisfied that a protest made by the Sultan of Johor against the activities of the Dutch East India Company in the waters around Pedra Branca/Pulau Batu Puteh in the middle of the seventeenth century had clearly indicated that the Sultan of Johor had held Pedra Branca/Pulau Batu Puteh within its territorial domain.[140]

It is necessary to detail the above incident here. In the middle of the seventeenth century, the Dutch Governor of Malacca wrote a letter to propose the Dutch East India Company to send two boats to cruise in the vicinity of Pedra Branca/Pulau Batu Puteh for preventing Chinese traders from entering Johor River.[141] According to this proposal, two Chinese junks were taken in the Straits and diverted to Malacca.[142] This incident triggered a protest from the Sultan. The Sultan sent an envoy to the Dutch Governor of Malacca to indicate his great displeasure regarding the seizure of the two Chinese junks, 'not without using offensive and threatening terms in the event that the same thing occurs in the future'.[143] On this basis of this single incident, the ICJ concluded that the Sultan of Johor had possessed sovereign authority over Pedra Branca/Pulau Batu Puteh.[144]

---

138 The ICJ has cited Grotius's words to *confirm* the sovereign status of the Sultan of Johor, which stated that: 'There is in India a kingdom called Johore, which has long been considered a sovereign principality [*supremi principatus*], so that its ruler clearly possessed the authority necessary to conduct a public war [against the Portugese]'. See Sovereignty over Pedra Branca/Pulau Batu Puteh, Middle Rocks and South Ledge, n 23, paras.52-53.

139 *Ibid.*, paras.62-67, 261.

140 *Ibid.*, para.55.

141 *Ibid.*, para.54.

142 *Ibid.*

143 *Ibid.*

144 *Ibid.*, para.55. It is noted that Malaysia and Singapore also disputed the relevance to the sovereignty issue of the construction and commissioning of the lighthouse on Pedra Branca/Pulau Batu Puteh around 1850. Malaysia claimed that Johor manifested its sovereignty over this island by having permitted the building of the lighthouse. Yet, the ICJ did

This conclusion obtained little doubt from inside the court,[145] and has not received open criticism from scholarly commentaries.[146] The ICJ's above conclusion, albeit not necessarily applicable in all circumstances, is arguable in terms of a small and uninhabited island like Pedra Branca/Pulau Batu Puteh in this case. This position is also in line with Schrijver and Prislan's analysis of a series of ICJ cases concerning island sovereignty. According to their analysis of international jurisprudence, in the case of small, remote and uninhabited islands, the ICJ has been satisfied with very little in the way of the actual exercise of sovereign rights, provided that the other State(s) cannot make a superior claim.[147]

2.4.3.2 The Time Element

The time element requires that the possession should be uninterrupted, unbroken and uncontested for a sufficiently long period of time.[148] It is, however, difficult to fix the time-limit as required for the establishment of a title based on immemorial possession. It is reasonable to expect that the time required would depend on specific circumstances. According to Fauchille, absent agreement between interested parties, the time-limit would vary according to the

---

not draw any conclusion about sovereignty based on the construction and commissioning of the lighthouse. See *ibid.*, paras.150, 162.

145 Almost all the individual opinions expressly agreed with the majority of the court on this point. See *ibid.*, Declaration of Judge Ranjeva, para.1; Separate Opinion of Judge Parra-Aranguren, para. 13; Joint Dissenting Opinion of Judges Simma and Abraham, para.4; Declaration of Judge Bennouna, para.1; and Dissenting Opinion of Judge ad hoc Dugard, para.3. The only criticism came from Judge Rao, who was the *ad hoc* judge appointed by Singapore on this case. In his view, 'Malaysia could not show that the Sultan of Johor had even a notional possession of Pedra Branca/Pulau Batu Puteh to sustain the claim of original title based on immemorial possession'. See *ibid.*, Separate Opinion of Judge ad hoc Sreenivasa Rao, para.25.

146 See *e.g.*, C.G. Lathrop, Sovereignty over Pedra Branca/Pulau Batu Puteh, Middle Rocks and South Ledge, 102(4) *AJIL* (2008), 830, 833–834; D.A. Colson and B.J. Vohrer, Introductory Note to International Court of Justice: Sovereignty over Pedra Branca/Pulau Batu Puteh, Middle Rocks and South Ledge (Malaysia/Singapore), 47 *International Legal Materials* (2008), 834; T. Hsien-Li, Case Concerning Sovereignty over Pedra Branca/Pulau Batu Puteh, Middle Rocks and South Ledge (Malaysia/Singapore), 12 *SYBIL* (2008), 259–262; S. Kopela, Case concerning Sovereignty over Pedra Branca/Pulau Batu Putech, Middle Rocks and South Ledge (Malaysia v. Singapore), 25(1) *IJMCL* (2010), 95, 110.

147 Schrijver and Prislan, n 112, 297.

148 Regarding 'uninterrupted', see Arbitration on Territorial Sovereignty and Scope of the Dispute, n 99, para.125. Regarding 'unbroken' and 'uncontested', see Meerauge, n 104, 391.

importance of the territory at stake, the manner of possession, and the attitudes of interested parties.[149]

In terms of the circumstances of *Malaysia/Singapore* where the island concerned is small and uninhabited, the ICJ considered two factors to be of significance. First, the ICJ noted that Pedra Branca/Pulau Batu Puteh evidently was not *terra incognita*.[150] This island was impossible to remain unknown or undiscovered by the local community, as it had always been known as a navigational hazard in the Straits of Singapore, which was an important channel for international navigation in east-west trade connecting the Indian Ocean with the South China Sea.[151] Thus, the ICJ concluded that it was reasonable to infer that Pedra Branca/Pulau Batu Puteh was viewed as one of the islands lying within the general geographical scope of the Sultan of Johor.[152] Second, the ICJ found that throughout the entire history of the Sultan of Johor, no competing claim had ever been advanced by other sovereigns.[153] Based on a combination of these geographical and historical contexts of the present case, the ICJ was satisfied that such a sufficiently prolonged absence of opposition by other sovereigns could lead to a conclusion that the possession of Pedra Branca/Pulau Batu Puteh by the Sultan of Johor had continued for so long a time that the origin of the territorial title to this island, though unknown, is beyond question. This finding indeed echoes the *Meerauge* arbitral award cited in the *Malaysia/Singapore* judgment, which defined 'immemorial possession' as 'the form of possession where no evidence can be adduced that the situation was ever different and no living person has ever heard of a different state of affairs'.[154] Distefano supported this position, commenting that immemorial possession indicated that one State's possession of territory was so ancient that other States could not put forward any adverse evidence.[155]

149 Though Fauchille's comments was pertinent to possession for prescription, it could equally apply to immemorial possession. See P. Fauchille, *Traité de Droit International Public*, Vol. i, Part ii (Paris: Rousseau 8th ed. 1925), 762.

150 Sovereignty over Pedra Branca/Pulau Batu Puteh, Middle Rocks and South Ledge, n 23, para.61.

151 *Ibid.*

152 *Ibid.*

153 *Ibid.*, para.62.

154 Meerauge, n 104, 391.

155 G. Distefano, The Conceptualization (Construction) of Territorial Title in the Light of the International Court of Justice Case Law, 19 *LJIL* (2006), 1069.

2.4.3.3 The Ties of Allegiance or Loyalty

Evidence of the ties of allegiance or loyalty between the inhabitants or regular users of the territory in dispute and the rulers of ancient kingdoms is not determinative but could confirm a historic title.[156] The *Malaysia/Singapore* judgment sheds light on the required level of the ties of allegiance or loyalty. Malaysia argued that the title of the Sultanate of Johor to Pedra Branca/Pulau Batu Puteh was confirmed by the ties of loyalty existing between the Sultanate and the Orang Laut, a nomadic people of the sea.[157] The Orang Laut, most of which constantly lived in their boats with a few having habitations onshore, frequently visited Pedra Branca/Pulau Batu Puteh and were engaged in various activities including fishing and piratical activities in the waters surrounding it.[158] The Orang Laut was one class of the Sultan's subjects. First, they were under the immediate control of two officers called Orang Kaya and Batin, the latter being subordinate to the former, which were appointed by the Sultan of Johor. Second, the Sultan could command their services on an emergency such as a war with a neighboring Chief.[159] Accordingly, the ICJ considered that the level of the ties of relationship between the Sultan of Johor and the Orang Laut proved sufficient political authority by the Sultan of Johor to qualify him as exercising sovereign authority over the Orang Laut, thereby confirming the title of the Sultanate of Johor to Pedra Branca/Pulau Batu Puteh.[160]

2.4.4 *Application to the Spratly Islands Setting*

China may base its territorial claim on the rule of historic title owing to its alleged historical contacts with the Spratly Islands. It is noted that the islands

156 It is noted that in *Indonesia/Malaysia* where Indonesia and Malaysia disputed the territorial sovereignty over two small islands in the Celebes Sea, namely Pulau Sipadan and Pulau Ligitan, Malaysia claimed that its predecessor – the Sultan of Sulu – originally held a historic title to these two disputed islands during the nineteenth and twentieth centuries based on the ties of loyalty between the Sultan of Sulu and the Bajau Laut, which was a local tribe that might have utilized these two islands from time to time. In this regard, the ICJ considered that even if the ties of loyalty between the Sultan of Sulu and the Bajau Laut were proved to be true, such ties were not in themselves sufficient to provide evidence that the Sultan of Sulu claimed territorial sovereignty over these two islands or considered them part of his possessions. See Sovereignty over Pulau Ligitan and Pulau Sipadan, n 30, paras.12-13, 98, 110. Schrijver and Prislan, n 112, 286.

157 Sovereignty over Pedra Branca/Pulau Batu Puteh, Middle Rocks and South Ledge, n 23, para.70.

158 *Ibid.*, paras.70-72.

159 *Ibid.*, para.73.

160 *Ibid.*, paras.74-75.

thereof are small and uninhabited similar to Pedra Branca/Pulau Batu Puteh. Hence, the *Malaysia/Singapore* formula for the application of the concept of historic title can offer useful guidance.[161] Two elements need to be satisfied in order to establish a historic title: the possession element and the time element. Moreover, evidence of the ties of allegiance or loyalty between the inhabitants or regular users of a contested land and the rulers of ancient kingdoms, albeit not determinative, could confirm a historic title.

2.4.4.1 The Possession Element

First, the possession should be completed by a sovereign that is capable of exercising authority over relevant land territory.[162] There is little dispute that China had begun to be admitted into the 'Family of Nations' at least by the end of the nineteenth century.[163] Moreover, by analogy to the ICJ's decision in *Malaysia/Singapore*, which admitted that the Sultan of Johor was a sovereign that could hold a particular territorial domain under its sovereignty since it came into existence in the early sixteenth century,[164] it is safe to conclude that China could be considered as a sovereign even in the time earlier than the late nineteenth century. This conclusion is also in line with Hébié's observation on international jurisprudence relating to the recognition of the legal personality of local political entities with non-western systems of social organizations. In his view, 'the tide has now turned in favour of admitting that local political entities enjoyed international legal personality during all relevant colonial periods'.[165]

---

161 The *Malaysia/Singapore* formula does not necessarily exclude the possibility of special rules or practices relating to territorial acquisition under non-Western normative systems. Yet, these special rules or practices are beyond the discussion of this chapter. For discussions about non-Western understanding of territorial acquisition, see *e.g.*, A. Carty and F.N. Lone, Some New Haven International Law Reflections on China, India and Their Various Territorial Disputes, 19 *Asia Pacific Law Review* (2011), 93–112 (regarding the Asian concepts of territorial sovereignty); B. Kwiatkowska, The Eritrea-Yemen Arbitration: Landmark Progress in the Acquisition of Territorial Sovereignty and Equitable Maritime Boundary Delimitation, 32 *ODIL* (2001), 15 (regarding the Islamic concepts of territorial sovereignty); D.W. Bowett, The Dubai/Sharjah Boundary Arbitration of 1981, 65 *BYIL* (1994), 123, 133 (regarding the Arabian concepts of territorial sovereignty).

162 R.Y. Jennings, *The Acquisition of Territory in International Law* (MUP. 1963), 26.

163 Schrijver and Prislan, n 112, 287. H.T. Hodgkin, *China in the Family of Nations* (George Allen & Unwin. 1923), 56. I.C.Y. Hsü, *China's Entrance into the Family of Nations: the Diplomatic Phase 1858–1880* (Harvard University Press. 1960).

164 Sovereignty over Pedra Branca/Pulau Batu Puteh, Middle Rocks and South Ledge, n 23, para.52.

165 M. Hébié, The Acquisition of Original Titles of Territorial Sovereignty in the Law and Practice of European Colonial Expansion, in M.G. Kohen and M. Hébié (eds.), *Research*

Second, establishing a historic title over small and uninhabited islands such as those in the Spratly Islands requires the manifestation of State authority over the islands concerned. In the present case, China had manifested its authority over these islands by protesting against the activities of the German government in this area in 1883.[166] Concerning small and uninhabited islands, possession does not necessarily mean maintaining a garrison at those places, but the power to hold such areas at will and to prevent other States from occupying them is sufficient.[167] Hence, it is arguable that a protest against the survey activities of the German government in the Spratly Islands suffices to demonstrate China's power to hold this area under its authority. Importantly, this event is similar to what happened to the Sultan of Johor in *Malaysia/Singapore*. In that case, the ICJ concluded that the Sultan of Johor enjoyed a territorial title to Pedra Branca/Pulau Batu Puteh since it had manifested its authority over this island by protesting against the activities of the Dutch East India Company in the waters around this island in the middle of the seventeenth century.[168] By analogy to this ICJ judgment, a protest against the survey activities of the German government in the Spratly Islands should, arguably, suffice to demonstrate China's power to hold this area under its authority.

2.4.4.2 The Time Element

It is difficult to fix the time-limit as required for the establishment of a title based on immemorial possession.[169] In *Malaysia/Singapore*, the ICJ considered two factors to be of significance, including: first, the geographical factor that Pedra Branca/Pulau Batu Puteh evidently was not *terra incognita*; and second, the historical factor that no competing claim had ever been advanced by other sovereigns throughout the entire history of the Sultan of Johor.

The Spratly Islands setting presents similar geographical and historical factors with Pedra Branca/Pulau Batu Puteh. First, the islands in this region were known as a navigational hazard in the South China Sea and thus were impossible to be *terra incognita*.[170] Second, no competing territorial claims regarding

---

Handbook on Territorial Disputes in International Law (Edward Elgar Publishing. 2018), 39–43.

166 Heinzig, n 35, 25–26, 72. Samuels, n 36, 52.

167 Minquiers and Ecrehos (France v. United Kingdom), Individual Opinion of Judge Basdevant of 17 November 1953 (ICJ), 78. Schwarzenberger, n 126, 316.

168 Sovereignty over Pedra Branca/Pulau Batu Puteh, Middle Rocks and South Ledge, n 23, para.55.

169 Fauchille, n 149, 762.

170 Heinzig, n 35, 22.

these islands had been put forward by other sovereigns until the twentieth century. Hence, by analogy to *Malaysia/Singapore*, it can be argued that such a sufficiently prolonged absence of opposition by other sovereigns could lead to a conclusion that the possession of the Spratly Islands by China had continued for so long a time that the origin of the territorial title to this island, though unknown, was beyond question at least until the twentieth century. This conclusion, albeit not necessarily applicable in all circumstances, is arguable in terms of small and uninhabited islands like those in the Spratly Islands.[171]

2.4.4.3 The Ties of Allegiance or Loyalty

Using the ties of allegiance or loyalty to confirm the historic title established by China, two conditions need to be fulfilled, including: first, Chinese fishers had regularly used the Spratly Islands; and second, the Chinese government had sufficient political authority over such fishers. As discussed below, these two conditions are fulfilled.

First, Chinese fishers had been conducting activities on or around the islands of the Spratly Islands at least since the nineteenth century. The crew of British surveying ships encountered Chinese fishers from Hainan on some islands thereof during surveys in the 1860s.[172] These surveys took place from 1862 until 1867 carried by *Royalist*. *The China Sea Directory* published in 1868 by the Britain Admiralty, when referring to the Tizard Bank and Reefs (Zhenghe

---

171 An analogy could be made to the time-limit element contained in the continuity requirement of *effectivités*. See section 2.5.1.4.

172 The French magazine *Le Monde Colonial Illustré* published in September 1933 gave support to the inhabitation of Chinese fishermen on the Spratly Islands as well. It was recorded that only Hainan natives from China inhabited the nine islands of the Spratly Islands and no people from other countries inhabited there. For example, there were seven inhabitants on South West Cay (two of them were children), five on Thitu Island, and four on Spratly Island (one more than that of 1930). There were worship stands and thatched cottages on Loaita Island, and a tablet with Chinese scripts on Itu Aba Island. This magazine analyzed the habitation situation on these islands and concluded that they were habitable because there was abundant vegetation (including coconut palms, banana trees, papaya trees, pineapples, green vegetables and potatoes), wells providing drinking water and poultry raised by the inhabitants. The *Asiatic Pilot*, Vol. IV, published by the United States Hydrographic Office in 1925, also had accounts about the inhabitation of Chinese fishers on the maritime features of the Spratly Islands. See China, n 34, paras.16-17. The presence of Chinese fishers on the maritime features of Spratly Islands was also confirmed in a Note dated 8 March 1928 from Mr Bourgouin, which acted in the capacity of representing French authority to respond to the Japanese claims to the Spratly Islands made in 1927. The original text reads as follows: 'The area [i.e. the Spratly Islands] is now visited only by a few Chinese fishermen from Hainan, who find an abundance of turtles and sea cucumbers there; it appears that some of them built temporary shelters'.

Qunjiao) in the Spratly Islands, observed that 'Hainan fishermen, who subsist by collecting trepang and tortoiseshell, were found upon most of these islands, some of whom remain for years amongst the reefs'.[173] Moreover, some historians claim that Chinese fishers had been compiling and circulating a book called 'Geng Lu Bu' (Manual of Sea Routes) at least since the sixteenth century, which was a navigation guidebook for the travelling between the coast of mainland China and the maritime features in the South China Sea.[174] This book records names given by Chinese fishers for at least seventy maritime features in the Spratly Islands.[175] Such names were mentioned and adopted by Western navigators and even marked in some official navigation guidebooks and charts published in the nineteenth and twentieth centuries. For example, the English names commonly used for Namyit Island, Sin Cowe Island and Subi Reef are originated respectively from 'Nanyi', 'Chenggou' and 'Chouwei' as pronounced in Hainan dialects.[176]

Second, China had exercised sufficient political authority over these fishers at least through household registration and fish tax. China had established a household registration system at least since the Western Zhou Dynasty (1045–771 B.C.), mainly for the purposes of collecting poll taxes and commanding military services when a need arose.[177] Chinese fishers operating in the Spratly Islands were called 'Dan Min' (or the Tankas, meaning 'the people of the sea') mainly from Hainan.[178] As shown by the official records of Ming Dynasty such

See Note dated 8 March 1928 from Mr Bourgouin, reproduced in: Chemillier-Gendreau, n 8, Annex 18.

173 Similar records were also contained in *The China Sea Directory* in 1906 and *The China Sea Pilot* in its editions of 1912, 1923 and 1937 published by the Britain Admiralty. See Hancox, n 37, 10. Heinzig, n 35, 23, 27. China, n 34, paras.12, 15.

174 Zhou and Tang, n 39, 117.

175 China, n 34, para.11.

176 *Ibid.*, para.12.

177 The existence of a household registration system in the Western Zhou Dynasty is evidenced by the records in a book – *Zhou Li* (*Rites of Zhou*) – credited to the Duke of Zhou, who was a member of the royal family of the Zhou dynasty who played a major role in consolidating the kingdom and acted as a capable and loyal regent for his young nephew King Cheng. According to these records, an officer called 'Simin' was responsible for implementing the household registration system. Females aged more than seven months after birth and males over eighth months must be registered in books. In addition, the birth and death of the population must be registered every year to reflect the natural changes, and a population survey verification was conducted every three years. See Zhou Li (Rites of Zhou) (in Chinese), available at <https://zh.wikisource.org/wiki/%E5%91%A8%E7%A6%AE/%E7%A7%8B%E5%AE%98%E5%8F%B8%E5%AF%87>.

178 Zhou and Tang, n 39, 128–129.

as 'Ming Tai Zu Shi Lu' ('Records of Hongwu Emperor') and 'Jiajing Guangdong Tong Zhi' ('General Records of Guangdong Ruled by Jiajing Emperor'), 'Dan Min' had become one class of the subjects that were required to be registered in the household registration system at least since the Ming Dynasty (1368–1644 A.D.).[179] China collected fish tax from 'Dan Min' at least in the Ming Dynasty and the Qing Dynasty (1644–1912 A.D.).[180] The Guangdong provincial government, whose administrative jurisdiction covered 'Dan Min' from Hainan, levied a fish tax on 'Dan Min' according to the number of vessels rather than the amount of catch.[181] An official entity called 'He Bo Suo' (the Office of Rivers and Lakes) was responsible for collecting the fish tax.[182]

2.4.4.4 Interim Conclusion

In terms of the small and uninhabited islands within the Spratly Islands, the preceding analysis concludes that two elements – the possession element and the time element – for establishing a historic title are, arguably, satisfied. It further concludes that China had been enjoying a historic title over the islands thereof at least until the twentieth century. This title is also confirmed by the ties of allegiance or loyalty between the Chinese government and the Chinese fishers who had regular activities in the region. Admittedly, this conclusion is built on a foundation that no competing territorial claims regarding these

179 These two books were both drafted and edited by officials authorized by the Emperors of China. See F. Xiao and Z. Liu, Clan, Market, Bandits and Dan Min: Clan Groups and Society in the Pearl River Delta Since the Ming Dynasty (in Chinese), 3 *Journal of Chinese Social and Economic History* (2004), 5. For example, it was recorded that 'in 1383, the Emperor ordered General Yong Zhao to register thousands of Dan Min from Guangzhou in the household registration system and further to recruit them into the navy'. See *Ming Tai Zu Shi Lu* (Records of Hongwu Emperor), Vol. 143, para. 456, available at <https://ctext.org/wiki.pl?if=gb&chapter=83442&remap=gb#p422 >.

180 See Q. Li, The Sea-related People in the Qiongzhou Strait Area and Their Marine Beliefs: Also on Some Issues in the Study of the History of the Straits (in Chinese) (28 November 2016), available at <http://www.sohu.com/a/120054012_523177>. P. Yang, Ocean Governance during the Qing Dynasty: The Evolution of Fisheries Tax Regulations in the Southeast Coast (in Chinese), 55(3) *Journal of Sun Yat-Sen University (Social Science Edition)* (2015), 142–143.

181 This method of taxation was recorded in a report from the Finance Minister, Ben Xu, addressed to the Qianlong Emperor, and also in Vol. 17 of the official records of Huilai County ruled by the Yongzheng Emperor. See Yang, n 180, 142, 143 and fn. 1.

182 For example, the fish tax collected from 'Dan Min' in all counties of Hainan in 1384 (the Ming Dynasty) was about 7632 Dan (i.e. an ancient volume unit of China, usually used to measure rice and pay official salaries and taxes), whereras in 1557 (the Qing Dynasty), it was equivalent to around 1871 taels of silver. See Li, n 180, Table 3.

islands in the Spratly Islands had been put forward by other sovereigns until the twentieth century. As mentioned at the beginning of this chapter, although this study has been careful not to overlook any available and relevant official documents and secondary literature, risks remain that evidence of significant importance might not be available to the public owing to confidentiality or other reasons. Thus, the above conclusion is valid unless adverse evidence, if any, is uncovered.

2.5 Effectivités

As the PCIJ has described in the 1933 *Eastern Greenland* judgment, a claim to sovereignty based not upon legal titles but merely upon continued display of authority namely *effectivités* requires two constituent elements: 'the intention and will to act as sovereign, and some actual exercise or display of such authority'.[183] The recent *Croatia/Slovenia* arbitral award has referred to the above description as 'two elements of *effectivités*'.[184]

2.5.1 *The Objective Element: Acts of Effectivités*

Effectivités require material acts exercising or displaying State authority. In international judicial practice, a wide range of acts has been invoked as evidence of the exercise of State sovereignty. In *Nicaragua v. Colombia*, the ICJ has summarized that 'acts and activities considered to be performed *à titre de souverain* are in particular, but not limited to, legislative acts or acts of administrative control, acts relating to the application and enforcement of criminal or civil law, acts regulating immigration, acts regulating fishing and other economic activities, naval patrols as well as search and rescue operations'.[185] These acts can be classified according to the three traditional powers of a State, namely the legislative power, the administrative or executive, and the judicial (subsection 2.5.1.1). Furthermore, to constitute relevant *effectivités*, these acts need to fulfil general requirements including being attributable to a State (subsection 2.5.1.2), peaceful (subsection 2.5.1.3), continuous, public, pertinent to the disputed territory (subsection 2.5.1.4), and sometimes, before the critical date (subsection 2.5.1.5).

183 Legal Status of Eastern Greenland, n 15, 45–46.
184 Arbitration between the Republic of Croatia and the Republic of Slovenia, n 22, para.341.
185 Territorial and Maritime Dispute, n 30, para.80.

2.5.1.1 Categories of Acts of Effectivités

2.5.1.1.1 *Legislative Acts*

As the PCIJ stated in *Eastern Greenland*, '[l]egislation is one of the most obvious forms of the exercise of sovereign power'.[186] In that case, the PCIJ held that the enactments including Ordinances of 1740–1751, 1758, 1776 and their operation had manifested the display of authority of the King of Denmark and Norway during the period from the founding of the colonies by Hans Egede in 1721 up to 1814 to an extent sufficient to give his country a valid claim to sovereignty over Greenland which was not limited to the colonized area.[187] In *Indonesia/Malaysia*, the ICJ considered that the Turtle Preservation Ordinance of 1917 and Land Ordinance of 1930 enacted by Malaysia, which regulated and controlled the collecting of turtle eggs and the establishment of a bird reserve, constituted regulatory assertions of authority over territory including the disputed Ligitan and Sipadan.[188]

2.5.1.1.2 *Administrative or Executive Acts*

Administrative or executive acts might comprise regulation of immigration or control of visits,[189] recognition of consular representations,[190] regulation of economic activities including fishing,[191] law enforcement measures,[192] naval visits and search and rescue operations,[193] marine incident investigation,[194] land reclamation projects,[195] and public works including the construction and operation of lighthouses and other navigational aids[196] over the disputed territory or within waters in its immediate vicinity.

---

186 Legal Status of Eastern Greenland, n 15, 48.

187 *Ibid.*, 48–51.

188 Sovereignty over Pulau Ligitan and Pulau Sipadan, n 30, paras.143-145.

189 See *e.g.*, Sovereignty over Pedra Branca/Pulau Batu Puteh, Middle Rocks and South Ledge, n 23, paras.235-239, 274.

190 See *e.g.*, Territorial and Maritime Dispute, n 30, paras.82-84.

191 See *e.g.*, Territorial and Maritime Dispute between Nicaragua and Honduras in the Caribbean Sea, n 30, para.195-196; Territorial and Maritime Dispute, n 30, paras.82-84.

192 See *e.g.*, Territorial and Maritime Dispute, n 30, paras.82-84.

193 See *e.g.*, *ibid.*

194 See *e.g.*, Sovereignty over Pedra Branca/Pulau Batu Puteh, Middle Rocks and South Ledge, n 23, paras.231-234.

195 See *e.g.*, *ibid.*, paras.249-250.

196 See *e.g.*, Maritime Delimitation and Territorial Questions between Qatar and Bahrain, n 114, paras.31-33, 197; Sovereignty over Pulau Ligitan and Pulau Sipadan, n 30, paras.130, 132, 147; Territorial and Maritime Dispute between Nicaragua and Honduras in the Caribbean Sea, n 30, para.205-207; Territorial and Maritime Dispute, n 30, paras.82-83.

2.5.1.1.3 *Judicial Acts*

Judicial acts include the exercise of jurisdiction by domestic courts in respect of the disputed territory. In *Minquiers and Ecrehos*, the ICJ concluded that 'Jersey courts have exercised criminal jurisdiction in respect of the Ecrehos during nearly a hundred years' based on the fact that five criminal proceedings were initiated in Jersey for criminal offences committed on the Ecrehos between 1826 and 1921.[197] Similarly, in *Nicaragua v. Honduras*, the ICJ held that the evidence provided by Honduras of criminal complaints before the courts of Honduras for criminal acts which occurred on the islands in dispute (South Cay and Savanna Cay) did have a bearing on the evaluation of *effectivités*.[198]

2.5.1.2 Acts Attributable to a State

First, in general, acts performed by State organs including both central and local governments and State agents acting in their official capacity are attributable to a State.[199] Second, acts performed by private entities cannot be attributed to a State unless they are acting on the instructions of or under the direction or control of that State.[200] In *Indonesia/Malaysia*, the ICJ did not consider Indonesian fishers' traditional use of the waters around Ligitan and Sipadan acts of *effectivités* on the ground that 'activities by private persons cannot be seen as *effectivités* if they do not take place on the basis of official regulations or under governmental authority'.[201]

The presence and activities of a population on a territory are not in themselves acts of *effectivités*.[202] For instance, in *Land, Island and Maritime Frontier Dispute*, the ICJ rejected El Salvador's contention that the private ownership of land by Salvadorians in the disputed area could indicate that this disputed area was not part of Honduras but part of El Salvador.[203] In contrast, the acts of State organs or agents regulating the activities of individuals on a territory can amount to *effectivités*. An example is *Malaysia/Singapore* where the ICJ considered that control of lighthouse visits conducted by the UK and

197 Minquiers and Ecrehos Case, n 94, 65.

198 Territorial and Maritime Dispute between Nicaragua and Honduras in the Caribbean Sea, n 30, paras.182-185.

199 UN Doc.: A/RES/56/83, ILC Articles on Responsibility of States for Internationally Wrongful Acts (28 January 2002), Articles 4 and 7.

200 *Ibid.*, Article 8.

201 Sovereignty over Pulau Ligitan and Pulau Sipadan, n 30, para.140.

202 Kohen, n 10, 160.

203 Land, Island and Maritime Frontier Dispute, n 97, para.97.

Singapore constituted acts *à titre de souverain* respecting Pedra Branca/Pulau Batu Puteh.[204]

2.5.1.3 Peaceful

The display of sovereign authority should be peaceful. It is evident that military action, albeit belonging to activities of administrative function in domestic law, is difficult to be considered as a peaceful and regular exercise of the functions of control over the territory concerned thereby constituting a relevant *effectivité*.[205] Moreover, a perusal of the ICJ jurisprudence shows that in the various cases when an international court or tribunal has upheld a party's territorial claim based upon *effectivités*, such *effectivités* are usually accompanied by another party's failure to protest, acquiescence or even recognition.[206] It is still, however, inconclusive to say that *effectivités* could only be considered peaceful in the absence of any disagreement or protest. Indeed, it is open to question whether diplomatic protests of an opposing State have the value of interrupting the peaceful possession maintained by a possessor State over the disputed territory.[207]

The 1911 *Chamizal* arbitral award has upheld that protests can preclude the peaceful character of the possession. In that case where Mexico and the US disputed the territorial title to the Chamizal Tract (land territory), the US based its territorial claim partly on prescription in addition to its title under the treaties of 1848 and 1853.[208] The tribunal dismissed the US's plea of prescription on the ground that it had been constantly challenged and questioned by Mexico through diplomatic protests.[209]

Scholars seem to hold a different opinion from the *Chamizal* award. According to Verykios, a diplomatic protest has a value of drawing the attention of international public opinion to the question, but a protest not followed by further steps, such as the settlement of the dispute, would become 'academic' and 'useless'.[210] Johnson agreed with Verykios and held that such further

204 Sovereignty over Pedra Branca/Pulau Batu Puteh, Middle Rocks and South Ledge, n 23, para.274.

205 For a similar view, see Kohen, n 10, 162.

206 Schrijver and Prislan, n 112, 296.

207 Shaw has pointed out that diplomatic protests will probably be sufficient to block any prescriptive claim, but he was aware that this position was not accepted by all academic writers. See Shaw, n 13, 375–376.

208 The Chamizal Case (Mexico/United States), Arbitral Award of 15 June 1911, RIAA Vol. XI, 328.

209 *Ibid.*, 328–329.

210 P.A. Verykios, *La prescription en droit international public* (Paris: Pedone. 1934), 101. ('ces protestations académiques finissent par ne plus avoir aucune utilité').

steps might include, where possible, a reference of the matter to the League of Nations or the PCIJ since 1919 or to the UN or the ICJ since 1945.[211] Johnson argued that the advent of new machinery for international dispute settlement since 1919 had largely reduced the significance of a protest in frustrating the peaceful display of the possession, and since then a protest could be said to have amounted to no more than a temporary bar.[212] Johnson further stated that how soon diplomatic protests should cease to be of value and become 'academic' and 'useless' was a matter of fact to be left to the determination of the court or tribunal concerned.[213]

However, no real inconsistency exists between the *Chamizal* award and the 'diplomatic protests plus further steps' formula purported by the scholars. Notably, the *Chamizal* award inferred that the circumstances in that case were such that for Mexico, diplomatic protests constituted the *only* feasible method of asserting its rights before the establishment of the International Boundary Commission in 1889, an international body created by the US and Mexico to determine the location of their international boundary and the commissioners of which also served as the arbitrators in this case.[214] The tribunal further pointed out that Mexico brought the dispute 'within a reasonable time' before the International Boundary Commission after it started to function. In this regard, MacGibbon has commented that this tribunal appeared to have required proof that 'the protesting State had taken some further steps [i.e. asserting a claim before the International Boundary Commission] as evidence of the seriousness and good faith of its intention to oppose encroachments on its rights'.[215] Hence, the *Chamizal* award does not differ from the 'diplomatic protests plus further steps' formula purported by the scholars.

The discussions contained in the *Chamizal* award and scholars' views, though pertaining to prescription or adverse possession, can entail analogical implications for *effectivités*. To this effect, diplomatic protests could not have the ultimate effect of obstructing peaceful possession unless followed by qualified further steps. Reducing the significance of diplomatic protests is reasonable because the costs of lodging diplomatic protests are so low that States might abuse them as 'unilateral and frequently opportunist instruments', thereby destabilizing the territorial order.[216] Thus, it is necessary and

---

211 Johnson, n 120, 346.

212 *Ibid.*

213 *Ibid.*

214 The Chamizal Case, n 208, 329.

215 I.C. MacGibbon, Some Observations on the Part of Protest in International Law, 30 *BYIL* (1953), 310.

216 *Ibid.*, 293.

reasonable to require further steps to show 'evidence of the seriousness and good faith' of the protesting State's 'intention to oppose encroachments on its rights'.[217] Otherwise, giving preference to mere periodical and ineffectual paper protests might prolong disputes indefinitely without good reason, which would be 'incompatible with the régime under which the rights of each State would be specified and guaranteed'.[218]

According to Johnson, there are two kinds of qualified further steps: a reference of the matter to the UN or the ICJ since 1945.[219] First, according to Article 35 of the UN Charter, a State, whether a member of the UN or not, can bring any dispute or any situation, which might lead to international friction or give rise to a dispute, before the General Assembly and Security Council for discussion to determine whether the continuance of the dispute or situation is likely to endanger the maintenance of international peace and security.[220] This article undoubtedly applies in the context of territorial disputes. Second, in case the possessor State does not accept the ICJ's jurisdiction, even if the opposing State brings the matter before the ICJ, the ICJ cannot exercise its jurisdictional power over the matter. In light of this, Judge Carneiro suggested in his individual opinion in *Minquiers and Ecrehos* that France could have and ought to have proposed arbitration to settle the territorial dispute regarding Minquiers and Ecrehos with the UK, in order to be adequate and effective in blocking the latter from claiming territorial titles based on its activities.[221] Hence, making an offer or proposal to settle the territorial dispute through an international court or tribunal amounts to one kind of qualified further steps.

A relevant question is whether there could be other kinds of qualified further steps, in addition to mechanisms involving the UN and international adjudication as proposed by Johnson about 70 years ago. Notably, Article 33(1) of the UN Charter sets forth other equally important peaceful means including negotiation, enquiry, mediation, conciliation, resort to regional agencies or arrangements, or other peaceful means of their own choice.[222] These peaceful means are of equal importance with mechanisms involving the UN and international adjudication in the sense that they can lead to the final settlement of a dispute. Nevertheless, the outcome of these peaceful means highly

217 *Ibid.*, 310.

218 Minquiers and Ecrehos (France/United Kingdom), Individual Opinion of Judge Levi Carneiro of 17 November 1953, 108.

219 Johnson, n 120, 346.

220 UN Charter, Article 35.

221 Minquiers and Ecrehos, n 218, 107.

222 UN Charter, Article 33(1).

depends on the political will of the disputant States. Consequently, similar to diplomatic protests, there is a risk that the disputant States might abuse these peaceful means to prolong disputes without good reason. Therefore, a balance must be struck between recognizing the importance of these peaceful means in dispute settlement and preventing the abuse of them to prolong disputes unreasonably. Schwarzenberger's suggestion is worth taking. In his view, to the extent that the opposing State has supplemented action by evidence that it has made every effort to induce the possessor State to agree to the peaceful settlement of the dispute through means enumerated in Article 33(1) of the UN Charter, such supplemented action amounts to qualified further steps to thwart the peaceful display of State authority alleged by the possessor State.[223]

However, one accepted exception to the 'diplomatic protests plus further steps' formula is that '[m]inor manifestations in the purported exercise of title might well adequately be met by protests'.[224] This position was stated by the agent for the UK in the oral proceedings of *Minquiers and Ecrehos* where it was argued that the character of the action taken by the protesting State should be related to and in proportion to the action taken by the State acquiring title.[225] Later, in the oral proceedings of *Anglo-Norwegian Fisheries*, the agent of the UK expressed a similar argument that '[t]he paper protest is at least as important as the paper decree'.[226] Such 'paper decree' include municipal legislation without actual enforcement. MacGibbon has commented that in the event of a paper decree, diplomatic protests are 'the proper and probably the only effective course open to an aggrieved State' because without the suffering of actual infringement of its rights, an aggrieved State would be unlikely to have any substantial cause of action before an international court or tribunal.[227] Hence, diplomatic protests would suffice at least until the attempt is made to enforce the paper decree.[228]

To conclude, diplomatic protests could generally act as a temporary bar to disturb the peaceful character of possession. Qualified further steps that can produce the ultimate effect of obstructing peaceful possession include mechanisms involving the UN, international adjudication, and other peaceful means enumerated in Article 33(1) of the UN Charter to the extent that the opposing State has demonstrated that it has made every effort to induce

223 Schwarzenberger, n 126, 323.
224 Minquiers and Ecrehos (France/United Kingdom), Oral Proceedings, 367.
225 *Ibid.*
226 Fisheries (United Kingdom v. Norway), Oral Proceedings, 37.
227 MacGibbon, n 215, 316.
228 *Ibid.*

the possessor State to agree on these peaceful means. One exception is that if the possessor State manifests its authority through municipal legislation without actual enforcement, diplomatic protests would suffice at least until the attempt is made to enforce the legislation.

2.5.1.4 Continuous, Public and Pertinent

The display of sovereign authority should be *continuous*. Continuity means that the performance of *effectivités* endures for a certain length of time. It is, however, impossible to point to any defined length of time.[229] The time-limit will rely on the specific circumstances of the case.[230] Isolated acts could become crucial depending on the nature of the territory and the existence of competing claims advanced by other sovereigns, including legal titles other than *effectivités* and the weight to be attributed to opposite *effectivités* performed by another sovereign over the same territory.[231]

First, the required degree of the display of sovereign authority should be in proportion to the nature of the territory concerned. The ICJ stated in *Nicaragua v. Honduras* that '[s]overeignty over minor maritime features ... may therefore be established on the basis of a relatively modest display of State powers in terms of quality and quantity'.[232] For example, though the construction and operation of lighthouses and other navigational aids were not considered as an act manifesting the exercise of State authority in *Minquiers and Ecrehos*,[233] the ICJ has concluded in several cases, including *Qatar v. Bahrain*, *Indonesia/Malaysia*, *Nicaragua v. Honduras* and *Nicaragua v. Colombia*, that these acts could be legally relevant and suffice to constitute a title in the event of tiny islands.[234] Scholars also comment that what act will suffice for the establishment of territorial sovereignty relies on the character of the territory: 'the bar

229 Shaw, n 13, 376.

230 *Ibid.*

231 Kohen, n 10, 157.

232 Territorial and Maritime Dispute between Nicaragua and Honduras in the Caribbean Sea, n 30, para.174.

233 Minquiers and Ecrehos Case, n 94, 70–71.

234 See *e.g.*, Maritime Delimitation and Territorial Questions between Qatar and Bahrain, n 114, paras.31-33, 197 (regarding a small island, Qit'at Jaradah); Sovereignty over Pulau Ligitan and Pulau Sipadan, n 30, paras.130, 132, 147 (regarding two tiny islands, Pulau Ligitan and Pulau Sipadan); Territorial and Maritime Dispute between Nicaragua and Honduras in the Caribbean Sea, n 30, para.205-207 (regarding Bobel Cay, Savanna Cay, Port Royal Cay and South Cay); Territorial and Maritime Dispute, n 30, paras.82-83 (regarding Alburquerque, Bajo Nuevo, East-Southeast Cays, Quitasueño, Roncador, Serrana and Serranilla).

with respect to remote and sparsely settled areas will be set lower than in the context of more heavily populated territory'.[235]

Second, the continuous requirement might be reduced in the absence of any superior competing claim made by other States. The PCIJ endorsed this position in *Eastern Greenland*, stating that:

> [i]t is impossible to read the records of the decisions in cases as to territorial sovereignty without observing that in many cases the tribunal has been satisfied with very little in the way of the actual exercise of sovereign rights, provided that the other State could not make out a superior claim. This is particularly true in the case of claims to sovereignty over areas in thinly populated or unsettled countries.[236]

In keeping the same approach with the PCIJ, the ICJ held in *Nicaragua v. Honduras* that 'a significant element to be taken into account is the extent to which any acts *à titre de souverain* in relation to disputed islands have been carried out by another State with a competing claim to sovereignty'.[237] In case there are two competing claims of *effectivités* over the same territory, the relatively stronger one should prevail. Nevertheless, the international courts or tribunals have rarely been compelled to decide on which party has made a superior claim in the presence of competing *effectivités*, either because the other party has not provided any evidence of acts *à titre de souverain* in relation to the disputed territory, or the evidence put forward by it has been deemed unpersuasive, inconclusive or otherwise has no bearing on the territory in dispute.[238]

The display of sovereign authority should be *public* so that interested States can be made aware of it.[239] In *Malaysia/Singapore*, Singapore claimed that its installation of military communications equipment on this island in 1977 could constitute an act of *effectivité*, while Malaysia argued that the installation was undertaken secretly.[240] The ICJ rejected this claim on the ground that it was unable to assess whether Malaysia had any knowledge of this installation.[241]

---

235 Crawford, n 3, 210.
236 Legal Status of Eastern Greenland, n 15, 46.
237 Territorial and Maritime Dispute, n 30, para.80.
238 For an account of the ICJ cases in this regard, see Schrijver and Prislan, n 112, 295.
239 Shaw, n 13, 375.
240 Sovereignty over Pedra Branca/Pulau Batu Puteh, Middle Rocks and South Ledge, n 23, para.247.
241 *Ibid.*, para.248.

The display of sovereign authority should be explicitly or undoubtedly *pertinent* to the territory in dispute. In *Indonesia/Malaysia*, the ICJ pronounced a general principle for assessing activities constituting *effectivités* that '[the court] can only consider those acts as constituting a relevant display of authority which leave no doubt as to their specific reference to the islands in dispute as such'.[242] Similarly, in *Minquiers and Ecrehos*, the ICJ considered that the fact that the Rolls of the Manorial Court of the fief of Noirmont in Jersey contained three entries for the years 1615, 1616 and 1617 regarding specific objects shipwrecked at the Minquiers indicated that these judicial activities specifically referred to the Minquiers, and could therefore constitute valid evidence of *effectivités*.[243] In *Malaysia/Singapore*, the ICJ rejected to regard an exploitation concession granted by the Malaysian government to an oil company as valid evidence of *effectivités* because of the lack of publicity of the coordinates in relation to the concession.[244]

2.5.1.5 Critical Date

The concept of critical date is a date after which a court or tribunal should not admit evidence of the activities of the parties.[245] It is a jurisprudential tool used to 'freeze' any territorial title at the moment of the crystallization of the dispute.[246] As the ICJ has explained in the 2002 *Indonesia/Malaysia* judgment, in appraising evidence of *effectivités*, acts having taken place after the critical date, on which the dispute between the parties crystallized, could not be taken into consideration unless such acts amount to 'a normal continuation of prior acts and are not undertaken for the purpose of improving the legal position of the Party which relies on them'.[247] The ICJ has reaffirmed this position in cases including *Nicaragua v. Honduras*, *Malaysia/Singapore* and *Nicaragua v. Colombia*.[248]

---

242 Sovereignty over Pulau Ligitan and Pulau Sipadan, n 30, para.136.

243 Minquiers and Ecrehos Case, n 94, 67–69.

244 Sovereignty over Pedra Branca/Pulau Batu Puteh, Middle Rocks and South Ledge, n 23, paras.251-253.

245 Argentine-Chile Frontier Case, Arbitral Award of 9 December 1966, RIAA Vol. XVI, 166.

246 G. Distefano, The Time Factor and Territorial Disputes, in M.G. Kohen and M. Hébié (eds.), *Research Handbook on Territorial Disputes in International Law* (Edward Elgar Publishing. 2018), 399–400, fn. 17.

247 Sovereignty over Pulau Ligitan and Pulau Sipadan, n 30, para.135.

248 See *e.g.*, Territorial and Maritime Dispute between Nicaragua and Honduras in the Caribbean Sea, n 30, para.117; Sovereignty over Pedra Branca/Pulau Batu Puteh, Middle Rocks and South Ledge, n 23, para.179-180; Territorial and Maritime Dispute, n 30, para.83-84.

The *raison d'être* of the concept of critical date includes two facets. The first facet is a pragmatic one, being the practical necessity to confine the dossier to the more relevant facts and thus to acts prior to the existence of a dispute.[249] The second facet is a logical one. The disputed character of a territory at stake should bar acts subsequent to the crystallization of the dispute from producing any effect on the territorial title, as a normal inference from the principle of good and fairness is that 'a state should be precluded in law to avail itself of a situation carried with the sole purpose of establishing its sovereignty while the latter [the sovereignty] is precisely and overtly challenged by another state'.[250]

The ultimate relevance or importance of the concept of critical date may, however, vary depending on the specific circumstances of the case.[251] International courts or tribunals have found this concept of little utility in three circumstances. The first circumstance is where a court or tribunal is asked to determine a *contemporary* title to the territory in question, instead of a title established in the past. For example, the *Dubai/Sharjah* arbitral tribunal stated that:

> In reality the concept of the critical date has only played a significant role in cases where it was necessary to establish exactly and precisely when in the past sovereignty was exercised by a State over a given territory, as in the *Island of Palmas* and *Eastern Greenland* cases. This is not the situation in the present dispute where the task of the Court, as has been indicated in Chapter II above, is to decide to whom the disputed boundary areas belong today.[252]

Bowett commented that this finding indicated that the tribunal rejected the application of the concept of critical date to disputes about a contemporary title to territory.[253] In a similar vein, the *Argentine/Chile* arbitral tribunal 'considered the notion of the critical date to be of little value in the present litigation and … examined all the evidence submitted to it, irrespective of the date of the acts to which such evidence relates', as the *compromiso* asked the tribunal to determine the contemporary course of the boundary between the territories of the parties in certain sectors.[254] The second circumstance is where

249 Crawford, n 3, 207.
250 Distefano, n 246, 399.
251 Distefano, n 246, 399. Shaw, n 13, 378–379. Crawford, n 3, 207.
252 Dubai/Sharjah arbitration of 1981, International Law Report, Vo. 91, 594–595.
253 Bowett, n 161, 114.
254 Argentine-Chile Frontier Case, n 245, 167.

the parties do not advance any critical date argument. In *Eritrea/Yemen*, since the parties had not sought to employ a critical date argument in relation to any of the questions involving the substance of the dispute, the arbitral tribunal followed the example of the *Argentine/Chile* award and examined all the evidence submitted to it.[255] The third circumstance occurs when the activities of the parties had remained unchanged for a long time. The ITLOS in *Ghana/Côte d'Ivoire* considered the concept of critical date irrelevant to the case because the activities of both parties in the maritime area under consideration had been unchanged over the years.[256]

2.5.2 *The Subjective Element: Intent to Act as a Sovereign*

The acts of *effectivités* must be accompanied with an intent to act as sovereign. For example, acts performed by a trustee according to Chapter XII of the UN Charter or by a belligerent occupant cannot be considered as acts *à titre de souverain*.[257] International courts and tribunals tend to deduce the intent of a State from relevant acts undertaken by it rather than merely rely on its declarations. In *Indonesia/Malaysia*, the ICJ held that the activities relied upon by Malaysia, which included the measures taken to regulate and control the collecting of turtle eggs, the establishment of a bird reserve and the construction and operation of lighthouses and navigational aids, 'show a pattern revealing an intention to exercise State functions in respect of the two islands in the context of the administration of a wider range of islands'.[258]

Conversely, naval patrols usually are not considered acts *à titre de souverain* but just a matter of geographical necessity to pass near areas in dispute. In *Malaysia/Singapore*, both Malaysia and Singapore claimed that naval patrols and exercises around the disputed island – Pedra Branca/Pulau Batu Puteh – constituted evidence of *effectivités*.[259] However, the ICJ held that these activities were a matter of geographical necessity since the naval vessels from Singapore harbor often had to pass near Pedra Branca/Pulau Batu Puteh and that some part of these activities belonged to the five power arrangements between Malaysia, Singapore, the UK,

255 Arbitration on Territorial Sovereignty and Scope of the Dispute, n 99, para.95.

256 Dispute Concerning Delimitation of the Maritime Boundary between Ghana and Côte d'Ivoire in the Atlantic Ocean (Ghana/Côte d'Ivoire), Judgment of 23 September 2017 (ITLOS), para.210.

257 M.G. Kohen and M. Hébié, Territory, Acquisition, *MPEPIL* (2011), para.32.

258 Sovereignty over Pulau Ligitan and Pulau Sipadan, n 30, para.148.

259 Sovereignty over Pedra Branca/Pulau Batu Puteh, Middle Rocks and South Ledge, n 23, para.240.

Australia and New Zealand, thereby being of a cooperative nature rather than *à titre de souverain*.[260]

2.5.3 *Application to the Spratly Islands Setting*

2.5.3.1 Relevant Activities in the Spratly Islands

The acts that can be invoked by the disputant States as evidence of *effectivités* mainly include legislative and administrative acts. There are no reported domestic cases involving any island in the Spratly Islands, probably because the only physical presences on most of these islands are military forces and facilities.

2.5.3.1.1 *Legislative Acts*

Most national legislation of the disputant States that is specifically pertinent to the islands within the Spratly Islands aims at declaring sovereignty, rather than regulating activities on or around such islands.[261] China has declared its sovereignty over the Spratly Islands in a series of legislative documents,[262] including the 1949 Regulations on the Organization of the Office of the Chief Executive of the Hainan Special District which placed the Spratly Islands under the jurisdiction of the Hainan Special District,[263] the 1958 Declaration on Territorial Sea,[264] and the 1992 Law on the Territorial Sea and the Contiguous Zone.[265] Vietnam has declared its sovereignty over the Spratly Islands in legislative documents including the 1974 Proclamation by the Government of the Republic of Vietnam,[266] the 1997 Statement on the Territorial Sea, the Contiguous Zone,

260 *Ibid.*, paras.241.

261 The author has only found one piece of legislation that is specifically pertinent to the Spratly Islands, that is, *Announcement on the 2012 Summer Ban on Marine Fishing in the South China Sea Maritime Space*, enacted by the Fishery Bureau of Nanhai District under the Chinese Ministry of Agriculture on 10 May 2012. The announcement provided for a fishing moratorium in the South China Sea areas from 12° north latitude up and further stipulated that during the fishing moratorium, any fishing boat that holds Nansha Special Fishing Permits and goes to conduct fishing production in the sea areas of Nansha Islands [Spratly Islands] south of 12° north latitude must strictly follow the reporting system in its entry and exit of sea ports. See China, Announcement on the 2012 Summer Ban on Marine Fishing in the South China Sea Maritime Space (10 May 2012), reproduced in: South China Sea Arbitration (Philippines v. China), the Philippines' Memorial – Volume VI, Annex 118.

262 For an account of relevant legislation and other official documents, see China, n 34, paras.29-42.

263 China, Regulations on the Organization of the Office of the Chief Executive of the Hainan Special District (6 June 1949).

264 China, Declaration on China's Territorial Sea (4 September 1958).

265 China, Law on the Territorial Sea and the Contiguous Zone (25 February 1992), Article 2.

266 South Vietnam, Proclamation by the Government of the Republic of Vietnam (14 February 1974), para.3.

the Exclusive Economic Zone and the Continental Shelf,[267] and the 2012 Law of the Sea of Viet Nam.[268] The Philippines has declared its sovereignty over the islands within an area that it calls 'Kalayaan Island Group', which comprises Flat Island, Nanshan Island, Thitu Island, West York Island, North-East Cay and Loaita Island, in its legislative documents including the 1978 Presidential Decree No. 1596,[269] and the 2009 Republic Act No. 9522.[270] Malaysia has indicated its sovereignty over some insular features in the southeastern portion of the Spratly Islands by publishing a map on its territorial waters and continental shelf in 1979, whereby a certain portion of the Spratly Islands was shown to be part of Malaysia.[271] The Malaysian government reaffirmed this position in its official statements in 1983 and 1988.[272] All the above national legislation of the disputant States are for declaring sovereignty and does not directly entail enforcement, which thus belongs to 'paper decree'.[273]

2.5.3.1.2 *Administrative Acts*

As mentioned in section 2.3, the disputant States employed military forces to occupy islands in the Spratly Islands in the 1970s, 1980s and 1990s. After occupying the islands through military action, the disputant States have constructed and maintained the operation of lighthouses on most of their controlled islands in the Spratly Islands. Other facilities built by the States on these islands mainly include military bases or other military installations. These States exercise control of visits to both the disputed islands and their lighthouses. Only two islands are currently accessible to the civilian population: Swallow Reef under the control of Malaysia, and Thitu Island controlled by the Philippines. Moreover, China, Malaysia, the Philippines and Vietnam all have undertaken land reclamation projects on their controlled islands (Table 5).

2.5.3.2 Evaluation of Effectivités

2.5.3.2.1 *Application of Critical Date*

The concept of critical date is, arguably, of little relevance in appraising *effectivités* in the Spratly Islands. First, the purpose of the evaluation of *effectivités*

267 Vietnam, Statement on the Territorial Sea, the Contiguous Zone, the Exclusive Economic Zone and the Continental Shelf (12 May 1977), para.1.

268 Vietnam, the Law of the Sea of Viet Nam (21 June 2012), Article 1.

269 The Philippines, Presidential Decree No. 1596 (11 June 1978).

270 The Philippines, Republic Act No. 9522 (10 March 2009) (clarifying that the Philippines' sovereignty and jurisdiction of the Kalayaan Island Group area must be determined according to Article 121 of UNCLOS).

271 Heinzig, n 35, 65.

272 Haller-Trost, n 79, 48–49.

273 Fisheries, n 226, 37.

in this section is to determine the contemporary title to the islands in the region, or in other words, to take a 'photograph' of the territorial situation[274] in the Spratly Islands as what it is today but not what it was at a precise moment in the past. Second, given the specific circumstance of the present case where the activities of each disputant State as evidence of *effectivités* have been met with constant protests from other disputant States since the very beginning, the critical date or the moment of the crystallization of the dispute, if relevant here (*quod non*), might be so early that almost all the activities of the disputant States would be deemed irrelevant to the determination of the territorial title. In light of this, the following evaluation of *effectivités* will examine all the activities of the disputant States without regard to their dates.

2.5.3.2.2 *Application of the Peaceful, Continuous, Public and Pertinent Requirements*

Given the small size of the disputed islands in the Spratly Islands, there is little doubt that the above legislative and administrative acts, including the enactment of domestic legislation, the construction and operation of lighthouses and other facilities, the control of visits to the islands and lighthouses, and land reclamation projects, can constitute acts *à titre de souverain* and easily fulfil the *continuous*, *public* and *pertinent* requirements. However, whether these acts meet the *peaceful* requirement might sometimes be difficult to tell. There is little chance that the military action employed by the disputant States in the 1970s, 1980s and 1990s to gain or regain control of the disputed islands could be regarded as a peaceful and regular exercise of State authority and thereby constituting a relevant *effectivité*. Yet, whether legislative and administrative acts other than military action fulfil the peaceful requirement might be open to question, as these acts have been accompanied by constant protests lodged by other disputant States since the very beginning.[275]

---

274 Frontier Dispute, n 12, para.30.

275 For example, in a letter addressed to the UN dated 3 March 2016, the Chinese government stated that: 'Viet Nam has long been engaged in large-scale construction projects and deployment of missiles and other offensive weapons on the Chinese islands and reefs of the Nansha Islands [the Spratly Islands] that it has illegally occupied. China firmly opposes these acts and has been lodging sustained protests for a long time'. See China, Annex to the letter dated 3 March 2016 from the Permanent Representative of China to the United Nations addressed to the Secretary-General (2016). For an account of protests against activities respecting the Spratly Islands area, see P. Kreuzer, A Comparison of Malaysian and Philippine Responses to China in the South China Sea, 9 *The Chinese Journal of International Politics* (2006), 239–276.

TABLE 5 Lighthouses, other facilities, control of visits and land reclamation projects in the Spratly Islands[a]

Controlling state	Island	The year when control began	Lighthouse	Other facilities	Controls of visits to the site of the island and the Lighthouse	Land reclamation project
China (6)	Itu Aba Island	1946	Yes	A landing strip, a coast guard station, a weather station and an army garrison.	Site closed; Lighthouse closed.	Yes[b]
	Fiery Cross Reef	1988	Yes	An airstrip.	Site closed; Lighthouse closed.	Yes
	McKennan Reef[c]	1988	Data Unknown	Data Unknown	Data Unknown	Data Unknown
	Gaven Reef (North)	1988	Yes	A military base.	Site closed; Lighthouse closed.	Yes
	Cuarteron Reef	1988	Yes	A military base.	Site closed; Lighthouse closed.	Yes
	Johnson Reef	1988	Yes	A military base and airfield.	Site closed; Lighthouse closed.	Yes
Malaysia (1)	Swallow Reef	1977	Yes	An airstrip, a small naval base, and more recently a 15-room scuba diving resort.	Site open; Lighthouse closed.	Yes

TABLE 5 Lighthouses, other facilities, control of visits and land reclamation projects in the Spratly Islands (*cont.*)

Controlling state	Island	The year when control began	Lighthouse	Other facilities	Controls of visits to the site of the island and the Lighthouse	Land reclamation project
Philippines (6)	Flat Island[d]	1970	Data Unknown	Data Unknown	Data Unknown	Yes
	Nanshan Island	1970	Data Unknown	An army garrison.	Data Unknown	Data Unknown
	Thitu Island	1971	Yes	A military airstrip and houses for a civilian population (184 people in 2015).	Site open; Lighthouse closed.	Data Unknown
	West York Island	1971	Data Unknown	A small military observation post.	Data Unknown	Data Unknown
	North-East Cay	1971	Yes	An army garrison.	Site closed; Lighthouse closed.	Data Unknown
	Loaita Island	1971	Data Unknown	Data Unknown	Data Unknown	Data Unknown

Vietnam (6)	Spratly Island	1975	Yes	A military base, a short landing strip for propeller aircraft.	Site closed; Lighthouse closed.	Yes
	South-West Cay	1975	Yes	A military base.	Site closed; Lighthouse closed.	Yes
	Sin Cowe Island	1975	Yes	A military base.	Site closed; Lighthouse closed.	Yes
	Sand Cay	1975	Yes	A military base.	Site closed; Lighthouse closed.	Yes
	Namyit Island	1975	Yes	An army garrison.	Site closed; Lighthouse closed.	Yes
	Amboyna Cay	1975	Yes	An army garrison.	Site closed; Lighthouse closed.	Yes

a (1) Sources of data regarding lighthouses, other facilities and control of visits in this table: Lighthouses of the Spratly Islands, available at <https://www.ibiblio.org/lighthouse/spr.htm >. The data provided therein were last checked and revised on 31 January 2019. (2) Sources of data regarding land reclamation projects: CSIS, Asia Maritime Transparency Initiative, available at <https://amti.csis.org/>.

b It was reported that Taiwan began a modest land reclamation effort on Itu Aba Island in April 2014, which had reclaimed at least approximately five acres of land near the island's airstrip. See the US Office of the Secretary of Defense, Annual Report to Congress: Military and Security Developments Involving the People's Republic of China 2015 (7 April 2015), 72.

c McKennan Reef is guarded by the Chinese soldiers stationed at the nearby Hughes Reef (regarded as a low-tide elevation by the *South China Sea Arbitration* award). The Philippines treats McKennan Reef and Hughes Reef as one single feature. See The South China Sea Arbitration, n 11, para.292.

d Flat Island is guarded by Philippine soldiers stationed at nearby Nanshan Island.

It might be helpful to briefly recap the peaceful requirement here. On the one hand, diplomatic protests would suffice to disturb the peaceful display of those legislative acts without actual enforcement until the attempt is made to enforce the legislation. Therefore, respecting the Spratly Islands, it would be difficult for a disputant State to claim islands that do not fall under its control based on the mere declaration of sovereignty through its domestic legislation. On the other hand, for those islands that a disputant State has actual control and exercises of administrative power, diplomatic protests could act as a temporary bar but not produce the ultimate effect of interrupting the peaceful character of possession unless followed by qualified steps such as mechanisms involving the UN and international adjudication, and other peaceful means under Article 33(1) of the UN Charter, to the extent that the relevant State has demonstrated that it has made every effort to induce the possessor State to agree on such peaceful means. Hence, it is necessary to investigate the question of whether the disputant States have been committed to or engaged in any peaceful means for settling their territorial dispute over the Spratly Islands.

First, the disputant States have neither been committed to nor ever used mechanisms involving the UN and international adjudication to settle the territorial dispute in relation to the Spratly Islands. The compulsory dispute settlement regime stipulated in Part XV of UNCLOS, including Annex VII arbitration, does not apply to this territorial dispute because UNCLOS is a treaty about sovereignty and sovereign rights over the sea, not the land.[276] Moreover, China, Vietnam and Malaysia do not accept the compulsory jurisdiction of the ICJ. Though the Philippines does, it has made a reservation that excludes disputes relating to territorial sovereignty or maritime entitlements claimed or exercised by it.[277] None of these four disputant States has ever agreed to submit this territorial dispute to any other international courts or tribunals through a special agreement or an arbitration *compromis*. Conversely, China has expressly stated that it does not accept any recourse to third-party settlement on issues concerning territory and maritime delimitation, including the territorial dispute involving the Spratly Islands.[278]

276 UNCLOS, Article 298(1)(a)(i). (providing that 'any dispute that necessarily involves the concurrent consideration of any unsettled dispute concerning sovereignty or other rights over continental or insular land territory shall be excluded from such submission').

277 Declarations made by the Philippines under Article 36, paragraph 2, of the Statute of the International Court of Justice (18 January 1972), available at <https://treaties.un.org/pages/ViewDetails.aspx?src=IND&mtdsg_no=I-4&chapter=1&clang=_en#EndDec>.

278 China, n 34, paras.83, 130.

Second, the disputant States have expressed their political commitments to settle the territorial dispute in the Spratly Islands through consultations and negotiations by signing a series of bilateral or multilateral documents, and have been implementing these bilateral consultations and negotiations in a sustained manner. Negotiations between States are usually carried out through 'normal diplomatic channels' including by competent authorities or representatives of each State party or by summit discussions between heads of State or foreign ministers.[279] Consultations, in theory, belong to one form of negotiations, which require a State to discuss with the affected State when it anticipates that a decision or a proposed course of action may harm that State.[280]

Firstly, in 1995, a joint statement was signed by the senior officials of the Philippines and China as a result of their first consultations on the South China Sea issue, stating that '[t]erritorial disputes between the two sides should not affect the normal development of their relations. Disputes shall be settled in a peaceful and friendly manner through consultations on the basis of equality and mutual respect'.[281] The subsequent bilateral documents signed between the Philippines and China reiterated this commitment.[282] Furthermore, a Bilateral Consultation Mechanism on the South China Sea, through which both governments meet regularly to discuss issues of concern to either side on the South China Sea, was established in October 2016,[283] and has held at least six meetings.[284]

---

279 For an account of forms of negotiation, see J.G. Merrills, *International Dispute Settlement* (CUP 6th ed. 2017), 8–12.

280 *Ibid.*, 2–8.

281 China and Philippines, Agreed Minutes on the First Philippines-China Bilateral Consultations on the South China Sea Issue (10 August 1995), reproduced in: The South China Sea Arbitration, n 261, Vol. VI, Annex 180.

282 See *e.g.*, China and Philippines, Joint Statement: Philippine-China Experts Group Meeting on Confidence Building Measures (23 March 1999); China and Philippines, Joint Statement: Framework of Bilateral Cooperation in the Twenty-First Century (16 May 2000); China and Philippines, Joint Statement: 3rd Philippines-China Experts' Group Meeting on Confidence-Building Measures (4 April 2001); China and Philippines, Joint Press Statement on the State Visit of H.E. President Gloria Macapagal-Arroyo to the People's Republic of China, 1–3 September 2004 (3 September 2004); China and Philippines, Joint Statement (1 September 2011). These documents are reproduced in: The South China Sea Arbitration, n 261, Vol. VI, Annexes 178, 188, Vol. IX, Annexes 505, 506, 507.

283 China and Philippines, Joint Statement (21 October 2016), available at <https://www.philstar.com/headlines/2016/10/21/1636345/full-text-joint-statement-philippines-and-china >.

284 China, Assistant Minister of Foreign Affairs Wu Jianghao Chairs the Sixth Meeting of the China-Philippines Bilateral Consultation Mechanism on the South China Sea (21 May 2021), available at <https://www.fmprc.gov.cn/mfa_eng/wjbxw/t1877878.shtml >.

Secondly, in the 1999 Joint Statement on the Framework for Future Bilateral Cooperation, China and Malaysia agreed to resolve the disputes in the South China Sea through bilateral consultations and negotiations according to recognized principles of international law.[285] The subsequent bilateral documents signed between China and Malaysia in 2004, 2014 and 2016 reiterated this commitment.[286]

Thirdly, in 2011, China and Vietnam signed a bilateral document where both parties agreed to resolve the disputes between them including those relating to South China Sea through negotiations and consultations, and to involve other interested parties in the negotiations as well if they are parties to the dispute.[287] Furthermore, in 2013, these two States established a working group for bilateral consultations in a joint statement.[288] This working group is responsible for negotiating the joint development issues in a broader sea area including not only the area near Beibu Gulf but also other areas in the South China Sea. Despite occasional interruptions owing to the unpleasant maritime conflicts between the two sides, this working group has held at least nine rounds of consultations.[289]

Fourthly, apart from bilateral mechanisms, China and ASEAN jointly declared in the 2002 DOC to settle the territorial dispute in the South China Sea through consultations and negotiations.[290] Furthermore, in August 2017, China and ASEAN formally announced the start of negotiations on the fine

285 China and Malaysia, Joint Statement on the Framework for Future Bilateral Cooperation (31 May 1999), Article 9, available at <https://www.mfa.gov.cn/nanhai/chn/zcfg/t1367523.htm>.

286 China and Malaysia, Joint Statement (29 May 2004) available at <http://www.china.org.cn/english/2004/May/96837.htm >; China and Malaysia, Joint Statement on the 40th Anniversary of the Establishment of Diplomatic Relations (1 June 2014), Article 30, available at <https://www.mfa.gov.cn/nanhai/chn/zcfg/t1161309.htm>; China and Malaysia, Joint Statement (3 November 2016), Article 26, available at <https://www.mfa.gov.cn/nanhai/chn/zcfg/t1412634.htm>.

287 China and Vietnam, Agreement on Basic Principles Guiding Resolution of Maritime Issues (11 October 2011), Article 3, available at <http://www.gov.cn/jrzg/2011-10/12/content_1966682.htm>.

288 China and Vietnam, Joint Statement (15 October 2013), available at <https://www.mfa.gov.cn/nanhai/chn/zcfg/t1089639.htm >.

289 China, The 12th Round of Consultation of the Working Group on Sea Area Outside the Mouth of Beibu Bay and the 9th Round of Consultation of the Working Group for Consultation on Maritime Joint Development Between China and Vietnam Held in Beijing (26 December 2019), available at <https://www.fmprc.gov.cn/mfa_eng/wjbxw/t1728521.shtml>.

290 ASEAN and China, Declaration on the Conduct of Parties in the South China Sea (2002), Article 4.

print of the COC, which was aimed to coordinate State conduct in the South China Sea.[291] Three months later, China and ASEAN adopted a framework of the COC, reaffirming these States' commitments to explore and undertake cooperative arrangements in the region.[292]

Based on the above analysis of the engagement of the disputant States in using peaceful means for the settlement of the territorial dispute in relation to the Spratly Islands, it is clear is that the disputant States have neither been committed to nor ever used mechanisms involving the UN and international adjudication to settle this territorial dispute. In contrast, the 2002 DOC and the bilateral agreements, though not being legally binding documents, have indicated the disputant States' political commitments to settle this territorial dispute through consultations and negotiations as a preferred, though not necessarily exclusive, form of peaceful means.[293] These documents, together with the implementation of bilateral consultations and negotiations, are conclusive to the existence of the territorial dispute. It is prudent to argue that the sustained diplomatic protests and consultations and negotiations, which have been operated by relevant States since the very beginning of the acts *à titre de souverain* conducted by the possessor States,[294] though not yet producing any substantive outcome in relation to the settlement of this territorial dispute, have shown that the former had made sufficient efforts to induce the latter to agree on these peaceful means. Therefore, the peaceful character of those acts *à titre de souverain* is deprived, thereby unable to constitute *effectivités*. This conclusion is perhaps unsurprising, given that the activities of each disputant State have been conducted and maintained in the presence of constant opposition lodged by other disputant States since the very beginning. This situation significantly differs from the settled international jurisprudence where the relevant acts *à titre de souverain* are usually accompanied by another party's failure to protest, acquiescence or even recognition.[295]

---

291 Y. Lee, A South China Sea Code of Conduct: Is Real Progress Possible? (18 November 2017), available at <https://thediplomat.com/2017/11/a-south-china-sea-code-of-conduct-is-real-progress-possible/>.

292 Prashanth Parameswaran, Will a China-ASEAN South China Sea Code of Conduct Really Matter? (5 August 2017), available at <https://thediplomat.com/2017/08/will-a-china-asean-south-china-sea-code-of-conduct-really-matter/>.

293 South China Sea Arbitration (The Philippines v. China), Award on Jurisdiction and Admissibility of 29 October 2015 (PCA), paras.217, 230–251.

294 For an account of protests against activities respecting the Spratly Islands area, see Kreuzer, n 275, 239–276. China, Annex to the letter dated 3 March 2016 from the Permanent Representative of China to the United Nations addressed to the Secretary-General (2016).

295 Schrijver and Prislan, n 112, 296.

2.6 Treaty Title

2.6.1 *Applicable Law*

Boundary treaties including peace treaties and boundary delimitation treaties, and more broadly, treaties of cession, 'whereby either additional territory is acquired or lost or uncertain boundaries are clarified by agreement between the states concerned', are themselves a root of territorial title.[296] These treaties are special in two senses. First, territorial titles created by boundary treaties are valid *erga omnes*. As stated by the *Eritrea/Yemen* arbitral tribunal:

> this special category of treaties [boundary treaties] also represents a legal reality which necessarily impinges upon third states, because they have effect *erga omnes*. If State A has title to territory and passes it to State B, then it is legally without purpose for State C to invoke the principle of *res inter alios acta*, unless its title is better than that of A (rather than of B). In the absence of such better title, a claim of *res inter alios acta* is without legal import.[297]

Second, a territorial title created by a boundary treaty would continue to exist even if the treaty expires.[298] The above two exceptional legal effects are based on the principle of the stability and finality of boundaries, the importance of which has been recorded in the law of treaties,[299] and repeatedly emphasized in various international jurisprudence including *Temple of Preah Vihear*, *Aegean Sea* and *Bangladesh v. India*.[300]

2.6.2 *Application to the Spratly Islands Setting*

2.6.2.1 The 1887 China-France Treaty

As a result of the Tokin War, China and France concluded a treaty in 1887 to delimit the frontier between China and northern Vietnam. The third clause of this treaty used the Paris meridian 105°43'E as the demarcation line and allocated the islands east of this line to China.[301] This clause specifies only the

296 Shaw, n 13, 73.

297 Arbitration on Territorial Sovereignty and Scope of the Dispute, n 99, para.153.

298 Territorial Dispute, n 15, para.72.

299 VCLT, Article 62(2)(a).

300 See *e.g.*, Temple of Preah Vihear (Cambodia v. Thailand), Judgment of 15 June 1962 (ICJ), 34; Aegean Sea Continental Shelf (Greece v. Turkey), Judgment of 19 December 1978 (ICJ), 36; Bay of Bengal Maritime Boundary Arbitration between Bangladesh and India, Award of 7 July 2014 (PCA), para.216.

301 The third clause provides that: 'In Kwangtung, it is agreed that the disputed points which lie east and north-east of Monkai, beyond the frontier as determined by the Delimitation

starting point of the demarcation line, namely 'the eastern point of the island of Tcha's Kou, or Ouan Chan (Tra Co)', but not the ending point.

The absence of the ending point of the demarcation line gave rise to debates between China and France in the 1930s, more than 40 years after the treaty was concluded. In reply to the French government' inquiry on the Paracel Islands in 1932, the Chinese government declared that the Paracel Islands was under the sovereignty of China partly because this archipelago lied east of the demarcation line established according to the third clause of the 1887 China-France Treaty.[302] France rejected this argument, on the ground that the purpose of the 1887 treaty was to allocate the territories and islands situated in the Monkai region or the Gulf of Tonkin but not beyond, and that extending the demarcation line beyond that region would cause absurd consequences because islands immediately off the Vietnamese coast would also be placed to China.[303]

Apparently, China and France disputed the interpretation of the third clause of the 1887 treaty regarding the question of whether the demarcation line could extend southwards to reach into the South China Sea to allocate the Paracel Islands and even the Spratly Islands (lying east to the Paracel Islands) to China. If China intends to base its territorial claims to the Spratly Islands on the 1887 treaty, it would have to prove that both parties had the intent to do so when concluding the 1887 treaty, now that the text is ambiguous. However, due to the absence or unavailability of rclcvant historical evidence, this study could not consider the relevance of the 1887 treaty to the territorial dispute involving the Spratly Islands.

2.6.2.2 The 1951 Treaty of Peace with Japan

Article 2(f) of the 1951 Treaty of Peace with Japan provides that Japan shall renounce all rights and claims to the Spratly Islands but does not specify the recipient.[304] Unfortunately, the drafting history of this provision also sheds

Commission, are allocated to China. The islands which are east of the Paris meridian 105°43'E, i.e. east of the north-south line passing through the eastern point of the island of Tcha's Kou, or Ouan Chan (Tra Co), which forms the boundary, are also allocated to China. The island of Gotho and other islands west of this meridian belong to Annam'. See Clause 3 of the China-France Treaty on the Delimitation the Frontier between China and Northern Vietnam (26 June 1887). Chemillier-Gendreau, n 8, 36.

302 Note of 29 September 1932 from the Legation of the Chinese Republic in France to the Ministry of Foreign Affairs, Paris, reproduced in: Chemillier-Gendreau, n 8, Annex 10.

303 Note from Paris of 10 October 1937 and Note by Mr Chargueraud-Hartmann for the Under-Directorate for Asia of 16 August 1933, quoted in: Chemillier-Gendreau, n 8, 85–86.

304 Treaty of Peace with Japan, Article 2(f).

little light on who was the recipient of the Spratly Islands.[305] Moreover, given that only the Philippines and Vietnam are parties to the Treaty of Peace,[306] it is doubtful what legal effects this treaty would have vis-à-vis Malaysia and China (especially the PRC government).[307] Therefore, it is difficult to determine the extent to which the 1951 Treaty of Peace with Japan alone would have a bearing on the territorial title to the Spratly Islands. Furthermore, strictly speaking, this treaty is not a boundary treaty properly so called or itself a root of a territorial title to the Spratly Islands. Nor should this treaty amount to a recognition of Japan's title to the Spratly Islands prior to 1951. During the drafting of this treaty, Mr. Fearey of the Office of Northeast Asian Affairs of the US indicated in an official memorandum, which was to be transmitted to Australian representatives, that Japan was not perceived by the drafters of the Treaty of Peace as the rightful holder of the Spratly Islands.[308] Hence, the Treaty of Peace should be understood as merely obliging Japan to renounce all rights and claims to the Spratly Islands, if any, but not a recognition of Japan's title prior to 1951. To conclude, whether the 1951 Treaty of Peace with Japan has a bearing on the territorial title to the Spratly Islands remains questionable.

2.7 Cession

2.7.1 *Two Cumulative Requirements*

It is a well-established rule under international law that a State with sovereignty over a particular area is entitled to cede such sovereignty to another State.[309] To confer the successor State with an indisputable claim by right of cession, two *cumulative* requirements need to be fulfilled.

---

305 For comprehensive discussions on the drafting history of Article 2(f), see Chen, n 6, 178–192.

306 Signatories to the Treaty of Peace with Japan, available at <https://treaties.un.org/Pages/showDetails.aspx?objid=080000028015 28c2>.

307 It is noted that the ROC, by entering into the Sino-Japanese Peace Treaty with Japan on 28 April 1952, has accepted Article 2(f) of the Peace Treaty to be effective between them. See Article 2 of the Sino-Japanese Peace Treaty (also known as the Treaty of Taipei, adopted 28 April 1952, entered into force 5 August 1952).

308 Undated Memorandum by Mr. Robert A. Fearey of the Office of Northeast Asian Affairs: Answers to Questions Submitted by the Australian Government Arising Out of the Statement of Principles Regarding a Japanese Treaty Prepared by the United States Government, *Foreign Relations of the United States (1950), East Asia and The Pacific*, Vol. VI, available at <https://history.state.gov/historicaldocuments/frus1950v06/d774>.

309 Jennings, n 162, 16. Shaw, n 13, 369–370. Murphy, n 4, 198.

The first requirement is that the territorial title/claim of the predecessor State is substantiated under international law. Since the successor State cannot receive greater rights than those enjoyed by the predecessor State (*nemo dat quod non habet*), the former can only claim a territorial title when the latter is entitled to enjoy one.[310] For example, in *Island of Palmas*, the US based its territorial claim to the disputed island on cession indicated in an 1898 treaty with Spain whereby all rights of sovereignty that Spain may have possessed in the region were transferred to the US.[311] However, the arbitrator held that this treaty was not conclusive in this case, as 'Spain could not transfer more rights than she herself possessed'.[312]

The second requirement is that as a 'bilateral mode of acquisition', the basis of cession is the agreement on the transfer between the predecessor State and the cessionary State, which is usually manifested in the form of a treaty of cession.[313] The cessionary State has a right to occupy the territory at any time after the treaty enters into force under international law.[314]

2.7.2 *Application to the Spratly Islands Setting*

According to the rule of cession, for Vietnam to claim a territorial title to the islands in the Spratly Islands by right of cession, two cumulative requirements need to be fulfilled: first, France's territorial title/claim to these islands is substantiated under international law; and second, France agrees to cede the territory to Vietnam.

It is necessary to introduce France's historical contacts with the Spratly Islands briefly. Prompted by the growing Japanese interest in the Spratly Islands in the 1920s, France started to pay attention to the maritime features thereof.[315] Subsequently, on 13 April 1930, the Governor-General of Indochina

---

310 Jennings, n 162, 16. Crawford, n 3, 205.

311 Island of Palmas (The United States of America v. The Netherlands), Award of 4 April 1928 (PCA), 842.

312 *Ibid.*

313 Jennings, n 162, 16–17.

314 *Ibid.*, 17.

315 In the 1920s, some Japanese people showed the commercial interest of collecting guano and fishing on or near Spratly Island (Nansha Island), a high-tide elevation feature in the Spratly Islands area. Consequently, in 1927, the Japanese consul in Hanoi arranged a discussion with the French authority about the status of some islands, including Spratly Island, Itu Aba and Amboyna Cay, but no conclusion was reached during this discussion. See Hancox, n 37, 52. The 1927 negotiation between Japan and France was also confirmed in a letter dated 26 December 1927 from the Acting Governor General of Indochina, Hanoi, to the Minister for the Colonies, Paris, and another letter dated 20 March 1930

sent the advice-boat, *La Malicieuse*, to Spratly Island (a maritime feature in the Spratly Islands).[316] The members of the expedition raised the French flag on this island, but they did not occupy it and left on the same day. On 23 September 1930, France notified other Great Powers that it declared the ownership of Spratly Island and Amboyna Cay.[317] The French government based its territorial claim over the islands in the Spratly Islands on effective occupation of *terra nullius*, stating that:

> If the island [i.e. Spratly Island] is at present *terra nullius*, the granting of a permit to prospect, followed by actual operations undertaken by the holder of the concession, and accompanied by any manifestation whatsoever of continuous occupation by the French State (visits by warships, flag, orders issued by the police) would be the kind of act establishing the sovereignty of France over the island in question ... The eventual solution might well also be applied to all or some of the other islands in the same group [i.e. the Spratly Islands].[318]

In 1933, French survey ships visited and surveyed some islands in the Spratly Islands.[319] By a decree of 26 July 1933, the French Government proclaimed the occupation of seven features thereof,[320] which prompted China's protest.[321] On 3 July 1938, France announced to occupy the whole archipelago of the Spratly Islands.[322]

---

from the Governor General of Indochina, Hanoi to the Minister for the Colonies, Paris. These two letters are reproduced in: Chemillier-Gendreau, n 8, Annex 5 & Annex 17.

316 Hancox, n 37, 56.

317 *Ibid.*, 52–53.

318 Note dated 26 November 1928 addressed to the Under-Directorate for Asia and Oceania regarding the Spratly Island or Strom Island, reproduced in: Chemillier-Gendreau, n 8, Annex 19. The plan to occupy the Spratly Islands was reaffirmed in the Letter of 30 March 1932 from the Minister for National Defence (Navy) to the Minister for Foreign Affairs – Directorate for Political Affairs and Trade (Asia-Oceania), reproduced in: *ibid.*, Annex 31.

319 Hancox, n 37, 84–88.

320 The French government claimed to occupy seven islands: (1) Spratly Island, possessed on 13 April 1930; (2) Amboyna Cay, possessed on 7 April 1933; (3) Itu Aba Island, possessed on 10 April 1933; (4) North-East Cay, possessed on 10 April 1933; (5) South-West Cay, possessed on 10 April 1933; (6) Loaita Island, possessed on 12 April 1933; (7) Thitu Island, possessed on 12 April 1933. See Republic of Vietnam, n 49, Chapter III. The occupation of these seven islands was also confirmed in Article 1 of the *Decree by the Governor of Cochin China (J. Krautheimer), Saigon*, dated 21 December 1933. This Decree is reproduced in: Chemillier-Gendreau, n 8, Annex 30.

321 Journal officiel de la Republique Francaise, No. 172 (25 July 1933), 7794.

322 Heinzig, n 35, 29.

Regarding the first requirement under the rule of cession, for France to claim a territorial title to the islands in the Spratly Islands, these islands must be *terra nullius* when France claimed to effectively occupy them in the 1930s. This matter depends on whether there had been any preexisting titles to the islands enjoyed by other sovereigns before the 1930s. As concluded in section 2.4, China had been enjoying a historic title over the islands thereof at least until the twentieth century. Therefore, there is little chance that such islands were *terra nullius* at the French occupation. In fact, the French occupation triggered protests from the Chinese government, who claimed that only Chinese fishers lived on these islands and that they belonged to China.[323]

The second requirement is also not fulfilled. France has never agreed to cede the territory to Vietnam.[324] France explicitly stated in 1951 and 1955 that its occupation of the Spratly Islands was conducted on behalf of France itself but not Vietnam.[325] A relevant passage reads:

> Since 1933, when the French Government forcefully took possession of the Spratlys on behalf of France and up to the present day, these islands were included, for administrative purposes, under the former Government General of Indochina to which they had been attached ... Indeed, at no point in its history did the former Empire of Annam [the predecessor of Vietnam] make any claim to these territories, which, furthermore, it has never occupied; and the fact that the Spratlys were for a time attached to Cochin China merely for administrative convenience cannot be relied on by the new State of Vietnam as jurisdiction for rights it never possessed ...

---

323 The protest from China was made through its ambassador WeiJune Gu. See Han, n 48, 261. Chen, n 6, 176–177.

324 Some scholars argued that in 1949 or 1950 the French government officially transferred the control of both the Spratly Islands and Paracel Islands to the South Vietnam authority. However, for the Spratly Islands, when making this statement, these scholars failed to cite or show any supporting evidence. See Chemillier-Gendreau, n 8, 41. L.T. Nguyen, *The South China Sea Dispute: A reappraisal in the Light of International Law* (University of Bristol PhD Dissertation. 2008), 107–108.

325 Letter of 7 May 1951 from the Minister of State with responsibility for relations with Associated States to the Minister for Overseas Territories. Letter of 16 June 1955 from General Jacquot, General Commissioner of France and Acting Commander-in-Chief in Indochina, to the Secretary of State with responsibility for relations with Associated States. These two Letters are reproduced in: Chemillier-Gendreau, n 8, Annex 39 & Annex 40.

> the Spratlys should now come under the French Department of Overseas Territories, on the same basis as other French territories in the Pacific.[326]

To conclude, since neither the first nor second requirement is satisfied, Vietnam's claim of a territorial title to the islands in the Spratly Islands by right of cession is untenable under international law.

2.8 Discovery of Terra Nullius

2.8.1 *Applicable Law*

The rule of discovery was developed in the fifteenth century to deal with the legal relationship between the European States on acquiring discovered territories during the colonial era.[327] The following three observations have been rarely contested in international law.

First, discovery, distinct from mere geographical awareness, should be accompanied by an affirmation of sovereignty, which is usually demonstrated and materialized through acts of symbolic annexation including erecting signs, hosting flags and reciting solemn declarations.[328]

Second, the rule of discovery applies to *terra nullius* ('nobody's land'), which undisputedly covers the territories with the absolute absence of a settled population that did not belong to any sovereign.[329] Admittedly, it is disputable whether the concept of *terra nullius* includes territories inhabited by population unknown to the colonial powers with non-western systems of social organizations.[330] However, tailored to the Spratly Islands setting, the analysis can be confined to uninhabited territories, since the islands therein have never been inhabited permanently by a settled population. Importantly, 'uninhabited territories' are not necessarily '*terra nullius*', as a possibility remains that the former, though not materially inhabited by any settled population, might belong to a sovereign.[331]

326 Letter of 7 May 1951 from the Minister of State with responsibility for relations with Associated States to the Minister for Overseas Territories, reproduced in: Chemillier-Gendreau, n 8, Annex 39.

327 M.G. Kohen and M. Hébié, Territory, Discovery, *MPEPIL* (2011), paras.1, 4, 5.

328 F.A.F. von der Heydte, Discovery, Symbolic Annexation and Virtual Effectiveness in International Law, 29 *AJIL* (1935), 452. Hébié, n 165, 58–59.

329 Hébié, n 165, 59.

330 For a comprehensive discussion on the application of the rule of discovery to inhabited territories, see Hébié, n 165, 61–72. Chemillier-Gendreau, n 8, 30, 50, 56.

331 Hébié, n 165, 76.

Third, discovery could constitute a valid title of territorial sovereignty until the middle of the sixteenth century.[332] The arbitrator, Huber, confirmed this position in *Island of Palmas*. In that case, the Netherlands and the US disputed the territorial sovereignty over the Island of Palmas, which was incidentally located not far from the Spratly Islands.[333] The US claimed itself to be a successor to the territorial title of Spain to the Island of Palmas established on the basis of discovery in the first half of the sixteenth century.[334] Huber held that the effect of discovery by Spain had to be appreciated in the light of the law contemporary with it, and thus a valid title to the island was created at that time.[335] However, since the middle of the sixteenth century, mere discovery does not suffice for the conferral of a territorial title and could only create an 'inchoate title' that needs to be perfected by actual occupation,[336] largely owing to the increasing competition between colonial powers as a result of the development of navigation technologies and the expansion of colonial presence.[337] As stated by Huber, absent the completion by actual occupation, 'an inchoate title could not prevail over the continuous and peaceful display of authority [namely an *effectivités*] by another state'.[338] Though the notion of

332 Jennings, n 162, 4. Kohen, n 10, 151. Crawford, n 3, 211.

333 Island of Palmas, n 311, 831.

334 *Ibid.*, 837.

335 *Ibid.*, 845.

336 *Ibid.*, 845–846. Von der Heydte, n 328, 460.

337 With the development of navigation technologies and the expansion of colonial presence since the middle of the sixteenth century, new colonial powers such as England and France desired a new theory about the rule of discovery to justify their occupation of overseas territories. These new colonial powers were concerned with infringing the rights enjoyed by Spain and Portugal under specific papal bulls including the bull *Inter Caetera* decreed by Pope Alexander VI in 1493, which granted Spain and Portugal exclusive rights to discover the lands located in each half of the world. Consequently, in the 1580s, the then British Queen, Elizabeth I, and her legal advisors refined the rule of discovery by adding one crucial new element, namely the requirement of actual occupation. This action was also followed by the successor of Elizabeth I, James I, who granted the British colonists property rights in America since such lands were 'not now actually possessed by any Christian Prince or People' in accordance with the 1606 First Charter of Virginia and the 1620 Charter to the Council of New England. Hence, an European State was required to actually occupy non-Christian lands to perfect their discovery title to discovered lands. See R.J. Miller and J. Ruru, *Discovering Indigenous Lands: The Doctrine of Discovery in the English Colonies* (Oxford Scholarship Online. 2010), 18. Hébié, n 165, 44. The Papal bull Inter Caetera Alexander VI (4 May 1493), available at <http://www.let.rug.nl/usa/documents/before-1600/the-papal-bull-inter-caetera-alexander-vi-may-4-1493.php>; First Charter of Virginia (10 April 1606), available at <http://avalon.law.yale.edu/17th_century/va01.asp>; Charter of New England (1620), available at <http://avalon.law.yale.edu/17th_century/mass01.asp>.

338 Island of Palmas, n 311, 846.

'inchoate title' might be misleading, the message is clear that effective occupation or *effectivités* rather than mere discovery matters in contemporary international law.[339]

2.8.2 *Application to the Spratly Islands Setting*

2.8.2.1 China

China claimed to be the first one to have discovered the Spratly Islands, which could date back to at least 225–230 A.D.[340] According to the rule of discovery of *terra nullius* before the middle of the sixteenth century, to confer a territorial title, discovery should be accompanied by an affirmation of sovereignty, which is usually demonstrated through acts of symbolic annexation including erecting signs, hosting flags and reciting solemn declarations.[341] However, no historical documents have been found recording any symbolic act conducted by China before the middle of the sixteenth century to demonstrate territorial sovereignty over the islands in this region. Hence, although little evidence is required as regards possession of tiny islands,[342] China's mere geographical awareness of these islands could not create a title unless there is evidence indicating the affirmation of sovereignty.

2.8.2.2 The Philippines

The Philippines claims a legal title arising from the occupation of some islands in 1956 by a Philippine citizen, Tomas Cloma, on the basis of the rule of discovery of *terra nullius*. However, Cloma's occupation did not constitute discovery because this conduct was not taken under the authorization of the Philippine government, thus lacking an affirmation of sovereignty. Even if the 1974 'Deed of Assignment Waiver of Rights' through which Cloma relinquished his territorial claim to the Philippine government could be considered as an affirmation of sovereignty, discovery could not be creative of a valid territorial title in the present case because discovery could entail a title until the middle of the sixteenth century. In other words, discovery was not a valid rule for acquiring a territorial title in 1956 when Cloma's occupation took place or in 1974 when the alleged affirmation of sovereignty occurred. As Sorensen commented: 'Unless otherwise indicated, the temporal sphere of application of any norm of public international law shall be determined in accordance with the general principle of law by which any fact, action or

339 Crawford, n 3, 211.
340 China, n 34, para.3.
341 Von der Heydte, n 328, 452.
342 Schrijver and Prislan, n 112, 297.

situation must be assessed in the light of the rules of law that are contemporaneous with it'.[343] Hence, discovery, which was a valid title until the middle of the sixteenth century, could not be an applicable law for appraising the events in 1956 or 1974. To conclude, the territorial claim of the Philippines based on discovery is untenable under international law.

2.9 Titles vis-à-vis Effectivités

The preceding analysis reveals that when evaluated against the contemporary law of territory, among all claims based on titles of territorial sovereignty, only China's territorial claim based on historic title is plausible. First, the acts *à titre de souverain* taken by the disputant States respecting the Spratly Islands fail to amount to *effectivités* in the present case, because such acts cannot fulfil the peaceful requirement owing to the presence of sustained diplomatic protests, consultations and negotiations, which have been operated by relevant States since the very beginning of the acts *à titre de souverain* conducted by the possessor States.[344] Second, there is no sufficient evidence to show that the 1887 China-France Treaty or the 1951 Treaty of Peace with Japan has a bearing on the disposition of the Spratly Islands.[345] Third, due to the presence of a pre-existing title enjoyed by China prior to the French occupation and the lack of agreement of cession between France and Vietnam, Vietnam's claim of a territorial title to the islands in the Spratly Islands by right of cession is untenable.[346] Fourth, China and the Philippines' territorial claims based on discovery of *terra nullius* are unsubstantiated under international law, owing to either the lack of an affirmation of sovereignty or the inapplicability of discovery after the middle of the 16th century.[347] According to the analytical framework as set forth in section 2.2, the present case coincides with the fifth type of the titles/*effectivités* relationship, where the historic title of China is not duplicated by subsequent *effectivités*, which thereby does not prevent the historic title from having a legal effect.

---

343 M. Sorensen (Rapporteur), *The Institute of International Law Resolution on The Intertemporal Problem in Public International Law* (11 August 1975), Article 1. For a further discussion on the application of intertemporal law and the South China Sea dispute, see X. Ma, The Intertemporal Principle in International Judicial Practice and Its Implications for the South China Sea Dispute, 3(1) *Edinburgh Student Law Review* (2016), 102–115.

344 See section 2.5.

345 See section 2.6.

346 See section 2.7.

347 See section 2.8.

The above appraisal results only describe, nevertheless, the territorial situation of the Spratly Islands as it is today. The territorial title might change with the development of the events and activities in the region. As showcased in *Malaysia/Singapore*, a legal title previously established may lapse due to a common understanding or tacit agreement developed between the disputant States, and in this circumstance, *effectivités* can come into play.[348] Hence, if China's alleged historic title lapses as a result of an 'evolving understanding' or 'a convergent evolution of the positions' shared by the claimant States,[349] to the extent that the conduct mentioned in section 2.5.3.1 could be considered as relevant *effectivités* if absent sustained protests, consultations and negotiations in the future, the third type of the titles/*effectivités* relationship might come to play, whereby these *effectivités* could be constitutive of a territorial title.

2.10 Conclusion

As observed by Huber, in a territorial dispute, 'only one of two conflicting interests is to prevail, because sovereignty can be attributed to but one of the Parties'.[350] Hence, it can never be a win-win situation for all the disputant States. Meanwhile, another point worth noting is that modern international law rejects the applicability of *terra nullius* and tends to attribute a certain territory to a country whenever possible. As observed by the PCIJ in *Eastern Greenland*: 'in many cases the tribunal has been satisfied with very little in the way of the actual exercise of sovereign rights, provided that the other State could not make out a superior claim'.[351] The rejection of *terra nullius* is necessary for attaining a stable territorial order across the globe and thus worth supporting, despite its side effect that picking the best argument out of a mediocre bunch might sometimes be difficult and thus has little chance to enjoy unanimous support.

Perhaps one of the few examples showcasing the farthest international law has gone in providing a 'creative diplomatic solution'[352] to territorial disputes

348 Sovereignty over Pedra Branca/Pulau Batu Puteh, Middle Rocks and South Ledge, n 23, para.276.

349 *Ibid.*

350 Island of Palmas, n 311, 870.

351 Legal Status of Eastern Greenland, n 15, 46.

352 H.W. Ohnesorge, A Sea of Troubles: International Law and the Spitsbergen Plus Approach to Conflict Management in the South China Sea, in E. Fels and T.-M. Vu (eds.), *Power*

is the approach taken in the century-old Spitsbergen Treaty that settled the territorial dispute over the Svalbard archipelago.[353] The Spitsbergen Treaty recognizes 'the full and absolute sovereignty' of Norway over the Svalbard archipelago.[354] This treaty also gives all countries that are parties to the treaty non-discriminatory rights of access, fishing and hunting in the territories of the Svalbard archipelago and their territorial waters,[355] while disputes exist about whether such non-discriminatory rights apply to the EEZ and continental shelf of the Svalbard archipelago.[356] Some scholars suggest using the Spitsbergen Treaty as a potential model for a negotiated solution to the territorial dispute in the Spratly Islands.[357] However, it is recognized that the claimant States are unlikely to concede on their respective positions on territorial sovereignty in the near future – '[t]he difficulty is political will'.[358]

The evidence available to this study suggests that China's territorial claim to the islands in the Spratly Islands based on historic title, among all the claims, is the most plausible one, albeit not necessarily an impeccable one, when evaluated against the law of territory. The extent or scope of China's established historic title, which covers all the islands in the Spratly Islands, can, arguably, be based on the group or unity principle in relation to territorial allocation, which the author has discussed in another paper by examining a series of relevant international cases in the past one hundred years.[359] Nevertheless, as Schrijver rightly pointed out, sovereignty, inevitably including territorial sovereignty, is 'not an absolute and static concept but more a relative and dynamic one'.[360] As mentioned earlier, if China's alleged historic title lapses as a result of an 'evolving understanding' or 'a convergent evolution of the positions' shared by the claimant States,[361] the acts

Politics in Asia's Contested Waters: Territorial Disputes in the South China Sea (Springer. 2016), 45.

353 Treaty concerning the Archipelago of Spitsbergen, adopted 9 February 1920, entered into force 14 August 1925, 2 *UNTS* 7.

354 *Ibid.*, art. 1.

355 *Ibid.*, arts. 2, 3.

356 Ø. Jensen, The Svalbard Treaty and Norwegian Sovereignty, 11 *Arctic Review on Law and Politics* (2020), 94.

357 Ohnesorge, n 352, 49. P. Dutton, Three Disputes and Three Objectives – China and the South China Sea, 64(4) *Naval War College Review* (2011), 60–61.

358 Ohnesorge, n 352, 50. T.L. McDorman, The Territorial Sovereignty Disputes in the South China Sea, in K. Zou (ed.), *Routledge Handbook of the South China Sea* (Routledge. 2021), 100.

359 X. Ma, International Jurisprudence Concerning the Group or Unity Principle in Territorial Allocation, 18(1) *CJIL* (2019), 165–178.

360 Schrijver, n 2, 98.

361 *Ibid.*

à titre de souverain taken by the disputant States in respect of the Spratly Islands might have a chance to be considered as relevant *effectivités* and thus constitutive of a territorial title, to the etxtent that protests, consultations and negotiations are absent in the future.

Furthermore, there appears to be little possibility of resolving this territorial dispute by either judicial or diplomatic methods in the foreseeable future,[362] owing to various factors such as China's resistance to any recourse to third-party settlement,[363] the foreseeable difficulties in negotiations for claimant States to compromise their territorial interests,[364] nationalist sentiments about territorial sovereignty,[365] the strategic location of the Spratly Islands,[366] and high economic stakes because of the abundance of natural resources therein.[367] Hence, the settlement of this territorial dispute cannot be counted on as the only method to achieve and maintain the peaceful coexistence of the disputant States in the region. It would thus be wise for the disputant States to set aside this territorial dispute and to figure out alternative solutions to coordinate their behaviours and to make efficient uses of marine natural resources in the Spratly Islands area pending the final settlement of this territorial dispute. Relevant alternative solutions may include exercising self-restraint on their respective unilateral activities (chapter 4), and entering into cooperative arrangements on managing the hydrocarbon resources, fishery resources, and marine pollution (chapters 5–8) respecting the Spratly Islands area in the absence of delimitation.

---

362 U. Hideshi, The Problems in the South China Sea, *Review of Island Studies* (2013), 2–3.

363 China, n 34, paras.83, 130.

364 M.Z. Ahmad and M.A. Mohd Sani, China's Assertive Posture in Reinforcing its Territorial and Sovereignty Claims in the South China Sea: An Insight into Malaysia's Stance, 18(1) *Japanese Journal of Political Science* (2017), 71.

365 Park, n 44, 34.

366 Murphy, n 4, 189.

367 U.S. Energy Information Administration, *South China Sea* (7 February 2013), available at <https://www.eia.gov/beta/international/analysis_includes/regions_of_interest/South_China_Sea/south_china_sea.pdf>.

CHAPTER 3

Identifying Disputed Marine Areas

3.1 Introduction

One of the essential respects of the management of the Spratly Islands area according to international law is the application of relevant international obligations preceding delimitation – such as the obligations to negotiate in good faith and not to jeopardize delimitation as stipulated in Articles 74(3) and 83(3) of UNCLOS – to regulate the unilateral behaviours of the disputant States. Identifying the seaward limit of the disputed marine areas in this region is necessary before applying such obligations to the disputant States and thus of relevance if the role of international law in the management of the Spratly Islands area is to be discussed. International courts and tribunals tend to define the areas of overlapping claims as disputed marine areas. For instance, in *Aegean Sea*, the ICJ considered the areas of overlapping claims, to which both Greece and Turkey claimed rights of exploration and exploitation, to be areas in dispute.[1] Similarly, the ITLOS decided in *Ghana/Côte d'Ivoire* that the spatial extent of the marine area in dispute between Ghana and Côte d'Ivoire for applying provisional measures was ' "a triangular disputed area" defined by the competing claims of the Parties'.[2]

The identification process can, however, sometimes be difficult, especially in the presence of ambiguous claims put forward by the disputant parties, or where other disputant parties view a claim as being excessive. This chapter terms these two difficulties 'ambiguity' and 'alleged excessiveness'. In terms of maritime claims, 'ambiguity', denoting the quality of being open to more than one interpretation,[3] means that when a State makes a claim, it does not specify either the scope of a claim or the legal basis on which a claim relies. 'Excessiveness' means that a claim exceeds what is entitled to the claimant according to international law. Accordingly, 'alleged excessiveness' means that

1 Aegean Sea Continental Shelf (Greece v. Turkey), Order of 11 September 1976, Request for the Indication of Interim Measures of Protection (ICJ), para.28.

2 Dispute Concerning Delimitation of the Maritime Boundary between Ghana and Côte d'Ivoire in the Atlantic Ocean (Ghana/Côte d'Ivoire), Order of 25 April 2015, Request for the prescription of provisional measures (ITLOS), para.45.

3 'Ambiguity', Oxford Dictionaries, available at <https://en.oxforddictionaries.com/definition/ambiguity>.

 | DOI:10.1163/9789004504332_004

other claimants view a claim as being excessive, regardless of whether there is final proof such as judicial findings or agreements mutually accepted by claimants. 'Ambiguity' and 'alleged excessiveness' are interconnected. A claim being ambiguous either in its scope or legal basis is prone to be viewed as being excessive by other claimants.

The maritime dispute in the Spratly Islands area is fraught with both difficulties, thereby making the identification of disputed marine areas therein a challenging task. Only a few pieces of literature have addressed how to identify disputed marine areas, often in an incidental manner, which adds more difficulties to this task.[4] This chapter aims to address this challenge. For this purpose, this chapter explores the typology of maritime claims put forward by the disputant States with respect to the Spratly Islands area and analyses the extent of ambiguity and alleged excessiveness associated with different types of claims (section 3.2). This chapter continues to discuss the application of two different approaches in identifying disputed marine areas in the Spratly Islands setting: (1) the areas of overlapping claims approach taking into account all claims, and (2) an alternative approach excluding unreasonable claims (section 3.3). The implementation of these two approaches requires an examination of three questions: What are the categories of maritime claims that ought to be taken into account under each approach? What are unreasonable claims? And what is the impact of *South China Sea Arbitration* on the categorization of disputed marine areas? (subsections 3.3.1–3.3.2) After tackling these questions, this chapter continues to discuss which approach is more apt for the Spratly Islands area (subsection 3.3.3).

3.2 Maritime Claims: Typology, Ambiguity and Alleged Excessiveness

3.2.1 *Typology*

According to different legal bases, the maritime claims put forward by the disputant States can be grouped into three types: (1) claims based on entitlements generated by mainland territories, (2) claims based on entitlements generated

4 See *e.g.* S.P. Kim, *Maritime Delimitation and Interim Arrangements in North East Asia* (Martinus Nijhoff Publishers. 2004), 56; BIICL, *Report on the Obligations of States under Articles 74(3) and 83(3) of UNCLOS in respect of Undelimited Maritime Areas* (2016), paras.100-107; S.D. Murphy, Obligations of States in Disputed Areas of the Continental Shelf, in T. Heider (ed.), *New Knowledge and Changing Circumstances in the Law of the Sea* (Brill. 2020), 185–187; Y. van Logchem, *Disputed Maritime Areas: The Rights and Obligations of States under International Law* (PhD Dissertation, Utrecht University, defended on 8 January 2019), 5–6.

by islands, and (3) claims based on the U-shaped line. For clarity, it might be helpful to point out the conceptual distinction between the terms 'claim' and 'entitlement' used in this section. A legal 'claim', as opposed to a factual claim, is an assertion, demand or request put forward by a legal entity (such as a State, individual, or organization) of something considered one's right or title.[5] An 'entitlement' describes the fact that a legal entity has a right to something specified especially by law or contract.[6] Whereas a legal 'claim' expresses a subjective belief of rights, an 'entitlement' corresponds to an objective assessment of whether a legal entity has a certain right in light of the law. An entitlement might be contingent on meeting certain factual conditions or requirements. For example, pursuant to Article 121(3) of UNCLOS, for an island to generate entitlements related to an EEZ and continental shelf, it must be capable of sustaining human habitation or economic life of its own. Moreover, an entitlement and its realization are two separate things. The realization of the maximum potential of entitlement cannot always be guaranteed. For example, a coastal State is entitled to a 200-M EEZ emanating from its mainland territory according to Article 57 of UNCLOS. However, in case this State's entitlement overlaps with the same entitlement held by another State with an opposite or adjacent coast, the former might not get a 200-M EEZ after delimitation.

3.2.1.1 Claims Based on Entitlements Generated by Mainland Territories

The first type of maritime claim is based on entitlements related to the EEZ and continental shelf, including the extended continental shelf, generated by mainland territories. In the South China Sea, Malaysia, Vietnam, the Philippines and Brunei assert this type of claim.

Malaysia first claimed a continental shelf from its mainland territory when it enacted the Continental Shelf Act in 1966.[7] In 1984, Malaysia enacted the Exclusive Economic Zone Act, claiming a 200-M EEZ from its mainland territory.[8] Malaysia claims a continental shelf extending beyond 200 M measured from the baselines along its mainland coast, which extends over the Spratly Islands area. Its joint submission with Vietnam to the Commission on the Limits of the Continental Shelf (CLCS) in 2009 defined these two coastal States' extended continental shelf claims in the southern part of the South China

5 'Claim', Oxford Dictionaries, available at <https://en.oxforddictionaries.com/definition/claim>.

6 'Entitlement', Oxford Dictionaries, available at <https://www.merriam-webster.com/dictionary/entitlement>.

7 Malaysia, Continental Shelf Act 1966 (28 July 1966).

8 Malaysia, Exclusive Economic Zone Act 1984 (1984).

Sea.[9] Malaysia's subsequent submission to the CLCS in 2019 further described its claimed outer limits of the continental shelf beyond 200 M in the northern part of the South China Sea.[10]

Vietnam uttered its official claim over the maritime spaces in 1977 when it issued the Statement on the Territorial Sea, the Contiguous Zone, the Exclusive Economic Zone and the Continental Shelf.[11] Vietnam further indicated the outer limits of its continental shelf derived from its mainland coast in the maps contained in its joint submission with Malaysia to the CLCS in 2009.[12] In this joint submission, Vietnam claims a continental shelf extending beyond 200 M measured from the baselines along its mainland coast, which extends over the Spratly Islands area.[13] In addition, in the same year, Vietnam also made another separate submission to the CLCS to claim a continental shelf extending beyond 200 M in the north area of the South China Sea.[14]

The Philippines, in its 1978 Presidential Decree No. 1599, claimed an EEZ emanating from its mainland coast that extends over the Spratly Islands area.[15] When the Philippines submitted information on the continental shelf beyond 200 M in the Benham Rise region to the CLCS in 2009, it declared that this submission was 'made without prejudice to the right of the Philippines to make other submissions for other areas at a future time'.[16] Hence, the Philippines might claim an extended continental shelf generated by its archipelago that extends over the Spratly Islands area in the future.

Brunei inherited a continental shelf partially delimited by the UK at its independence in 1984, which laid between parallel lines drawn to the 100-fathom isobath.[17] In 1993, Brunei published the Declaration on the Exclusive Economic

---

9 Malaysia and Vietnam, Joint Submission to the Commission on the Limits of the Continental Shelf pursuant to Article 76, paragraph 8 of the United Nations Convention on the Law of the Sea 1982 in respect of the southern part of the South China Sea (7 May 2009).

10 Malaysia, Partial Submission to the Commission on the Limits of the Continental Shelf pursuant to Article 76, paragraph 8 of the United Nations Convention on the Law of the Sea 1982 in the South China Sea (12 December 2019).

11 Vietnam, Statement on the Territorial Sea, the Contiguous Zone, the Exclusive Economic Zone and the Continental Shelf (12 May 1977).

12 Malaysia and Vietnam, n 9.

13 Malaysia and Vietnam, n 9.

14 Vietnam, Outer Limits of the Continental Shelf beyond 200 nautical miles in respect of the North Area (VNM-N) (7 May 2009).

15 The Philippines, Presidential Decree No. 1599 establishing an Exclusive Economic Zone and for other purposes (11 June 1978).

16 The Philippines, A Partial Submission of Data and Information on the Outer Limits of the Continental Shelf in Benham Rise Region (8 April 2009), para.1.

17 D.J. Dzurek, *The Spratly Islands Dispute: Who's On First?* (IBRU. 1996), 35.

Zone, establishing a 200-M EEZ measured from its mainland coast.[18] Moreover, in its preliminary submission to the CLCS concerning the outer limits of the continental shelf in 2009,[19] Brunei made a general claim to a continental shelf extending beyond 200 M measured from the baselines along its mainland coast.[20] The preliminary submission does not specify the coordinates of the outer limits of the continental shelf, and Brunei has not yet sent a full submission to the CLCS.[21] Nevertheless, due to Brunei's geological setting, its alleged extended continental shelf would undoubtedly extend over the Spratly Islands area (Map 2).

China does not have this type of claim because its mainland territory is so distant from the Spratly Islands area that it could not generate maritime entitlements extending over the latter.

3.2.1.2 Claims Based on Entitlements Generated by Islands

The second type of claim is connected with maritime entitlements generated by islands. As mentioned in chapter 2, China, Malaysia, Vietnam and the Philippines claim territorial titles to part or all of the islands in the Spratly Islands, and therefore, these four States assert entitlements emanating from islands.

Entitlements derived from islands in this region can be further divided into two sub-types: (1) entitlements related to the territorial sea and contiguous zone, and (2) entitlements related to the EEZ and continental shelf, including the extended continental shelf. Both sub-types are contingent on the sovereignty of the islands concerned. However, the relationships between these two sub-types and territorial sovereignty have a critical difference. The sovereignty over islands would undoubtedly entail entitlements related to the territorial sea and contiguous zone, but on its own does not necessarily lead to entitlements related to the EEZ and continental shelf. It is because apart from sovereignty, the latter depends on an extra requirement that the islands at issue must be capable of sustaining human habitation or economic life of their own

18 *Ibid.*, 58.

19 The reason why Brunei, Malaysia, the Philippines and Vietnam all made submissions to the CLCS in 2009 was probably to catch the submission deadlines. For more details, see chapter 5, section 5.3.2.1.

20 Brunei, Preliminary Submission concerning the Outer Limits of its Continental Shelf (12 May 2009).

21 Submissions, through the UN Secretary-General, to the Commission on the Limits of the Continental Shelf, pursuant to article 76, paragraph 8, of the United Nations Convention on the Law of the Sea of 10 December 1982 (as of 6 July 2021), available at <https://www.un.org/Depts/los/clcs_new/commission_submissions.htm>.

according to Article 121(3) of UNCLOS. For this reason, when a State claims sovereignty over a specific island, it is natural to expect that this State also claims maritime entitlements related to the territorial sea and contiguous zone generated around that island, but whether this State can have entitlements connected with the EEZ and continental shelf would require further examination. Hence, the following analysis places more focus on entitlements related to the EEZ and continental shelf generated around islands.

Turning to specific claims, China made its first official claim on the maritime entitlements over the Spratly Islands area through the Declaration on Territorial Sea in 1958. In that Declaration, China claimed a 12-M territorial sea for all its territories including the Spratly Islands.[22] In 1992, China reiterated this position in the Law on the Territorial Sea and the Contiguous Zone.[23] In 1998, China enacted the Law on the Exclusive Economic Zone and the Continental Shelf, which set out a 200-M EEZ and continental shelf for its land territories including the Spratly Islands.[24] China publicly stated that: 'China's Nansha Islands [the Spratly Islands] is fully entitled to Territorial Sea, Exclusive Economic Zone (EEZ) and Continental Shelf'.[25] Moreover, when China submitted the information on the limits of the continental shelf beyond 200 M in the East China Sea to the CLCS in 2012, it declared that '[t]his submission of the Chinese Government is without prejudice to any future submission by China on delineation of the outer limits of the continental shelf in [the] East China Sea and other seas'.[26]

Malaysia did not explicitly claim the EEZ or continental shelf from islands under its control in the Spratly Islands area in its 1966 Continental Shelf Act and 1984 Exclusive Economic Zone Act. However, in its joint submission with Vietnam to the CLCS in 2009, Malaysia drew the outer limits of its alleged continental shelf generated only from its mainland coast but not from any island in the Spratly Islands.[27] Schofield commented that these outer limits as shown in this joint submission implied that Malaysia did not claim any continental shelf generated by the islands therein.[28] Moreover, Malaysia claims

22 China, Declaration on China's Territorial Sea (1958), para.1.
23 China, Law on the Territorial Sea and the Contiguous Zone (25 February 1992).
24 China, Law on the Exclusive Economic Zone and the Continental Shelf (26 June 1998).
25 China, Note Verbale No. CML/8/2011 (14 April 2011).
26 China, Submission on the Outer Limits of the Continental Shelf in Part of the East China Sea (14 December 2012).
27 Malaysia and Vietnam, n 9.
28 C. Schofield, Untangling A Complex Web: Understanding Competing Maritime Claims in the South China Sea, in I. Storey & C.Y. Lin (eds.), *The South China Sea Dispute: Navigating Diplomatic and Strategic Tensions* (Singapore: ISEAS Yusof Ishak Institute. 2016), 31–32.

a single maritime boundary for its EEZ and continental shelf according to its Declaration upon the Ratification of UNCLOS on 14 October 1996.[29] It follows that Malaysia might not claim any EEZ emanating from the islands therein either.[30]

As to Vietnam, its 1977 Statement on the Territorial Sea, the Contiguous Zone, the Exclusive Economic Zone and the Continental Shelf stipulated that Vietnam's islands and archipelagos, including the Spratly Islands, had their own territorial sea, contiguous zone, EEZ and continental shelf.[31] In a note *verbale* dated 30 March 2020, Vietnam stated that the maritime entitlement of each high-tide feature in the Spratly Islands shall be determined according to Article 121(3) of UNCLOS.[32] However, Vietnam has indicated the outer limits of its continental shelf generated only by its mainland territory but not by any island in the Spratly Islands in the maps contained in its joint submission with Malaysia to the CLCS in 2009.[33] Similar to the situation of Malaysia, these outer limits as shown in the joint submission probably implies that Vietnam does not claim any continental shelf generated by the islands.[34]

Whether the Philippines intended to claim entitlements related to the EEZ or continental shelf for the Kalayaan Island Group in the Spratly Islands was not evident before the *South China Sea Arbitration* case. In the 2009 Republic Act No. 9522, the Philippines stated that its jurisdiction over the Kalayaan Island Group should be determined according to Article 121 of UNCLOS.[35] However, during the merits hearing of *South China Sea Arbitration* in 2015, the Philippines clarified that it would not claim 200-M maritime entitlements measured from the baselines of the islands in the Spratly Islands, probably for ensuring the tribunal's jurisdiction over its submissions.[36] Notably, China's reservation in relation to UNCLOS excluded the tribunal's jurisdiction over disputes 'relating to sea boundary delimitation'.[37] The tribunal admitted that it would not have jurisdiction over some of the Philippines' submissions if any

29 Malaysia, Declaration upon the ratification of UNCLOS (14 October 1996).

30 Schofield, n 28, 31–32.

31 Vietnam, n 11.

32 Vietnam, Note Verbale No. 22/HC-2020 (30 March 2020).

33 Malaysia and Vietnam, n 9.

34 Schofield, n 28, 31–32.

35 The Philippines, Republic Act No. 9522 (10 March 2009).

36 Transcript on Merits Hearing of the Republic of Philippines v. the People's Republic of China Arbitration, 24 November 2015.

37 UNCLOS, Article 298. China, *Declaration made after ratification of UNCLOS* (25 August 2006), available at <http://www.un.org/depts/los/convention_agreements/convention_declarations.htm#China after ratification>.

disputed island therein was entitled to an EEZ or continental shelf, because such an EEZ or continental shelf would extend over most of the Spratly Islands area, whereby relevant submissions could be characterized as 'relating to sea boundary delimitation'.[38]

3.2.1.3 Claims Based on the U-shaped Line

In addition to the above two types of claims, China appears to assert maritime claims based on a U-shape line. China published the first U-shaped line map titled 'Map of South China Sea Islands' in 1947,[39] and it attached a U-shaped line map to its note *verbale* addressed to the UN in 2009 as a response to the joint submission to the CLCS made by Malaysia and Vietnam regarding their alleged extended continental shelf in the Spratly Islands area.[40] China itself has never clarified its claim in relation to the U-shaped line.[41] Nevertheless, as the *South China Sea Arbitration* tribunal pointed out, even though China had not clarified the meaning of the U-shaped line, it was apparent that China had 'a seemly expansive claim to maritime entitlements' based on the U-shaped line, which the Philippines disputed.[42]

3.2.1.4 Summary

Table 6 summarizes three types of maritime claims put forward by the disputant States respecting the Spratly Islands area.

3.2.2 *Ambiguity and Alleged Excessiveness*

For the first type of maritime claim, namely claims based on entitlements generated by mainland territories, Brunei, Malaysia, the Philippines and Vietnam

---

38 The South China Sea Arbitration (The Philippines v. China), Award on Jurisdiction and Admissibility of 29 October 2015 (PCA), paras.156, 368–369.

39 OES, China: Maritime Claims in the South China Sea, *Limits in the Seas* (5 December 2014), 3.

40 China, Note Verbale No. CML/17/2009 (7 May 2009).

41 As pointed out by Xue, '[a]lthough the U-shaped line has long been on official Chinese maps, China neither explained the exact legal value of the line nor the status of the waters inside the line'. See G. Xue, The South China Sea: Competing Claims and Conflict Situations, in C. Schofield, *et al.* (eds.), *The Limits of Maritime Jurisdiction* (Brill. 2014), 243. Usuki also opined that it was '*prima facie* not known' whether the U-shaped line meant to indicate the assertion for historic titles to waters or merely for historic rights falling short of historic titles. See E. Usuki, China's Three Distinctive Assertions under the 'Nine-dash-line' Claims and the Annex VII Arbitral Tribunal's Interpretation of Article 121 Regarding an Island and Rocks under the 1982 UN Convention on the Law of the Sea, 21 *Asian Yearbook of International Law* (2015), 146–147.

42 The South China Sea Arbitration, n 38, para.167.

TABLE 6 Three types of maritime claims advanced by the disputant States

	(1) Claims based on entitlements generated by mainland territories	(2) Claims based on entitlements generated by islands	(3) Claims based on the U-shaped line
Brunei	√	--	--
China	--	√	√
Malaysia	√	√	--
Philippines	√	√	--
Vietnam	√	√	--

Notes: The symbol '√' means that the State concerned advances the maritime claim, and the symbol '--' indicates the opposite.

have published coordinates of the baselines along their mainland coasts and the 200-M outer limits of their respective EEZ and continental shelf. Since the sovereignty over their mainland territories is not disputed, these States undoubtedly have entitlements to the EEZ and continental shelf generated by such territories. Hence, in general, these claims are neither ambiguous nor viewed as being excessive. There is one exception, that is, the claims or potential claims regarding the extended continental shelf. Neither Brunei nor China or the Philippines has specified the outer limits of their alleged continental shelf extending over the Spratly Islands area. Hence, potential claims of these three States regarding the areas of the extended continental shelf in this region remain ambiguous in their scope. Malaysia and Vietnam's claims on the extended continental shelf are regarded as being excessive by China and the Philippines.[43]

The situation becomes complicated when it comes to the second type of maritime claim, namely claims based on entitlements generated by the islands. The legal basis for these claims is clear, namely the alleged sovereignty over relevant islands. However, the scope of these claims remains undefined, since none of the countries claiming sovereignty has published coordinates for baselines that can be used to measure the maritime entitlements that they may claim in this region. Moreover, the four States dispute the sovereignty over

43 China, n 40. The Philippines, Note Verbale No. 000819 (4 August 2009), para.2.

the islands in the Spratly Islands area as well as the question of whether these islands could generate entitlements related to the EEZ and continental shelf. As a result, among these States, one views another's claims based on entitlements generated by the islands as being excessive.

With respect to the third type of maritime claim, namely China's potential claim based on the U-shaped line, it is patent that both the scope of and legal basis for this claim remain ambiguous, as China has not provided any clarification. Other claimants have viewed this claim as being excessive.[44]

Neither the ambiguity nor the alleged excessiveness of a party's claim affects the existence of a dispute. In *Cameroon v. Nigeria*, the ICJ stated that 'the exact scope of this dispute cannot be determined at present; a dispute nevertheless exists between the two Parties'.[45] The *South China Sea Arbitration* tribunal endorsed this position, concluding that the 'existence of a dispute over [relevant] issues is not diminished by the fact that China has not clarified the meaning of the nine-dash line or elaborated on its claim to historic rights'.[46] Whether a claim is excessive under international law is also of no relevance to the existence of a dispute. International jurisprudence has widely recognized the necessity to 'distinguish between the dispute itself and arguments used by the parties to sustain their respective submissions on the dispute'.[47] The *South China Sea Arbitration* tribunal pointed out that international law did not require a State to expound its legal arguments in order for a dispute to arise.[48]

The diplomatic correspondence between and among China, Vietnam, Malaysia and the Philippines dating back to 2009–2011 have already shown that these claimants are positively against one another's maritime claims in relation to the Spratly Islands area, whereby a maritime dispute apparently exists.[49] In

44 Examples include: Vietnam, Note Verbale No. 86/HC-2009 (8 May 2009), para.3; The Philippines, Note Verbale No. 000228 (5 April 2011).

45 Land and Maritime Boundary (Cameroon v. Nigeria), Judgment of 11 June 1998 (Preliminary Objections) (ICJ), para.93.

46 The South China Sea Arbitration, n 38, para.167.

47 Fisheries Jurisdiction (Spain v. Canada), Judgment of 4 December 1998 (ICJ), para.32. The South China Sea Arbitration, n 38, para.170.

48 *Ibid.*

49 The key to finding the existence of a dispute is that 'the claim of one party is positively opposed by the other'. Such positive opposition is normally apparent from the diplomatic correspondence of the parties, as views are exchanged and claims are made and rejected. See Mavrommatis Palestine Concessions (Greece v. Britain), Judgment of 30 August 1924, PCIJ Series A No. 2, 11; South West Africa (Ethiopia/Liberia v. South Africa), Judgment of 21 December 1962 (ICJ), 328; Fisheries Jurisdiction, n 47, para.31; Armed Activities on the Territory of the Congo (New Application: 2002) (Democratic Republic of the Congo v. Rwanda), Judgment of 3 February 2006 (Jurisdiction of the Court and Admissibility of the Application) (ICJ), para.90; Application of the International Convention on the

2009, Malaysia and Vietnam submitted jointly to the CLCS the information on the limits of the continental shelf beyond 200 M from the baselines along their mainland coasts, which extended over the Spratly Islands area.[50] The joint submission received strong protests from China and the Philippines.[51] China attached a U-shaped line map in its response to the joint submission,[52] which fuelled strong objections from Vietnam and the Philippines.[53] Brunei did not express its objection to the joint submission, probably because the maritime boundaries between Brunei and Malaysia out to 200 M have been delimited by an exchange of letters dated 16 March 2009.[54] These letters, however, are not publicly available,[55] and neither Malaysia nor Brunei has given the due publicity to these maritime boundaries as required by Articles 75(2) and 84(2) of UNCLOS.[56] Even so, Brunei and Malaysia still dispute the continental shelf beyond 200 M,[57] which is confirmed in Brunei's preliminary submission concerning the outer limits of the continental shelf in 2009.[58] A maritime dispute also exists between China and Brunei.[59] For instance, when China conducted survey research in the Spratly Islands area in 2003, Brunei affirmatively opposed and rejected the maritime claims of China by making protests against China's conduct in its alleged EEZ.[60]

Elimination of All Forms of Racial Discrimination (Georgia v. Russian Federation), Judgment of 1 April 2011 (Preliminary Objections) (ICJ), para.23; The South China Sea Arbitration, n 38, para.159.

50 Malaysia and Vietnam, n 9.

51 China, n 40, para.2. The Philippines, n 43, para.2.

52 China, n 40, para.2.

53 Vietnam, n 44, para.3. The Philippines, n 44.

54 Brunei, n 20, para.10. Schofield, n 28, 31.

55 Scholars comment that the absence of this exchange of letters between Malaysia and Brunei in the public domain may explain why China did not make a formal response to it. See *e.g.*, I. Storey, Brunei's Contested Sea Border with China, in B. Elleman, *et al.* (eds.), *Beijing's Power and China's Borders: Twenty Neighbors in Asia* (Taylor and Francis. 2014), 41. J.A. Roach, Malaysia and Brunei: An Analysis of their Claims in the South China Sea, *Center for Naval Analyses Occasional Paper* (2014), 4, fn. 23.

56 Malaysia, Submission in Compliance with the Deposit Obligations Pursuant to the United Nations Convention on the Law of the Sea, available at <http://www.un.org/depts/los/LEGISLATIONANDTREATIES/STATEFILES/MYS.htm>. Brunei, Submission in Compliance with the Deposit Obligations Pursuant to the United Nations Convention on the Law of the Sea, available at <http://www.un.org/depts/los/LEGISLATIONANDTREATIES/STATEFILES/BRN.htm>.

57 Brunei, n 20, para.12.

58 *Ibid.* Brunei stated that 'there may exist areas of potential overlapping entitlements in respect of its continental shelf beyond 200 nautical miles'.

59 Storey, n 55, 41–43.

60 O. Ward, The Silent Claimant in the South China Sea (16 July 2017), available at <https://www.aseantoday.com/2017/07/the-silent-claimant-in-the-south-china-sea/>.

3.3 Two Competing Approaches to Identifying Disputed Marine Areas

Though the presence of ambiguity and alleged excessiveness associated with maritime claims does not impact the existence of the maritime dispute in the Spratly Islands area, it may add difficulties to identifying the exact geographical extent of disputed marine areas therein. As mentioned at the beginning of this chapter, areas of overlapping claims would normally be identified as disputed marine areas. This approach can be attractive to the disputant States because the spatial scope of contested areas is determined solely based on the overlapping areas of their unilateral claims. However, if without any constraint, a State may abuse this approach by making plainly unreasonable claims or mere assertions of rights manifestly incapable of existing under international law. For example, China's claims in relation to the U-shaped line are often criticized as 'expansive'.[61] An alternative approach is to exclude unreasonable claims when determining the spatial extent of contested marine areas. In light of this, this section discusses the applicability of two different approaches in the Spratly Islands setting.

3.3.1 *The Areas of Overlapping Claims Approach: Taking into Account All Claims*

3.3.1.1 Categorization of Disputed Marine Areas

Implementing the areas of overlapping claims approach in the Spratly Islands setting requires taking into account all the three types of maritime claims as specified in section 3.2.1. Accordingly, the disputed marine areas therein can be categorized into two general groups: (1) areas of overlapping claims related to the same type of maritime zone, and (2) areas of overlapping claims related to different types of maritime zones. This categorization is of critical importance to the analysis of applicable international law preceding delimitation in chapter 4.

3.3.1.1.1 *Areas of Overlapping Claims Related to the Same Type of Maritime Zone*

The claims of the disputant States can be associated with the same type of maritime zone, being either the territorial sea, contiguous zone, EEZ or continental shelf.

---

61 D. French, In the Matter of the South China Sea Arbitration: Republic of Philippines v People's Republic of China, Arbitral Tribunal Constituted under Annex VII to the 1982 United Nations Law of the Sea Convention, Case No. 2013-19, Award of 12 July 2016, 19(1) *Environment Law Review* (2017), 49.

One category of disputed areas in this group is the disputed areas of the territorial sea or contiguous zone generated around the disputed islands. The overlapping claims can occur in two scenarios. First, since the claimants dispute the sovereignty over the islands in this region, each territorial sea or contiguous zone generated by any one of these islands is itself a contested area. Second, the territorial sea or contiguous zone generated by one island might overlap with the same type of maritime zone generated by another island.

Another category is the disputed areas of the EEZ or continental shelf including the extended continental shelf. First, to the extent that only China claims entitlements to an EEZ or a continental shelf emanating from the islands in the Spratly Islands area, this claim would overlap with entitlements to the EEZ or continental shelf generated by the mainland territories of Brunei, Malaysia, the Philippines and Vietnam opposing to the coasts of these islands.[62] Second, though neither Brunei nor China or the Philippines has specified the outer limits of their alleged areas of the extended continental shelf extending over the Spratly Islands area, potential overlaps between or among the disputant States' claims related to the areas of the extended continental shelf might occur in the future.

3.3.1.1.2 *Areas of Overlapping Claims Related to Different Types of Maritime Zones*

In the context of the Spratly Islands area, the claim of a territorial sea generated by an island might overlap with the claim of a contiguous zone, EEZ or continental shelf generated by another island, or with the claim of an EEZ or continental shelf derived from a mainland territory. However, this overlap would not lead to a disputed marine area, because in no case can a contiguous zone, EEZ or continental shelf of one State encroach upon a territorial sea of another State. This position, albeit not stipulated in UNCLOS, has been widely supported by international jurisprudence, State practice and legal commentators.[63] For instance, in *Bangladesh/Myanmar*, the ITLOS

62 Some pronouncements of international jurisprudence might be taken to suggest that small islands are not given much weight in maritime boundary delimitation. However, this does not apply to the situation of the Spratly Islands, since the islands therein are 'one of the principal elements in the delimitation and not an incidental feature in a larger geographical setting'. For more discussions in this regard, see A.G. Oude Elferink, The Islands in the South China Sea: How Does Their Presence Limit the Extent of the High Sea and Area and the Maritime Zones of the Mainland Coasts, 32(2) *ODIL* (2001), 178–182.

63 For relevant international jurisprudence, see *e.g.*, Dubai/Sharjah Border Arbitration, Award of 19 October 1981, 91 *International Law Reports* 674 (The tribunal found that Abu Musa as an island was entitled 'ex principio to a belt of territorial sea quite independently

decided that Bangladesh had the right to a 12-M territorial sea around St. Martin's Island in the area where an overlap occurred with the EEZ or continental shelf claims of Myanmar.[64] The underlying rationale, according to the ITLOS, is that in case of an overlap, more weight has to be attributed to sovereignty over the territorial sea rather than sovereign rights over the EEZ or continental shelf.[65]

The second category is the areas of overlapping claims related to a contiguous zone and an EEZ. The claim of a contiguous zone generated by an island might overlap with the claim of an EEZ generated by another island, or with an EEZ emanating from a mainland territory.

Third, an EEZ claimed by one party might overlap with a continental shelf claimed by another. This overlap may occur because according to Article 56(1) of UNCLOS, the rights of a coastal State in the EEZ consists of 'sovereign rights for the purpose of exploring and exploiting, conserving and managing the natural resources, whether living or non-living, of the waters superjacent to the seabed and *of the seabed and its subsoil*'[66] (emphasis added). Three scenarios are relevant here. Firstly, an EEZ generated by an island overlaps with a continental shelf generated by another island. Secondly, an EEZ generated by

and separately from either the actual or potential continental shelf claims of neighbouring states'.); Second Stage of the Proceedings between Eritrea/Yemen (Maritime Delimitation), Decision of 17 December 1999, paras.160-161 (The tribunal concluded that the maritime boundary line must not cut through the 12-M territorial sea generated by Zuqar and Hanish, respectively.); Dispute concerning delimitation of the maritime boundary between Bangladesh and Myanmar in the Bay of Bengal (Bangladesh/Myanmar), Judgment of 14 March 2012 (ITLOS), para.169. For relevant State practices, which mainly include treaties concerned with the delimitation of EEZs or continental shelves which establish the boundary in such a way that islands are attributed at least a 12-M territorial sea, see *e.g.*, Agreement Concerning the Sovereignty over the Islands of Al-'Arabiyah and Farsi and the Delimitation of the Boundary Line Separating the Submarine Areas Between the Kingdom of Saudi Arabia and Iran, adopted 24 October 1968, entered into force 29 January 1969, 696 *UNTS* 212; Agreement concerning Joint Development of the Southern Part of the Continental Shelf Adjacent to Japan and South Korea (with map, appendix, agreed minutes and exchanges of notes), adopted 30 January 1974, entered into force 22 June 1978, 1225 *UNTS* 113. For relevant scholarly literature, see *e.g.*, A.G. Oude Elferink, Does Undisputed Title to a Maritime Zone Always Exclude its Delimitation: The Grey Area Issue, 3 *IJMCL* (1998), 153–154, 159–160, 164–165. Oude Elferink, n 62, 175. van Logchem, n 4, 22.

64 Dispute concerning delimitation of the maritime boundary between Bangladesh and Myanmar in the Bay of Bengal, n 63, para.169.

65 *Ibid.*

66 UNCLOS, Article 56(1).

an island overlaps with a continental shelf derived from a mainland territory. Thirdly, an EEZ derived from a mainland territory overlaps with a continental shelf based upon another mainland territory, or the other way around. For instance, as shown in Map 2, Malaysia's outer limits of the EEZ emanating from its mainland territory intersect with the outer limits of the extended continental shelf jointly claimed by Malaysia and Vietnam.

Fourth, the maritime zones encompassed by the U-shaped line overlap with all maritime zones generated by the islands in the Spratly Islands and with the EEZ and continental shelf derived from the mainland territories of Brunei, Malaysia, the Philippines and Vietnam.

3.3.1.2 Mapping the Extent of Disputed Marine Areas

The geographical extent of disputed marine areas identified according to the areas of overlapping claims approach must take into account two categories of disputed marine areas as specified in section 3.3.1.1: (1) areas of overlapping claims related to the same type of maritime zone, and (2) areas of overlapping claims related to different types of maritime zones. Accordingly, Map 2 depicts the extent of disputed marine areas in the Spratly Islands area, which basically covers the whole of the Spratly Islands area.

3.3.2 *An Alternative Approach: Excluding Unreasonable Claims*

3.3.2.1 Standard Setting: What Are 'Unreasonable Claims'?

The key to the alternative approach is defining and excluding 'unreasonable claims'. Some scholars regard claims not asserted in good faith as 'unreasonable claims', arguing that contested marine areas must only be 'zones of overlapping boundaries claimed *bona fide*'.[67] This argument is, arguably, inappropriate. Even if there is no possible legal basis for a State's claims, this State may still have asserted these claims in good faith. Yet, what matters here is not whether relevant claims have not been genuinely held but whether the claims are unreasonable. Hence, the good faith argument could be omitted.

The test of plausibility, which is widely recognized and used as a criterion for the indication of provisional measures in international jurisprudence

67 Kim, n 4, 56. N.A. Ioannides, The China-Japan and Venezuela-Guyana Maritime Disputes: How the Law on Undelimited Maritime Areas Addresses Unilateral Hydrocarbon Activities, *EJIL: Talk!* (25 January 2019), available at <https://www.ejiltalk.org/the-china-japan-and-venezuela-guyana-maritime-disputes-how-the-law-on-undelimited-maritime-areas-addresses-unilateral-hydrocarbon-activities/>.

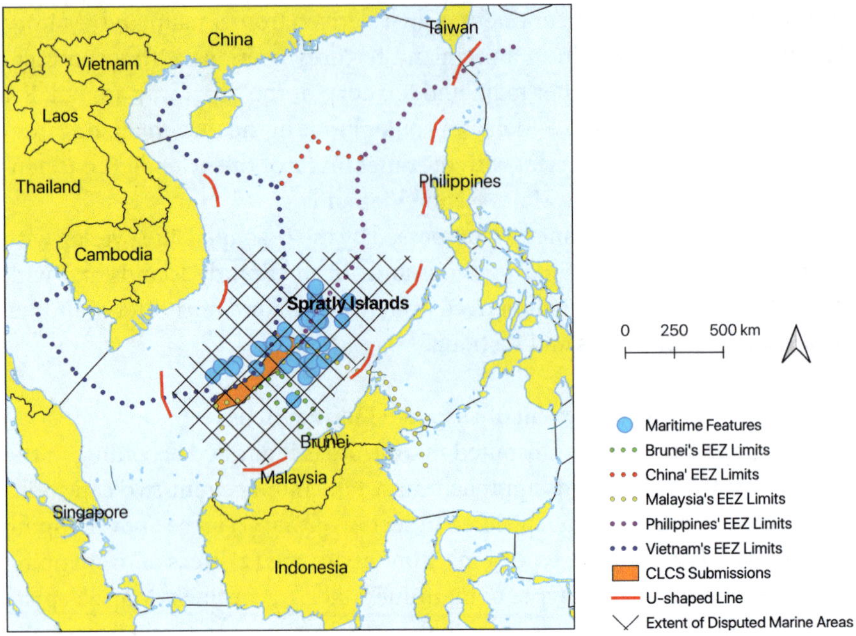

MAP 2 The extent of disputed marine areas in the Spratly Islands area according to the areas of overlapping claims approach
Notes: The author produced this illustrative map using the QGIS software. The coordinates of the maritime features are obtained from GoogleEarth. The data about the CLCS Submissions are obtained from: ESRI shapefile data for Malaysia and Vietnam ECS polygons, available online at <http://continentalshelf.org/onestopdatashop/6350.aspx>. The data about the EEZ limits are obtained from: Flanders Marine Institute (2018) Maritime Boundaries Geodatabase: Maritime Boundaries and Exclusive Economic Zones (200NM), version 10, available online at <https://doi.org/10.14284/312>.

which requires that the rights a party seeks to protect are plausible,[68] can be a good criterion for filtering out unreasonable claims.[69] The arbitral tribunal in *Guyana v. Suriname* has used the test of plausibility to guide itself in deciding

68 See *e.g.*, Questions relating to the Obligation to Prosecute or Extradite (Belgium v. Senegal), Order of 28 May 2009 (Request for the indication of provisional measures) (ICJ), para.57; Certain Activities carried out by Nicaragua in the Border Area (Costa Rica v. Nicaragua), Provisional Measures Order of 8 March 2011 (ICJ), paras.53, 57; Request for Interpretation of the Judgment of 15 June 1962 in the Case concerning the Temple of Preah Vihear (Cambodia v. Thailand) (Cambodia v. Thailand), Order of 18 July 2011 (Request for the Indication of Provisional Measures) (ICJ), para.33; Dispute Concerning Delimitation of the Maritime Boundary between Ghana and Côte d'Ivoire in the Atlantic Ocean, n 2, para.58.

69 Murphy, n 4, 185–186.

what types of activities are permissible in disputed marine areas.[70] In the tribunal's view, provisional measures can only be prescribed in exceptional circumstances.[71] It means that a court or tribunal will not prescribe provisional measures unless it finds there is 'a real and imminent risk that irreparable prejudice may be caused to the rights of the parties in dispute'.[72] On this basis, the tribunal has further concluded that the regime of provisional measures is 'far more circumscribed' than the regime that regulates activities in disputed marine areas.[73] It follows that if a claim could justify the use of exceptional power of a court or tribunal to indicate provisional measures, then such a claim must not be deemed unreasonable in the context of disputed marine areas.[74]

An important question is to what exact extent the rights that a State claims over a disputed area can be considered as 'plausible' and thus being 'reasonable'. The 'possibility' standard rather than 'probability' is more appropriate and widely accepted in international jurisprudence.[75] For instance, in *Belgium v. Senegal*, in examining the link between the right protected and the measures requested, the ICJ held that 'the power of the Court to indicate provisional measures should be exercised only if the Court is satisfied that the rights asserted by a party are at least plausible'.[76] The ICJ further explained that it did not need to establish *definitively* the existence of the rights that Belgium sought to be protected.[77] Rather, provided that the rights asserted by Belgium were grounded in a *possible* interpretation of the Convention against Torture, the ICJ considered such rights to be plausible.[78] Therefore, a disputant State's rights over the area in dispute would be considered plausible and thus reasonable, to the extent that such rights constitute a *possible* interpretation and application of the applicable international law such as UNCLOS provisions.

70 Guyana v. Suriname, Arbitral Award dated 17 September 2007 (PCA), para.469.
71 *Ibid.* Aegean Sea Continental Shelf, n 1, para.31.
72 Dispute Concerning Delimitation of the Maritime Boundary between Ghana and Côte d'Ivoire in the Atlantic Ocean, n 2, para.41. Guyana v. Suriname, n 70, para.469.
73 Guyana v. Suriname, n 70, para.469.
74 *Ibid.*
75 See *e.g.*, Passage through the Great Belt (Finland v. Denmark), Separate Opinion of Judge Shahabuddeen attached to Order of 29 July 1991 (Request for the Indication of Provisional Measures) (ICJ), 31, 36; Questions relating to the Obligation to Prosecute or Extradite, n 68, para.60; Dispute Concerning Delimitation of the Maritime Boundary between Ghana and Côte d'Ivoire in the Atlantic Ocean, n 2, paras.61–62.
76 Questions relating to the Obligation to Prosecute or Extradite, n 68, para.57.
77 *Ibid.*, para.60.
78 *Ibid.*

3.3.2.2 The Impact of the South China Sea Arbitration

In implementing the alternative approach in the Spratly Islands setting, the *South China Sea Arbitration* award might deem some of China's maritime claims implausible, thereby excluding these claims from consideration in determining disputed marine areas.

In *South China Sea Arbitration*, the Philippines argued that China's alleged U-shaped line contradicted UNCLOS, and that China could not enjoy any maritime entitlement based on the U-shaped line.[79] The Philippines also claimed that none of the nine selected maritime features in the Spratly Islands (including Mischief Reef, Second Thomas Shoal, Subi Reef, Gaven Reef, McKennan Reef, Hughes Reef, Johnson Reef, Cuarteron Reef and Fiery Cross Reef) constituted islands that could generate an entitlement to an EEZ or continental shelf.[80]

The tribunal concluded that China's maritime claim based on the U-shaped line was unsubstantiated under international law, because UNCLOS superseded any historic rights or other sovereign rights or jurisdiction in excess of the limits imposed therein.[81] Moreover, in addition to the nine maritime features mentioned in the Philippines' submissions, the tribunal took a *proprio motu* move to examine the factual conditions of all the other maritime features in the Spratly Islands and concluded that none of them was capable of sustaining human habitation or an economic life of their own within the meaning of those terms in Article 121(3) of UNCLOS so as to generate an entitlement to an EEZ or continental shelf.[82]

Obviously, the above arbitral decisions have an adverse impact on the plausibility of some of China' maritime claims. These decisions entail that China's maritime claims, including those based on the U-shaped line and entitlements to the EEZ and continental shelf generated by the islands in the Spratly Islands, cannot be a possible interpretation and application of UNCLOS. Therefore, according to the *South China Sea Arbitration* award, these maritime claims would be deemed implausible and thus unreasonable. Though the decisions in this case only bind upon the Philippines and allegedly China, these decisions, by impacting China's maritime claims, might also affect the maritime disputes between China and other claimants, namely Vietnam, Malaysia and Brunei.[83]

---

79 The South China Sea Arbitration, n 38, para.101.
80 *Ibid.*
81 The South China Sea Arbitration (The Philippines v. China), Award of 12 July 2016 (PCA), para.278.
82 *Ibid.*, para.646.
83 L. Reed and K. Wong, Marine Entitlements in the South China Sea: The Arbitration Between the Philippines and China, 110 *AJIL* (2016), 760.

Some scholars commented that 'the award has succeeded in clearly demarcating the disputed areas in the South China Sea as being confined to the territorial sea around each disputed high-tide feature'.[84] This comment does not necessarily capture a precise picture. Importantly, the *South China Sea Arbitration* award only affects part of the second type of maritime claim (China's claims based on entitlements related to the EEZ and continental shelf generated by the islands) and the third type of maritime claim (China's potential claim based on the U-shaped line), as identified in section 3.2.1. By contrast, the first type of maritime claim (claims based on entitlements generated by mainland territories) and the rest of the second type of maritime claim (claims based on entitlements generated by the islands) remain unaffected. Thus, even taking full account of the *South China Sea Arbitration* award, the disputed marine areas therein would consist of not only (1) 'the territorial sea around each disputed high-tide feature', but also other types of disputed marine areas, including, at least: (2) the contiguous zone generated around the disputed islands; (3) the overlaps between the contiguous zone generated around the disputed islands and the EEZ generated by the mainland territories of Brunei, Malaysia, the Philippines and Vietnam; (4) the overlaps between an EEZ derived from a mainland territory and a continental shelf based upon another mainland territory (*e.g.*, the intersect of Malaysia's outer limits of the EEZ emanating from its mainland territory with the outer limits of the extended continental shelf jointly claimed by Malaysia and Vietnam, as shown in Map 2); and (5) the potential disputed areas of the extended continental shelf. Table 7 compares the categories of disputed marine areas before and after taking full account of the impact of the *South China Sea Arbitration* award.

It needs to be clarified that the *South China Sea Arbitration* award itself does not go so far to address all disputed marine areas in the Spratly Islands area. In fact, both the Philippines' submissions and the tribunal's award are rather cautious and limit most of the disputes discussed to concern only a few particular locations around several offshore features such as Mischief Reef and Second Thomas Shoal.[85] The underlying rationale is to avoid triggering

---

84 *Ibid.*, 759.

85 The South China Sea Arbitration, n 81, paras. 169 (submissions No. 1–2 concerning nine-dash line and historic rights), 281, 385 (submissions No. 3-7 concerning the status of features), 649, 652–667, 669, 679 (submission No. 8 concerning the activities of Chinese officials and vessels in the areas of several petroleum blocks declared by the Philippines, Mischief Reef, and Second Thomas Shoal), 718 (submission No. 9 concerning China's toleration of fishing by its vessels in the areas of Mischief Reef and Second Thomas Shoal), 758 (submission No. 10 concerning the territorial sea of Scarborough Shoal), 815

TABLE 7 The categories of disputed marine areas before and after taking into account the impact of the South China Sea Arbitration award

Categories			Before	After
General categories	Types of maritime zones that overlap	Specific scenarios		
Areas of overlapping claims related to the same type of maritime zone	TS-TS	Disputed TS generated by an island	√	√
		A TS generated by an island overlaps with a TS generated by another island	√	√
	CZ-CZ	Disputed CZ generated by an island	√	√
		A CZ generated by an island overlaps with a CZ generated by another island	√	√
	EEZ-EEZ	An EEZ generated by an island overlaps with an EEZ generated by a mainland territory	√	--
	CS-CS	A CS generated by an island overlaps with a CS generated by a mainland territory	√	--
		A CS generated by a mainland territory overlaps with a CS generated by another mainland territory (mainly involving extended CS)	√	√

Areas of overlapping claims related to different types of maritime zones	TS-Others	A TS generated by an island overlaps with a CZ/EEZ/CS generated by another island/mainland territory	--	--
	CZ-EEZ	A CZ generated by an island overlaps with an EEZ generated by another island	√	--
		A CZ generated by an island overlaps with an EEZ generated by a mainland territory	√	√
	EEZ-CS	An EEZ generated by an island overlaps with a CS generated by another island	√	--
		An EEZ generated by an island overlaps with a CS generated by a mainland territory, or the other way around	√	--
		An EEZ generated by a mainland territory overlaps with a CS generated by another mainland territory	√	√
	U-shaped line-Others	Areas encompassed by the U-shaped line overlap with all maritime zones generated by the islands and with the EEZ s/CS s emanating from the mainland territories	√	--

Notes: (1) 'TS' stands for 'territorial sea', 'CZ' for 'contiguous zone', and 'CS' for 'continental shelf'; (2) The symbol '√' means that the category of disputed marine area exists in the Spratly Islands area, and the symbol '--' indicates the opposite.

the jurisdictional exception under Article 298(1)(a)(i) of UNCLOS in case of overlapping entitlements that would call for the application of Articles 15, 74 and 83 to delimit the overlap.[86] Consequently, the locations that the tribunal explicitly established as undisputed parts of the EEZ and continental shelf of the Philippines are only a few, namely the areas of Mischief Reef and Second Thomas Shoal, and several petroleum blocks (i.e., the GSEC101 block, Area 3, Area 4, and the SC58 block).[87]

3.3.2.3 Mapping the Extent of Disputed Marine Areas

Taking into full account the impact of the *South China Sea Arbitration* award, the extent of disputed marine areas according to the alternative approach must reflect the categories of disputed marine areas as identified in Table 7, including: (1) the territorial sea generated around the disputed islands; (2) the contiguous zone generated around the disputed islands; (3) the overlaps between the contiguous zone generated around the disputed islands and the EEZ generated by the mainland territories of Brunei, Malaysia, the Philippines and Vietnam; (4) the overlaps between an EEZ derived from a mainland territory and a continental shelf based upon another mainland territory; and (5) the potential disputed areas of the extended continental shelf. Accordingly, Map 3 depicts the extent of disputed marine areas in the Spratly Islands area. This figure allows three remarks.

First, the size of disputed marine area identified according to the alternative approach is smaller than that using the areas of overlapping claims approach (see a comparison of Maps 2 and 3, or Table 7).

Second, the size of disputed marine area according to the alternative approach can vary depending on the drawing of the baselines from which the territorial sea and contiguous zone generated around the disputed islands are measured. Many States, most of which are non-parties to the Spratly Islands disputes, have applied baselines to encompass geographical features within a dependent archipelago or an island group for measuring maritime

(submission No. 11 concerning the protection and preservation of the marine environment at Scarborough Shoal, Second Thomas Shoal, Cuarteron Reef, Fiery Cross Reef, Gaven Reef, Johnson Reef, Hughes Reef and Subi Reef), 816, 994 (submission No. 12 concerning China's occupation of and construction activities on Mischief Reef), 1044 (submission No. 13 concerning China's operation of its law enforcement vessels near Scarborough Shoal), 1110 (submission No. 14 concerning China's actions since the commencement of the arbitration), and 1182 (submission No. 15 concerning the future conduct of the parties).

86 *Ibid.*, para.6.

87 *Ibid.*, paras. 633, 647, 1025, 1153, 1203(B)(7) (concerning Mischief Reef and Second Thomas Shoal), and 694, 697 (concerning the GSEC101 block, Area 3, Area 4, and the SC58 block).

entitlements.[88] A possible legal argument relates to the regime of straight baselines as outlined in Article 7(1) of UNCLOS, which provides that the method of straight baselines 'joining appropriate points' may be used in localities 'where the coastline is deeply indented and cut into', or 'if there is a fringe of islands along the coast in its immediate vicinity'.[89] Article 7(1) does not set limits on water-land ratio and baseline length.[90] Moreover, the phrase 'joining appropriate points' leaves room for employing straight baselines to enclose a group of offshore islands.[91]

It is noted that the *South China Sea Arbitration* tribunal briefly addressed the interpretation of Article 7(1) of UNCLOS in the merits award. The tribunal pointed out that it was aware of 'the practice of some States in employing straight baselines with respect to offshore archipelagos'.[92] The tribunal further underlined that this provision could provide for the application of straight baselines only in 'localities where the coastline is deeply indented and cut into, or if there is a fringe of islands along the coast in its immediate vicinity'.[93] Without making a serious inquiry into specific practices of offshore archipelagos, the tribunal jumped to a conclusion that '[t]hese conditions [sufficing the application of straight baselines] do not include the situation of an offshore

---

88 Relevant practices can be divided into three categories. The first and also the most popular category is to apply a set of straight baselines to enclose a dependent archipelago as a whole. Examples include: Canary Islands – Spain, Coco Islands and Preparis Islands – Myanmar, Falkland Islands – the United Kingdom, Faroe Islands – Denmark, Galapagos Islands – Ecuador, Lakshadweep Islands – India, Paracel Islands – China, and Svalbard Archipelago – Norway. The second category is to apply a combination of straight baselines and normal baselines to encircle a dependent archipelago as a whole. Examples include: Guadeloupe – France, Houtman Abrolhos Islands – Australia, Kerguelen Islands – France, and Turks and Caicos Islands – the United Kingdom. The third category does not enclose an archipelago as a whole but applies several sets of straight baselines to encompass subgroups of islands within a dependent archipelago separately. Examples include: Azores and Madeira Islands – Portugal, Balearic Islands – Spain, Diaoyu (Senkaku) Islands – China, Falkland Islands – Argentina, and New Caledonia – France. See S. Kopela, *Dependent Archipelagos in the Law of the Sea* (Martinus Nijhoff Publishers. 2013), 99–148. OES, Straight Baselines: The Faeroes, *Limits in the Seas* (12 March 1970), 2–4. OES, Straight Baselines: Ecuador, *Limits in the Seas* (23 May 1972), 2. OES, Straight Baselines Claim: China, *Limits in the Seas* (9 July 1996), 8. OES, Straight Baselines: Svalbard, *Limits in the Seas* (6 March 1972), 2. China, Statement on the Territorial Sea Baselines for Diaoyu Dao and Its Affiliated Islands (10 September 2012), *Law of the Sea Bulletin No. 80* (2012).

89 UNCLOS, Article 7.

90 This is in contrast to the regime of archipelagic baselines as stipulated in Article 47 of UNCLOS.

91 The South China Sea Arbitration, n 81, para.575.

92 *Ibid.*, para.575.

93 *Ibid.*

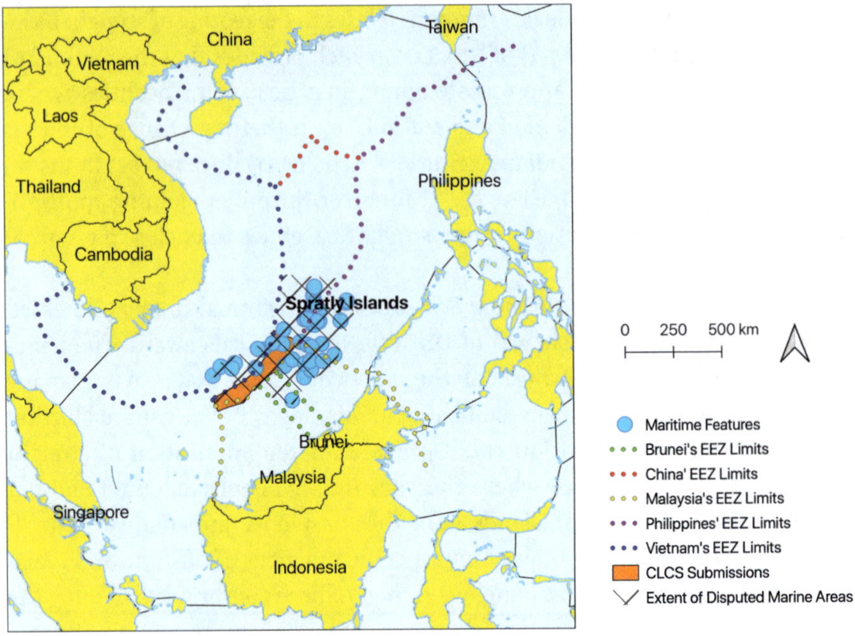

MAP 3 The extent of disputed marine areas in the Spratly Islands area according to the alternative approach excluding unreasonable claims
Notes: The author produced this illustrative map using the QGIS software. The coordinates of the maritime features are obtained from GoogleEarth. The data about the CLCS Submissions are obtained from: ESRI shapefile data for Malaysia and Vietnam ECS polygons, available online at <http://continentalshelf.org/onestopdatashop/6350.aspx>. The data about the EEZ limits are obtained from: Flanders Marine Institute (2018) Maritime Boundaries Geodatabase: Maritime Boundaries and Exclusive Economic Zones (200NM), version 10, available online at <https://doi.org/10.14284/312>.

archipelago'.[94] However, the tribunal's conclusion is unconvincing because under certain circumstances, the geometric circumstances of an offshore archipelago might satisfy either of the two preconditions as outlined in Article 7(1) of UNCLOS.[95] For instance, France has adopted a combination of straight baselines and normal baselines to enclose the Kerguelen Islands, which is a French overseas archipelago in the southern Indian Ocean and comprises the main island, namely Grande Terre, and 300 smaller islands.[96] The smaller islands

94 *Ibid.*
95 Kopela, n 88, 122.
96 France, *Decree No. 2015-635 of 5 Jun 2015 defining the baselines from which the breadth of the French territorial sea adjacent to the Kerguelen Islands (French Southern and Antarctic*

are located close to the coast of the main island and thus are likely to be considered as fringing the coast. Therefore, the application of straight baselines to encompass the Kerguelen Islands may be deemed compatible with Article 7(1) of UNCLOS.[97] Accordingly, some scholars commented that 'straight baselines may be employed in localities on individual islands of a[n] offshore archipelago that meet the applicable geographic criteria in Article 7'.[98] Whomersley also commented that the tribunal's above statement was *obiter dictum* since it was not related to either the Philippines' submissions or the final decisions reached in the award.[99] In fact, the tribunal made the above conclusion relating to Article 7(1) of UNCLOS when addressing the legal status of features as rocks or islands in the South China Sea (submissions No. 3, 5 and 7).[100] It is evident that Article 7(1) of UNCLOS has nothing to do with the determination of the legal status of features as rocks or islands (the applicable law in this regard should be Article 121 of UNCLOS). Hence, the tribunal's statement about Article 7(1) of UNCLOS was *obiter dictum*. Therefore, albeit not without controversies, it is arguable that the disputant States are entitled to apply one set or several sets of baselines to enclose the whole or part of the offshore features in the Spratly Islands area according to Article 7(1), to the extent that any of the disputed islands could be regarded as having a deeply indented and cut-into coastline or a fringe of islands along the coast in their immediate vicinity.

Third, it is difficult to know exactly how large or small the high seas (not necessarily equivalent to the applicable scope of high seas freedoms) remain in the Spratly Islands area because none of the claimant States has ever established baselines for the islands therein from which the limits of the territorial sea and contiguous zone shall be measured. Notably, the *South China Sea Arbitration* award has, at least, identified 19 maritime features in the Spratly Islands area as 'above water at high tide' under Article 121(1) of UNCLOS, which, thereby, as islands, are entitled to generate a territorial sea and contiguous zone.[101] Having

---

Territories) is measured (2015), available at <http://www.un.org/depts/los/LEGISLATIONANDTREATIES/PDFFILES/DEPOSIT/fra_kerguelen_en.pdf>.

97 Kopela, n 88, 117.

98 J.A. Roach, Offshore Archipelagos Enclosed by Straight Baselines: An Excessive Claim?, *ODIL* (2018), 3. C. Whomersley, The Award on the Merits in the Case Brought by the Philippines against China Relating to the South China Sea: A Critique, 16 *CJIL* (2017), 387–423, para.55.

99 Whomersley, n 98, 387–423, para.50.

100 The South China Sea Arbitration, n 81, para.575.

101 There are at least 19 islands in the entire Spratly Islands area: Itu Aba Island, Thitu Island, West York Island, Spratly Island, North-East Cay, South-West Cay, Sin Cowe Island, Nanshan Island, Sand Cay, Loaita Island, Swallow Reef, Namyit Island, Amboyna Cay,

said that, one thing is sure that a narrow selection of high seas freedoms especially those regarding navigation and overflight enjoyed by all States (either parties or non-parties to the Spratly Islands territorial and maritime disputes) remains applicable in this region according to Articles 58 and 87 of UNCLOS,[102] except in the territorial sea generated around islands where third States enjoy only a right of innocent passage pursuant to Article 17 of UNCLOS.[103] Moreover, one has to bear in mind that the Spratly Islands area is part of the South China Sea, a semi-enclosed sea primarily covered by the EEZs of surrounding countries. In terms of the Spratly Islands area (not the whole South China Sea), only a part (which approximates the orange zone indicated in Map 3) remains susceptible to the status of high seas. Furthermore, the remaining part susceptible to the status of high seas may well be partially covered by the territorial seas and contiguous zones generated around the disputed islands. Admittedly, the extent of jurisdictional overlaps involving the contiguous zone is much less significant than those involving the territorial sea. It is because distinct from the territorial sea where a State enjoys exclusive jurisdiction over extensive matters,[104] a State's jurisdiction to the contiguous zone is confined to solely preventing or punishing infringements occurring within its territory or territorial sea of its customs, fiscal, immigration or sanitary laws and regulations.[105] Article 86 of UNCLOS corroborates this point by inferring that jurisdictional rights associated with the contiguous zone shall not interfere with navigation and other rights and freedoms enjoyed by other States on high seas.[106] Despite

Flat Island, Fiery Cross Reef, McKennan Reef, Gaven Reef (North), Cuarteron Reef, and Johnson Reef. This list is based on the *South China Sea Arbitration* award: first, the tribunal has conducted a detailed examination on the status of eleven (11) maritime features identified in the Philippines' submissions and concluding that Scarborough Shoal (not a part of the Spratly Islands), Fiery Cross Reef, McKennan Reef, Gaven Reef (North), Cuarteron Reef and Johnson Reef are high-tide elevations and hence islands in the sense of Article 121 of UNCLOS; and second, by passage, the tribunal has confirmed that Itu Aba Island, Thitu Island, West York Island, Spratly Island, North-East Cay, South-West Cay, Sin Cowe Island, Nanshan Island, Sand Cay, Loaita Island, Swallow Reef, Namyit Island, Amboyna Cay and Flat Island are high-tide elevations. See The South China Sea Arbitration, n 81, paras.382 (regarding Fiery Cross Reef, McKennan Reef, Gaven Reef (North), Cuarteron Reef and Johnson Reef), 401 (regarding Itu Aba Island), 402 (regarding Thitu Island), 403 (regarding West York Island), 404 (regarding Spratly Island), 405 (regarding North-East Cay), 406 (regarding South-West Cay), 407 (regarding Amboyna Cay, Flat Island, Loaita Island, Namyit Island, Nanshan Island, Sandy Cay, Sin Cowe Island, and Swallow Reef).

102 D. Guilfoyle, The High Seas, in D.R. Rothwell *et al.* (eds.), *The Oxford Handbook of the Law of the Sea* (OUP. 2015), 212.

103 UNCLOS, Articles 17, 58 and 87.

104 UNCLOS, Articles 2.

105 UNCLOS, Article 33.

106 UNCLOS, Article 86.

the limited coastal State rights concerning the contiguous zone, the disputed areas involving the territorial sea generated around the disputed islands alone can reduce the remaining part susceptible to the status of high seas in the Spratly Islands area (which approximates the orange zone indicated in Map 3), especially when taking into account the possible application of one set or several sets of baselines to enclose the whole or part of the offshore features according to Article 7(1) of UNCLOS, as mentioned earlier.

3.3.3 *'Areas of Overlapping Claims' versus 'Excluding Unreasonable Claims'*

This subsection analyses the pros and cons of the two approaches and figures out which approach is the most appropriate in the Spratly Islands setting.

The bright side of the areas of overlapping claims approach is that almost all the unilateral action undertaken by the claimants in the undelimited areas, which may be detrimental to the legal interests of others, are put under regulation. A research project undertaken by the British Institute of International and Comparative Law (BIICL) echoed this approach by using undelimited maritime areas as the geographical extent to apply Articles 74(3) and 83(3) of UNCLOS.[107] According to the BIICL report, '"undelimited" marine areas are areas where the continental shelves or EEZs of States overlap or may potentially overlap, and no final delimitation is in place'.[108] The report has clarified that the geographical scope of the obligation should cover the whole undelimited area including both those actively disputed areas and areas where the competing claim is implausible.[109] However, a considerable drawback of this approach is that States with a stronger claim would be reluctant to accept this argument. For instance, Mischief Reef, a low-tide elevation located in the Spratly Islands area, is currently under the control of China. However, the *South China Sea Arbitration* merits award concluded that the Philippines enjoyed exclusive sovereign rights over Mischief Reef.[110] Hence, the Philippines is probably unwilling to abandon this favourable finding and regard Mischief Reef as in dispute with China.

The alternative approach, which excludes unreasonable claims, can eliminate the risk of the States' abuse of the areas of overlapping claims approach to enlarge the geographical extent of contested marine areas. Adopting this approach, the *South China Sea Arbitration* award would deem China' maritime claims related to the U-shaped line and the EEZ and continental shelf

107 BIICL, n 4, para.12.
108 *Ibid.*, para.4.
109 *Ibid.*, para.107.
110 The South China Sea Arbitration, n 81, para.751.

generated by the islands in the Spratly Islands implausible under international law, thereby excluding these claims from being considered in determining the spatial extent of disputed marine areas. However, China has explicitly rejected the *South China Sea Arbitration* award as 'null and void'.[111]

The preceding analysis indicates that both approaches have little chance of obtaining unanimous support from the disputant States. The main difference between these two approaches is that the former encompasses a larger disputed marine area, and the latter a smaller one. Some scholars vouched for the latter and commented that a big success of the *South China Sea Arbitration* award was confining the disputed areas in the South China Sea to the territorial sea around each disputed island, which could facilitate cooperation.[112] However, chances of reaching cooperative arrangements respecting such confined disputed areas are slim, given China's non-acceptance and non-recognition of the award.[113] Arguably, a larger disputed marine area is a better and probably more realistic choice for four reasons.

First, excluding unreasonable claims probably would not prevent States from undertaking unilateral conduct in areas over which they assert such unreasonable claims. The other States with stronger claims in these areas are likely to take measures to suspend such unilateral conduct. As a result, excluding unreasonable claims might complicate and even intensify conflicts in the Spratly Islands area.

Second, the primary goal of the transitional period pending determination is to achieve and maintain the peaceful coexistence of the disputant States in the Spratly Islands area. As will be discussed in chapter 4, States are obliged to exercise mutual restraint and not to take unilateral conduct that could jeopardise or hamper the reaching of the final determination in disputed marine areas.[114] A larger disputed marine area amounts to imposing constraints on broader areas, thus more apt for achieving and maintaining peace in the region.

Third, identifying specific areas as in dispute for the application of certain international obligations in the transitional period does not alert or require predetermination of the plausibility of relevant claims and will not affect the final maritime delimitation.

111 China, Statement on the Award of 12 July 2016 of the Arbitral Tribunal in the South China Sea Arbitration Established at the Request of the Republic of the Philippines (12 July 2016), available at <https://www.fmprc.gov.cn/nanhai/eng/snhwtlcwj_1/t1379492.htm>.

112 Reed and Wong, n 83, 759.

113 China, n 111.

114 UNCLOS, Articles 74(3) and 83(3).

Fourth, legally speaking, the *South China Sea Arbitration* award only binds upon the Philippines and allegedly China, and does not directly apply to disputes between China and other claimants. Instituting a new litigation between China and other claimants regarding the South China Sea is not absolutely impossible, although the chance might be relatively small. For example, a senior government official from Vietnam was reported to have publicly mentioned possible legal action against China over the South China Sea dispute on 6 November 2019.[115] Admittedly, such a new litigation, even if it happens, cannot directly concern or affect the rights of the Philippines, because judicial decisions are only binding *inter partes*.[116] However, it cannot be ruled out that future possible litigation might deal with some disputes that were addressed in the *South China Sea Arbitration* award, especially those which are difficult to be considered as exclusively between the parties to the proceedings. Examples may include disputes regarding China's maritime claim based on the U-shape line, and the evaluation of the legal status of the maritime features in the Spratly Islands according to Article 121 of UNCLOS. Some scholars have doubts as to whether there is much room left for alternative argument in terms of decisions on maritime entitlements for particular maritime features according to Article 121 of UNCLOS, which are often considered as 'a matter of objective determination'.[117] However, there is no absolute guarantee that a new litigation would definitely have the same findings as the *South China Sea Arbitration* award, since the principle of *res judicata* – which requires that a question having been finally juridically decided on its merits cannot be litigated again between the same parties – does not apply in this circumstance.[118] As Tanaka commented, 'as typically shown in the law of maritime delimitation, an accumulation of case law will be needed to elaborate the interpretation of norms of international law', and 'the same applies to Article 121' of UNCLOS.[119] Thus, the alternative approach excluding claims that are deemed impossible based solely on the *South China Sea Arbitration* award might not necessarily be appropriate.

---

115 See *e.g.*, J. Pearson and K. Vu, Vietnam mulls legal action over South China Sea dispute (6 November 2019), available at <https://www.reuters.com/article/us-vietnam-southchina sea/vietnam-mulls-legal-action-over-south-china-sea-dispute-idUSKBN1XG1D6>.

116 See *e.g.*, the ICJ Statute, Article 59; UNCLOS, Annex VII, Article 11.

117 Y. Tanaka, *The South China Sea Arbitration: Toward an International Legal Order in the Oceans* (Hart Publishing. 2019), 191. N.B. O'Sullivan, The Case Law's Handling of Issues Concerning Third States, in A.G. Oude Elferink, T. Henriksen and S.V. Busch (eds.), *Maritime Boundary Delimitation: The Case Law: Is it Consistent and Predictable?* (CUP. 2018), 273.

118 W.S. Dodge, Res Judicata, *MPEPIL* (2006), paras.4-10.

119 Tanaka, n 117, 113.

Therefore, tailored to the Spratly Islands setting, the areas of overlapping claims approach that takes account of all claims, plausible or implausible, is a better and more realistic choice.

3.4 Conclusion

By sorting out relevant maritime claims of disputant States through the lens of international law, especially the law of the sea, the preceding analysis leads to four main conclusions. First, the presence of ambiguity and alleged excessiveness associated with maritime claims put forward by the disputant States adds difficulties to the identification of disputed marine areas in the Spratly Islands area. Second, as a result of the significantly divided interests of these States in the region, neither the areas of overlapping claims approach nor the alternative approach would obtain unanimous support from these States. Third, the areas of overlapping claims approach taking into account all claims is more apt for the Spratly Islands setting. The main underlying reason is that a larger disputed marine area contributes more to maintaining the peaceful coexistence of these States in the region by imposing constraints on State conduct in broader areas than the choice for a more limited area based upon excluding unreasonable claims. Fourth, following this approach, the geographical extent of disputed marine areas basically amounts to the entire Spratly Islands area. Accordingly, the disputant States are obliged to observe specific international obligations as set out in chapter 4 when behaving unilaterally in this region absent delimitation.

CHAPTER 4

The Permissible Scope for Unilateralism

4.1 Introduction

On 27 March 2017, a speedboat, presumably operated by the China Coast Guard, fired seven times upon a Philippine fishing trawler – *Princess Johann* – when the latter was operating near the Union Banks in the Spratly Islands area, to which both China and the Philippines have maritime claims.[1] This incident is not an isolated case. Due to the maritime dispute among multiple States, clashes and standoffs have been frequent and risked destabilizing the Spratly Islands area.[2] Clarifying the permissible scope for unilateralism under international law within the disputed marine areas in this region is thus necessary for reducing the risk of such clashes and standoffs. In light of this, setting out the legal parameters to determine what sort of unilateral conduct should be prohibited and what should be permissible in the Spratly Islands area is the key to maintaining the peaceful coexistence of the disputant States therein, thereby laying down a solid foundation for the sustainable utilisation and management of this region.

For this purpose, this chapter analyses the UNCLOS regulatory framework in relation to unilateral conduct taken by the claimant States within disputed marine areas, identifies its regulatory limitations and proposes solutions to remedy such limitations (section 4.2). Beyond UNCLOS, some general principles in customary international law are also of particular relevance to disputed marine areas. Such principles include the no-harm principle, the principle of peaceful settlement of disputes, the principle of the prohibition of the threat or use of force, the good faith principle, and the principle of non-aggravation of a dispute. This chapter discusses the application of these principles in the Spratly Islands setting (Section 4.3).

1 Radio Taiwan International, Philippine Fishermen Accused China Coastal Guard of Shooting (21 April 2017), available at <http://news.rti.org.tw/news/detail/?recordId=339630>. D.J. Yap, China shoots away Pinoys from Spratlys (21 April 2017), available at <http://globalnation.inquirer.net/155120/china-shoos-away-pinoys-spratlys>.

2 G. Torode, Chinese Coast Guard Involved in Most South China Sea Clashes: Research (7 September 2016), available at <https://www.reuters.com/article/us-southchinasea-china-coastguard/chinese-coast-guard-involved-in-most-south-china-sea-clashes-research-idUSKCN11C2LA>.

 | DOI:10.1163/9789004504332_005

As to the analytical scope, this chapter focuses on three types of unilateral conduct that have been frequently taken by the disputant States or their nationals within the Spratly Islands area: (1) offshore activities related to hydrocarbon resources, (2) fisheries-related conduct, and (3) law enforcement measures responding to another disputant State's resource-related activities. Based on the applicable law as identified in sections 4.2 and 4.3, this chapter addresses the permissible scope for these three types of unilateral conduct under international law, respectively (sections 4.4–4.6).

4.2 Regulatory Framework under UNCLOS

4.2.1 *Overlapping Areas of Territorial Sea*

At UNCLOS III, the Seventh Negotiation Group (NG7) was mandated to negotiate on 'Delimitation of maritime boundaries between adjacent and opposite States and settlement of disputes thereon', including the interim regime prior to the territorial sea delimitation.[3] Despite the broad mandate, negotiations within NG7 focused primarily on the delimitation of the EEZ and the continental shelf. In contrast, there was hardly any debate on the interim regime preceding the territorial sea delimitation, probably because this matter was less controversial compared with matters associated with the EEZ/ continental shelf delimitation. As a result, the final text of Article 15 of UNCLOS, which provides a broad contour for the interim regime prior to the territorial sea delimitation, is virtually identical to Article 12(1) of the Convention on the Territorial Sea and Contiguous Zone (CTS).[4]

The textual analysis of Article 15 of UNCLOS entails three observations. First, regarding the ambit of application, a literal reading of Article 15 suggests that this provision is limited to overlapping areas of the territorial sea claimed by States with opposite or adjacent coasts. Strictly speaking, this provision does not apply to a territorial sea generated by a disputed territory, in which circumstance the overlapping claims emanate from the same coast of that disputed territory. Second, when failing to reach a delimitation agreement, States

3 UN Doc.: A/CONF.62/61, Report of the General Committee on the Organization of the Work of the Seventh Session (11 April 1978), para.5.

4 Arbitration between the Republic of Croatia and the Republic of Slovenia, Final Award of 29 June 2017 (PCA), para.950. Maritime Delimitation and Territorial Questions between Qatar and Bahrain, Judgment of 16 March 2001 (ICJ), para.176. Convention on the Territorial Sea and the Contiguous Zone, adopted 29 April 1958, entered into force 10 September 1964, 516 *UNTS* 205, Article 12.

are obliged not to extend their territorial seas beyond the equidistance line or median line. The equidistance line is the line every point of which is equidistant from the nearest points on the baselines from which the breadth of the territorial seas of each of these States is measured.[5] Third, there is an exception to the equidistance rule, that is, the presence of 'historic title or other special circumstances' can weaken and qualify the primacy of the equidistance rule.

However, Article 15 has two limitations. First, this provision does not clarify the specific implication of designating a temporary boundary on the unilateral conduct of claimants within undelimited areas. Whether the claimants are obliged to refrain from performing acts of sovereignty beyond the equidistance line is open to question.[6] This matter was mentioned neither during UNCLOS III nor in the *travaux préparatoires* related to Article 12(1) of CTS during the First UN Conference on the Law of the Sea (UNCLOS I, 1958).[7] Second, the text of Article 15 itself is not informative as to who has the power to determine on the presence or absence of 'historic title or other special circumstances', which could prevail over the equidistance line and lead to another boundary line. This caveat is thus a backdoor which might introduce significant uncertainties, cause confusion and encourage States to claim 'historic title or other special circumstances' for reasons of self-interest.[8]

4.2.2 *Overlapping Areas of Contiguous Zone*

Article 24(3) of CTS provides for an interim regime preceding the delimitation of overlapping contiguous zones claimed by States with opposite or adjacent coasts.[9] Accordingly, a claimant shall refrain from extending its contiguous zone beyond the equidistance line or median line. The formulation of Article 24(3) of CTS is substantively similar to that of Article 15 of UNCLOS or Article 12(1) of CTS, except that it does not contain the 'historic title or other special circumstances' caveat.

The matter regarding an interim regime preceding the contiguous zone delimitation was not discussed during the negotiations at UNCLOS III. As a

5 UNCLOS, Article 15.

6 N. Antunes, *Towards the Conceptualisation of Maritime Delimitation: Legal and Technical Aspects of a Political Process* (Martinus Nijhoff, 2003), 98.

7 See the First United Nations Conference on the Law of the Sea (Geneva, 24 February – 27 April 1958), Volume III: First Committee (Territorial Sea and Contiguous Zone), available at <http://legal.un.org/diplomaticconferences/1958_los/vol3.shtml>.

8 This risk was underlined by Yugoslavia, Portugal and Norway at UNCLOS I related to the negotiation on Article 12(1) of CTS. See UN Doc.: A/CONF.13/C.1/SR.56-60, Summary Records of the 60th meeting of 22 April 1958, 187, 190, paras.8, 12, 44.

9 CTS, Article 24(3).

result, UNCLOS contains no provision on this matter. Pursuant to Article 311(2), UNCLOS shall not alter the rights and obligations of States that arise from other agreements compatible with this convention.[10] Hence, Article 24(3) of CTS remains relevant to those States that are parties to CTS. However, among the claimant States respecting the Spratly Islands dispute, only Malaysia is a party to CTS.[11] Therefore, Article 24(3) of CTS does not apply between the disputant States in the Spratly Islands setting unless there is evidence that this provision can be deemed constituting customary international law.

4.2.3 *Overlapping Areas of EEZ/Continental Shelf*

It is clear from the titles of Articles 74 ('Delimitation of the exclusive economic zone between States with opposite or adjacent coasts') or 83 ('Delimitation of the continental shelf between States with opposite or adjacent coasts') that the applicable scopes of these two provisions are overlapping areas of the EEZ or continental shelf between States with opposite or adjacent coasts.[12] In other words, strictly speaking, these two provisions do not apply where the areas of overlapping claims are related to different types of maritime zones (for example, where one State claims the area concerned to be the contiguous zone, and the other State the EEZ) or where the disputed areas of the EEZ or continental shelf are generated by the same coast of a disputed island.

Furthermore, Articles 74(3) and 83(3) of UNCLOS, being two identically phrased provisions, oblige disputant States to cooperate and abstain from behaviours that may frustrate the reaching of a final delimitation agreement in the disputed areas of the EEZ and continental shelf. These provisions entail two interlinked obligations 'during this transitional period': (1) the obligation to 'make every effort to enter into provisional arrangements of a practical nature', and (2) the obligation to '[make every effort] not to jeopardize or hamper the reaching of the final agreement'. The former amounts to an obligation to negotiate provisional arrangements in good faith. For simplicity, the latter is referred to as the obligation 'not to jeopardize or hamper delimitation' throughout the book. These two obligations are interlinked in two aspects.

First, the disputant States are not obliged to negotiate in good faith with respect to activities that do not have the effect of jeopardizing the final delimitation agreement. In other words, acts that comply with the obligation 'not to jeopardize or hamper delimitation' can be unilaterally undertaken by a

---

10 UNCLOS, Article 311(2).

11 CTS, List of Parties (as of 11 July 2019), available at <https://treaties.un.org/pages/ViewDetails.aspx?src=TREATY&mtdsg_no=XXI-1&chapter=21&clang=_en>.

12 UNCLOS, Articles 74 and 83.

disputant State without negotiating with others. This conclusion is logical because otherwise, there would be no need to set forth the equally important obligation 'not to jeopardize or hamper delimitation' next to the obligation to negotiate provisional arrangements in good faith, if the latter were intended to eschew all unilateral actions in the absence of provisional arrangements.

Second, acts having the jeopardizing or hampering effect can still be permissible under international law, provided that they are undertaken pursuant to a provisional arrangement agreed between the States concerned.[13] It follows that a provisional arrangement regarding certain acts can deprive these acts of the jeopardizing or hampering effect. To that effect, only acts that are carried out in the absence of a provisional arrangement are required not to frustrate the reaching of a final delimitation agreement. Tailored to the Spratly Islands setting, owing to the absence of any binding provisional arrangement at the moment, all activities, including resource-related conduct and law enforcement measures, are of a unilateral nature, and thus, must observe the obligation 'not to jeopardize or hamper delimitation'.

The drafting history of Articles 74(3) and 83(3) reveals that two different lines of argumentation relating to the obligation 'not to jeopardize or hamper delimitation' existed during the negotiations at UNCLOS III. Some delegations advocated a moratorium on economic activities within areas in dispute pending delimitation.[14] However, others did not accept the idea of a moratorium due to the concern that a moratorium would severely impede the economic development of coastal States.[15] Despite the divergence, all States generally recognized that 'mutual restraint should be exercised pending final agreement

13 Guyana v. Suriname, Arbitral Award dated 17 September 2007 (PCA), para.467.

14 For example, Ireland proposed a complete ban of any exploration or exploitation activities within disputed marine areas, stating that: 'Pending an [delimitation] agreement … no State is entitled to carry on exploration or exploitation activities in any areas which are claimed bona fide by any other State except with the express consent of that State'. Papua New Guinea also endorsed this position, claiming that: 'Pending agreement of settlement, the States concerned shall, either (a) make provisional arrangements taking into account the provisions of paragraph 1, or (b) establish a moratorium against economic activities within the area under dispute'. See UN Doc.: A/CONF.62/C.2/L.43, Ireland: draft article on delimitation of areas of continental shelf between neighbouring States (6 August 1974), 221, para.3. Also see Informal Document, NG7/15 (9 May 1978), Article 83, paragraph 3 (Papua New Guinea), quoted in: Y. van Logchem, The Scope for Unilateralism in Disputed Maritime Areas, in C. Schofield, *et al.* (eds.), *The Limits of Maritime Jurisdiction* (Brill. 2014), 180.

15 UN Doc.: A/CONF.62/SR.108, 108th Plenary meeting (15 September 1978), para.40.

or settlement in order not to impede the completion of the final delimitation'.[16] Consequently, States reached a consensus at the 126th plenary meeting in 1980 that they must avoid recourse to a moratorium against exploration and exploitation activities in the disputed zones.[17] Meanwhile, as a balance, States are obliged not to undertake activities that may have the effect of jeopardizing or hampering the reaching of the final delimitation agreement as provided in the final provision of Articles 74(3) and 83(3) of UNCLOS.[18] To this effect, the drafting history indicates that States did not intend to interrupt or suspend all economic activities in disputed zones,[19] but which activities should be allowed and which should be prohibited remain largely undefined.[20]

4.2.4 *Regulatory Limitations and Remedies*

The UNCLOS regulatory framework, notably Articles 15, 74(3) and 83(3), has two major limitations in providing a legal order for disputed marine areas preceding delimitation: (1) the limited applicable scope, and (2) the vagueness in the substantive content.

4.2.4.1 Limited Applicable Scope

The first regulatory limitation is that relevant UNCLOS provisions have a fairly limited applicable scope. Articles 15, 74(3) and 83(3) are designed to apply to specific categories of disputed marine areas. Firstly, these provisions only apply to areas of overlapping claims related to the same type of maritime zone, being either the territorial sea, EEZ or continental shelf. Secondly, a literal reading of these provisions suggests that they only apply to areas of overlapping claims emanating respectively from the adjacent or opposing coasts of the States concerned, rather than areas of overlapping claims generated around the same coast of a disputed island. However, according to section 3.3.1.1, the Spratly Islands area involves not only areas of overlapping claims related to the same type of maritime zone covered by Articles 15, 74(3) and 83(3), but also other

---

16 UN Doc.: A/CONF.62/RCNG/2, Reports of the Committees and Negotiating Groups on negotiations at the resumed seventh session contained in a single document both for the purposes of record and for the convenience of delegations (1978), 171.

17 UN Doc.: A/CONF.62/SR.126, 126th Plenary meeting (2 April 1980), para.123.

18 M.H. Nordquist, *et al.* (eds.), *United Nations Convention on the Law of the Sea, 1982: A Commentary. Vol. 2: Articles 1 to 85, Annexes I and II, Final Act, Annex II* (Nijhoff. 1993), 815.

19 Guyana v. Suriname, n 13, para.465.

20 Van Logchem, n 14, 179–181. N.A. Ioannides, The China-Japan and Venezuela-Guyana Maritime Disputes: How the Law on Undelimited Maritime Areas Addresses Unilateral Hydrocarbon Activities, *EJIL: Talk!* (25 January 2019).

atypical categories of disputed marine areas.[21] Such *atypical* disputed marine areas include: (1) the areas of overlapping claims related to different types of maritime zones in this region, such as the overlapping areas of maritime claims related to a contiguous zone and EEZ, and (2) the disputed areas of the territorial sea or contiguous zone generated around a disputed island.

To address this regulatory limitation, some scholars have suggested widening the scope of Articles 74(3) and 83(3) of UNCLOS to cover other categories of disputed marine areas such as those involving claims to a territorial sea.[22] A proposal of a similar idea was introduced by Morocco in 1978 during the negotiations at UNCLOS III. Morocco suggested that the obligation to 'endeavour to reach mutually acceptable provisional arrangements' and the obligation to refrain from unilateral activities that could prejudge a final solution or would aggravate the maritime boundary dispute should apply to States whose territorial sea claims overlapped.[23] Morocco's proposal was geared towards one purpose, that is, to bring substantive uniformity between Article 15 and Articles 74/83 of UNCLOS. The idea of bringing substantive uniformity across the disputed territorial sea, EEZ or continental shelf was supported by Argentina, Bangladesh and Venezuela in 1980, though these States placed more emphasis on the delimitation matter rather than the interim regime preceding delimitation.[24] Yet, these attempts were dismissed by the majority of States, largely due to fears that reopening discussions on streamlining different delimitation rules contained in Articles 15, 74 and 83 might put the earlier negotiated package at risk.[25]

However, implementing a unified regulatory standard across disputed marine areas as a whole is highly desirable in the Spratly Islands area owing to its special situation. First, the situation in this region is complicated owing to the presence of complex overlapping claims resulting in diverse categories of

21 See chapter 3, section 3.3.1.1.

22 See *e.g.*, R. Lagoni, Interim Measures Pending Maritime Delimitation Agreements, 78(2) *AJIL* (1984), 367; I. Papanicolopulu, Enforcement Action in Contested Waters: the Legal Regime, paper presented at the 6th IHO-IAG ABLOS Conference (2010), 3; Y. van Logchem, *Disputed Maritime Areas: The Rights and Obligations of States under International Law* (PhD Dissertation, Utrecht University, defended on 8 January 2019), 99–100.

23 NG 7/3 April 1978 (Morocco), reproduced in: R. Platzöder, Third United Nations Conference on the Law of the Sea: Documents, Vol. IX (Oceana Publications. 1983), 395, quoted in: van Logchem, n 22, 93.

24 UN Doc.: A/CONF.62/SR.126, Summary Records of 126th Plenary Meeting (2 April 1980), para.88(Argentina), para.137 (Venezuela); UN Doc.: A/CONF.62/SR.162, Summary Records of 162nd Plenary Meeting (31 March 1982), para.5 (Bangladesh).

25 Van Logchem, n 22, 94.

disputed marine areas involving a range of alleged maritime entitlements as specified in section 3.3.1.1. Second, even if the disputed marine areas therein can be carefully fragmented into various pieces where different interim regimes apply, it is inconvenient and difficult for the users of these areas to comply with this piecemeal approach. It is especially so considering that most ocean-related activities are not motionless and would inevitably involve categories of disputed marine areas. Third, it would also be very difficult for the disputant States to enforce fragmented interim regimes against target unilateral activities that span multiple categories of disputed marine areas. Due to these compelling reasons, it seems prudent to accept a unified regulatory standard to be implemented across disputed marine areas in the Spratly Islands area as a whole, regardless of the category of disputed marine area.

Furthermore, compared with Article 15 of UNCLOS, Articles 74(3) and 83(3) would be a better regulatory rule to be applied across the Spratly Islands area, as the latter prescribes relatively more precise and specific obligations than the former, including, for example, the obligation 'not to jeopardize or hamper delimitation'.[26] Moreover, unlike Article 15, the interpretation and application of Articles 74(3) and 83(3) have been addressed in some international cases, which could, therefore, assist in clarifying the meaning of these provisions.[27] A more in-depth discussion can be found in section 4.4.

4.2.4.2 Vagueness in Substantive Content

The second regulatory limitation is that the language of Articles 15, 74(3) and 83(3) of UNCLOS, for example, '[not] to extend its territorial sea beyond the median line' and 'not to jeopardize or hamper the reaching of the final agreement', contains a certain degree of vagueness that implies a very wide range of possible obligations and actions. For instance, whether fishing or the exploitation of hydrocarbon resources is permissible within disputed marine areas is not straightforward from a literal reading or a *prima facie* understanding of these provisions.

---

26 *Ibid.*, 100.

27 See *e.g.*, Guyana v. Suriname, n 13; Dispute Concerning Delimitation of the Maritime Boundary between Ghana and Côte d'Ivoire in the Atlantic Ocean (Ghana/Côte d'Ivoire), Order of 25 April 2015, Request for the prescription of provisional measures, and Judgment of 23 September 2017 (ITLOS).

4.2.4.2.1 *Relationship between Vagueness and Legal Uncertainty*

A common critique of vagueness is that imprecision results in legal uncertainty.[28] This critique is in line with Judge Sørensen's statement in *North Sea Continental Shelf* that '[t]he clearer the rule, and the more automatic its application, the less the seed of discord is sown'.[29] However, vagueness is not necessarily an affliction of regulatory frameworks, because rules with rigid specificity do not always lead to greater legal certainty than vague rules with less specificity and more flexibility.

Rules with rigid specificity, in Dworkin's words, are 'applicable in an all-or-nothing fashion', as these rules are crafted to include all of their exceptions exhaustively: 'If the facts a rule stipulates are given, then either the rule is valid, in which case the answer it supplies must be accepted, or it is not, in which case it contributes nothing to the decision'.[30] Therefore, rules with rigid specificity usually have a limited applicable scope. Thus, for simple and stable patterns of action that involve neither high stakes nor unpredictable changes across time, rules with rigid specificity can produce admirable reliance as to what the legal obligations are.[31]

Conversely, when it comes to complex actions in changing environments where large economic interests are at stake, rules with less specificity and more flexibility are more likely to enable legal certainty than rules with rigid specificity.[32] Relying heavily on rules with rigid specificity to regulate complex action might, on the one hand, create loopholes owing to these rules' failure to cover all variety of regulatory phenomena, and on the other hand, lead to paper compliance without real compliance as a result of the neglect of a systematic understanding of the complex regulatory phenomena at issue.

The mechanism, via which the vagueness and flexibility of rules functions to enable legal certainty, relies on an unarticulated premise that a case-by-case analysis of each regulatory phenomenon can be effectively carried out whenever a need arises. This premise is normally not a problem within a domestic legal system, as a centralized authority could enact legislation to authorize a competent court or any other organ to deal with the dispute concerning

---

28 C.S. Diver, Regulatory Precision, in K. Hawkins and J. Thomas (eds.), *Making Regulatory Policy* (University of Pittsburgh Press. 1989), 200.

29 North Sea Continental Shelf (Federal Republic of Germany/Netherlands), Dissenting Opinion of Judge Sørensen (ICJ), 255.

30 R. Dworkin, The Model of Rules, 35 *University of Chicago Review* (1967), 25.

31 J. Braithwaite, Rules and Principles: A Theory of Legal Certainty, 27 *Australian Journal of Legal Philosophy* (2002), 52.

32 *Ibid.*, 53.

rules with less specificity whenever it occurs. However, the international legal system, distinct from a domestic legal system, operates largely through the consent of sovereign States, and there is no universally accepted centralized authority to enact and enforce international law. UNCLOS is no exception to this, despite its Part XV.[33]

4.2.4.2.2 *Non-applicability of Compulsory Dispute Settlement Mechanism under UNCLOS*

Tailored to the Spratly Islands setting, it has to be admitted that vague rules with flexibility might, to some extent, be more viable for this region than those with rigid specificity, owing to the considerable economic interests at stake and the complex nature of the unilateral action involved, which could be embedded in diverse specific circumstances and connected with different categories of disputed marine areas. Vague rules with flexibility would allow a delicate and case-by-case analysis of each circumstance occurred therein. However, the lack of a mechanism to carry out the case-by-case analysis of each regulatory phenomenon whenever a need arises diminishes the effectiveness of vague rules with flexibility. Unfortunately, this is the case in the Spratly Islands setting, because as discussed below, the compulsory dispute settlement mechanism entailing binding decisions as provided in Section 2 of Part XV of UNCLOS does not necessarily apply to disputes arising from the interpretation and application of Articles 15, 74(3) and 83(3) in relation to the Spratly Islands area.[34]

According to Article 298(1)(a)(i) of UNCLOS,[35] 'disputes concerning the interpretation or application of articles 15, 74 and 83 relating to sea boundary

---

33 UNCLOS, Part XV (Settlement of Disputes).

34 UNCLOS, Part XV, section 2.

35 Article 298(1)(b) stipulates that 'disputes concerning military activities' and 'disputes concerning law enforcement activities in regard to the exercise of sovereign rights and jurisdiction excluded from the jurisdiction of a court or tribunal under article 297, paragraph 2 or 3' can be exempt from the compulsory dispute settlement mechanism. According to Article 297(2) and (3), the second type of disputes mentioned in Article 298(1)(b) refer to those concerning law enforcement activities with regard to marine scientific research arising out of the discretionary power of a coastal State to regulate, authorize and conduct marine scientific research in its EEZ or continental shelf, as well as with regard to fisheries relating to the sovereign rights of a coastal State respecting the living resources in the EEZ. Since Article 298(1)(b) does not specify whether it applies to disputed areas of the EEZ or continental shelf, the relevance of this provision to the specific context of the Spratly Islands area is open to question. Nevertheless, the author does not feel it necessary to address this matter herein, as all the activities with regard to disputed marine areas potentially covered by Article 298(1)(b) would fall inside the scope of Article 298(1)(a)(i).

delimitations' can be exempt from the compulsory dispute settlement mechanism entailing binding decisions under UNCLOS.[36] Thus, the point of debate is whether disputes arising from unilateral action in the Spratly Islands area concerning Articles 15, 74(3) and 83(3) could be regarded as 'relating to sea boundary delimitations'. Despite divided opinion among scholars,[37] international jurisprudence tends to provide an answer in the affirmative. For instance, in *Timor-Leste/Australia*, Timor-Leste requested the compulsory conciliation commission (the Commission) to assist the parties to agree on appropriate transitional arrangements in the disputed marine areas, in order to bring the parties from their current temporary arrangements to the full implementation of their newly agreed permanent maritime boundary.[38] Australia argued that the matters concerning transitional arrangements had exceeded the competence of the Commission because they were not 'relating to sea boundary delimitations'.[39] The Commission considered that Articles 74/83 'address not only the actual delimitation of the sea boundary between States with opposite or adjacent coasts, but also the question of the transitional period pending a final delimitation and the provisional arrangements of a practical nature that the Parties are called on to apply pending delimitation'.[40] Therefore, the Commission regarded disputes concerning provisional arrangements preceding delimitation as 'relating to sea boundary delimitations' and thus falling inside the scope of Article 298(1)(a)(i).[41] It can be equally argued that disputes arising from unilateral activities in the period preceding delimitation concerning Articles 74(3) or 83(3) could also be regarded as 'relating to sea boundary delimitations'.[42]

---

36 UNCLOS, Article 298(1)(a)(i).

37 For opinions supporting that such disputes are 'relating to sea boundary delimitations', see *e.g.*, Lagoni, n 22, 368; Papanicolopulu, n 22, 7; E. Milano and I. Papanicolopulu, State Responsibility in Disputed Areas on Land and at Sea, 71 *Zeitschrift* (2011), 621; BIICL, *Report of Conference on Obligations of States in Undelimited Maritime Areas* (2016), 26–27; N. Klein, Provisional Measures and Provisional Arrangements, in A.G. Oude Elferink, *et al.* (eds.), *Maritime Boundary Delimitation: The Case Law: Is it Consistent and Predictable?* (CUP. 2018), 124–125. For the opposite opinion, see *e.g.*, van Logchem, n 14, 195.

38 Conciliation between The Democratic Republic of Timor-Leste and The Commonwealth of Australia, Decision on Competence of 19 September 2016 (PCA), para.93.

39 *Ibid.*, para.94.

40 *Ibid.*, para.97.

41 *Ibid.*, paras.97-99.

42 The *South China Sea Arbitration* jurisdiction award has also entertained a similar issue to some extent. In its Submission No. 13, the Philippines requested the tribunal to declare that 'China has breached its obligations under the Convention by operating its law enforcement vessels in a dangerous manner causing serious risk of collision to Philippine vessels navigating in the vicinity of Scarborough Shoal'. The tribunal considered that

China has declared that it 'does not accept any of the procedures provided for in Section 2 of Part XV of the Convention with respect to all the categories of disputes referred to in paragraph 1 (a) (b) and (c) of Article 298 of the Convention'.[43] The Philippines, Malaysia and Brunei have not made such a reservation.[44] Vietnam has simply declared in its declaration upon ratification of UNCLOS that it would like to settle the territorial and maritime disputes relating to the Spratly Islands area 'through peaceful negotiations', but not explicitly excluded such disputes from the compulsory dispute settlement mechanism.[45] Therefore, any dispute that involves China as a party, which arises from unilateral activities in the transitional period preceding delimitation concerning the interpretation and application of Articles 15, 74(3) or 83(3), is exempt from the compulsory dispute settlement mechanism entailing binding decisions as set forth in Section 2 of Part XV of UNCLOS.[46] The non-applicability of this compulsory mechanism, to some extent, reduces the effectiveness of vague rules, namely Articles 15, 74(3) or 83(3) in the present case, in regulating unilateral conduct carried out by disputant States in the Spratly Islands area.

---

this dispute principally related to events occurring in the territorial sea surrounding Scarborough Shoal, noting that Article 298(1)(b) did not apply to territorial seas. Thus, the tribunal concluded that it had jurisdiction to address this submission *to the extent* that the claimed dispute occurred *within the territorial sea* of Scarborough Shoal. The tribunal did not explicitly address whether it would have jurisdiction over the interference occurring *beyond the scope of the territorial sea*. Nevertheless, by conditioning its jurisdiction to the dispute on law enforcement measures in respect of territorial sea only, this award seems to suggest that the tribunal's jurisdiction might become problematic when it comes to a dispute occurring beyond the territorial sea, as it might be regarded as a dispute 'relating to sea boundary delimitations' and thus trigger the application of Article 298(1)(b). See The South China Sea Arbitration (The Philippines v. China), Award on Jurisdiction and Admissibility of 29 October 2015 (PCA), paras.101, 410.

43 China, Declaration made after ratification of UNCLOS (25 August 2006).

44 The Philippines, Understanding made upon signature (10 December 1982) and confirmed upon ratification (8 May 1984). Malaysia, n 29.

45 Vietnam, Declaration upon Ratification of UNCLOS (25 July 1994).

46 Disputes concerning the interpretation or application of Articles 15, 74 and 83 relating to sea boundary delimitations that are exempt from compulsory procedures entailing binding decisions shall be subject to compulsory conciliation procedures under Article 298(1)(a)(i) of UNCLOS. However, such compulsory conciliation procedures are of little assistance in providing definitive settlements for disputes arising from unilateral activities occurring within the Spratly Islands area, because such procedures can only give non-binding recommendations. See Institut de droit international, Resolution on International Conciliation (Thirtieth Commission, Rapporteur: Mr Henri Roulin), Session of Salzburg (1961), Article 1. S. Yee, Conciliation and the 1982 UN Convention on the Law of the Sea, 44(4) *ODIL* (2013), 316.

4.2.4.2.3 *Interpretative Methods under VCLT*

Despite the absence of a compulsory mechanism to carry out the case-by-case analysis of each regulatory phenomenon, the interpretative methods as provided in VCLT may contribute to clarifying the meaning of Articles 15, 74(3) or 83(3) of UNCLOS in two ways.

First, according to Article 31(2) of VCLT, the interpretation of a treaty provision shall take into account its context, which undoubtedly includes other provisions of the same treaty.[47] Thus, other provisions of UNCLOS, especially Part XII, can inform the interpretation of Articles 15, 74(3) or 83(3).[48] In particular, Part XII of UNCLOS applies to all marine areas, regardless of whether they are disputed or not,[49] and confer States with various obligations in relation to the protection and preservation of the marine environment as well as the obligation to take active measures to achieve that aim.[50]

Second, according to Article 31(3)(c) of VCLT, a treaty shall be interpreted by taking into account 'any relevant rules of international law applicable in the relations between the parties'.[51] The logic underlying 'systemic integration' as required by Article 31(3)(c) is that a treaty provision is not constructed in a vacuum but rather is intended to be interpreted and applied against the background of the general principles of international law.[52] There is little doubt that treaty-based rules, customary international law, and general principles of law as listed in Article 38(1) of the ICJ Statute are of relevance to the interpretation

---

47 Vienna Convention on the Law of Treaties, adopted 23 May 1969, entered into force 27 January 1980, 1155 *UNTS* 331, Article 31(2).

48 In 1979, Oxman suggested framing an interim regime by making cross-references to other provisions in UNCLOS that could be equally applicable to disputed marine areas. He opined that this alternative approach had the advantages of not requiring a precise definition of a disputed area as well as being consistent with the positions of competing claimants. Unfortunately, this suggestion was not considered by the drafters of UNCLOS. However, the absence of cross-references to other provisions in UNCLOS does not necessarily mean that these provisions cannot apply with equal force to disputed marine areas. See B. Oxman, The Third United Nations Conference on the Law of the Sea: The Seventh Session (1978), 73 *AJIL* (1979), 23.

49 The South China Sea Arbitration (The Philippines v. China), Award of 12 July 2016 (PCA), para.940.

50 UNCLOS, Part XII.

51 VCLT, Article 31(3)(c).

52 See B. McNair, *The Law of Treaties* (Clarendon Press. 1961), 466; C. Mclachlan, The Principle of Systemic Integration and Article 31(3)(c) of The Vienna Convention, 54(2) *ICLQ* (2005), 280–281; UN Doc.: A/CN.4/L.682, *Fragmentation of International Law: Difficulties Arising from the Diversification and Expansion of International Law*, Report of the Study Group of the International Law Commission (13 April 2006), para.172.

of a treaty pursuant to Article 31(3)(c) of VCLT.[53] One point must be clarified that Article 31(3)(c) of VCLT should not be considered to be a universal panacea that can be used to reconcile principles and rules in all circumstances. Article 31(3)(c) cannot apply where there are true conflicts between norms in international law because the gist of this provision is to accommodate values underlining different norms but 'not the triumph of one norm over another'.[54] In other words, the systemic integration principle operates to harmonize norms of international law through treaty interpretation before an irreconcilable or genuine conflict of norms has arisen.[55] In terms of disputed marine areas, Article 31(3)(c) can be applied to reconcile or harmonize the principles and rules that are applicable to such areas, to the extent that these principles and rules do not manifest genuine conflicts and that none of them can be held superior to the others. Consequently, the interpretation of Articles 15, 74(3) or 83(3) of UNCLOS can take into account relevant general principles under customary international law. A more detailed discussion is provided in the following section.

4.3 Regulatory Framework beyond UNCLOS: General Principles

Beyond UNCLOS, some general principles in customary international law are of particular relevance to disputed marine areas. Such principles include the no-harm principle, the principle of peaceful settlement of disputes, the principle of the prohibition of the threat or use of force, the good faith principle, and the principle of non-aggravation of a dispute. These principles can be informative to the interpretation and application of Articles 74(3) and 83(3) of UNCLOS in the Spratly Islands setting pursuant to Article 31(3)(c) of VCLT.

53 See *e.g.*, UN Doc. A/CN.4/L.702, Fragmentation of International Law: Difficulties Arising from the Diversification and Expansion of International Law, Report of the Study Group of the International Law Commission (18 July 2006), paras.19-20; UN Doc. A/61/10, Report of the International Law Commission, 58th session, 1 May – 9 June and 3 July – 11 August 2006, 413, paras.18-21. Also see P. Merkouris, *Article 31(3)(c) VCLT and the Principle of Systemic Integration: Normative Shadows in Plato's Cave* (Brill. 2015), 19–20.

54 Arrest Warrant of 11 April 2000 (Democratic Republic of the Congo v. Belgium), Joint separate opinion of Judges Higgins, Kooijmans and Buergenthal of 14 February 2002 (ICJ), para.79. Mclachlan, n 52, 318; J. Pauwelyn, *Conflict of Norms in Public International Law: How WTO Law Relates to other Rules of International Law* (CUP. 2003), 272.

55 Mclachlan, n 52, 318.

4.3.1 *Principle of No-Harm*

The no-harm principle, or in the Latin maxim *sic utere tuo ut alienum non laedas*, is embodied in Article 194(2) of UNCLOS, providing that pollution arising from incidents or activities under a State's jurisdiction or control shall not spread beyond the areas where they exercise sovereign rights.[56] The no-harm principle has been accepted as a rule of customary international law in international cases including *Trail Smelter Arbitration*, *Corfu Channel*, *Legality of the Threat or Use of Nuclear Weapons* and *Gabčíkovo-Nagymaros Project*.[57]

Before the 1970s, the application of the no-harm principle was limited to activities occurring in the 'territory' of a State that cause transboundary harm to the 'territory' of another State.[58] However, the Stockholm Declaration of 1972 expanded the application of this principle to activities occurring in areas under *a State's sovereignty or jurisdiction* that might cause damage to *the environment of other States or of areas beyond the limits of national jurisdiction*.[59] Nearly the same language was used in the 1992 Rio Declaration.[60] This position is also endorsed by the ICJ in *Legality of the Threat or Use of Nuclear Weapons* and *Gabčíkovo-Nagymaros Project*, where it concluded that 'the general obligation of States to ensure that activities within their jurisdiction and control respect the environment of other States or of areas beyond national control is now part of the corpus of international law relating to the environment'.[61] Scholars have commented that the change since the 1970s shows that the no-harm principle is no longer solely bilateral in nature, but instead, operates *erga omnes*, as it can relate to the protection of areas beyond national jurisdiction which concerns common interests of the international community as a whole.[62]

---

56 UNCLOS, Article 194(2).

57 Trail Smelter arbitration (the US/Canada), Decisions of 16 April 1938 and 11 March 1941; Corfu Channel (United Kingdom of Great Britain and Northern Ireland v. Albania), Judgment of 9 April 1949 (Merits) (ICJ), 22; Legality of the Threat or Use of Nuclear Weapons, Advisory Opinion of 8 July 1996 (ICJ), para.29; Gabčíkovo-Nagymaros Project (Hungary/Slovakia), Judgment of 25 September 1997 (ICJ), para.53.

58 See *e.g.*, Trail Smelter arbitration, n 57; Corfu Channel n 57, 22.

59 Stockholm Declaration (16 June 1972), Principle 21.

60 UN Doc.: A/CONF.151/26 (Vol. I), Rio Declaration on Environment and Development (3–14 June 1992), Principle 2. ('States have ... the responsibility to ensure that activities within their jurisdiction or control do not cause damage to the environment of other States or of areas beyond the limits of national jurisdiction'.).

61 Legality of the Threat or Use of Nuclear Weapons, n 57, para.29; Gabčíkovo-Nagymaros Project, n 57, para.53.

62 See *e.g.*, Y. Tanaka, *The International Law of the Sea* (CUP 3rd ed. 2019), 330; P.W. Birnie and A.E. Boyle, *International Law and the Environment* (OUP 1994), 145.

Tailored to the Spratly Islands setting, the no-harm principle as understood in the usual sense does not neatly apply to activities occurring within a disputed marine area, since the area concerned is or will not necessarily be under a claimant State's exclusive jurisdiction or control. However, a broader interpretation or *mutatis mutandis* application of this principle to disputed marine areas would entail that a disputant State should refrain from spreading pollution arising from incidents or activities under its jurisdiction or control beyond the disputed marine areas where they claim sovereignty or sovereign rights.[63] This principle is relevant to all types of activities in the Spratly Islands area. According to the systemic integration approach under Article 31(3)(c) of VCLT, the interpretation of Articles 74(3) and 83(3) of UNCLOS must take into account the no-harm principle. Thus, acts violating the no-harm principle are not compatible with the obligation 'not to jeopardize or hamper delimitation' under Articles 74(3) and 83(3) of UNCLOS.

4.3.2 *Principles of Peaceful Settlement and Prohibition of Threat or Use of Force*

Peaceful settlement of international disputes is a general principle formulated in Article 2(3) of the UN Charter, according to which all member States are obliged to settle their international disputes by peaceful means in a way that does not endanger international peace and security, and justice.[64] Article 2(4) of the UN Charter deems threat of use of force against the territorial integrity or political independence of any State or inconsistent with the purposes of the UN to be an unlawful means to settle a dispute.[65] A corollary of enjoining force as a traditional means of settling international disputes is a corresponding obligation to resolve differences peacefully. In this sense, the principle of peaceful settlement of international disputes is complementary to the principle of prohibition of the threat or use of force.[66] It follows that an action violating the latter cannot be compatible with the former under current international law. The principles of peaceful settlement of international disputes and prohibition of the threat or use of force are also reiterated in Articles 279 and 301 of UNCLOS.[67]

63 For similar discussions, see *e.g.*, van Logchem, n 22, 84–86.

64 UN Charter, Article 2(3).

65 *Ibid.*, Article 2(4).

66 J.G. Merrills, The Principle of Peaceful Settlement of Disputes, in M. Akehurst, *et al.* (eds.), *The United Nations and the Principles of International Law: Essays in Memory of Michael Akehurst* (Routledge. 1994), 41.

67 UNCLOS, Articles 279 and 301.

The Declaration on Principles of International Law concerning Friendly Relations and Co-operation among States (Friendly Relations Declaration) of 1970 reaffirms the complementary relationship between these two principles.[68] This declaration further relates the principle of prohibition of the threat or use of force to international boundary disputes, stipulating that this principle applies to 'territorial disputes and problems concerning frontiers of States'.[69] There is little doubt that the wording 'problems concerning frontiers of States' should be interpreted so as to include maritime disputes.[70] The compatibility between the principle of prohibition of the threat or use of force and disputed areas is also confirmed in international jurisprudence. As the Eritrea-Ethiopia Claims Commission explained, border disputes between States were so frequent that making an exception to the principle of prohibition of the threat or use of force for a territory that was allegedly occupied unlawfully would significantly weaken this fundamental principle of international law.[71] This opinion has been cited with endorsement in the *Guyana v. Suriname* award.[72]

Tailored to the Spratly Islands setting, the principles of peaceful settlement of international disputes and prohibition of the threat or use of force entail that the disputant States should settle their disputes by peaceful means and should refrain from using the threat or use of force in contravention of Article 2(4) of the UN Charter. These two principles are more relevant to law enforcement measures, where forcible action might be involved, than to the resource-related conduct. Nonetheless, it needs to be noted that not all forcible action is unlawful *per se*. For instance, law enforcement activities might contain some forcible action, and such forcible action might be deemed lawful to the extent that it was 'unavoidable, reasonable and necessary'.[73] Yet, drawing a line between unlawful threat or use of force and mere law enforcement can sometimes be difficult.[74] This matter is discussed more in-depth in section 4.6. Moreover, acts violating these two principles amount to a breach of the obligation 'not to jeopardize or hamper delimitation' under Articles 74(3) and 83(3)

68 UN Doc.: A/RES/2625(XXV), Declaration on Principles of International Law concerning Friendly Relations and Co-operation among States (24 October 1970), para.1.

69 *Ibid.*

70 See *e.g.*, van Logchem, n 22, 72–73.

71 Eritrea-Ethiopia Claims Commission – Partial Award: Jus Ad Bellum – Ethiopia's Claims 1–8, 19 December 2005, RIAA, Vol. XXVI, 465, para.10.

72 Guyana v. Suriname, n 13, para.423.

73 Guyana v. Suriname, n 13, para.445. S. S. 'I'm Alone' (Canada, United States), Awards of 30 June 1930, 5 January 1935 (Arbitration), 1617.

74 T. Ruys, The Meaning of 'Force' and the Boundaries of the Jus Ad Bellum: Are 'Minimal' Uses of Force Excluded from UN Charter Article 2(4)?, 108 *AJIL* (2014), 210.

of UNCLOS.[75] This position is exemplified in the *Guyana v. Suriname* award. In that case, the tribunal concluded that Surname's warning against Guyana's oil rig and drilling ship in a disputed marine area, while also violating the principle of prohibition of the threat or use of force, constituted a breach of the obligation 'not to jeopardize or hamper delimitation' under Articles 74(3) and 83(3) of UNCLOS.[76] The underlying rationale, as the tribunal explained, was that 'Suriname had a number of peaceful options to address Guyana's authorisation of exploratory drilling', instead of resorting to self-help by threatening Guyana's oil rig and drilling ship.[77]

4.3.3 *Principle of Good Faith*

Good faith is a principle of customary international law and affirmed in the UN Charter and Friendly Relations Declaration.[78] This principle applies to diverse facets of international law, including the interpretation and implementation of generally recognized principles and rules of international law.[79] It is also echoed in Article 300 of UNCLOS, providing that States shall fulfil the obligations under this convention in good faith and shall not abuse the rights recognized in this convention.[80]

Tailored to the Spratly Islands setting, when the claimants agree to enter into a negotiation or are obliged to negotiate a solution to their dispute, the good faith principle requires the negotiation to be carried out in good faith 'with a genuine intention to achieve a positive result'.[81] As Thirlway put it, 'to negotiate otherwise than in good faith is surely not to negotiate at all'.[82] This

---

75 The obligation to refrain from using the threat or use of force under Article 2(4) of the UN Charter and the obligation 'not to jeopardize or hamper delimitation' under Articles 74(3) and 83(3) of UNCLOS are interlinked. See D.H. Anderson, Some Aspects of the Use of Force in Maritime Law Enforcement, in N. Boschiero *et al.* (eds.), *International Courts and the Development of International Law: Essays in Honour of Tullio Treves* (Springer. 2013), 239.

76 Guyana v. Suriname, n 13, para.484.

77 *Ibid.* J. Gao, Comments on Guyana v. Suriname, 8(1) *CJIL* (2009), 203.

78 UN Charter, Article 2(2); UN Doc.: A/RES/2625(XXV), Declaration on Principles of International Law concerning Friendly Relations and Co-operation among States (24 October 1970), para.1.

79 G. White, The Principle of Good Faith, in M. Akehurst, *et al.* (eds.), *The United Nations and the Principles of International Law: Essays in Memory of Michael Akehurst* (Routledge. 1994), 164.

80 UNCLOS, Article 300.

81 Delimitation of the Maritime Boundary in the Gulf of Maine Area (Canada/United States of America), Judgment of 12 October 1984, para.87.

82 H. Thirlway, The Law and Procedure of the International Court of Justice 1960–1989: Part One, 60 *BYBIL* (1989), 25.

obligation to negotiate in good faith is an obligation of conduct (*pactum de negotiando*), as distinct from an obligation of result (*pactum de contrahendo*).[83] In *Kingdom of Greece v. Federal Republic of Germany*, the arbitral tribunal for the Agreement on German External Debts spelt out the material content of this obligation as follows:

> both sides would make an effort, in good faith, to bring about a mutually satisfactory solution by way of a compromise, even if that meant the relinquishment of strongly held positions earlier taken. It implies a willingness for the purpose of negotiation to abandon earlier positions and to meet the other side part way.[84]

Articles 74(3) and 83(3) oblige the disputant States to negotiate in good faith provisional arrangements in the period preceding delimitation. However, as concluded in section 4.2.3, the disputant States are not obliged to negotiate in good faith with respect to activities that do not have the effect of jeopardizing the final delimitation agreement. Hence, the obligation to negotiate in good faith is not informative as to the interpretation of the obligation 'not to jeopardize or hamper delimitation' because it only applies *after* activities amount to a violation of the obligation 'not to jeopardize or hamper delimitation'.

Nevertheless, the *Guyana v. Suriname* award offers non-exhaustive procedural guidelines that the disputant States may follow to avoid a breach of the obligation to negotiate in good faith.[85] On the one hand, before undertaking activities that violate the obligation 'not to jeopardize or hamper delimitation' in a disputed area, a claimant should give another party to the dispute official and detailed notice of the planned activities (prior information) instead of a mere announcement in the press, seek cooperation of another party in

83 Dispute Concerning Delimitation of the Maritime Boundary between Ghana and Côte d'Ivoire in the Atlantic Ocean (Ghana/Côte d'Ivoire), Judgment of 23 September 2017 (ITLOS), para.627.

84 Case concerning Claims Arising Out of Decisions of the Mixed Graeco-German Arbitral Tribunal set up under Article 304 in Part X of the Treaty of Versailles (Between Greece and the Federal Republic of Germany), Decision of 26 January 1972, RIAA, Vol. XIX, 56.

85 Guyana v. Suriname, n 13, paras.476-477. Davenport commented that 'decision in Guyana v. Suriname undeniably gives some teeth to the obligation to negotiate provisional arrangements in Articles 74(3) and 83(3) and is a welcome clarification of a provision which had not been subject to judicial interpretation before'. See T. Davenport, The Exploration and Exploitation of Hydrocarbon Resources in Areas of Overlapping Claims, in R. Beckman, *et al.* (eds.), *Beyond Territorial Disputes in the South China Sea Legal Frameworks for the Joint Development of Hydrocarbon Resources* (Edward Elgar Publishing. 2013), 103–104.

undertaking the activities, offer to share the results of these activities and give another party an opportunity to observe the activities, and offer to share all financial benefits received from the activities.[86] On the other hand, as a response to another claimant's such activities in a disputed area, a claimant should take the initiative to bring that claimant to the negotiating table, and it could insist on the immediate cessation of the activities at issue as a condition to participating in further talks.[87] The compliance with these procedural guidelines is required by the obligation to negotiate in good faith provisional arrangements, but such compliance cannot replace provisional arrangements to deprive unlawful unilateral acts of their jeopardizing or hampering effect.[88] In other words, unless a provisional arrangement is agreed, fulfilling the above procedural guidelines does not give a disputant State a 'permit' to undertake unilateral activities that would jeopardize the reaching of the final delimitation agreement.

4.3.4 *Principle of Non-aggravation of a Dispute*

In elaborating the principle of peaceful settlement of international disputes, both the Friendly Relations Declaration and the Manila Declaration on the Peaceful Settlement of Disputes (Manila Declaration) stipulate that States parties to an international dispute shall refrain from any action that may aggravate the situation so as to endanger the maintenance of international peace and security.[89] It is evident that an act leading to a breach of the prohibition of the threat or use of force principle would undoubtedly put international peace and security at risk. However, whether other acts such as the severance of diplomatic relations and economic sanctions have the effect of endangering the maintenance of international peace and security is left largely undefined in these two instruments.

86 Guyana v. Suriname, n 13, para.477.

87 *Ibid.*, para.476.

88 Scholars have different opinions on this matter. For example, van Logchem argued that procedural guidelines could not justify the unilateral taking of activities having the effect of jeopardizing or hampering. Conversely, Redgwell and Rajamani argued that 'where there is notice given of such activities and there is sharing of the results', exploratory drilling could be allowed despite its jeopardizing or hampering effect. See van Logchem, n 22, 222–223; C. Redgwell and L. Rajamani, Energy Underground: What's International Law Got to Do With It?, in D. Zillman *et al.* (eds.), *The Law of Energy Underground: Understanding New Developments in Subsurface Production, Transmission, and Storage* (OUP. 2014), 119, fn. 124.

89 UN Doc.: A/RES/2625(XXV), Declaration on Principles of International Law concerning Friendly Relations and Co-operation among States (24 October 1970), para.1; UN Doc.: A/RES/37/10, Peaceful Settlement of Disputes between States (15 November 1982), para.8.

In contrast, the material content of the obligation of non-aggravation of a dispute associated with dispute resolution proceedings is clearly defined in international jurisprudence.[90] That is, parties engaged in the conduct of dispute resolution proceedings are obliged to refrain from aggravating or extending the dispute pending the completion of these proceedings. The dispute settlement procedures mentioned here should be interpreted so as to include negotiation. The obligation of non-aggravation of a dispute is derived from the good faith principle.[91] As mentioned above, a claimant shall negotiate in good faith when entering into a negotiation or is obliged to negotiate a solution to a dispute. Another requirement derived from the principle of good faith is that a State shall refrain from aggravating or extending the dispute so as to defeat the object and purpose of negotiation.[92]

Tailored to the Spratly Islands setting, the principle of non-aggravation of a dispute entails that when the disputant States agree to enter into a negotiation or are obliged to negotiate a solution to their dispute, they shall refrain from aggravating or extending the dispute in a manner that the object and purpose of negotiation are defeated. This principle only applies to activities that violate the obligation 'not to jeopardize or hamper delimitation', because the disputant States are not obliged to negotiate in good faith with respect to activities that comply with the obligation 'not to jeopardize or hamper delimitation'. Moreover, it is clear that not all the actions that detrimentally affect States' relations with one another would violate the obligation of non-aggravation of a dispute.[93] For instance, China banned the importation of fruits from the Philippines after the latter initiated a case against it regarding their maritime dispute in the South China Sea in 2013.[94] Yet, it is difficult to say that China's fruit ban violated the obligation of non-aggravation of a dispute associated with the *South China Sea arbitration* proceedings. For example, when the tribunal in *South China Sea arbitration* was asked by the Philippines to decide

90 See *e.g.*, Electricity Company of Sofia and Bulgaria (Belgium v. Bulgaria), Interim Measures of Protection, Order of 5 December 1939, PCIJ Series A/B, No. 79, 199; LaGrand (Germany v. United States of America), Judgment of 27 June 2001 (ICJ), paras.102-103; Dispute Concerning Delimitation of the Maritime Boundary between Ghana and Côte D'Ivoire in the Atlantic Ocean, Provisional Measures, Order of 25 April 2015 (ITLOS), para.108(1)(e); The South China Sea Arbitration, n 49, para.1174.

91 The South China Sea Arbitration, n 49, para.1171.

92 For similar discussions, see *e.g.*, van Logchem, n 22, 81.

93 The South China Sea Arbitration, n 49, para.1174.

94 K. Lema, Philippines Looks to China for Farms 'Windfall' When Fruit Ban Ends (9 October 2016), available at <https://www.reuters.com/article/us-philippines-china-agriculture-idUSKCN1290PV>.

whether China's intensified construction of artificial islands on seven features aggravated the disputes submitted in that case, the tribunal rightly pointed out:

> Neither the Convention, nor international law, go so far as to impose a legal duty on a State to refrain from aggravating generally their relations with one another, however desirable it might be for States to do so.[95]

Rather, only those actions that have a 'specific nexus' with the rights and claims making up the parties' dispute in the conduct of negotiation can violate this obligation.[96] Therefore, as Tanaka rightly pointed out, 'breaches of the obligations of non-aggravation must be decided on a case-by-case basis, taking account of particularities of each case'.[97] In concrete cases, such a 'specific nexus' can manifest in two ways. First, in the course of negotiation, the conduct of a claimant may aggravate a dispute where that claimant continues during the pendency of the proceedings with actions that violate the rights of the other in such a way as to render the alleged violation more serious. Second, a claimant may also aggravate a dispute by taking actions that would frustrate the effectiveness and integrity of the negotiation, including by rendering the progress or work of negotiation significantly more onerous, taking other actions that decrease the likelihood of the negotiation leading to the resolution of the parties' dispute, or rendering the implementation of the outcome significantly more difficult.[98]

4.3.5 *Summary*

In terms of the Spratly Islands area, Article 31(3)(c) of VCLT can be used to reconcile or harmonize the principles and rules that are applicable to the disputed marine areas therein, as these principles and rules do not manifest genuine conflicts, and none of them can be held superior to the others.[99] Accordingly, the interpretation of Articles 74(3) and 83(3) of UNCLOS should be informed by the general principles including the no-harm principle, the principle of peaceful settlement of disputes, the principle of the prohibition of the threat or use of force, the good faith principle, and the principle of non-aggravation of a dispute. As a result, any unilateral action taken by a disputant State within

95 The South China Sea Arbitration, n 49, para.1174.

96 *Ibid.*

97 Y. Tanaka, *The South China Sea Arbitration: Toward an International Legal Order in the Oceans* (Hart Publishing. 2019), 160.

98 The South China Sea Arbitration, n 49, para.1176.

99 Arrest Warrant of 11 April 2000, n 54, para.79. Mclachlan, n 52, 318. Pauwelyn, n 54, 272.

disputed marine areas shall not cause pollution spread beyond these areas, and shall not involve forcible acts that are prohibited under Article 2(4) of the UN Charter. In contrast, the principles of good faith and non-aggravation of a dispute are more relevant *after* relevant unilateral activities are deemed a breach of the obligation 'not to jeopardize or hamper delimitation'. Thus, these two principles are not informative as to whether certain unilateral action violates the obligation 'not to jeopardize or hamper delimitation' or not.

4.4 The Permissible Scope for Unilateral Offshore Hydrocarbon Activities

This section aims to clarify the permissible scope for unilateral offshore hydrocarbon activities under international law in the Spratly Islands setting. For this analytical purpose, this section begins with an account of the stages of hydrocarbon resources development (subsection 4.4.1). It then delves into the interpretation of Articles 74(3) and 83(3) informed by relevant international jurisprudence, including *Aegean Sea Continental Shelf*, *Guyana v. Suriname* and *Ghana/Côte d'Ivoire* (subsection 4.4.2). This section then explores the application of Articles 74(3) and 83(3) to unilateral offshore hydrocarbon activities in the Spratly Islands setting (subsection 4.4.3).

4.4.1 *Stages of Hydrocarbon Resources Development*

In chronological order, hydrocarbon resources development can roughly be divided into four stages: designating oil blocks and granting concessions, seismic surveys, exploratory drilling, and exploitation. The general rule of thumb is that progressing through these four stages, the marine environment will be put increasingly at risk.[100]

4.4.1.1 Designating Oil Blocks and Granting Concessions

Designating oil blocks and granting concessions constitute the preparatory phase of hydrocarbon resources development. Actual work is meant to be carried out subsequent to the activation of a concession. In the Spratly Islands area, some disputant States have designated oil lease blocks extending over part of the contested waters. For instance, in 2012, the Chinese state-owned oil company, China National Offshore Oil Corporation (CNOOC), introduced oil

100 Y. van Logchem, The Status of a Rule of Capture under International Law of the Sea with regard to Offshore Oil and Gas Resource Related Activities, 26 *Michigan State International Law Review* (2018), 231–239.

lease blocks opposite the coast of Vietnam and almost going along the margin of the U-shaped line.[101] China claimed that these blocks were in 'waters under [its] jurisdiction'.[102] This incident raised strong protests from Vietnam.[103] Similarly, Vietnam has declared several oil lease blocks within its alleged 200-M EEZ.[104] The Philippines has also designated an oil block – GSEC101 – at Reed Bank in the Northeast of the Spratly Islands area.[105]

4.4.1.2 Seismic Surveys

Seismic surveys are often employed as a primary tool to clarify the potential of hydrocarbon resources during the exploration phase because of their lower costs than exploratory drilling. A seismic survey involves small explosions aimed to send sound waves through the seabed and to obtain information about the geophysical structure of the earth beneath it.[106] Seismic surveys are reported to have occurred at times in the Spratly Islands area.[107] A recent one was reported in July 2019 that a Chinese survey ship – *Haiyang Dizhi 8* (*Marine Geology 8*) – entered waters near a Vietnamese-controlled reef (Vanguard Bank) in the Spratly Islands to conduct seismic survey operation, which triggered a week-long standoff between Chinese and Vietnamese coastguard vessels.[108]

4.4.1.3 Exploratory Drilling

After sites with a high probability of finding hydrocarbon resources have been identified through seismic surveys, exploratory drilling is used at such sites to further confirm the location of *in situ* hydrocarbon resources and to obtain

---

101 OES, China: Maritime Claims in the South China Sea, *Limits in the Seas* (5 December 2014), 16.

102 CNOOC, Notification of Part of Open Blocks in Waters under Jurisdiction of the People's Republic of China Available for Foreign Cooperation in the Year of 2012 (23 June 2012), available at <http://www.cnooc.com.cn/art/2014/9/25/art_6241_1148011.html>.

103 *Ibid.*

104 Crisis Group, Stirring up the South China Sea (IV): Oil in Troubled Waters (27 January 2016), available at <https://medium.com/@CrisisGroup/stirring-up-the-south-china-sea-iv-oil-in-troubled-waters-7d4b7286aac0>.

105 The South China Sea Arbitration, n 49, para.652.

106 Aegean Sea Continental Shelf (Greece v. Turkey), Order of 11 September 1976, Request for the Indication of Interim Measures of Protection (ICJ), para.30.

107 For more details about the oil-related practices within the South China Sea, see J. Li, *et al.*, Hydrocarbon Resources within the U-Shaped Line in the Southern China Sea: Distribution Characteristics and Development Status, 1 *China Oceans L. Rev.* (2013), 41–58.

108 L. Zhen, China and Vietnam in stand-off over Chinese survey ship mission to disputed reef in South China Sea (12 July 2019), available at <https://www.scmp.com/news/china/diplomacy/article/3018332/beijing-and-hanoi-stand-over-chinese-survey-ship-mission>.

actual temperature measurements, rock samples and fluid samples for chemical analysis.[109] Exploratory drilling provides the most accurate information during the exploration process, but it is also the most expensive method, and is usually the last phase of the exploration process. Since it utilizes drill holes, the physical condition of seabed and subsoil will be impacted. The drill holes used in this phase are normally not as deep, smaller, and quicker to drill compared with the production and injection wells used in the exploitation phase. No exploratory drilling activities are reported to have taken place in the contested areas of the Spratly Islands. The absence of exploratory drilling in this region might be well explained by the possibility that sporadic seismic surveys undertaken unilaterally by the disputant States have not yet led to any conclusive result, and thus, it would be premature to conduct exploratory drilling at this stage.

4.4.1.4 Exploitation

Exploitation refers to drilling hydrocarbon resources from production and injection wells.[110] It will inevitably impact the structure of the seabed and subsoil. Due to its high costs, exploitation would not take place in the absence of conclusive results accrued from the exploration process. For this reason, it might be understandable why no exploitation drilling activities are reported to have occurred in the contested areas of the Spratly Islands.[111] Another factor contributing to the absence of exploitation in this region is that the disputed status of marine areas usually scares away oil companies, which would refrain from investing vast sums in areas of high political risk.

4.4.2 *Relevant International Jurisprudence*

After introducing the stages of hydrocarbon resources development, this chapter now turns to the interpretation of Articles 74(3) and 83(3) informed by relevant international jurisprudence. Two international cases, namely *Guyana v. Suriname* and *Ghana/Côte d'Ivoire*, have directly addressed the interpretation and application of Articles 74(3) and 83(3) of UNCLOS. These two cases

109 OpenEI, Exploration Technique: Exploration Drilling, available at < https://openei.org/wiki/Exploration_Drilling >.

110 UNEP, Environmental Management in Oil and Gas Exploration and Production, *UNEP IE/PAC Technical Report 37* (1997), 7–8.

111 D. Letts and D.R. Rothwell, Challenges for the law of the sea in South East Asia: resolving current controversies and addressing horizon threats, in D.R. Rothwell and D. Letts (eds.), Law of the Sea in South East Asia: Environmental, Navigational and Security Challenges (Routledge. 2019), 244.

are specifically associated with unilateral offshore hydrocarbon activities within contested waters. Moreover, though *Aegean Sea Continental Shelf* was adjudicated before the adoption of UNCLOS and thus did not directly relate to the interpretation of Articles 74(3) and 83(3) of UNCLOS, the ICJ's pronouncement in this case has been cited with endorsement in the subsequent *Guyana v. Suriname* award to support the interpretation of the obligation 'not to jeopardize or hamper delimitation' under Articles 74(3) and 83(3).[112] Besides, the ongoing *Somalia v. Kenya* case might also be of relevance, as the motivating factor behind Somalia's submission of the maritime boundary dispute with Kenya to the ICJ was that Kenya had acted unilaterally to undertake, or authorise private companies to undertake, extensive seismic research in their disputed areas.[113] Nevertheless, this case is not discussed in detail because the ICJ has not yet made decisions on the merits.

4.4.2.1 Aegean Sea Continental Shelf

In *Aegean Sea Continental Shelf*, Greece instituted proceedings against Turkey in a dispute over the Aegean Sea continental shelf. Greece requested the ICJ to order interim measures that Turkey should refrain from all exploration activity or any scientific research with respect to the disputed area of continental shelf pending the final decision upon the dispute.[114] The 'exploration activity or any scientific research' that Greece referred to mainly included seismic exploration undertaken by or under licence from Turkey within the disputed area of the continental shelf.[115]

In the interim measures order, the ICJ distinguished between activities of a transitory character and activities that risked irreparable prejudice to the other party's rights. The ICJ considered that according to Article 41 of the ICJ Statute, its exceptional power to indicate provisional measures presupposed that 'the circumstances of the case disclose the risk of an irreparable prejudice to rights in issue in the proceedings'.[116] Accordingly, the ICJ declined to indicate the requested interim measure on the ground that the alleged form of seismic exploration did not risk irreparable prejudice to the rights in issue,[117] citing three factors that such seismic exploration: (1) did not involve any risk

112 Guyana v. Suriname, n 13, para.470.

113 Maritime Delimitation in the Indian Ocean (Somalia v. Kenya), Memorial of Somalia, 13 July 2015, paras.8.27-8.28.

114 Aegean Sea Continental Shelf, n 106, para.2.

115 *Ibid.*, para.24.

116 *Ibid.*, para.32.

117 *Ibid.*, paras.32-33.

of physical damage to the seabed or subsoil; (2) was of the transitory character that did not involve the establishment of installations on or above the seabed of the continental shelf; and (3) did not embark upon any operations involving the actual appropriation or other use of the natural resources of the disputed area of the continental shelf.[118]

4.4.2.2 Guyana v. Suriname

In *Guyana v. Suriname*, Guyana instituted proceedings against Suriname concerning the delimitation of the maritime boundary between them and the alleged breaches of international law by Suriname in the disputed marine areas. As a response, Suriname claimed that Guyana violated the obligation 'not to jeopardize or hamper delimitation' under Articles 74(3) and 83(3) of UNCLOS by allowing its concession holder to undertake exploratory drilling in marine areas that were in dispute between them.[119]

In interpreting the legal parameters of the obligation 'not to jeopardize or hamper delimitation' under Articles 74(3) and 83(3), the tribunal spelt out a review standard 'in the context of activities surrounding hydrocarbon exploration and exploitation'.[120] The tribunal drew a distinction between activities 'having a permanent physical impact on the marine environment' and those that do not.[121] Based on this distinction, the tribunal considered that unilateral acts which did not cause a permanent physical change to the marine environment would generally be permissible within the contested waters.[122]

Accordingly, the tribunal concluded that Guyana authorizing exploratory drilling in disputed marine areas fell short of its obligation 'not to jeopardize or hamper delimitation', because these activities might jeopardize or hamper the reaching of a final delimitation agreement as a result of the perceived change to the *status quo* that they would engender.[123] The tribunal further held that a substantive legal difference existed between two kinds of oil exploration activities, namely exploratory drilling and seismic testing.[124] In the view of the tribunal, whereas exploratory drilling might cause a permanent physical change to the marine environment and thus should be prohibited in disputed

118 *Ibid.*, para.30.
119 *Ibid.*, para.479.
120 *Ibid.*, para.466.
121 *Ibid.*, para.470.
122 *Ibid.*, para.467.
123 *Ibid.*, para.480.
124 *Ibid.*, para.469.

waters, seismic testing was permissible because it usually would not change the marine environment.[125]

Two main points of debate may arise regarding the review standard, including: (1) to what extent the tribunal has clarified the precise threshold required by the review standard; and (2) whether the tribunal's conclusion could be read as indicating that all seismic exploration activities are permissible irrespective of the circumstances surrounding a dispute or case.

The first point of debate pertains to the precise threshold required by the review standard. In other words, to what extent a specific act could be considered as causing 'permanent physical change to the marine environment'? In trying to find an answer to this question, the tribunal considered that this review standard was reminiscent of the preceding international jurisprudence on interim/ provisional measures. The tribunal considered that the 'permanent physical change to the marine environment' test was consistent with the jurisprudence of international courts and tribunals on interim measures. The tribunal cited the ICJ's decision in *Aegean Sea Continental Shelf* to clarify that the power to indicate interim measures only applied to those activities that could cause irreparable prejudice to another party's rights.[126]

At this point, one may ask whether 'permanent physical change to the marine environment' is tantamount to 'irreparable prejudice to another party's rights'. The answer is in the negative, as the tribunal continued to conclude that 'the regime of interim measures is far more circumscribed than that surrounding activities in disputed waters generally', owing to the exceptional nature of the power to indicate provisional measures.[127] Although 'permanent physical change to the marine environment' was not exactly the same as 'irreparable prejudice to another party's rights', the tribunal stated that the latter could still be informative as to which types of activities were permissible in disputed waters preceding delimitation. The tribunal explained the rationale behind this statement as follows: 'Activities that would meet the standard required for the indication of interim measures ... would easily meet the lower threshold of hampering or jeopardising the reaching of a final agreement'.[128] Said differently, activities that risk irreparable prejudice to another party's rights thereby justifying the use of exceptional power to indicate provisional measures would undoubtedly constitute a breach of the obligation 'not to jeopardize or hamper delimitation' under Articles 74(3) and 83(3) of UNCLOS.

125 *Ibid.*, para.481.
126 *Ibid.*
127 *Ibid.*, para.469.
128 *Ibid.*

Nevertheless, the converse is not necessarily true. Activities that do not trigger the use of exceptional power to indicate provisional measures might still constitute a breach of the obligation 'not to jeopardize or hamper delimitation'. This conclusion is a corollary of the presumption established by the *Guyana v. Suriname* tribunal that the regime of provisional measures is far more *circumscribed* than regulating unilateral activities in contested marine areas. For example, a court or tribunal may find that explanatory drilling capable of reparation by appropriate means *ex post* does not trigger the exercise of its exceptional power to indicate provisional measures to suspend such activities. However, such explanatory drilling would cause a permanent physical impact on the marine environment and thus violates the obligation 'not to jeopardize or hamper delimitation'.

To this effect, it can be said that the *Guyana v. Suriname* award clearly indicates that the *ceiling* threshold for unilateral conduct to be permissible within disputed zones is that such conduct does not risk irreparable prejudice to another party's rights so as to trigger the indication of provisional measures. However, this award is of little help in clarifying the *floor* threshold of the review standard. Put differently, for unilateral conduct that does not reach the high threshold of triggering the indication of provisional measures, the extent to which such unilateral conduct amounts to causing 'permanent physical change to the marine environment' remains largely undefined.

The second point of debate concerns whether the tribunal's conclusion could be read as indicating that all seismic exploration activities are permissible irrespective of the circumstances surrounding a dispute or case. Arguably, the answer is in the negative. It needs to be noted that the *Guyana v. Suriname* tribunal carefully constructed the language of its reasoning in this regard to be limited to the 'the circumstances at hand', and did not specify whether a seismic survey by its very definition was permissible in a disputed area.[129] Accordingly, as rightly pointed out by van Logchem, the possibility of amounting unilateral seismic activity to a breach of the obligation 'not to jeopardize or hamper delimitation' under a certain constellation of circumstances could not be precluded.[130] This position is also complemented by the results of scientific research that seismic testing may have adverse effects on marine life under certain circumstances.[131] As a result, it is difficult to generalize unilateral seismic exploration activities as (not) infringing the obligation

129 Van Logchem, n 14, 185.

130 *Ibid.*

131 I. Udoinyang and M.U. Igboekwe, The Impacts of Seismic Activities on Marine Life and its Environment, 2 *International Archive of Applied Sciences and Technology* (2011), 1–10.

'not to jeopardize or hamper delimitation'. Rather, the assessment is always circumstance-dependent.

4.4.2.3 Ghana/Côte d'Ivoire

In *Ghana/Côte d'Ivoire*, Ghana and Côte d'Ivoire submitted their maritime boundary dispute in the Atlantic Ocean to a Special Chamber of ITLOS (Chamber) based on a special agreement concluded between them in 2014. The proceedings of this case consist of two stages: provisional measures proceedings and merits proceedings.

4.4.2.3.1 *Provisional Measures Proceedings*

During the provisional measures proceedings, Côte d'Ivoire requested Ghana to be ordered to suspend all *ongoing* oil exploration and exploitation operations and refrain from granting any *new* operations in the disputed area.[132] The Chamber admitted that both the ongoing and future exploration and exploitation activities would result in significant and permanent modification of the physical characteristics of the area in dispute, thus creating a risk of irreversible prejudice to the rights of Côte d'Ivoire and also causing harm to the marine environment.[133] However, the Chamber also noted that suspending Ghana's ongoing activities in respect of which drilling had already taken place would not only entail the risk of considerable financial loss to Ghana and its concessionaires but also pose a serious danger to the marine environment particularly caused by the deterioration of equipment.[134] Therefore, the Chamber considered that an order suspending all ongoing activities would cause prejudice to the rights claimed by Ghana and create an undue burden on it.[135] Hence, the Chamber issued an order of provisional measures requesting that Ghana should refrain from conducting any *new* drilling in the disputed area and that Ghana could continue the *ongoing* drilling as long as it carried out strict and continuous monitoring of all activities undertaken by Ghana or with its authorization in the disputed area 'with a view to ensuring the prevention of serious harm to the marine environment'.[136]

132 Dispute Concerning Delimitation of the Maritime Boundary between Ghana and Côte d'Ivoire in the Atlantic Ocean, n 90, para.25.
133 *Ibid.*, para.95.
134 *Ibid.*, para.99.
135 *Ibid.*, para.100.
136 *Ibid.*, para.108.

At first glance, the above decision made by the Chamber seems to contradict the *Guyana v. Suriname* award.[137] The latter explicitly concluded that Guyana's authorisation of its concession holder to undertake exploratory drilling within contested areas violated the obligation 'not to jeopardize or hamper delimitation' because it would cause permanent physical change to the marine environment.[138] In contrast, in the former, albeit admitting that Ghana's ongoing drilling would result in significant and permanent modification of the physical characteristics of the area in dispute, the Chamber did not order Ghana to suspend its ongoing drilling.

Nevertheless, some difference exists between *Guyana v. Suriname* and *Ghana/Côte d'Ivoire*. The hydrocarbon resources development activities involved in the former case included only exploratory drilling and did not include any actual exploitation operation. Consequently, the suspension of such activities would not entail the risk of considerable financial loss to Guyana and its concessionaires and pose a serious danger to the marine environment. In comparison, the hydrocarbon resources development practices in *Ghana/Côte d'Ivoire* comprised oil concessions, seismic surveys, exploration and drilling activities. The extent and intensity of the unilateral activities undertaken by Ghana were much more substantial than those of Guyana. Consequently, suspending Ghana's activities would cause prejudice to the rights claimed by Ghana and create an undue burden on it.[139]

It is generally accepted that a provisional measure could not itself cause prejudice to the rights of both parties in dispute. Thus, before the final settlement of the maritime dispute, the legal protection through provisional measures during such a transitional period must not be exclusive to any one of the disputant States. The remedies through provisional measures are available only if the applicant can show that 'the potential injury to the applicant outweighs the potential injury to the respondent'.[140] In this sense, it is understandable why the Chamber had refused to order Ghana to stop all *ongoing* drillings in the disputed area in its order of provisional measures.

137 Dispute Concerning Delimitation of the Maritime Boundary between Ghana and Côte d'Ivoire in the Atlantic Ocean, n 83, paras.210, 619. X. Ma, *Ghana/Côte d'Ivoire: Unilateral Oil Activities in Disputed Marine Areas*, Opinio Juris (9 November 2017), available at <http://opiniojuris.org/2017/11/09/ghana-v-cote-divoire-unilateral-oil-activities-in-disputed-marine-areas/>.

138 Guyana v. Suriname, n 13, para.482.

139 Dispute Concerning Delimitation of the Maritime Boundary between Ghana and Côte d'Ivoire in the Atlantic Ocean, n 90, para.100.

140 Lord Collins of Mapesbury (Rapporteur), Provisional Measures, 78 *Annuaire de l'Institut de Droit international* (2017), 3.

However, as concluded in section 4.4.2.2, activities that do not trigger the indication of provisional measures might still constitute a breach of the obligation 'not to jeopardize or hamper delimitation'. As a result, the fact that the Chamber did not order the suspension of ongoing oil exploration and exploitation operations as a provisional measure in *Ghana/Côte d'Ivoire* does not necessarily lead to the conclusion that such ongoing activities did not violate the obligation 'not to jeopardize or hamper delimitation'.

4.4.2.3.2 *Merits Proceedings*

In the merits proceedings, Côte d'Ivoire had requested the Chamber to declare that unilateral activities undertaken by Ghana after the issuance of the provisional measures 'in the Ivorian maritime area' constituted a violation of the obligation 'not to jeopardize or hamper delimitation' under Article 83(3) of UNCLOS.[141] However, the Chamber brushed this issue aside by simply concluding that the activities of Ghana did not meet the qualification of the relevant submission of Côte d'Ivoire since such activities did not take place 'in the Ivorian maritime area' but in an area attributed to Ghana.[142]

The majority of the bench could have stopped here. But it went further to conclude that activities undertaken unilaterally by a State in an area of the continental shelf which had been attributed to another State by an international judgment could not be considered as a violation of the sovereign rights of the latter if two cumulative conditions were met: first, such activities were carried out before the judgment was delivered; and second, the area concerned was the subject of claims made in good faith by both States.[143]

The above decision infers that unilateral oil exploitation activities carried out within contested waters would not be deemed unlawful provided that relevant areas are found to belong to the party who has undertaken these activities. This finding is *obiter dictum* since it is irrelevant to the submission made by Côte d'Ivoire, which, according to the Chamber, only pertains to activities 'in the Ivorian maritime area' instead of contested waters or the area that was attributed to Ghana.

Aside from its *obiter dictum* status, this finding has sent a misleading signal to States that undertook or planned to commit unilateral conduct within disputed waters. First, the obligation 'not to jeopardize or hamper delimitation' under Article 83(3) was designed to oblige States to exercise caution and

141 Dispute Concerning Delimitation of the Maritime Boundary between Ghana and Côte d'Ivoire in the Atlantic Ocean, n 83, para.606.

142 *Ibid.*, para.633.

143 *Ibid.*, para.592.

restraint in the area yet to be delimited.[144] Exonerating activities having the jeopardizing or hampering effect, simply because the relevant area is ultimately attributed to a State undertaking such activities, would significantly impair the value of this obligation.[145] Second, by taking this obligation lightly, this finding might entail negative implications for States in a disputed area elsewhere since they saw less reason to exercise constraints on their unilateral conduct within contested waters.[146]

This finding is also inconsistent with the *Guyana v. Suriname* award.[147] In the provisional measures order, the Chamber did admit Ghana's ongoing oil exploitation conduct risked irreparable prejudice due to the significant and permanent modification of the physical characteristics of the contested area that could not be adequately compensated by financial reparations.[148] Hence, according to the review standard ('permanent physical change to the marine environment') established in *Guyana v. Suriname*, Ghana's ongoing oil exploitation conduct should amount to a breach of the obligation 'not to jeopardize or hamper delimitation'.

To conclude, *Ghana/Côte d'Ivoire* fails to clarify the interpretation of the obligation 'not to jeopardize or hamper delimitation' under Articles 74(3) and 83(3) of UNCLOS. Instead, it might cause more confusion by sending a misleading signal that if a relevant area is ultimately found to be attributed to a State, this finding could condone the unilateral conduct undertaken by that State.

4.4.3 *Application to the Spratly Islands Setting*

The drafting history of Articles 74(3) and 83(3) of UNCLOS clearly indicates that States did not intend to interrupt or suspend all economic activities in contested waters. The *Guyana v. Suriname* award articulates that the review standard for unilateral offshore hydrocarbon activities to be permissible within disputed zones is that such activities do not cause 'permanent physical change to the marine environment'. Though uncertainty remains as to the threshold required by this review standard, the *Guyana v. Suriname* award suggests that unilateral conduct that risks irreparable prejudice to another party's rights so

144 *Ibid.*, Separate opinion of Judge Paik (ITLOS), para.17.

145 *Ibid.*

146 *Ibid.*, paras.18-19.

147 B. Zhao, The Curious Case of Ghana/Côte d'Ivoire: A Consistent Approach to Hydrocarbon Activities in the Disputed Area?, *Asian Journal of International Law* (2019), 30.

148 Dispute Concerning Delimitation of the Maritime Boundary between Ghana and Côte d'Ivoire in the Atlantic Ocean, n 90, para.89.

as to trigger the indication of provisional measures undoubtedly falls into the scope of 'permanent physical change to the marine environment'.

Both *Guyana v. Suriname* and *Ghana/Côte d'Ivoire* admitted that extracting oil or gas reserves in contested waters, including exploitation and exploratory drilling, belongs to activities that would risk irreparable prejudice to another party's rights.[149] Scholars also endorse this position.[150] For example, Lagoni commented that any activity having the effect of causing an irreparable prejudice to the final delimitation agreement, such as the 'establishment of installations on or above the seabed' or the 'actual appropriation or other use of the natural resources', would undoubtedly violate the obligation under Articles 74(3) and 83(3).[151]

As to whether exploration activities with a less invasive effect such as seismic testing is permissible under international law, *Guyana v. Suriname* has provided limited clarification. The fact that the *Guyana v. Suriname* tribunal has carefully constructed its reasoning in the particular circumstances of that case seems to indicate that a different conclusion might have been reached if the circumstances were not the same.[152] In certain circumstances, less invasive activities undertaken in a unilateral manner could also cause severe tension between disputant States, thus harming the prospects of the delimitation agreement.[153] However, for the following two reasons, the author finds it difficult to agree with the position that unilateral hydrocarbon resources development activities, invasive or not, should be prohibited, merely because they cause or intensify the tension between the disputant States.[154]

First, as stated in the *South China Sea Arbitration* merits award, neither UNCLOS nor general international law has gone 'so far as to impose a legal duty on a State to refrain from generally aggravating their relations with one

149 Guyana v. Suriname, n 13, para.469. Dispute Concerning Delimitation of the Maritime Boundary between Ghana and Côte d'Ivoire in the Atlantic Ocean, n 90, para.89.

150 See *e.g.*, Lagoni, n 22, 366; van Logchem, n 14, 196.

151 Lagoni, n 22, 366.

152 Van Logchem, n 14, 196.

153 Dispute Concerning Delimitation of the Maritime Boundary between Ghana and Côte d'Ivoire in the Atlantic Ocean (Ghana/Côte d'Ivoire), Separate opinion of Judge Paik (ITLOS), para.7.

154 For a different position, see *e.g.*, K. Zou, Realizing Sustainability in the South China Sea, in K. Zou and S. Wu (eds.), *Non-Traditional Security Issues and the South China Sea: Shaping a New Framework for Cooperation* (Routledge. 2014). In Zou's view, '[f]or the multiple claimed part of the South China Sea, a best option for regional cooperation at present is to negotiate a scheme of moratorium in which each claimant will agree not to explore and exploit any mineral resource including oil and gas beyond its territorial sea for at least 50 years so as to realize sustainability in the South China Sea'.

another, however desirable it might be for States to do so'.[155] It follows that not all conduct causing or intensifying the tension between the disputant States would violate the principle of non-aggravation of a dispute. Moreover, as concluded in section 4.3.4, the principle of non-aggravation of a dispute is of little relevance to the interpretation and application of the obligation 'not to jeopardize or hamper delimitation', as the former only applies *after* the latter has been violated.

Second, this position entails that the same activities might be permissible if disputant States are in a harmonious relationship, which indeed requires unilateral conduct to receive no protest from other States concerned in order to be allowable under international law. Yet, obtaining assent or no protest from the other claimants can be an extremely difficult task. Consequently, there would be little chance for unilateral activities to be deemed lawful within contested marine areas, and thus, the above position is almost tantamount to a moratorium against all economic activities within the contested areas. This result would contradict what is indicated in the drafting history of Articles 74(3) and 83(3) of UNCLOS and confirmed in the *Guyana v. Suriname* award: UNCLOS does not aim to exclude all economic activities within contested areas preceding delimitation. Rather, the review standard for the obligation 'not to jeopardize or hamper delimitation' under Articles 74(3) and 83(3) must reflect a delicate balance between ensuring a party's ability to pursue economic development and preventing irreparable harm to another party's rights.

Thus, for the above reasons, some less invasive activities including seismic surveys, to the extent of not causing irreversible harm to the marine environment, must generally be allowed within contested marine areas. Nevertheless, the unilateral taking of seismic surveys, if causing or intensifying the tension between the disputant States, would risk disrupting the peaceful order that is hard to achieve in disputed marine areas. Hence, to reduce and even eliminate this risk, it is suggested that unilateral seismic surveys are permissible under international law provided that the information in relation to marine natural resources collected through such activities is shared with other disputant States.[156] Albeit not explicitly required by UNCLOS or other treaties, the

155 The South China Sea Arbitration, n 49, para.1174.

156 To avoid a breach of the obligation to negotiate in good faith, one procedural guideline proposed in the *Guyana v. Suriname* award is to offer to share the results obtained from unilateral activities at issue. See Guyana v. Suriname, n 13, paras.476-477. Moreover, a precedent supporting this idea is the tripartite Joint Marine Seismic Undertaking entered into by the oil companies of China, the Philippines and Vietnam in 2005. The parties signed this tripartite agreement because they wanted to undertake joint surveys on hydrocarbon resources in a vast area of the South China Sea. The information collected

information-sharing requirement is not excessive, because the environment of the disputed marine areas concerned can be viewed as 'commons' in the sense that it is not subject to the exclusive jurisdiction of any claimant States, but instead, is used by all claimant States and their nationals.[157]

Tailored to the Spratly Islands setting, it can be concluded that exploitation and exploratory drilling of hydrocarbon resources should not be allowed in this region according to the review standard as articulated in *Guyana v. Suriname*. So far, there has not been any reported drilling in this region. The disputant States must refrain from licensing or operating exploitation and exploratory drilling activities unilaterally, especially in view of the fragile and precious marine environment in the region. Nevertheless, to the extent of not causing irreversible harm to marine life, seismic surveys unilaterally conducted by the disputant States are permissible, provided that the information related to marine natural resources collected through such activities is communicated to other disputant States. Another relevant issue is that some disputant States have declared or issued oil lease blocks over part of the contested waters in the Spratly Islands. According to the above review standard, it is arguable that the mere issuance or declaration of oil blocks without further action is unlikely to directly cause a permanent physical change to the marine environment and thus are permissible under international law.[158] This conclusion is also an inevitable result if seismic surveys are deemed lawful within contested waters, as in regular practice, States would need to designate oil lease blocks and grant concessions before seismic surveys can actually take place.

---

through surveys were shared among all three parties. For more detailed discussions, see chapter 5, section 5.3.1.2.

157 N. Schrijver, *Development Without Destruction: The UN and Global Resource Management* (Indiana University Press. 2010), 6.

158 The unilateral issuance of oil blocks respecting the Spratly Islands area must be differentiated from the unilateral promulgation of legislation pertaining to the South China Sea as addressed in *South China Sea Arbitration*. In that case, the Philippines claimed that China's extension of its fisheries jurisdiction in the South China Sea by promulgating the 2012 moratorium on fishing constituted a violation of the Philippines' sovereign rights in the EEZ under Article 56 of UNCLOS. The tribunal upheld this claim on the ground that the 2012 moratorium was 'without exception for areas of the South China Sea falling within the [EEZ] of the Philippines and without limiting the moratorium to Chinese flagged vessels'. Put differently, the tribunal deemed China's alleged promulgation of unlawful because this legislation covered non-Chinese flagged vessels in respect of undisputed areas falling within the EEZ of the Philippines. Therefore, to the extent that the issuance of oil lease blocks relates to the disputed marine area, such issuance is permissible. See The South China Sea Arbitration, n 49, paras.709, 712, 716 and 1203(B)(7).

4.5 The Permissible Scope for Unilateral Fisheries-Related Conduct

The absence of adequate management on fishery resources tends to attract more fishers and therefore, sooner or later, causes depletion or overfishing in disputed waters, because unlike hydrocarbon resources, the exploitation of fishery resources does not require sizable investments or advanced technologies.[159] This is the current situation in the Spratly Islands area. Under the influence of alternating monsoons, this area is a rich fishing ground with the cohabitation of various species.[160] Fishery vessels from all the disputant States have been fishing here.[161] The Food and Agriculture Organization of the United Nations (FAO) stock assessments report indicates that some species, notably dermal and surimi species, are depleted or overfished in this region.[162] Hence, clarifying the scope of fishing that can be unilaterally permitted, licensed or authorized by the disputant States is of critical importance to the sustainable utilisation and conservation of the fishery resources in the Spratly Islands area.

Given that international courts and tribunals have not yet been requested to determine the compatibility of unilateral fisheries-related conduct with Articles 74(3) and 83(3) of UNCLOS, this section adopts three approaches for analytical purposes. First, after discussing two key characteristics of fishery resources (subsection 4.5.1), this section resorts to Part XII of UNCLOS in relation to environmental protection to inform the legal constraints applicable to unilateral fishing within the disputed marine areas of the Spratly Islands area (subsection 4.5.2). Second, it explores the *mutatis mutandis* application of the review standard, which has been developed in the specific context of unilateral hydrocarbon activities through *Aegean Sea Continental Shelf* and *Guyana v. Suriname*, to unilateral fisheries-related conduct (subsection 4.5.3). Third, this section relies on two international cases, namely *Icelandic Fisheries Jurisdiction* and *Southern Bluefin Tuna*, which concern the permissible scope for unilateral fishing pending the final settlement of a dispute, to provide useful guidance (subsection 4.5.4).

---

159 R.R. Churchill, Fisheries Issues in Maritime Boundary Delimitation, 17 *Marine Policy* (1993), 45.

160 FAO Asia-Pacific Fishery Commission, *Regional Overview of Fisheries and Aquaculture in Asia and the Pacific* (2012), RAP Publication 2012/26.

161 A. Greer, The South China Sea Is Really a Fishery Dispute (20 July 2016), available at <https://thediplomat.com/2016/07/the-south-china-sea-is-really-a-fishery-dispute/>. For example, China issues a 'Nansha Certificate of Fishing Permit' to its nationals for fishing in the Spratly Islands area. See The South China Sea Arbitration, n 49, para.747.

162 FAO Asia-Pacific Fishery Commission, n 160.

Moreover, considering that a majority of the fisheries activities carried out in the Spratly Islands area is likely to be of a traditional or artisanal nature, this section also analyses the permissible scope for unilateral traditional or artisanal fishing across the Spratly Islands area (subsection 4.5.5). The last part of this section explores the implications of the above analysis for the unilateral fisheries-related conduct in the Spratly Islands setting (subsection 4.5.6).

4.5.1 *'Renewable' and 'Exhaustible' Characteristics*

Fishery resources, which provide an increasingly important source of protein for humankind, are normally renewable in terms of their ability to recover.[163] International law tends to be more tolerant towards unilateral fishing than unilateral oil-related activities in contested areas. It is widely accepted that States assume no obligation under customary international law to prevent its nationals from fishing in contested marine areas in normal circumstances.[164] This conclusion is exemplified by *Ghana/Côte d'Ivoire* where both parties did not protest against each other's fisheries-related conduct within the contested waters in the absence of any agreed fishery arrangement.[165]

However, it does not necessarily entail that there should be no constraints upon unilateral fishing activities within contested waters since 'renewable' natural resources can also be 'exhaustible'.[166] As stated by the WTO appellate body in *US-Import Prohibition of Certain Shrimp and Shrimp Products*, 'renewable' and 'exhaustible' natural resources are not mutually exclusive, as one lesson learned from modern biological sciences is that 'living species, though in principle, capable of reproduction and, in that sense, "renewable", are in certain circumstances indeed susceptible of depletion, exhaustion and extinction, frequently because of human activities'.[167]

4.5.2 *Part XII of UNCLOS in Relation to Environmental Protection*

Part XII of UNCLOS prescribes substantive provisions applicable to the marine environment in all areas, irrespective of whether these areas are disputed or not.[168] With respect to the utilization and conservation of fishery resources, Articles 192-194 are of particular relevance.

163 Tanaka, n 62, 281.
164 Churchill, n 159, 51.
165 Dispute Concerning Delimitation of the Maritime Boundary between Ghana and Côte d'Ivoire in the Atlantic Ocean, n 83, para.197.
166 Schrijver, n 157, 2–3.
167 US-Import Prohibition of Certain Shrimp and Shrimp Products, WT/DS58/AB/R, Appellate Body Report of 12 October 1998 (WTO), para.128.
168 UNCLOS, Part XII. The South China Sea Arbitration, n 49, para.940.

Article 192 provides that States have a general obligation to protect and preserve the marine environment.[169] This general obligation comprises 'protection' of the marine environment from future damage and 'preservation' in terms of maintaining or improving its present condition.[170] The content of the general obligation in Article 192 with respect to fishing is further detailed in Articles 193 and 194(5). Article 193 stipulates that States are required to comply with their duty to protect and preserve the marine environment when exercising their sovereign rights to exploit marine natural resources.[171] Article 194(5) sets forth that the measures taken by States to prevent, reduce and control pollution of the marine environment shall include those 'necessary to protect and preserve rare or fragile ecosystems as well as the habitat of depleted, threatened or endangered species and other forms of marine life'.[172]

As informed by Articles 193 and 194(5), Article 192 of UNCLOS can be interpreted as entailing a due diligence obligation to protect and preserve depleted, threatened or endangered species. The *South China Sea Arbitration* merits award has clarified the material content of this due diligence obligation as including two aspects: first, this obligation prevents the *direct* harvest of depleted, threatened or endangered species; and second, this obligation also extends to prevention of harms that would affect depleted, threatened, or endangered species *indirectly* through the destruction of their habitat.[173] Accordingly, any disputant State engaging in the direct exploitation of depleted, threatened or endangered species or any activities that may indirectly destroy the habitats of such species would undoubtedly fall short of its obligation under Article 192 of UNCLOS, and thus amount to a breach of the obligation 'not to jeopardize or hamper delimitation' under Articles 74(3) and 83(3) of UNCLOS.[174]

---

169 UNCLOS, Article 192.

170 The South China Sea Arbitration, n 49, para.941.

171 UNCLOS, Article 193.

172 UNCLOS, Article 194(5).

173 The South China Sea Arbitration, n 49, para.959.

174 This obligation is also consistent with Article 61(2) of UNCLOS, which provides that a coastal State shall consider the best scientific evidence available to it and take proper conservation and management measures to ensure that the fishery resources within its EEZ are not endangered by over-exploitation. Arguably, this provision should equally apply to the marine area over which a State claims to be its EEZ. Accordingly, once the best scientific evidence shows that relevant fish species within the Spratly Islands area are endangered by over-exploitation, disputant States are obliged to take proper conservation and management measures, including preventing their nationals from exploiting these endangered species. See UNCLOS, Article 61(2).

4.5.3 *Mutatis Mutandis Application of the Review Standard*

In addition to the environmental protection obligations as outlined in Part XII of UNCLOS, one might wonder whether the 'permanent physical change to the marine environment' review standard developed in the specific context of unilateral hydrocarbon activities could be transposed to evaluate the lawfulness of unilateral fisheries-related conduct. Some scholars have doubts, arguing that the *mutatis mutandis* application of this review standard to fisheries-related conduct might run into difficulties, because, in their view, fishing usually would not cause permanent physical change to the marine environment, and thus, this review standard would basically deem all fisheries activities to be permissible in a disputed marine area.[175]

However, similar to hydrocarbon resources development activities, certain harmful fishing practices could cause permanent physical change and irreparable damage to the marine environment, such as degrading habitats of important species and destroying the structure of seabed and subsoils by using explosives. The *mutatis mutandis* application of this review standard would deem such harmful fishing practices impermissible under international law. This application is also consistent with the *South China Sea Arbitration* merits award. In that case, the tribunal considered that Chinese fishing vessels' widespread harvesting of giant clams through the use of boat propellers to break through the coral substrate in search of buried clam shells caused irreparable harm to the coral reef habitat.[176] Consequently, the tribunal concluded that the Chinese government's failure to prevent such harmful fishing practices violated its obligation under Article 192 of UNCLOS in relation to the protection and preservation of the marine environment.[177]

4.5.4 *Relevant International Jurisprudence*

The 'permanent physical change to the marine environment' review standard requires a prohibition of harmful fishing practices but does not constrain non-harmful fishing practices. Yet, it is common sense that the harvest or catch as a result of non-harmful fishing activities cannot be limitless, in order to avoid the exhaustion of relevant resources. Thus, a further question is what is the permissible scope for non-harmful fishing activities. *Icelandic Fisheries Jurisdiction* and *Southern Bluefin Tuna*, which concern the permissible scope

175 T.N. Dang, Fisheries Co-operation in the South China Sea and the (Ir)relevance of the Sovereignty Question, 2 *Asian Journal of International Law* (2012), 71. van Logchem, n 22, 315.

176 The South China Sea Arbitration, n 49, paras.953, 958, 1178.

177 *Ibid.*, paras.965-966. UNCLOS, Article 192.

for unilateral fishing pending the final settlement of a dispute, might provide some useful guidance.

4.5.4.1 Icelandic Fisheries Jurisdiction Cases

In the *Icelandic Fisheries Jurisdiction* cases, which occurred in the pre-UNCLOS III period, the UK and Federal Republic of Germany instituted proceedings against Iceland concerning a dispute over the proposed extension by Iceland of the limits of its exclusive fisheries jurisdiction from a distance of 12 M to a distance of 50 M. In the provisional measures proceedings, both applicants claimed that the fishing vessels under their registration should be allowed to fish pending the final judgment in the marine areas where Iceland alleged to apply the contemplated exclusion measures.[178]

The ICJ upheld the applicants' claim and decided that the UK and Federal Republic of Germany should ensure that vessels under their registration did not take an annual catch of more than 170,000 and 119,000 metric tons, respectively, of fish from the marine area discussed in this case.[179] These figures were calculated on the basis of the available statistical information for the five years (1967–1971) immediately before initiating the proceedings of provisional measures. The ICJ considered that these figures could reflect the *status quo* concerning fisheries of different species in the marine area of discussion.[180] This finding is perhaps unsurprising, as 'international law is biased towards preserving the status quo' to pursue stability unless otherwise provided.[181]

4.5.4.2 Southern Bluefin Tuna

In *Southern Bluefin Tuna*, Australia and New Zealand jointly instituted proceedings against Japan concerning the conservation of the population of Southern Bluefin Tuna (SBT). The applicants claimed that the SBT species was significantly overfished and below commonly accepted thresholds for biologically

---

178 Fisheries Jurisdiction (United Kingdom of Great Britain and Northern Ireland v. Iceland), Order of 17 August 1972, Provisional Measures (ICJ), para.1. Fisheries Jurisdiction (Federal Republic of Germany v. Iceland) – Provisional Measures, Order of 17 August 1972 (ICJ), para.1.

179 Fisheries Jurisdiction (United Kingdom of Great Britain and Northern Ireland v. Iceland), n 178, dispositif, para.(1)(e). Fisheries Jurisdiction (Federal Republic of Germany v. Iceland), n 178, dispositif, para.(1)(e).

180 Fisheries Jurisdiction (United Kingdom of Great Britain and Northern Ireland v. Iceland), n 178, para.26. Fisheries Jurisdiction (Federal Republic of Germany v. Iceland), n 178, para.27.

181 R. Hanania, Norms Governing the Interstate Use of Force: Explaining the Statu Quo Bias of International Law, 27(2) *Emory International Law Review* (2013), 861.

safe parental biomass, and that Japan failed to comply with its obligation to cooperate in the conservation of this stock.[182] In the provisional measures proceedings, the applicants requested the ITLOS to order provisional measures that Japan should immediately cease unilateral experimental fishing for SBT pending the final settlement of this dispute.[183]

The ITLOS did not uphold the applicants' request on the ground that scientific uncertainty existed regarding measures to be taken to conserve the stock of SBT, and that there was no agreement among the parties as to whether the conservation measures taken so far had led to the improvement in the stock of SBT.[184] Instead, the ITLOS decided that Japan could continue to conduct unilateral fishing for SBT pending the final settlement of this dispute, provided that its catches did not exceed the *annual national allocation* at the level last set for Japan.[185]

4.5.4.3 Summary

The preceding two cases indicate that unilateral fisheries-related conduct is, in general, permissible pending the final settlement of a dispute. Yet, there are some constraints. In the presence of agreed national allocations, the amount of catch by each State should not exceed such *agreed national allocations*. In the absence of any agreement, the amount of catch should not exceed the *current annual catch*. Although the disputes over the Spratly Islands area are not submitted for adjudication, it would be reasonable to argue that the above conclusions based on the analysis of *Icelandic Fisheries Jurisdiction* and *Southern Bluefin Tuna*, concerning the permissible scope for unilateral fishing pending the final settlement of the dispute, could apply equally to the disputed marine areas in the Spratly Islands area.

4.5.5 *Traditional or Artisanal Fishing*

A total of over 1.77 million vessels fish in the South China Sea, with 86 per cent of such vessels being small-scale vessels (1.5 million).[186] It is difficult to have an accurate estimation of the employment in small-scale fisheries and large-scale or more commercial type fisheries.[187] However, considering that small-scale

182 Southern Bluefin Tuna Cases (New Zealand v. Japan; Australia v. Japan), Order of 27 August 1999, Provisional Measures (ITLOS), paras.28-29.
183 *Ibid.*, paras.31-32.
184 *Ibid.*, para.79.
185 *Ibid.*, paras.81, 90(1)(c).
186 FAO Asia-Pacific Fishery Commission, n 160.
187 *Ibid.*, 27.

fisheries provide direct employment for over twice the workforce on average compared with commercial fisheries for the same fish catch,[188] the majority of vessels being small-scale vessels indicates that small-scale fisheries rather than commercial fisheries are a more significant form of employment in the South China Sea including the Spratly Islands area. A majority of the fishing activities carried out in the Spratly Islands area is also likely to be of a traditional or artisanal nature. Therefore, it is important to clarify the permissible scope for unilateral traditional or artisanal fishing activities under international law in the Spratly Islands setting. Two cases, namely *South China Sea Arbitration* and *Eritrea/Yemen*, might provide useful guidance, as they have addressed the lawfulness of traditional or artisanal fishing within maritime zones of a State's sovereignty or sovereign rights.

4.5.5.1 Main Characteristics

Traditional fishing is also referred to as artisanal fishing.[189] Despite the lack of a universally accepted definition of artisanal fishing,[190] one of its most distinguishing characteristics is that artisanal fishing, as opposed to industrial fishing, is simple and carried out on a small scale, 'using fishing methods that largely approximate those that have historically been used in the region'.[191] This characteristic does not mean that artisanal fishing practices cannot gradually change with the advent of technology. Indeed, as stated in *Eritrea/Yemen*, artisanal fishing does not exclude 'improvements in powering the small boats, in the techniques of navigation, communication or in the techniques of fishing'.[192] However, there are two constraints. First, the improvements do not transform the fishing regime into large-scale commercial or industrial fishing.[193] Second, the fishing methods broadly follow the manner of fishing that has been carried out for generations and reflecting the traditions and customs of the region.[194]

Another main characteristic of artisanal fishing is that these rights are private rights enjoyed by relevant fishers but not held by sovereign States. As Tanaka commented, traditional fishing rights are different from historic rights

188 FAO, *Securing Sustainable Small-scale Fisheries: Sharing Good Practices from around the World* (2019), FAO Fisheries and Aquaculture Technical Paper 644, 10.

189 Second Stage of the Proceedings between Eritrea/Yemen (Maritime Delimitation), Decision of 17 December 1999, para.105.

190 The South China Sea Arbitration, n 49, para.797.

191 *Ibid.*

192 Second Stage of the Proceedings between Eritrea/Yemen, n 189, para.106.

193 *Ibid.*

194 The South China Sea Arbitration, n 49, para.806.

or titles of States.[195] As stated in the *South China Sea Arbitration* merits award, the legal basis for protecting artisanal fishing stems from 'the notion of vested rights and the understanding that, having pursued a livelihood through artisanal fishing over an extended period, generations of fishermen have acquired a right, akin to property, in the ability to continue to fish in the manner of their forebears'.[196] This characteristic indicates that the nationality of relevant fishers is not a decisive factor in determining whether they could enjoy traditional fishing rights. Instead, what matters is whether relevant fishers have practised artisanal fishing for such a long time that traditional livelihoods and cultural patterns have been formed.[197] Hence, fishers entitled to traditional fishing rights in a contested area could come from a disputant State or a third State.

4.5.5.2 Relevant International Jurisprudence

In *South China Sea Arbitration*, the Philippines submitted that China had unlawfully prevented Philippine fishers from pursuing their livelihoods by interfering with traditional fishing activities within the territorial sea of Scarborough Shoal.[198] To address this submission, the tribunal concluded that UNCLOS accorded varying treatment to traditional fishing rights across maritime zones: (1) in archipelagic waters, traditional fishing rights were expressly protected by Article 51(1); (2) in territorial seas, traditional fishing rights remain protected by international law; and (3) in EEZ s, traditional fishing rights were extinguished except that these rights constitute a factor to be taken into account by the coastal State in giving access to any surplus in the allowable catch under Article 62(3).[199]

In *Eritrea/Yemen*, both parties claimed traditional fishing rights in the Red Sea and requested the tribunal to clarify the extent of their rights.[200] The tribunal concluded that traditional fishing rights could continue to apply not only in territorial seas but also in EEZ s.[201] While the reasoning of the tribunal on this matter appears to be succinct, the tribunal considered that the traditional fishing regime had 'existed for the benefit of the fishermen of both countries throughout the region', which 'by its very nature … [was] not qualified by the maritime zones specified under [UNCLOS]'.[202]

195 Tanaka, n 97, 160.
196 The South China Sea Arbitration, n 49, para.798.
197 *Ibid.*, para.794.
198 *Ibid.*, para.758.
199 *Ibid.*, para.804.
200 Second Stage of the Proceedings between Eritrea/Yemen, n 189, paras.87-88.
201 *Ibid.*, para.109.
202 *Ibid.*

The decisions of these two cases apparently contradict each other.[203] The *South China Sea Arbitration* tribunal recognized the divergence between its decision and that made by the *Eritrea/Yemen* tribunal but attributed such divergence to the difference in the applicable law with which the two tribunals were obliged to comply.[204] Being an arbitral tribunal established under Annex VII to UNCLOS, the *South China Sea Arbitration* tribunal could only apply UNCLOS and rules of law not incompatible therewith according to Article 293(1). By contrast, the proceedings of *Eritrea/Yemen* were initiated based on a special agreement between the parties, which prescribed a broad scope of applicable law including 'the opinion that it will have formed on questions of territorial sovereignty, the United Nations Convention on the Law of the Sea, and any other pertinent factor'.[205] Thus, in the *South China Sea Arbitration* tribunal's view, the arbitral tribunal in *Eritrea/Yemen* was empowered to and did go beyond the law on traditional fishing as it would exist under UNCLOS.[206]

However, the above explanation given by *South China Sea Arbitration* tribunal is somewhat problematic. This explanation is based on two premises: first, traditional fishing rights are incompatible with the UNCLOS provisions relating to the EEZ regime, and thus do not fall inside Article 293(1) of UNCLOS, which provides for the scope of international law that a court or tribunal having jurisdiction under UNCLOS shall apply; and second, judicial proceedings established outside Annex VII of UNCLOS or non-judicial proceedings are not necessarily bound by Article 293(1) of UNCLOS on the scope of applicable law. Following this rationale, if the same case is addressed by another court or tribunal such as the one formed in *Eritrea/Yemen*, then traditional fishing rights could be applicable law, and thus traditional fishing practices might be regarded as permissible in EEZ s. A major downside of this rationale is that the outcome of a particular dispute becomes unpredictable and highly dependent on which dispute settlement proceeding has been selected. Besides, the reasoning of the *South China Sea Arbitration* tribunal also neglects the references to general international law which UNCLOS itself mentions, for example, in the preamble.[207]

---

203 E.L. Enyew, The South China Sea Award and the Treatment of Traditional Fishing Rights within the Territorial Sea, *JCLOS Blog* (10 August 2016).

204 The South China Sea Arbitration, n 49, paras.259 and 803.

205 Second Stage of the Proceedings between Eritrea/Yemen, n 189, Annex I – The Arbitration Agreement, Article 2(3).

206 The South China Sea Arbitration, n 49, para.259.

207 UNCLOS, preamble (providing that 'matters not regulated by this Convention continue to be governed by the rules and principles of general international law').

To better understand the issue at hand, it may be helpful to have a close look at why the *South China Sea Arbitration* tribunal has concluded that traditional fishing rights in EEZs were incompatible with UNCLOS. The tribunal noted that Article 62(3) stipulated that in giving access to other States to the surplus of the allowable catch in the EEZ, the coastal State should take account of 'the need to minimize economic dislocation in States whose nationals have habitually fished in the zone'.[208] The tribunal considered that 'the inclusion of this provision – which would be entirely unnecessary if traditional fishing rights were preserved in the exclusive economic zone – confirms that the drafters of the Convention did not intend to preserve such rights'.[209] Tanaka commented that the tribunal's approach minimized the role of historical element in the law of the sea and might be 'an option well worth considering to avoid any controversy with regard to historical evidence'.[210]

However, this interpretation is not necessarily the only and most 'eligible interpretation' inferred from the text of Article 62(3).[211] Even if traditional fishing rights are not extinguished by the UNCLOS provisions relating to the EEZ, it is still necessary and reasonable to request the coastal State to pay due regard and not to abuse its rights of allocating surplus to hamper traditional fishing rights. For example, if the surplus in the EEZ is 1,000 tons, and the amount of fish harvested by fishers who have habitually fished in the zone is 500 tons, then as a possible interpretation of this provision, the coastal State is obliged to take the 500 tons fished by these habitual fishers into account before allocating fishing quota to other States in the subregion or region. Instead, the interpretation of Article 62(3) as proposed by *South China Sea Arbitration* might be somewhat problematic.

First, as mentioned earlier, the tribunal in *South China Sea Arbitration* considered that traditional fishing rights remained unaffected in areas of archipelagic waters and territorial seas.[212] It is important to note that a coastal State enjoys territorial sovereignty over these two types of areas, which are much stronger and more extensive than sovereign rights that a State enjoys over the EEZ. Thus, if it can be accepted that traditional fishing rights can perpetuate

208 The South China Sea Arbitration, n 49, para.804.

209 *Ibid.*

210 Tanaka, n 97, 71–72.

211 For more information about the theory of 'eligible interpretation', see: R. Dworkin, *Law's Empire* (Harvard University Press. 1986), 225–275; A. Roberts, Traditional and Modern Approaches to Customary International Law: A Reconciliation, 95(4) *AJIL* (2001), 774–784.

212 The South China Sea Arbitration, n 49, para.804.

these stronger rights, *a priori*, it might be reasonable to expect that these traditional fishing rights could also survive the introduction of the EEZ regime.

Second, as the tribunal persistently underlined in *South China Sea Arbitration*, '[t]he attention paid to traditional fishing rights in international law stems from the recognition that traditional livelihoods and cultural patterns are fragile in the face of development and modern ideas of interstate relations and warrant particular protection'.[213] Considering that the fragility of traditional or artisanal fishing does not change across different maritime zones, it is reasonable to expect that protection of traditional or artisanal fishing should be warranted not only in the context of archipelagic waters and territorial seas but also in EEZ s, especially when considering that in reality, many fish stocks easily migrate across these different maritime zones.

Third, as pointed out by the tribunal, 'the vast majority of traditional fishing takes place in close proximity to the coast'.[214] It means that few traditional fishing activities occur in the EEZ. Thus, it is likely that the coexistence of traditional fishing rights would not cause an overwhelming impact on the EEZ regime. Hence, the tribunal's reasoning is somewhat unconvincing that UNCLOS drafters would intend to terminate these almost harmless traditional or artisanal fishing rights in order to protect the newly introduced regime of the EEZ that has apparently not been at risk.

Fourth, during the negotiations at UNCLOS III, 'maritime powers' or 'distant water fishing nations', such as Japan, the US and the USSR, were concerned that the introduction of the EEZ regime would cause them to lose their traditional freedom of fishing in these waters.[215] To tackle the potential conflicts between the EEZ regime and the traditional fishing freedom, the 'Working Paper of the Second Committee: Main Trends', adopted in the 1974 Caracas session, proposed in its Provision 103 that for ensuring full utilization of renewable resources within the EEZ, the coastal State shall permit nationals of other States to fish for a portion of the allowable catch of the renewable resources not fully utilized by its nationals, with priorities given to 'States that have normally fished for a resource'.[216] To elaborate on the modalities of granting such priorities, the Provision 104 of this working paper further proposed three *alternative* formulas, namely formulas A, B and C.[217] The formulas A and B recognize

213 *Ibid.*, para.794.

214 *Ibid.*, para.804.

215 Tanaka, n 62, 150.

216 UN Doc.: A/CONF.62/L.8/Rev.1, Working Paper of the Second Committee: Main Trends (17 October 1974), UNCLOS III, Official Records, Vol. 3, 123, Provision 103, Formula C.

217 *Ibid.*, 123, Provision 104.

the fishing rights of the non-coastal State based on 'long and mutually recognized usage', which might not be limited to the small-scale traditional or artisanal fishing. In comparison, the formula C differentiates 'traditional subsistence fishing' from fishing 'on a substantial scale'. Paragraph 1 of the formula C obliges the coastal State to take account of 'traditional subsistence fishing', which approximates the traditional or artisanal fishing discussed here, when adopting measures respecting the EEZ. Paragraph 2, by contrast, provides for a phase-out regime for fishing 'on a substantial scale' for a period of no less than ten years. Therefore, a plain reading of the formula C suggests that 'traditional subsistence fishing' *not* 'on a substantial scale' shall remain protected within the EEZ. The commonality shared by these three formulas is that a coastal State shall respect, at least, traditional subsistence fishing in the EEZ.

Subsequently, while Provision 103 was incorporated into the Informal Single Negotiating Text (ISNT) in the 1975 Geneva session and subsequently the final provision of UNCLOS, Provision 104 was left unconsidered.[218] Some scholars opined that this indicated that UNCLOS drafters intended to exclude 'the granting of transitional and phase-out arrangements to fishermen from other states'.[219] However, one has to bear in mind that UNCLOS was a package deal and that the language used in its provisions might be deliberately left with ambiguity and flexibility so as to produce a compromise that could be acceptable to as many States as possible.[220] Therefore, it might be improper to simply interpret the neglect of Provision 104 as a negation or denial. Arguably, to the extent that the small-scale traditional or artisanal fishing is concerned and that a surplus of the allowable catch exists, the coastal State shall respect the traditional fishing rights that exist within the EEZ.

Based on the foregoing reasons, the regime of traditional or artisanal fishing rights should coexist with the EEZ regime introduced by UNCLOS. Accordingly, traditional or artisanal fishing is permissible across different types of maritime zones, including areas of archipelagic waters, the territorial sea and EEZ. Admittedly, the resultant coexistence of a coastal State's resource rights over

---

218 J.R. Stevenson and B.H. Oxman, The Third United Nations Conference on the Law of the Sea: The 1974 Caracas Session, 69(1) *AJIL* (1975), 15–18. J.R. Stevenson and B.H. Oxman, The Third United Nations Conference on the Law of the Sea: The 1975 Geneva Session, 69(4) *AJIL* (1975), 774–781.

219 H. Tseng and C. Ou, The Evolution and Trend of the Traditional Fishing Rights, 53(5–6) *OCM* (2010), 274. L. Bernard, The Effect of Historic Fishing Rights in Maritime Boundaries Delimitation, *Proceedings from the 2012 LOSI-KIOST Conference on Securing the Ocean for the Next Generation*, 7–9.

220 B. Buzan, Negotiating by Consensus: Developments in Technique at the United Nations Conference on the Law of the Sea, 75(2) *AJIL* (1981), 324.

the EEZ and traditional fishing rights enjoyed by the nationals of another State might have a trade-off. That is, the coexistence might lead to conflicts and thus, to some extent, is unconducive to the peaceful development of the area concerned. However, the benefit from supporting traditional or artisanal fishing rights, which warrants legal protection to artisanal fishers who are usually poor and among the most vulnerable and whose livelihoods highly depend on fisheries,[221] outweighs the trade-off.

4.5.6 *Application to the Spratly Islands Setting*

Tailored to the Spratly Islands setting, the preceding analysis entails three *cumulative* legal parameters that unilateral fisheries-related conduct taken therein needs to fulfil in order to be permissible under international law.

First, a general constraint as entailed from Article 192 of UNCLOS requires the disputant States not to engage in direct exploitation of depleted, threatened or endangered species or any activities that may indirectly destroy the habitats of such species.

Second, as a result of the *mutatis mutandis* application of the review standard developed in *Guyana v. Suriname*, harmful fishing practices that could cause permanent physical change and irreparable damage to the marine environment, such as degrading habitats of important species and destroying the structure of seabed and subsoils by using explosives, should be prohibited within the Spratly Islands area.

Third, for other fishing activities that do not involve harmful practices, international jurisprudence suggests that they are generally permissible in disputed marine areas. Yet, the amount of harvest should not exceed agreed national allocations, or in the absence of such agreement, the current annual catch. In the specific context of the Spratly Islands area, since the disputant States have not reached any agreement on national allocations of fishing quota respecting this region, the amount of catch by the nationals of each disputant State should not exceed the current annual catch, unless the scientific evidence suggests otherwise.

When it comes to traditional or artisanal fishing activities, they are permissible across different types of maritime zones, including areas of archipelagic waters, the territorial sea and EEZ. Consequently, traditional or artisanal fishing practices, if any, are permissible across different types of maritime zones within the Spratly Islands area.[222] Nevertheless, such rights are not

221 FAO, *A Fishery Manager's Guidebook* (2009), 82.

222 On the one hand, in theory, the right of traditional fishing at issue would not be extinguished regardless of which State would finally enjoy sovereign rights over the areas concerned. Requesting fishermen to suspend their artisanal fishing practices pending

impervious to regulation. The above three *cumulative* legal constraints applicable to fishing in general apply with equal force to traditional or artisanal fishing.[223]

4.6 The Permissible Scope for Unilateral Law Enforcement Measures

It is common in practice that a disputant State takes law enforcement measures within contested marine areas, especially to fight against the resource-related activities conducted or authorized unilaterally by another disputant State. This section aims to clarify the permissible scope for unilateral law enforcement measures under international law in the Spratly Islands setting. Unlike resource-related activities that might cause a physical change to the marine environment, law enforcement measures normally do not have that effect. Thus, the 'permanent physical change to the marine environment' review standard cannot apply to assess the lawfulness of unilateral enforcement action. Rather, two elements are relevant to the analytical purpose. First, since most law enforcement incidents, as described in section 4.6.1, involve the use of forcible action against merchant vessels, a question that presents itself is whether such forcible acts violate the principle of the prohibition of the threat or use of force under Article 2(4) of the UN Charter. Second, the principles applicable to law enforcement measures in general – such as principles of reasonableness, necessity, and proportionality – might also provide some useful guidance for determining the permissible scope for unilateral enforcement action within disputed marine areas.

the resolution of the dispute would create a risk of injuring their rights. On the other hand, international jurisprudence has long recognised that in the absence of an explicit agreement to the contrary, the change or development of sovereignty should refrain from modifying private rights as much as possible. Following this established practice, before the legal status of the marine areas in dispute is figured out, the right of traditional fishing, being a private right enjoyed by fishermen, remains protected. See Award between the United States and the United Kingdom relating to the Rights of Jurisdiction of United States in the Bering's Sea and the Preservation of Fur Seals Decision of 15 August 1893, 271. German Settlers in Poland, Advisory Opinion of 10 September 1923, PCIJ Series B No. 6, 36. Award in the Arbitration regarding the Delimitation of the Abyei Area between the Government of Sudan and the Sudan People's Liberation Movement/Army, Award of 22 June 2009, para.766. The South China Sea Arbitration, n 49, para.799.

223 *Ibid.*, para.809. Second Stage of the Proceedings between Eritrea/Yemen, n 189, para.108.

4.6.1 *Presenting the Stakes in the Spratly Islands Area*

Unilateral uses of law enforcement measures by a disputant State to disturb the activities carried out by private vessels flying the flag of another disputant State have been sources of conflicts in the Spratly Islands area.[224] Most law enforcement measures that have occurred in this region are aimed at suspending the fishing or seismic survey activities undertaken by a vessel registered with another disputant State. For example, on 3 July 2019, four Vietnamese coastguard vessels pursued a Chinese survey ship – *Haiyang Dizhi 8* – which was escorted by two Chinese coastguard vessels when entering waters near a Vietnamese-controlled reef (Vanguard Bank) in the Spratly Islands to conduct seismic survey operation.[225] Similarly, on 25 February 2011, a Chinese naval vessel – *Dongguan 560* – instructed Philippine fishing vessels to leave the area around Jackson Atoll in the Spratly Islands.[226] The Philippine side claimed that the Chinese naval vessel fired shots at the Philippine fishing vessels.[227] On 2 March 2011, a Philippine research vessel – *M/V Venture* – was conducting a seismic survey in the waters near Reed Bank in the Spratly Islands.[228] Philippine officials claimed that two Chinese patrol boats – *CMS 71* and *CMS 75* – threatened to ram the *M/V Venture*. The Philippine navy dispatched three vessels to assist the *M/V Venture*, and in the end, the Chinese patrol vessels left the area.[229]

Occasionally, a disputant State might use law enforcement measures to prevent fishing vessels of another disputant State from entering the disputed marine area, but for purposes other than suspending their fishing activities. For instance, on 28 February 2016, it was reported that the China Coast Guard chased Philippine fishers away from Jackson Atoll in the Spratly Islands and

224 As rightly pointed out by Sicun Wu, 'the claimant states continue to consolidate their presence and claims via increased law enforcement activities in the disputed areas of the South China Sea', which 'creates a continuing potential for rising tensions'. See S. Wu, China's Maritime Law Enforcement Practice in the South China Sea: Challenges and Prospects, in M.H. Nordquist, *et al.* (eds.), *Legal Order in the World's Oceans: UN Convention on the Law of the Sea* (Brill|Nijhoff, 2017), 452.

225 Zhen, n 108.

226 GMA, China fired at Filipino fishermen in Jackson atoll (4 June 2011), available at <http://www.gmanetwork.com/news/news/specialreports/222519/china-fired-at-filipino-fishermen-in-jackson-atoll/story/>.

227 J. Gomez, China to neighbors: Stop oil search in Spratlys (9 June 2011), available at <http://globalnation.inquirer.net/3595/china-to-neighbors-stop-search-for-spratlys-oil>.

228 J. Laude, China gunboats harass RP vessel (4 March 2011), available at <http://www.philstar.com/headlines/662502/china-gunboats-harass-rp-vessel>.

229 Stratfor, Philippines and China: An Encounter in Reed Bank (4 March 2011), available at <https://worldview.stratfor.com/article/philippines-and-china-encounter-reed-bank>.

prevented the Philippine fishing vessels from entering the fishing areas near this atoll until 2 March 2016.[230] However, the Chinese government clarified that the China Coast Guard was in the area to tow a grounded foreign ship which was abandoned near Jackson Atoll in 2015.[231] The Chinese authority decided to tow this vessel away due to the concern that 'it might cause possible impediment to navigation safety and damage to the marine environment'. During the operation, the Chinese side advised fishing boats including the Philippine fishing vessels to avoid this area for the reason of navigation security.

In all the above examples, it is coast guard vessels that have undertaken law enforcement measures. However, military or navy vessels can also get involved in enforcement action. For example, on 9 May 2016, a Malaysian naval vessel – *Lakshamana Tun Abdul Jamil* (*F-135*) – intercepted a Philippine fishing vessel which was operating 29 km southwest of Commodore Reef in the Spratly Islands.[232] It was reported that the Malaysian naval officers captured, restrained, and beat the Philippine fishers from that vessel, claiming that they were encroaching upon the Malaysian waters.[233] These fishers were released on the same day by the Malaysian forces with a written warning stating 'Last warning! Aggressive action will be taken if we meet you again'.[234] On 27 May 2016, the Malaysian government expressed regret over the incident and agreed to pay compensation to the fishers and punish the responsible naval personnel.[235]

---

230 M. Mogato, Philippine officials say China blocked access to disputed South China Sea atoll (2 March 2016), available at <https://www.reuters.com/article/us-southchinasea-china-philippines/philippine-officials-say-china-blocked-access-to-disputed-south-china-sea-atoll-idUSKCN0W402A>.

231 Foreign Ministry Spokesperson Hong Lei's Regular Press Conference on March 2, 2016, available at <http://www.fmprc.gov.cn/mfa_eng/xwfw_665399/s2510_665401/t1344679.shtml>.

232 Reuters, PH military: Malaysian Navy detains three fishermen in South China Sea (25 May 2016), available at <http://cnnphilippines.com/news/2016/05/25/Malaysian-Navy-detains-three-fishermen-in-South-China-Sea.html>.

233 GMA, Filipino fishermen allegedly beaten up by Malaysian navymen in Spratlys get medical attention (25 May 2016), available at <http://www.gmanetwork.com/news/news/nation/567536/filipino-fishermen-allegedly-beaten-up-by-malaysian-navymen-in-spratlys-get-medical-attention/story/>.

234 T. Torres-Tupas, PH fishermen 'mauled' by Malaysian Navy, seek DOJ help (5 July 2016), available at <http://globalnation.inquirer.net/140686/ph-fishermen-mauled-by-malaysian-navy-ask-doj-for-help>.

235 See V. Barcelo, KL regrets fishers' beating (27 May 2016), available at <http://www.manilastandard.net/news/-main-stories/top-stories/206636/kl-regrets-fishers-beating.html>. Also see ChinaPower, Are maritime law enforcement forces destabilizing Asia?, available at <https://chinapower.csis.org/maritime-forces-destabilizing-asia/>.

It needs to be noted that almost all the above law enforcement incidents involve the use of forcible acts by a State against a private vessel of another State. The notion of 'forcible acts' contemplated in this chapter refers to the physical coercion exercised by governmental vessels and officials against private vessels or personnel navigating within the Spratly Islands area.[236] A question of relevance is whether and to what extent such forcible acts in the conduct of law enforcement measures amount to a breach of the principle of the prohibition of the threat or use of force. This question is addressed in the following section.

4.6.2 *Principle of Prohibition of Threat or Use of Force*

Law enforcement measures can be defined as acts that are aimed to enforce laws including domestic or international law and to this end, satisfy various technical requirements.[237] This working definition does not exclude forcible acts. Drawing a line between forcible acts allowed within the paradigm of law enforcement and unlawful forcible acts constituting a threat or use of force can sometimes be a difficult task.[238]

No international jurisprudence has ever rendered unequivocal support to the position that Article 2(4) of the UN Charter should be constructed broadly so as to encompass forcible action of all scales and effects. The ICJ's statement in *Nicaragua* that it is necessary 'to distinguish the most grave forms of the use of force (those constituting an armed attack) from other less grave forms'[239] has sometimes been taken to imply that the ICJ did not support the existence of a *de minimis* threshold for Article 2(4), as 'forcible acts need not be especially grave to qualify as the use of force'.[240] However, one might refrain from reading too much into the *Nicaragua* judgment, as the wording 'other less grave forms' is used by the ICJ as opposed to 'the most grave forms of the use of force' constituting armed attacks, and this wording is not tantamount to all 'other forms' of the use of force regardless of the gravity threshold.

In several international cases where a State used forcible acts to enforce its sovereignty or sovereign rights and jurisdiction against vessels flying the flag of another State, such forcible acts were characterized as violations of

---

236 M. Tondini, The Use of Force in the Course of Maritime Law Enforcement Operations, 4(2) *Journal on the Use of Force and International Law* (2017), 255.

237 Fisheries Jurisdiction (Spain v. Canada), Judgment of 4 December 1998 (ICJ), para.68.

238 Ruys, n 74, 210.

239 Military and Paramilitary Activities in and against Nicaragua (Nicaragua v. United States of America), Judgment of 27 June 1986 (ICJ), para.191.

240 See *e.g.*, Ruys, n 74, 165–166.

international law applicable to law enforcement measures in general (such as the principles of necessity and proportionality) but not as infringements of the principle of prohibition of threat or use of force.[241]

More importantly, *Guyana v. Suriname* has explicitly confirmed a divide between minimum uses of forcible action in the pursuit of law enforcement and the prohibited threat or use of force under Article 2(4) of the UN Charter.[242] In *Guyana v. Suriname*, two officials of the Surinamese Navy ordered Guyana's oil licensee – an oil rig and drilling ship – to leave the disputed marine area between these two countries and announced that if they refused to fulfil this demand, the responsibility for unspecified consequences would be theirs.[243] Guyana and Suriname had different views on the nature of Suriname's action. Guyana claimed that Suriname violated the obligation not to jeopardize or hamper the reaching of the final agreement under Articles 74(3) and 83(3) of UNCLOS due to its threat of use of force as a response to Guyana's exploratory drilling.[244] Suriname argued that its action was 'of the nature of reasonable and proportionate law enforcement measures to preclude unauthorized drilling in a disputed area of continental shelf'.[245]

The tribunal concluded without much explanation that the action mounted by Suriname constituted a threat of use of force by imposing an explicit threat that force might be used if the order was not obeyed, and that this action also jeopardised the reaching of a final delimitation agreement as a breach of the obligation 'not to jeopardize or hamper delimitation' under Articles 74(3) and 83(3) of UNCLOS.[246] Having said that, the tribunal explicitly admitted that law enforcement activities might contain a threat or use of force and that such force could be deemed legal to the extent that it was 'unavoidable, reasonable and necessary'.[247]

The above decision gives rise to two observations. First, the above decision indicates the tribunal's support for a divide between minimum uses of forcible action in the pursuit of law enforcement and the prohibited threat or use of

241 See *e.g.*, S. S. 'I'm Alone', n 73, 1617; Investigation of Certain Incidents Affecting the British Trawler Red Crusader (UK/Denmark), Report of 23 March 1962 (Commission of Enquiry), RIAA, Vol. XXIX, 524, 526, 537, 538.

242 See *e.g.*, C.D. Gray, *International Law and the Use of Force* (OUP. 2008), 30; O. Corten, *The Law Against War: The Prohibition on The Use of Force in Contemporary International Law* (Bloomsbury Publishing. 2010), 73; Milano and Papanicolopulu, n 37, 600.

243 Guyana v. Suriname, n 13, para.439.

244 *Ibid.*, para.483.

245 *Ibid.*, para.441.

246 *Ibid.*, paras.439, 484.

247 *Ibid.*, para.445.

force under Article 2(4) of the UN Charter.[248] To that effect, Article 2(4) should be interpreted as having a *de minimis* threshold, and as a result, the forcible action involved in the conduct of law enforcement measures beneath such a *de minimis* threshold is not in contravention of Article 2(4). Second, the above decision found that the warning given by the two officials of the Surinamese Navy against Guyana's authorized oil rig and drilling ship amounted to a breach of Article 2(4). Scholars have commented that this finding introduces a relatively low threshold for forcible measures against merchant vessels to be qualified as a threat of the use of the force under Article 2(4).[249] As rightly pointed out by Anderson, this finding might come as a surprise to the readers of the award because the summaries of evidence indicated that the officials of the Surinamese Navy 'did not board the rig at any stage or fire warning shots or attach a hawser to a leg [of any person on the oil rig and drilling ship]'.[250]

Scholars' opinions are sharply divided regarding the existence of a *de minimis* threshold for a forcible action to be qualified as a threat or use of force under Article 2(4) of the UN Charter. Among legal scholars, the objection to a general gravity threshold has been most staunchly defended by Ruys. He has argued that excluding 'minimal' uses of force from the scope of Article 2(4) because of their small scale or confined purposes, is conceptually confused, inconsistent with customary practice, and undesirable as a matter of policy.[251] In his view, the acceptance of a general *de minimis* threshold may open Pandora's box by making it far easier for States to justify their forcible action against foreign aircraft, vessels, or troops, and thus threatens to erode the legal constraints on the use of force, which is a very real concern in the age of drone warfare.[252] It needs to be noted that Ruys, albeit rejecting a general *de minimis* threshold, has agreed that enforcement action against merchant vessels under another State's flag undertaken by the coastal State in its *undisputed* EEZ or continental shelf was 'presumed not to affect the international relations between those states and accordingly remains beyond the reach of Article 2(4)'.[253] However, in other circumstances especially in the presence of territorial or maritime disputes, he has opined that if the force used in the enforcement action 'directly arises from a dispute between sovereign States',

248 See *e.g.*, Gray, n 242, 30; Corten, n 242, 73; Milano and Papanicolopulu, n 37, 600.

249 See *e.g.*, A. Aizenstatd, Guyana v Suriname Maritime Boundary Arbitration, *MPEPIL* (2011), para.12; Ruys, n 74, 205; van Logchem, n 22, 224.

250 Anderson, n 75, 239.

251 Ruys, n 74, 159.

252 *Ibid.*, 210.

253 *Ibid.*, 206.

then such action could amount to a threat or use of force in the sense of Article 2(4).[254] Similarly, the BIICL report on the use of force in relation to sovereignty disputes over land territory has also opposed the calls for a general *de minimis* threshold to be met before forcible acts constitute a threat or use of force.[255] This report has posited that an armed incursion in the disputed land territory, even if small in scale, that reflects a coercive intent, might come within the ambit of Article 2(4), irrespective of whether the other claiming State chooses to respond by force or not.[256] This report defines 'coercive intent' as 'a State deliberately engages in forcible acts as a means of coercion against another State'.[257]

In comparison, some scholars have supported the existence of a *de minimis* threshold inherent in Article 2(4) of the UN Charter to trigger the prohibition on the threat or use of force.[258] O'Connell has argued that Article 2(4) is narrower than it might appear on its face, and that minimal or *de minimis* uses of force are likely to fall below the threshold of the Article 2(4) prohibition.[259] The examples of *de minimis* uses of force given by O'Connell include the forcible action in the conduct of law enforcement measures used by a coastal State to arrest pirates, hijackers, terrorists and smugglers, and to stop foreign vessel suspected of illicit fishing or causing coastal pollution.[260] Corten, also in support of the existence of a *de minimis* threshold in Article 2(4), has argued that minimal forcible acts typically include law enforcement measures applied by a State to individuals or merchant vessels, instead of acts of force by one State against another.[261] According to his observation, such law enforcement measures usually are condemned as violations of a State's sovereignty or as noncompliance with specific treaty-based provisions, rather than as a breach of the prohibition of the threat or use of force between States.[262]

It can be seen that scholars supporting a *de minimis* threshold have not specified whether their conclusion – that law enforcement measures at sea should

254 *Ibid.*, 206–207.

255 BIICL, *Report on the Use of Force in relation to Sovereignty Disputes over Land Territory* (2018), paras.60-84.

256 *Ibid.*, para.76.

257 *Ibid.*

258 M.E. O'Connell, The Prohibition on the Use of Force, in N.D. White and C. Henderson (eds.), *Research Handbook on International Conflict and Security Law: Jus ad Bellum, Jus in Bello and Jus post Bellum* (Edward Elgar Publishing. 2013), 102. Corten, n 242, 55.

259 O'Connell, n 258, 102.

260 *Ibid.*

261 Corten, n 242, 56.

262 *Ibid.*, 55.

be generally regarded as outside the reach of Article 2(4) – applies equally to disputed and undisputed marine areas. Scholars opposing a *de minimis* threshold suggest that the forcible action in the conduct of law enforcement measures would be considered in contravention of Article 2(4) to the extent that such forcible action 'directly arises from a dispute between sovereign States' or 'a State deliberately engages in forcible acts as a means of coercion against another State'. In terms of disputed marine areas, forcible acts in the conduct of law enforcement measures usually arise from the maritime dispute between States. A disputant State often uses such forcible acts as a means of coercion against another State to obstruct the latter and its nationals from fishing or conducting any other activities in the areas concerned. In this sense, the approach endorsed by scholars opposing a *de minimis* threshold would lead to a prohibition of any forcible action within disputed marine areas.

However, the author finds it difficult to agree with a ban on all forcible action within disputed marine areas and argues that the *de minimis* threshold for a forcible act to be qualified as a threat or use of force should equally apply to disputed and undisputed marine areas.

First, the unified implementation of the *de minimis* threshold across disputed and undisputed marine areas is consistent with the *Guyana v. Suriname* award. In that case, Suriname's forcible action was carried out within a disputed marine area. It was in this circumstance that the tribunal stated that law enforcement activities might contain a threat or use of force and that such force could be deemed legal to the extent that it was 'unavoidable, reasonable and necessary'.[263] Therefore, the tribunal's confirmation of a divide between mere law enforcement and the threat or use of force under Article 2(4) applies equally to forcible action taken in undisputed areas and disputed areas.

Second, depriving the disputant States of the right to take forcible acts in the pursuit of law enforcement would significantly weaken their ability in deterring unlawful conduct occurring within disputed marine areas preceding delimitation. These forcible acts, albeit likely to have the risk of intensifying conflicts, could be essential to the protection of their legitimate interests in those areas, especially when the rescue through the compulsory dispute settlement mechanism as outlined in UNCLOS is not available in certain circumstances.

Third, as described by Ong, where a maritime boundary has been delimited or where it is absent are two different phases on the 'time-space continuum'.[264] Built on Ong's 'time-space continuum', van Logchem argued that 'it seems

263 Guyana v. Suriname, n 13, para.445.

264 D. Ong, Joint Development of Common Offshore Oil and Gas Deposits: 'Mere' State Practice or Customary International Law?, 93(4) *AJIL* (1999), 783.

more prudent to approach the period before and after delimitation in terms of degrees rather than absolutes' since these two phases fall on the same continuum after all.[265] Agreeing with Ong and Van Logchem, it would be unpersuasive to amount all forcible acts, which would fall below the reach of Article 2(4) of the UN Charter if conducted in uncontested marine areas, to a breach of Article 2(4) simply because of their presence in disputed marine areas.

Based on the foregoing analysis, there should be a *de minimis* threshold for a forcible act taken within a disputed marine area to be qualified as a threat or use of force. A forcible act enforced by a disputant State against a foreign vessel, which falls below the *de minimis* threshold of the Article 2(4) prohibition, should not be generally prohibited.

A follow-up question is how to determine the *de minimis* threshold required by Article 2(4) of the UN Charter, or put differently, how to determine whether a particular forcible act remains within the paradigm of legitimate law enforcement measures or whether it brings Article 2(4) into play. It can be argued that the appropriate characterization of relevant forcible acts requires a case-by-case assessment, taking into consideration various factors, including: 'the political context; the gravity or intensity of the acts (including the means used), as well as whether they are isolated or recurring events; the author; the level of decision making'.[266] Two general observations can be made. First, forcible acts undertaken by police units such as coast guard administrations are less likely to be considered a threat or use of force under the UN Charter than those by military units. Second, compared with forcible acts ordered by the top of the command chain, the threat or use of force initiated at the initiative of the individual coastguard or police officer are also less likely to trigger the application of Article 2(4).

4.6.3 *Principles Applicable to Law Enforcement Measures in General*

For law enforcement measures that do not amount to the prohibited threat or use of force under Article 2(4) of the UN Charter, their legality ought to be decided in light of the principles applicable to law enforcement measures in general.[267] The *Arctic Sunrise Arbitration* award has made it clear that law enforcement measures taken by Russia in its EEZ against the *Arctic Sunrise*, a vessel flying the flag of the Netherlands, and the thirty persons on board that

265 Van Logchem, n 22, 317.

266 Ruys, n 74, 207.

267 F. Francioni, Use of Force, Military Activities, and the New Law of the Sea, in A. Cassese (ed.), *The Current Legal Regulation of the Use of Force* (Martinus Nijhoff Publishers. 1986), 377.

vessel, shall comply with a four-pronged test: (1) international law (such as treaties and custom) provides 'a legal basis' for the measures at issue; and such measures are carried out in accordance with general principles of (2) 'reasonableness', (3) 'necessity', and (4) 'proportionality'.[268] The prongs (1) and (2) apply to all law enforcement measures, irrespective of whether they involve forcible acts or not. Conversely, the prongs (3) and (4) only apply where forcible acts are contained in the conduct of law enforcement measures, because the objective of the principles of necessity and proportionality is to regulate the level of violence or force used.

First, 'legitimate interests' of a coastal State normally derives from its sovereignty or sovereign rights, which provide a legal basis for its law enforcement measures undertaken within areas under its national jurisdiction.[269] For disputed marine areas such as the Spratly Islands area, international jurisprudence has widely recognised that a State can enjoy 'legitimate interests' over the area in dispute, even though the rights which it wishes to seek protection for have not yet been proved to exist.[270]

Second, the reasonableness of law enforcement measures depends on whether the circumstances under which these measures are taken 'could reasonably be considered as constituting an interference with' the legitimate interests of a State that takes these measures.[271] The reasonableness derives from the specific circumstances that cause a State to have a reasonable belief that relevant vessels at which its law enforcement measures are targeted might be involved in activities infringing the legitimate interests of this State.[272]

Third, the principle of necessity requires the exhaustion of non-violent means and the use of minimum necessary force. It follows that forcible acts

---

268 Arctic Sunrise Arbitration (Netherlands v. Russia), Award on the Merits of 14 August 2015 (PCA), para.224. Also see Russia and the Netherlands, Joint Statement on Scientific Cooperation in the Russian Arctic Region and the Settlement of a Dispute (17 May 2019) (requiring that the coastal State's measures 'must fulfil the tests of reasonableness, necessity and proportionality').

269 Arctic Sunrise Arbitration (Netherlands v. Russia), n 268, para.327.

270 See *e.g.*, Dispute Concerning Delimitation of the Maritime Boundary between Ghana and Côte d'Ivoire in the Atlantic Ocean, n 90, para.57; Questions relating to the Obligation to Prosecute or Extradite (Belgium v. Senegal), Order of 28 May 2009 (Request for the indication of provisional measures) (ICJ), para.57; Certain Activities carried out by Nicaragua in the Border Area (Costa Rica v. Nicaragua), Provisional Measures Order of 8 March 2011 (ICJ), paras.53, 57; Request for Interpretation of the Judgment of 15 June 1962 in the Case concerning the Temple of Preah Vihear (Cambodia v. Thailand) (Cambodia v. Thailand), Order of 18 July 2011 (Request for the Indication of Provisional Measures) (ICJ), para.33.

271 Arctic Sunrise Arbitration (Netherlands v. Russia), n 268, para.327.

272 *Ibid.*

can be used as law enforcement measures only when 'strictly necessary' and in exceptional circumstances.[273] Non-violent means shall be first exhausted, including verbal notice, warning, persuasion or communication.[274] For instance, in *Red Crusader*, the Commission of Enquiry was constituted to address the legality of the open firing by a Royal Danish Navy vessel, *Niels Ebbesen*, against a British trawler, *Red Crusader*.[275] The Commission concluded that the open firing 'exceeded legitimate use of armed force ... without proved necessity', because the commanding officer of *Niels Ebbesen* should have attempted other means to persuade *Red Crusader* to stop and revert to the normal procedure which it had previously followed.[276]

Fourth, the principle of proportionality only comes into play when the principle of necessity has been satisfied.[277] The use of violence or force as law enforcement measures shall be in proportion to the gravity of the offence and the legitimate objective to be achieved.[278] As entailed by this principle, the tribunal concluded in the *South China Sea Arbitration* award that law enforcement measures must be taken proportionately to the seriousness of the offence, in the sense that if the suspected offence was just a pre-existing threat rather than an immediate danger, a State was obliged not to take law enforcement measures in a dangerous manner, in order to prevent serious risk of collision and ensure navigation safety.[279]

---

273 UN Doc.: A/RES/34/169, Commentary on Article 3, Code of Conduct for Law Enforcement Officials (17 December 1979), Article 3. Also see UN Doc.: A/CONF.144/28/REV.1, Basic Principles on the Use of Force and Firearms by Law Enforcement Officials, adopted by the Eighth United Nations Congress on the Prevention of Crime and the Treatment of Offenders (27 August to 7 September 1990), Article 4.

274 Geneva Academy of International Humanitarian Law and Human Rights, Use of Force in Law Enforcement and the Right to Life: the Role of the Human Rights Council, *Academy In-Brief No. 6* (November 2016), 7.

275 Investigation of Certain Incidents Affecting the British Trawler Red Crusader, n 241, 524.

276 *Ibid.*, 538.

277 Geneva Academy of International Humanitarian Law and Human Rights, n 274, 9.

278 Basic Principles on the Use of Force and Firearms by Law Enforcement Officials, Adopted by the Eighth United Nations Congress on the Prevention of Crime and the Treatment of Offenders, n 273, Article 5(a). Also see Commentary on Article 3, Code of Conduct for Law Enforcement Officials, n 273, Commentary (b).

279 The *South China Sea Arbitration* award can be considered as a recent example of the application of this principle, though it did not explicitly use the term of proportionality. See The South China Sea Arbitration, n 49, para.1095.

4.6.4 *Application to the Spratly Islands Setting*

Tailored to the Spratly Islands setting, the preceding analysis entails three implications for the unilateral law enforcement measures taken within the disputed marine areas therein.

First, it can be seen that law enforcement measures occurring within the Spratly Islands area, as described in section 4.6.1, have often been taken unilaterally by coast guard administrations, rather than military units, of the disputant States. Therefore, even if these measures contain forcible acts, they are less likely to be considered as a threat or use of force under the UN Charter.

Second, according to the principle of reasonableness, law enforcement measures taken by a State can only be deemed reasonable when that State has a reasonable belief that another State or its nationals may be involved in activities infringing its legitimate interests. However, as concluded in sections 4.4 and 4.5, the disputant States or their nationals are, in general, entitled to conduct fishing and seismic surveys unilaterally within contested waters. Therefore, unless such legitimate activities are carried out in a way that infringes the rights of others, it is difficult for a disputant State taking law enforcement measures to have a reasonable belief that such permissible activities would infringe its legitimate interests, as otherwise, it would negate the lawfulness of these activities. One may argue that pursuant to Article 22 of the ILC Articles on Responsibility of States for Internationally Wrongful Acts, the wrongfulness of these law enforcement measures can be precluded if they constitute countermeasures.[280] However, this argument is untenable in the present case because countermeasures can only be taken against a State that is responsible for an internationally wrongful act.[281] Thus, to the extent that unilateral fishing and seismic surveys are permissible within contested waters and not carried out in a way that infringes the rights of others, a State cannot rely on countermeasures as argumentation to justify its unilateral taking of law enforcement measures for blockading another State's legitimate activities.

Third, having said that, it does not necessarily mean that a State can never undertake any law enforcement measure when another State is fishing or conducting seismic surveys in contested areas. For example, if a State has a reasonable belief that another State is fishing endangered fishery species or its seismic survey could cause harm to the marine environment, that State may use law enforcement measures to halt these activities. Arguably, law enforcement measures that are aimed at preventing possible impediment to navigation safety

280 UN Doc.: A/RES/56/83, ILC Articles on Responsibility of States for Internationally Wrongful Acts (28 January 2002), Article 22.

281 *Ibid.*, Article 49.

or damage to the marine environment should be deemed reasonable. A relevant example is that the China Coast Guard prevented the Philippine fishing vessels from entering into the fishing areas near Jackson Atoll in the Spratly Islands between 28 February and 2 March 2016.[282] The Chinese side claimed that its law enforcement measures in the relevant area were not aimed to stop the Philippine fishers from fishing in the area but to tow a grounded foreign ship to prevent possible impediment to navigation safety and damage to the marine environment.[283] To the extent that this claim is true, China's unilateral taking of enforcement actions is not unlawful.

4.7 Conclusion

The UNCLOS regulatory framework is inadequate in determining the permissible scope for unilateralism under international law within the disputed marine areas in the Spratly Islands area, owing to the limited applicable scope and vagueness in the substantive content of relevant provisions. To remedy the limitation in applicable scope, it is recommended to implement Articles 74(3) and 83(3) of UNCLOS as a unified regulatory standard across the Spratly Islands area, regardless of the different categories of disputed marine areas. To remedy the vagueness in the substantive content of Articles 74(3) and 83(3), their interpretation and application to the Spratly Islands setting can take into account other UNCLOS provisions especially Part XII concerning environmental protection and relevant general principles in customary international law, pursuant to Article 31(2) and (3)(c) of VCLT. Accordingly, the permissible scope for different types of unilateral acts in the Spratly Islands setting has been clarified as follows.

First, relevant international jurisprudence indicates that the 'permanent physical change to the marine environment' test is the review standard for assessing the lawfulness of the unilateral offshore hydrocarbon activities. It follows that in general, exploitation and exploratory drilling are prohibited in the disputed marine areas pending delimitation. Nevertheless, to the extent of not causing irreversible harm to marine life, seismic surveys unilaterally conducted by the disputant States are permissible, provided that the information related to marine natural resources collected through such activities is communicated to other disputant States. The mere issuance or declaration of oil

282 Mogato, n 230.

283 Foreign Ministry Spokesperson Hong Lei's Regular Press Conference on March 2, 2016, n 231.

blocks without further action is unlikely to cause a permanent physical change to the marine environment directly and thus are generally allowed.

Second, according to a general constraint as entailed from Article 192 of UNCLOS, the disputant States shall not engage in direct exploitation of depleted, threatened or endangered species or any activities that may indirectly destroy the habitats of such species. Furthermore, as a result of the *mutatis mutandis* application of the 'permanent physical change to the marine environment' review standard to unilateral fisheries-related conduct, harmful fishing practices that could cause permanent physical change and irreparable damage to the marine environment, such as degrading habitats of important species and destroying the structure of seabed and subsoils by using explosives, should be prohibited. For non-harmful fishing activities, relevant international jurisprudence suggests that they are generally permissible but should not exceed the current annual catch within the Spratly Islands area, unless the scientific evidence suggests otherwise. Traditional or artisanal fishing practices, if any, are permissible across the entire Spratly Islands area.

Third, the obligation 'not to jeopardize or hamper delimitation' also curtails how the disputant States can respond to another State's unilateral resources-related conduct. A forcible act enforced by a disputant State against a foreign vessel falling below the *de minimis* threshold of the Article 2(4) prohibition is not generally prohibited within the Spratly Islands area. Most law enforcement measures occurring in this region have been taken unilaterally by coast guard administrations of the disputant States, and thus are less likely to trigger the application of Article 2(4) of the UN Charter. Moreover, according to the principles applicable to law enforcement measures in general, a disputant State cannot take unilateral enforcement actions to halt another disputant State's fishing or seismic surveys, unless this State has a reasonable belief that the latter breaches its obligations under international law such as the obligation to protect and preserve the marine environment.

Considering that a binding COC for this region may be yet to come, the analysis of this chapter contributes to providing guidance for the disputant States to consider when behaving unilaterally in the region. The disputant States must refrain from undertaking unlawful unilateral conduct. Otherwise, the unlawful conduct would entail State responsibility. However, as mentioned in subsection 4.2.4, owing to China's reservation, such a conflict cannot be submitted to the compulsory dispute settlement mechanism as outlined in UNCLOS to the extent that the conflict relating to unilateral conduct involves China as a party. Nevertheless, the parties to the conflict can still resort to other peaceful settlement means as indicated in Article 33(1) of the UN Charter, including negotiation, enquiry, mediation, conciliation, regional arrangements or other peaceful means of their own choice.[284] Alternatively, the disputant States can coordinate their activities through cooperative arrangements, which are addressed in chapters 5–8.

284 UN Charter, Article 33(1).

PART 2

Cooperation: Facilitating Resource and Pollution Management

CHAPTER 5

Duty to Cooperate

5.1 Introduction

Despite the wide recognition that the claimants have obvious incentives such as the reduced risk of conflicts and economic and environmental benefits to enter into cooperation, joint development is a niche topic in the general literature on the South China Sea dispute.[1] Most studies tend to view this prospect merely in aspirational terms, as the transformation of economic and environmental incentives into action highly depends on whether all the interested parties have enough political will to exert necessary efforts in reaching an agreement.[2] In light of this, this chapter explores the extent to which international law can guide cooperation in resource and pollution management concerning the Spratly Islands area (section 5.2). This chapter also discusses whether the political will of the disputant States is in favour of cooperation at the moment (section 5.3), and on this basis, it further maps out a theoretical framework on institutionalized cooperation, which calls for a paradigm shift from the balance of power to more organized international collaboration (section 5.4).

5.2 Duty to Cooperate

The duty to cooperate is theoretically tied with Friedman's idea that international law has been primarily divided between the law of coexistence and the law of cooperation since the end of WWII.[3] The main feature of the law

---

1 C. Santamaria, Sino – Philippine Joint Development in the South China Sea: Is Political Will Enough?, 10(2) *Asian Politics & Policy* (2018), 327–328.

2 Miyoshi seemed to be pessimistic about hydrocarbon cooperation in the Spratly Islands area. See M. Miyoshi, *The Joint Development of Offshore Oil and Gas in Relation to Maritime Boundary Delimitation* (IBRU. 1999), 46. Zou, who was more confident in joint development in this region than Miyoshi, opined that 'some kind of joint development, in no matter what form, can be arranged for the disputed area in the South China Sea provided that all the interested parties have the intention and good will to exert necessary efforts in researching the agreement'. See K. Zou, Joint Development in the South China Sea: A New Approach, 21 *IJMCL* (2006), 108.

3 W. Friedmann, *The Changing Structure of International Law* (Columbia University Press. 1964), 297.

 | DOI:10.1163/9789004504332_006

of cooperation is the duty of States to cooperate with each other.[4] During the negotiations of the Friendly Relations Declaration, 'cooperation' was described as 'a form of active coexistence' and 'one practical way of giving effect to coexistence', meaning that 'States should not merely tolerate the existence of other States, but should be prepared to help them as best they could'.[5] Yet, treaties or resolutions of international organizations, including the Friendly Relations Declaration, have never defined the term 'cooperation' and instead proceed with a preconceived terminology.[6] Drawing on the Friendly Relations Declaration, Wolfrum has defined the term 'cooperation' as 'the voluntary co-ordinated action of two or more States which takes place under a legal regime and serves a specific objective', and accordingly, has amounted the duty to cooperate to the obligation to 'enter into such co-ordinated action so as to achieve a specific goal'.[7] Tailored to the Spratly Islands setting, a question of relevance is to what extent the disputant States are obliged to cooperate in resource and pollution management in this region. To address this question, this section first discusses whether States have a general obligation to cooperate with one another in general international law (subsection 5.2.1). It further analyses the duty to cooperate in the specific context of the law of the sea (subsection 5.2.2).

5.2.1 *Duty to Cooperate in General International Law*

Whether States have a general obligation to cooperate with one another in general international law was the focus of debate in the course of negotiations on the Friendly Relations Declaration. The UN General Assembly adopted the Friendly Relations Declaration in 1970 through Resolution 26/25 (XXV).[8] The then president of General Assembly, Edvard Hambro, stated that the purpose of the Friendly Relations Declaration was to clarify the basic principles of the UN Charter based on 'many years of effort for the progressive development and codification of the concepts' derived from these principles.[9] The final version of the Friendly Relations Declaration contains seven principles including

4 R. Wolfrum, Cooperation, International Law of, *MPEPIL* (2010), para.1.

5 UN Doc.: A/6230, Report of the 1966 Special Committee on Principles of International law concerning Friendly Relations and Co-operation among States (the Second Report) (27 June 1966), 85, para.420.

6 Wolfrum, n 4, para.2.

7 *Ibid.*

8 UN Doc.: A/RES/2625(XXV) (24 October 1970).

9 Statement made by Mr. Edvard Hambro (Norway), President of the General Assembly, following the adoption of the Declaration, available at < http://legal.un.org/avl/ha/dpilfrcscun/dpilfrcscun.html >.

the duty of States to cooperate with one another in accordance with the UN Charter.[10] However, in the course of the negotiations, the views of the States were significantly divided on the legal status of the duty to cooperate.

Representatives of developing countries and the socialist States expressed the view that the duty to cooperate was neither an optional activity nor merely a moral obligation, but rather had developed into a principle of contemporary international law.[11] These representatives argued that the duty to cooperate had become an objective necessity in the process of adjustment to the existing patterns and requirements of international relations, resulting from the common interest of the international community as a whole.[12] The legal basis for the duty to cooperate was found in the provisions of the UN Charter, particularly in Article 56. In their view, Article 56 spelt out two sets of obligations in relation to the principle of cooperation: the obligations of States to cooperate among themselves for the achievement of the purposes of international cooperation, and the obligation of States to cooperate with the UN itself for the attainment of those same purposes.[13] They further noted that the duty to cooperate had been referred to in various other international instruments such as the constitutions of international organizations, resolutions and recommendations adopted by the UN and its specialized agencies, and several regional conferences.[14]

In contrast, representatives of western industrialized countries argued that the duty to cooperate was not a legal duty recognized in customary international law but rather a moral duty with a realistic pattern of international behavior.[15] These representatives gave several lines of reasoning to justify their position. First, Article 1(1) and (3) of the UN Charter entails that part of the purposes of the UN system is to achieve international cooperation in three aspects: (1) maintaining international peace and security, (2) solving international problems of an economic, social, cultural or humanitarian character, and (3) promoting and encouraging respect for human rights and for fundamental freedoms for all without distinction as to race, sex, language or religion.[16] Whereas Article 1 of the UN Charter describes the objectives of the

10 UN Doc.: A/RES/2625(XXV) (24 October 1970).

11 UN Doc.: A/6230 (27 June 1966), 87, para.435; UN Doc.: A/6799, Report of the 1966 Special Committee on Principles of International law concerning Friendly Relations and Co-operation among States (the Third Report) (26 September 1967), 25, para.140.

12 UN Doc.: A/6230 (27 June 1966), 87, para.435.

13 *Ibid.*

14 UN Doc.: A/6799 (26 September 1967), 25, para.137.

15 UN Doc.: A/6230 (27 June 1966), 87, paras.436-437; UN Doc.: A/6799 (26 September 1967), 25, para.138.

16 UN Charter, Article 1(1) and (3).

UN as an international organization, Article 2 prescribes the relevant legal principles that both the UN and its member States are obliged to respect for the achievement of the purposes enshrined in Article 1. However, promoting international cooperation is only given legal expression in Article 1 but not in Article 2. Some representatives argued that the omission to list cooperation among the legal principles contained in Article 2 of the UN Charter gave the duty to cooperate a declaratory nature.[17] Second, the UN Charter provisions regarding international cooperation, including Article 56, constituted a general declaration of the UN's competence.[18] Article 55 established an obligation binding on the UN rather than on member States, and Article 56 only refers to cooperation as being the basis for the entire system of the UN as set out in Article 55.[19] To this effect, Article 56 concerned only the duties of States in relation to the obligation of the UN rather than a general duty of States to cooperate with each other in their international relations. Third, though admitting the necessity of cooperation owing to the absence of an overall government in the international community which could legally compel its members to cooperate as was the case in the sphere of national law, some representatives argued that a general duty to cooperate did not exist as a norm of customary international law. In their view, the necessity for a rule growing out of the present situation of the interdependence of States should not be equated with the existence of a rule the formulation of which might be therefore regarded as a part of contemporary international law.[20] Fourth, some representatives opined that it would not seem necessary to treat the general duty to cooperate as an obligation under customary international law, as every country would, in general, profit from cooperation, so that it would voluntarily undertake cooperation when it desired to do so.[21] In exceptional cases where States did not desire to cooperate, the binding character of a general duty to cooperate might have the effect of creating for certain countries obligations which they might not be in a position to fulfil given their economic or material resources.[22]

As a result of the negotiations, the final version of the Friendly Relations Declaration contained a section entitled 'The duty of States to cooperate with one another in accordance with the Charter'. The section comprises three paragraphs. The first paragraph provides that 'States have the duty to cooperate

17 UN Doc.: A/6799 (26 September 1967), 25, para.138.
18 UN Doc.: A/6230 (27 June 1966), 87, para.437.
19 Wolfrum, n 4, para.16.
20 UN Doc.: A/6799 (26 September 1967), 25, para.139.
21 UN Doc.: A/6230 (27 June 1966), 87, para.436.
22 UN Doc.: A/6799 (26 September 1967), 25, para.141.

with one another ... in the various spheres of international relations'. As to the second paragraph, subsections (a), (b) and (d) are basically replicas of Articles 1(1), (3) and 56 of the UN Charter, and subsection (c) prescribes the relation between the duty to cooperate and other principles, stipulating that 'States shall conduct their international relations ... in accordance with the principles of sovereign equality and non-intervention'. The third paragraph sets forth that 'States should cooperate in the economic, social and cultural fields as well as in the field of science and technology'.

The use of the wording 'should' in the third paragraph shows that this paragraph only formulates recommendations instead of prescribing legal obligations. In this sense, the third paragraph negates the content of the first paragraph, which postulates that 'States have the duty to cooperate with one another ... in the various spheres of international relations'.[23] Therefore, the final provisions on the duty to cooperate adopted in the Friendly Relations Declaration indeed reflect the position of western industrialized countries during the negotiating process that opposed posing upon States a general legal duty to cooperate with one another. In light of this, Wolfrum has, with the endorsement of other scholars,[24] drawn a distinction between a general duty to cooperate and a duty to cooperate in specific areas of international law.[25] He has further pointed out that the former has not yet existed in customary international law due to the failure to meet the necessary acceptability among all groups of States.[26] It follows that if a duty to cooperate has been established, such an obligation has to be in relation to a specific field.[27] The following section examines whether a duty to cooperate exists in the field of the law of the sea, particularly in UNCLOS.

5.2.2 *Duty to Cooperate in the Law of the Sea*

The purpose of this subsection is to analyse the duty to cooperate in the specific context of the law of the sea. In the Spratly Islands setting, since all the disputant States are parties to UNCLOS, debates have long persisted as to

23 Wolfrum, n 4, para.17.

24 See *e.g.*, J. Delbrück, The International Obligation to Cooperate–An Empty Shell or a Hard Law Principle of International Law?–A Critical Look at A Much Debated Paradigm of Modern International Law, in H. Hestermeyer and R. Wolfrum (eds.), *Coexistence, Cooperation and Solidarity: Liber Amicorum Rüdiger Wolfrum* (Brill. 2012), 4; M.A. Young and S.R. Sullivan, Evolution through the Duty to Cooperate: Implications of the Whaling Case at the International Court of Justice, 16 *Melb. J. Int'l L.* (2015), 333.

25 Wolfrum, n 4, para.6.

26 *Ibid.*, paras.25, 40.

27 *Ibid.*, para.40.

whether provisions of UNCLOS, especially Articles 123, 74(3) and 83(3), impose on these States an obligation to cooperate in resource and pollution management therein.[28]

5.2.2.1 Duty to Cooperate in Semi-enclosed Seas: Article 123 of UNCLOS

The South China Sea is a semi-enclosed sea as defined by Article 122 of UNCLOS, which means 'a gulf, basin or sea surrounded by two or more States and connected to another sea or the ocean by a narrow outlet or consisting entirely or primarily the territorial seas and exclusive economic zones of two or more coastal States'.[29] Article 123 addresses the need for cooperation between States bordering semi-enclosed seas in respect of living resources, marine environment and scientific research.[30] It reads as follows:

> States bordering an enclosed or semi-enclosed sea *should* cooperate with each other in the exercise of their rights and in the performance of their duties under this Convention. To this end they *shall endeavour*, directly or through an appropriate regional organization:
> (a) to coordinate the management, conservation, exploration and exploitation of the living resources of the sea;
> (b) to coordinate the implementation of their rights and duties with respect to the protection and preservation of the marine environment;
> (c) to coordinate their scientific research policies and undertake where appropriate joint programmes of scientific research in the area;
> (d) to invite, as appropriate, other interested States or international organizations to cooperate with them in furtherance of the provisions of this article.[31] [emphasis added]

28 See *e.g.*, C. Linebaugh, Joint Development in a Semi-Enclosed Sea: China's Duty to Cooperate in Developing the Natural Resources of the South China Sea, 52 *Columbia J. Transnatl. Law* (2014), 561; R. Beckman and L. Bernard, Framework for the Joint Development of Hydrocarbon Resources (2010), 7; R. Lagoni, Interim Measures pending Maritime Delimitation Agreements, 78 *AJIL* (1984), 78.

29 UNCLOS, Article 122. The South China Sea Arbitration (The Philippines v. China), Award of 12 July 2016 (PCA), 82. Zou, n 2, 83.

30 S.N. Nandan and S. Rosenne (eds.), *United Nations Convention on the Law of the Sea, 1982: A Commentary. Vol. 3: Articles 86 to 132 and Documentary Annexes* (Nijhoff. 1995), 343.

31 UNCLOS, Article 123.

5.2.2.1.1 *Textual Analysis*

Reading the text alone, the first sentence of Article 123 uses the word 'should', which means an exhortation in the legal context.[32] Consequently, the proper reading of the first sentence should be that bordering States are encouraged, rather than obliged, to cooperate with each other in the exercise of their rights and in the performance of their duties under UNCLOS. In comparison, the second sentence uses the word 'shall', which imposes a legal obligation.[33] A plain reading of the second sentence suggests that such a legal obligation applies to activities listed in subsection (a)-(c), namely management of the living resources, protection and preservation of the marine environment, and marine scientific research. The text of Article 123 does not explicitly mention non-living resources or hydrocarbon resources, and international jurisprudence has not touched upon this matter.[34] Scholars have differing opinions as to whether this provision applies to the management of hydrocarbon resources in a semi-enclosed sea such as the Spratly Islands area.[35] The preparatory work of Article

---

32 Nandan and Rosenne, n 30, 362. Also see 'should' (meaning giving advice or suggesting what the right thing to do is), Longman English Dictionary, available at <http://www.ldoceonline.com/dictionary/should>.

33 The English language group of the Drafting Committee in UNCLOS III, which had harmonized the use of the word 'shall' throughout the whole convention, pointed out that: 'The Group recalled its earlier recommendation that references to imperative duties and obligations, positive or negative, should contain the word 'shall'... In principle the word 'shall' should not be used where the present tense adequately conveys the meaning'. M.H. Nordquist, *et al.* (eds.), *United Nations Convention on the Law of the Sea, 1982: A Commentary. Vol. 4: Articles 192 to 278, Final Act, Annex VI* (Nijhoff. 1991), xli – xlii, 'Note on the Use of the Word "Shall" '.

34 So far, *South China Sea Arbitration* is the only case that has interpreted this provision. However, this case did not touch upon the application of Article 123 to the management of hydrocarbon resources. Rather, the tribunal 'merely cited the provision in its entirety without providing any interpretative guidance as to its application'. See The South China Sea Arbitration, n 29, paras.906 and 984. Also see N. Oral, The South China Sea Arbitral Award, Part XII of UNCLOS, and the Protection and Preservation of the Marine Environment, in S. Jayakumar, *et al.* (eds.), *The South China Sea Arbitration: The Legal Dimension* (Edward Elgar Publishing. 2018), 242.

35 A majority of scholars hold that Article 123 'merely establishes the duty of cooperation regarding the coordination of activities concerning living resources, protection and preservation of the marine environment, and scientific research, excluding non-living resources'. See *e.g.*, V. Becker-Weinberg, *Joint Development of Hydrocarbon Deposits in the Law of the Sea* (Springer. 2014), 64; J. Symonides, The Legal Status of the Enclosed and Semi-Enclosed Seas, 27 *German YB Int'l L.* (1984), 315, 328; D.M. Ong, Joint Development of Common Offshore Oil and Gas Deposits: 'Mere' State Practice or Customary International Law?, 93 *AJIL* (1999), 782; A.E. Bastida, *et al.*, Cross-Border Unitization and Joint Development Agreements: An International Law Perspective, 29 *Houston Journal of International Law* (2007), 355, 377; Beckman and Bernard, n 28, 12. Some argue that even

123 and the circumstances of its conclusion may shed light on the interpretation of this provision.

5.2.2.1.2 *Drafting History*

The discussion about whether the provisions on enclosed and semi-enclosed seas should be incorporated in UNCLOS began at the second session of negotiations in 1974 during UNCLOS III.[36] Among thirteen States which expressed their opinions on this issue at the 38th meeting of the Second Committee,[37] only France and Greece explicitly objected to including these provisions into the future convention.[38] These two countries argued that the disadvantages would outweigh the advantages of introducing this concept into the law of the sea because the concept of the enclosed and semi-enclosed seas was not a traditional concept of international law which lacked appropriate legal rules.[39] They further argued that creating special rules for the enclosed or semi-enclosed seas would amount to resuscitating 'the Roman formula of *mare nostrum* ["our sea", referring to the Mediterranean to the ancient Romans], with the consequent risk of establishing a *mare clausum* ["closed sea", meaning a sea under the jurisdiction of a State that is closed or not accessible to others]'.[40]

---

if Article 123 does not apply directly to nonliving resources, it can serve 'a useful function in finding an analogous cooperative nature in the legal regime applicable to' nonliving resources. See Ong, n 35, 782. Some seem to consider Articles 123(a)-(c) to be 'specific examples of areas of cooperation' or 'highlight activities', which implies that the list of activities as set forth by Article 123 is non-exhaustive. See M.H. Nordquist, *et al.*, *Recent Developments in the Law of the Sea and China* (Martinus Nijhoff Publishers. 2006), 174. Some even go further to assert that 'the best interpretation of Article 123 is that it imposes a duty on coastal States to cooperate in developing natural resources [including hydrocarbon resources] in an enclosed or semi-enclosed sea'. See Linebaugh, n 28, 561.

36 UN Doc.: A/CONF.62/29, Organization of the second session of the Conference and allocation of items: decisions taken by the Conference at its 15th meeting on 21 June 1974.

37 These States include: Iran (Mr. Kazemi), Israel (Mr. Rosenne), Denmark (Mr. Andreasen), Sweden (Mr. Heyman), Thailand (Mr. Panupong), France (Mr. Queneudec), Iraq (Mr. Al-Qadhi), German Democratic Republic (Mr. Goerner), Turkey (Mr. Tuncel), Union of Soviet Socialist Republics (Mr. Barabolya), Greece (Mr. Theodoropoulos), Algeria (Mr. Mesloub), and Democratic Yemen (Mr. Fares). See Third United Nations Conference on the Law of the Sea, Official Records, Vol. II (1973–1982), 273–278. Also see UN Doc.: A/CONF.62/C.2/SR.38, Summary Records of Meetings of the Second Committee 38th Meeting (10 December 1982).

38 *Ibid.*, 276, paras.34-37 (France), 277, paras.52-54 (Greece).

39 *Ibid.*, 276, para.34 (France), 277, para.52 (Greece).

40 This position was expressed by the French delegate, Mr. Queneudec, and was endorsed by the Greek delegate, Mr. Theodoropoulos. See *ibid.*, 276, para.35 (France), 277, para.52 (Greece).

Other delegates, on the contrary, explained why they believed that it was of importance for coastal States bordering the enclosed and semi-enclosed seas to enter into cooperation in managing living resources and preserving the marine environment. For example, the delegate from Thailand, Mr. Panupong, stated that the narrowness of the enclosed or semi-enclosed seas entailed that fragmentation of the area would be impractical and would be of little service to the States concerned when it comes to exploitation and conservation of living resources and preservation of the marine environment.[41] In other words, it was the unique circumstances of the enclosed and semi-enclosed seas that required a higher level of cooperation among coastal States in these areas of activities.[42] A number of other delegates endorsed this position.[43]

Mr. Panupong went further to state that exploitation of hydrocarbon resources was *not* included in the proposed cooperation regime but instead should be 'precisely determined by agreement among the parties concerned in the light of special circumstances'.[44] No one had explicitly opposed to this position. Quite the opposite, when talking about the necessity and importance of cooperation in the enclosed and semi-enclosed seas, other delegates also only referred to activities including management of living resources, preservation of the marine environment and scientific research and excluding management of hydrocarbon resources.[45] Therefore, the drafting history of Article 123 indicates that the drafters did not intend to include the management of hydrocarbon resources as an area of cooperation in the enclosed and semi-enclosed seas. This area was intentionally left to be determined by parties on the basis of agreement. Moreover, for those activities covered by Article 123, the use of the wording 'shall endeavor ... to' indicates that the duty to cooperate under this provision also amounts to an obligation of conduct rather than an obligation of result to enter into cooperation eventually.[46]

---

41 *Ibid.*, 275, para.32.

42 *Ibid.*, 273, para.7.

43 For example, see *ibid.*, 273, paras.2-7 (Iran), 274, para.10 (Israel), 275, para.19 (Denmark), 275, para.24 (Sweden).

44 *Ibid.*, 275–276, para.32.

45 For example, see *ibid.*, 273, paras.2-8 (Iran), 274, para.10 (Israel), 275, para.19 (Denmark), 275, para.24 (Sweden).

46 Symonides, n 35, 315, 327. The South China Sea Arbitration, n 29, paras.906 and 984.

5.2.2.2 Duty to Cooperate in Disputed Marine Areas: Articles 74(3) and 83(3) of UNCLOS

Articles 74(3) and 83(3) of UNCLOS provide that pending agreement reached between States with opposite or adjacent coasts on the delimitation of the EEZ or continental shelf, 'the States concerned, in a spirit of understanding and cooperation, shall make every effort to enter into provisional arrangements of a practical nature'.[47]

5.2.2.2.1 *'Shall Make Every Effort to Enter Into'*

A plain reading of the provision suggests that the wording 'shall' indicates a legal obligation. However, a question of relevance is to what precise extent States are required to make efforts towards entering into provisional arrangements preceding delimitation. In other words, is it an obligation of result, meaning that States are required to reach an arrangement successfully, or is it an obligation of conduct, meaning that a sincere attempt to negotiate an arrangement would suffice regardless of the eventual outcome of the negotiation?

The Special Chamber of the ITLOS in the *Ghana/Côte d'Ivoire* judgment has made it clear that this obligation is an obligation of conduct, as evidenced by the wording 'shall make every effort'.[48] In that case, Côte d'Ivoire claimed that the unilateral hydrocarbon activities undertaken by Ghana in the disputed area constituted violations of the obligation to make every effort to enter into provisional arrangements of a practical nature under Article 83(3) of UNCLOS.[49] The Chamber pointed out that the wording 'shall make every effort' clearly indicated that it did not amount to an obligation to reach an agreement on provisional arrangements but an obligation to act in good faith, which was enhanced by the wording that such acts had to be undertaken 'in a spirit of understanding and cooperation'.[50]

The above interpretation is in line with a previous finding made by the arbitral tribunal in the *Guyana v. Suriname* award that the language of this obligation under Articles 74(3) and 83(3) of UNCLOS was framed to impose on States a duty to negotiate a provisional arrangement in good faith preceding delimitation.[51] Scholars also endorse this interpretation, arguing that if this

47 UNCLOS, Articles 74(3) and Article 83(3).

48 Dispute Concerning Delimitation of the Maritime Boundary between Ghana and Côte d'Ivoire in the Atlantic Ocean (Ghana/Côte d'Ivoire), Judgment of 23 September 2017 (ITLOS), para.627.

49 *Ibid.*, para.606.

50 *Ibid.*, para.627.

51 Guyana v. Suriname, Arbitral Award dated 17 September 2007 (PCA), para.461.

obligation had been intended to be an obligation of result, the language of the relevant provisions could have been drafted differently, for example, 'the States concerned shall enter into provisional arrangements of a practical nature'.[52]

5.2.2.2.2 *'Provisional Arrangements of a Practical Nature'*

The term 'provisional' indicates that relevant arrangements are interim measures, which usually are only applicable in the period preceding delimitation, and cannot be deemed as a renunciation or modification of any party's claims on territorial sovereignty and maritime entitlements.[53] This position is echoed by the last sentence of Articles 74(3) and 83(3) of UNCLOS: 'Such arrangements shall be without prejudice to the final delimitation'.[54] This 'without prejudice' provision serves as a safeguard and assuages concerns about losing a battle about sovereignty or sovereign rights when entering into provisional arrangements.[55]

The term 'arrangement' includes the form of a binding agreement entered into by and between States. For example, in *Guyana v. Suriname*, the tribunal took note of a number of examples of agreements for the joint exploration and exploitation of maritime resources.[56] However, as rightly pointed out by some scholars, the term 'arrangement' is understood as indicating 'co-operative mechanism between States or the instruments which provide a legal basis for such mechanism regardless of their nomenclatures'.[57] An 'arrangement' might also include something less formal than a treaty such as a memorandum of understanding without legally binding force.[58]

The phrase 'of a practical nature' indicates that the provisional arrangement at issue must have a certain functionality as opposed to being purely theoretical. However, this phrase seems to provide little assistance for States in designing a provisional arrangement because almost all forms of provisional

---

52 See *e.g.*, BIICL, *Report on the Obligations of States under Articles 74(3) and 83(3) of UNCLOS in respect of Undelimited Maritime Areas* (2016); Lagoni, n 28, 356; S.P. Kim, *Maritime Delimitation and Interim Arrangements in North East Asia* (Martinus Nijhoff Publishers. 2004), 54.

53 Lagoni, n 28, 356. Beckman and Bernard, n 28, 10.

54 UNCLOS, Articles 74(3) and 83(3).

55 Beckman and Bernard, n 28, 17.

56 Guyana v. Suriname, n 51, para.462.

57 See *e.g.*, Kim, n 52, 43; BIICL, n 52, para.61; Y. van Logchem, *Disputed Maritime Areas: The Rights and Obligations of States under International Law* (PhD Dissertation, Utrecht University, defended on 8 January 2019), 142–143.

58 BIICL, n 52, para.61.

arrangements would be deemed to have certain practicality owing to the low threshold inferred by this phrase.[59]

5.2.3 *Interim Conclusion*

The preceding analysis concludes that States do not have a general duty to cooperate with one another in their international relations under customary international law. However, States are obliged to negotiate in good faith a provisional arrangement in respect of disputed marine areas in a period preceding delimitation according to Articles 74(3) and 83(3) of UNCLOS (covering all kinds of resource and pollution management activities), or within a semi-enclosed sea according to Article 123 of UNCLOS (in terms of activities including management of living resources and marine pollution but excluding hydrocarbon resources development activities). Tailored to the Spratly Islands setting, the disputant States are obliged to negotiate in good faith a provisional arrangement concerning resource and pollution management therein.

Some issues, however, remain unsolved.[60] First, good-faith negotiation might take years without any result. Under this circumstance, international law is impotent because the obligation under Articles 74(3), 83(3) and 123 is an obligation of conduct rather than an obligation of result, which means that the disputant States are not obliged to reach an arrangement eventually after negotiations. Second, this obligation does not mandate the substantive content of a particular provisional arrangement but leaves it to be determined by the disputant States based on mutual consent.[61] In light of this, the following section explores whether at this stage, the disputant States have the political will to cooperate in resource and pollution management in the Spratly Islands area.

5.3 Momentum for Cooperation

As concluded in section 5.2, the final achievement of cooperative arrangements between or among the disputant States on resource and pollution management in the Spratly Islands area is not mandated in international law but

59 D. Attard, *The Exclusive Economic Zone in International Law* (Oxford: Clarendon Press. 1987), 228.

60 T. Davenport, The Exploration and Exploitation of Hydrocarbon Resources in Areas of Overlapping Claims, in R. Beckman, *et al.* (eds.), *Beyond Territorial Disputes in the South China Sea Legal Frameworks for the Joint Development of Hydrocarbon Resources* (Edward Elgar Publishing. 2013), 104.

61 Beckman and Bernard, n 28, 9.

highly reliant on the political will of such States. Thus, this section addresses the question of whether momentum has been generated at this stage for cooperation in resource and pollution management in the Spratly Islands area, through the examination of important events that could reflect the positive or negative willingness to cooperate of the claimants. The foreign relations between the disputant States have experienced ups and downs in the past three decades. Three periods can be divided according to changes in cooperative willingness, namely between 1992 and 2008 (subsection 5.3.1), between 2009 and 2016 (subsection 5.3.2), and post-2016 (subsection 5.3.3). Notably, the analysis of important events during these three periods goes beyond pure description of historical details and covers two facets: on the one hand, the analysis involves a holistic examination of motivations, causes, backdrops, genesis and development in relation to relevant legal documents – including binding treaties, non-binding international instruments, and judicial documents – in order to facilitate a better understanding of the roles that such documents have played or will play in the relations between or among relevant disputant States; and on the other hand, the analysis includes the interpretation of relevant legal documents, and their implications for the prospect for cooperative arrangements in the Spratly Islands setting. The lessons learned during the adoption and implementation of relevant legal documents will also be used as a reference when designing the cooperative institutions for resource and pollution management in chapters 6–8.

5.3.1 *First Attempts of Cooperation: 1992–2008*

The first period lasted from 1992 to 2008. The year 2002 witnessed the most favourable political atmosphere for cooperation, when China and ASEAN, to which Vietnam, the Philippines, Malaysia and Brunei are members, entered into the DOC for promoting a peaceful, friendly and harmonious environment and enhancing peace, stability, economic growth and prosperity in the South China Sea. Another important milestone in this period was the tripartite agreement for Joint Marine Seismic Undertaking (JMSU) concluded among the State-owned oil companies of China, Vietnam and the Philippines in 2005.

5.3.1.1 Declaration on Conduct (1992–2002)

In July 1992, the ASEAN States pronounced the idea of exploring the possibility of cooperation in the South China Sea at the 25th ASEAN Ministerial Meeting (AMM).[62] In the resultant Manila Declaration on the South China Sea, the

62 S. Wu and H. Ren, More than a Declaration: A Commentary on the Background and the Significance of the Declaration on the Conduct of the Parties in the South China Sea, 2(1) *CJIL* (2003), 312–313.

foreign ministers of ASEAN were committed to 'explor[ing] the possibility of cooperation in the South China Sea' in a list of specified fields, which consisted of 'the safety of maritime navigation and communication, protection against pollution of the marine environment, coordination of search and rescue operations, efforts towards combatting piracy and armed robbery as well as collaboration in the campaign against illicit trafficking in drugs'.[63] Exploration and exploitation of hydrocarbon resources were not included in this list.

In July 1996, the ASEAN foreign ministers further raised an official proposal of formulating a regional code of conduct 'to lay the foundation of long term stability' in the South China Sea at the 29th AMM.[64] A draft ('the ASEAN draft') was approved at the ASEAN Senior Officials' Meeting (SOM) held in November 1999. The ASEAN draft allows three observations. First, with an attempt to obtain China's approval, the ASEAN draft adopted the Philippine proposal on the definition of disputed areas as including the Spratly Islands only and without any reference to the Paracel Islands, which was contested by Vietnam.[65] Second, the ASEAN draft did not include exploration and exploitation of hydrocarbon resources in disputed areas in the list of potential areas of cooperation, which was originally included in the Philippines' proposal.[66] Third, the ASEAN draft adopted the Philippine proposal on the ban on the occupation of new islands, reefs and shoals.[67]

In November 1999, the ASEAN draft was submitted for consideration by heads of government of China and ASEAN at the 3rd ASEAN informal summit. China objected to most provisions of the ASEAN draft and circulated its own version of the draft code of conduct at the summit ('the Chinese draft').[68] In particular, China objected to the ban on the occupation of new maritime features contained in the ASEAN draft and insisted on the inclusion of a provision that 'parties should refrain from conducting any military exercises directed against other countries in the Spratly Islands and their adjacent waters'.[69] Yet, similar to the ASEAN draft, the Chinese draft also excluded the Paracel Islands from the geographical scope.

63 Manila Declaration on the South China Sea, adopted on 22 July 1992.

64 Joint Communiqué of the 29th ASEAN Ministerial Meeting, adopted on 21 July 1996.

65 L. Buszynski, ASEAN, the Declaration on Conduct, and the South China Sea, 25(3) *Contemporary Southeast Asia* (2003), 355.

66 Wu and Ren, n 62, 313.

67 Buszynski, n 65, 355–356.

68 *Ibid.*, 356.

69 *Ibid.*

Both the ASEAN draft and the Chinese draft were presented for consideration at the ASEAN-Chinese SOMs held in March 2000 and May 2001. However, no consensus was reached at these SOMs, as differences seemed irreconcilable both within ASEAN and in relation to China. For instance, within ASEAN, Vietnam still pressed for the inclusion of the Paracel Islands into the scope of disputed areas, while between ASEAN and China, the Philippines insisted on the ban on the occupation of new maritime features, which was opposed by China.

At the 35th AMM in July 2002, Malaysia moved to resolve the deadlock by proposing a declaration on the conduct in the South China Sea, which would be non-binding compared with a code, as a further concession to China. The foreign ministers of ASEAN approved this proposal at the meeting and agreed to work closely with China with a view to adopting a declaration.[70] China accepted the idea of a declaration and negotiated certain details with ASEAN before the document was finally adopted at the 8th ASEAN Summit in November 2002.

The final version of the DOC reflects a compromise between China and ASEAN.[71] First, the DOC simply refers to the South China Sea as its applicable geographical scope, without naming either the Spratly Islands or the Paracel Islands. Second, the Philippine proposal on the ban of the occupation of new maritime features is not included and is replaced in the first paragraph of Article 5 with an agreement on 'refraining from action of inhabiting on the presently uninhabited islands, reefs, shoals, cays, and other features'. Third, the Chinese proposal on the ban of military exercises is not accepted and is replaced in the second paragraph of Article 5 with a voluntary option to 'notify … other Parties concerned of any impending joint/combined military exercise'. Fourth, Article 6 provides for five areas of cooperation, which serve as a non-exhaustive list, including: (1) marine environmental protection, (2) marine scientific research, (3) safety of navigation and communication at sea, (4) search and rescue operation, and (5) combating transnational crime. Exploration and exploitation of hydrocarbon resources are not included in this list. Fifth, China did not accept an obligation to work on a code of conduct after the conclusion of the DOC and demanded including a provision that the eventual adoption

70 Joint Communiqué of the 35th ASEAN Ministerial Meeting, adopted on 30 July 2002.

71 T. Vu, The Logic of Strategic Restraint and Prospects for Joint Development in the South China Sea, in A. Gerstl and M. Strašáková (eds.), *Unresolved Border, Land and Maritime Disputes in Southeast Asia: Bi- and Multilateral Conflict Resolution Approaches and ASEAN's Centrality* (Brill. 2017), 238.

of a code of conduct should be 'on a basis of consensus', which is reflected in Article 10 of the DOC.

The DOC is the first multilateral document involving all the disputant States to work towards regional cooperation in respect of the South China Sea. It signifies a start for the disputant States to reduce a potential source of threat in this region through respect of standard international norms.[72] The motivation behind cooperation was the desire for economic growth and prosperity shared by the ASEAN States and China. Most ASEAN States, including Brunei, Malaysia and the Philippines, were impacted by the Asian financial crisis which occurred in 1997 and confronted with domestic crises including economic recession, terrorism and social unrest. China's fast-growing economy made the ASEAN countries begin to realize that China, as a rising power in the region, could be an opportunity for them to regain prosperity. China embraced cooperation with ASEAN because it was aware that a stable regional environment was conducive to its economic development. When China established diplomatic relations with ASEAN States in the 1970s and the 1980s, China's former leader, Xiaoping Deng (in office from 1978 to 1992), announced the proposal of 'setting aside [the] dispute and pursuing joint development' with regard to the South China Sea.[73] This proposal has been repeatedly emphasized in China's official statements of its policies towards ASEAN.[74] The core motive underlying this proposal is to defuse the potential for conflict among sovereign States through economic interdependence, in order to promote a peaceful, secure and stable regional environment to safeguard China's economic growth.[75]

Nevertheless, being merely a political statement without legally binding force, the DOC falls short of a code of conduct with the legal status that the ASEAN States had initially sought.[76] It does not mandate the modalities, scope or locations in respect of cooperation but leaves them to be agreed upon by the parties concerned prior to their actual implementation. In light of this, the DOC serves as a starting point for cooperation, but further initiatives will be

---

72 Wu and Ren, n 62, 319.

73 Ministry of Foreign Affairs of People's Republic of China, *Set aside Dispute and Pursue Joint Development*, available at < https://www.fmprc.gov.cn/mfa_eng/ziliao_665539/3602_665543/3604_665547/t18023.shtml>.

74 M. Yahuda, *The International Politics of the Asia Pacific* (Routledge. 2011), 216. T. Kivimäki, *War Or Peace in the South China Sea?* (NIAS. 2002), 91.

75 V. Chheang, Joint Development Prospects in the South China Sea: Divergent and Convergent Forces, in S. Wu and N. Hong (eds.), *Recent Developments in the South China Sea Dispute: the Prospect of a Joint Development Regime* (Routledge. 2014), 175. Kivimäki, n 74, 91.

76 Buszynski, n 65, 357.

required to formulate concrete cooperative arrangements and eventually put them into implementation.

5.3.1.2 Joint Marine Seismic Undertaking (2004–2008)

Bilateral ties between China and the Philippines registered a significant upturn in 2004 when the president of the later, Arroyo, agreed to undertake joint development in some areas in the South China Sea during her State visit to China, along with China's commitment to financing several infrastructure construction projects in the Philippines.[77] As a follow-up of this state visit, CNOOC and Philippine National Oil Company (PNOC), which are the State-owned oil companies of China and the Philippines, respectively, signed an agreement for Joint Marine Seismic Undertaking (JMSU) in September 2004, 'with a view of engaging in a joint research of petroleum resource potential of certain areas of the South China Sea as a pre-exploration activity'.[78] Perhaps it was unsurprising that China and the Philippines were the first ones to make the joint development efforts, given that these two countries, unlike the other claimants, have always been oil importers. The 2004 JMSU was never implemented,[79] as in less than six months after its adoption, it expanded into a tripartite JMSU in March 2005 when PetroVietnam, the State-owned oil company of Vietnam, joined the agreement.[80] The Philippine president, Arroyo, showed her optimism in this tripartite agreement by calling it 'a historic event' and 'a diplomatic breakthrough' in implementing the 2002 DOC.[81]

China, the Philippines and Vietnam had sufficient motives to enter into joint development of hydrocarbon resources in the South China Sea. First, these countries were interested in economic revenues accrued by oil and gas

77 Official Gazette, The President's Day: September 1, 2004, available at <https://www.officialgazette.gov.ph/2004/09/01/the-presidents-day-september-1-2004/>.

78 Agreement for Joint Marine Seismic Undertaking in Certain Areas in the South China Sea by and between CNOOC and PNOC, adopted on 1 September 2004, preambular paragraph 4.

79 Notably, Article 10 of the 2004 JMSU stipulates that CNOOC and PNOC agree to negotiate with a third country's national oil company with a view of allowing the latter's participation under this agreement provided that the latter formally expresses its desire to participate in the joint marine seismic undertaking contemplated under this agreement. This provision was included to leave room for other disputant States to participate in the joint exploration after the execution of the agreement. See *ibid.*, Article 10.

80 A Tripartite Agreement for Joint Marine Seismic Undertaking in Certain Areas in the South China Sea by and among CNOOC, PetroVietnam, and PNOC, adopted on 14 March 2005.

81 Radio Free Asia, China, Philippines, Vietnam Sign Joint South China Sea Oil Search Accord (14 March 2005), available at < https://www.rfa.org/english/news/business/china_vietnam_spratlys-20050314.html >.

especially in the era when the price of a barrel of crude oil was hovering at around 100 US dollars.[82] Second, China was politically driven by the goal to drag at least some of the other disputant States away from the US sphere of influence, with an aim to preventing them from forging an alliance with the US and to avoiding destabilizing the situation in the South China Sea.[83] The governments of the Philippines and Vietnam were interested because they could demonstrate economic development by using tangible benefits gained from enhanced cooperation with China on investments, trade and official development assistance (ODA) that were not contingent upon human rights record, progress towards democratization or accountability linked to governance, which the US and the EU often tied their aid to.[84]

The content of tripartite JMSU is substantively similar to that of the 2004 JMSU. First, the tripartite JMSU establishes a Joint Operating Committee (JOC) as a cooperative institution to implement the tripartite cooperation. The JOC, with equal representatives of each party, is empowered to represent the parties to sign subcontracts and service contracts for seismic line acquisition and procession.[85] However, the JOC is neither an autonomous decision-making entity nor with independent legal personality, as it is subject to directions given by the parties, and the power to designate concessionaires remains with CNOOC, PetroVietnam and PNOC.[86] Second, the term of the tripartite JMSU was three years.[87] Yet, this agreement provides that the parties can negotiate a more definitive agreement for further cooperation prior to or during the period of ninety days following the expiration of the agreement.[88] Third, without directly mentioning sovereignty and sovereign rights, the tripartite JMSU provides that this agreement 'shall not undermine the basic position held by the Government of each Party on the South China Sea issue'.[89]

82 International Crisis Group, *Stirring up the South China Sea (IV): Oil in Troubled Waters*, Report No. 275 (26 January 2016), 18.

83 H. Zhao, Sino-Philippine Relations: Moving Beyond South China Sea Dispute, 26(2) *Journal of East Asian Affairs* (2012), 69–72.

84 C. Santamaria, Sino-Philippine Joint Development in the South China Sea: Is Political Will Enough?, *Asian Politics & Policy* (2018), 327–328. E. Bower, The JMSU: A Tale of Bilateralism and Secrecy in the South China Sea, 1(23) *Centre for Strategic and International Studies – Southeast Asia Program* (27 July 2010), 3.

85 A Tripartite Agreement for Joint Marine Seismic Undertaking in Certain Areas in the South China Sea, n 80, Article 5.4.6.

86 *Ibid.*, Articles 5.6, 6.

87 *Ibid.*, Article 1.

88 *Ibid.*, Article 8.

89 *Ibid.*, Preamble.

However, the implementation of the tripartite JMSU did not turn out to be a success. To implement the agreement, CNOOC vessels collected data that was sent to be processed in Vietnam and was subsequently brought to the Philippines for further interpretation.[90] Despite costly expenses, the results generated from the joint seismic research conducted under this JMSU were not conclusive enough for the parties to move on to the next phase of exploiting the hydrocarbon reserves.[91] The three national oil companies were to share equally the costs resulting from conducting the joint seismic research within the agreed area, which came to around 7 million US dollars over the three-year period.[92]

In 2008 when it was time to decide whether the JMSU would be extended or not, several interrelated political scandals surfaced in the Philippines. First, Article 2 of the tripartite JMSU defines an agreed area for conducting seismic research, which spanned 142,886 km^2 west of Palawan covering a vast area off the coast of the Philippines.[93] This provision sparked controversy in early 2008 when news broke out that the agreed area comprised parts of the South China Sea not claimed by China or Vietnam.[94] Second, the JMSU was further put into the spotlight when the Philippine media accused Arroyo allies of corruption by making concessions to China in exchange for graft-ridden shady business deals with China and profiting from 'windfall of Chinese investment and loan projects that followed the signing of JMSU'.[95] The support for the Arroyo administration from the domestic audience in the Philippines thus fell to the bottom. Third, suspicion subsequently surfaced of the secrecy involved in the course of concluding the JMSU. Both the Philippine Constitution of 1987 and the Philippine Petroleum Act of 1949 provide that only companies with at least 60% of the capital owned by Philippine citizens can explore and exploit hydrocarbon resources within Philippine national territory.[96] To circumvent possible legal obstacles caused by the Philippine legislation, the parties avoided using the wording 'exploration' in the language of the JMSU and instead used

90 International Crisis Group, n 82, 19.

91 Santamaria, n 84, 330.

92 N.H. Thao and R. Amer, A New Legal Arrangement for the South China Sea?, 40 *ODIL* (2009), 338.

93 A Tripartite Agreement for Joint Marine Seismic Undertaking in Certain Areas in the South China Sea, n 80, Article 2. Bower, n 84, 4.

94 A. Baviera, The Influence of Domestic Politics on Philippine Foreign Policy Since 2004, *RSIS Working Paper No. 241* (5 June 2012), 15.

95 Santamaria, n 84, 331.

96 The Philippines, Constitution (1987), section 2. Also see the Philippines, Petroleum Act, Republic Act 387 (1949), Article 31.

the wording 'seismic line acquisition and processing', 'joint studies' and 'data exchange'.[97] Moreover, to circumvent Senate approval in the Philippines, the JMSU was designed to be a commercial agreement between the State-owned oil companies rather than a government-to-government agreement.[98] These legal nuances prompted two nationalist members to the legislative branch to bring a case before the Philippine Supreme Court in 2008, requesting the court to declare the JMSU null and void based on its violation of the 60% capital cap as stipulated in the Constitution and Petroleum Act. The Philippine Supreme Court has yet to rule on this case, albeit it was re-petitioned in 2014.

Due to the political pressure within the domestic realm in the Philippines, the tripartite JMSU expired in 2008 rather than being extended. The joint development option came to an end in March 2009 when Arroyo signed Republic Act 9522, which reiterated the Philippines' sovereignty and jurisdiction over the Kalayaan Island Group in the Spratly Islands.[99] Strictly speaking, as rightly pointed out by some scholars, the tripartite JMSU does not constitute a joint development agreement in the sense of 'provisional arrangements of a practical nature' under Articles 74(3) and 83(3) of UNCLOS, as it is not entered into by the claimant States but by their oil companies.[100] However, the tripartite JMSU is still a milestone in the process of regional cooperation on the South China Sea issues because it has demonstrated the desire and capabilities of the disputant States to conclude and carry out cooperative arrangements in the region. As commented by Manalac, the then PNOC president and under-secretary of the Philippine Energy Department who signed the tripartite JMSU, '[o]ne of the strongest incentives of the tripartite agreement was the confidence building among the countries. We worked together to demonstrate it could be done. We succeeded at that'.[101]

5.3.2 *Standoffs between the Claimants: 2009–2016*

The friendly political atmosphere, however, did not last long. The second period was between 2009 and 2016 when standoffs occurred. The disputant States exchanged a series of diplomatic notes from 2009 to 2011, through which these States argued for their own claims and against other States' claims relating to the South China Sea. In this period, the relations between China and

97 A Tripartite Agreement for Joint Marine Seismic Undertaking in Certain Areas in the South China Sea, n 80, Article 5.4.
98 Santamaria, n 84, 330.
99 The Philippines, Republic Act No. 9522 (10 March 2009), Section 2. Santamaria, n 84, 330.
100 Thao and Amer, n 92, 343.
101 International Crisis Group, n 82, 19.

other disputant States deteriorated, and conflicts frequently occurred within the Spratly Islands area. The 2012 Scarborough Shoal standoff between China and the Philippines prompted the instigation by the Philippines of arbitration against China in 2013.

5.3.2.1 CLCS Correspondence (2009–2011)

On 7 May 2009, Malaysia and Vietnam jointly submitted to the CLCS the information on the limits of the continental shelf beyond 200 M from the baselines along their mainland coasts, which extended over the Spratly Islands area.[102] The timing of this submission was selected probably to catch the deadline of submission to the CLCS, namely 13 May 2009, as set according to Annex II, Article 4 of UNCLOS together with a decision adopted at the 11th Meeting of States Parties on UNCLOS (SPLOS) on 29 May 2001 (SPLOS/72).[103] The joint submission received strong protests from China and the Philippines.[104] China attached a U-shaped line map in its response to the joint submission. Though China did not make any official claims in relation to the U-Shaped line, China's growing assertiveness demonstrated through the U-shaped line fuelled debates among the claimant States. Between 2009 and 2011, China, Malaysia, the Philippines and Vietnam had been asserting their own claims and attacking

102 Malaysia and Vietnam, Joint Submission to the Commission on the Limits of the Continental Shelf pursuant to Article 76, paragraph 8 of the United Nations Convention on the Law of the Sea 1982 in respect of the southern part of the South China Sea (7 May 2009).

103 Annex II, Article 4 of UNCLOS sets the timeline for the submission to the CLCS to be within 10 years of the entry into force of UNCLOS for the submitting State. However, considering that some coastal States, in particular developing countries including small island developing States, had difficulties in meeting their deadlines calculated based on 10-year period, the 11th Meeting of SPLOS adopted a decision on 29 May 2001 (SPLOS/72), providing that for a State for which UNCLOS entered into force before 13 May 1999, the deadline for making submissions to the CLCS was extended to 13 May 2009. Since Malaysia and Vietnam ratified UNCLOS on 14 October 1996 and 25 July 1994, respectively, and UNCLOS entered into force on 16 November 1994, the dates of the entry into force of UNCLOS for Malaysia and Vietnam were both before 13 May 1999. Therefore, according to SPLOS/72, the deadline for Malaysia and Vietnam to make a joint submission to the CLCS was 13 May 2009. In the end, these two countries made the joint submission six days before the deadline. See UNCLOS, Annex II, Article 4. SPLOS/72 (29 May 2001), Decision regarding the date of commencement of the ten-year period for making submissions to the Commission on the Limits of the Continental Shelf set out in article 4 of Annex II to the United Nations Convention on the Law of the Sea.

104 China, Note Verbale No. CML/17/2009 (7 May 2009), para.2; The Philippines, Note Verbale No. 000819 (4 August 2009), para.2.

others' claims relating to the South China Sea through sending several rounds of note *verbales* addressed to the Secretary-General of the UN.[105]

The relations between China and other disputant States deteriorated, and conflicts frequently occurred within the Spratly Islands area. One of the most famous standoffs in this period was the 2012 Scarborough Shoal standoff between China and the Philippines, which was said to light the fuse for the arbitration initiated by the Philippines against China in 2013.[106] On 10 April 2012, a Philippine warship intercepted several Chinese fishing vessels at the Scarborough Shoal, which was an island close to the Spratly Islands disputed between China and the Philippines, leading to an intense standoff when two Chinese law enforcement vessels arrived before the Philippine warship could complete the arrest.[107] Lasting for nearly two months, this standoff has been one of the longest standoffs in the South China Sea in the past two decades.[108]

The Philippines' foreign policy toward China was largely driven by its domestic politics.[109] President Aquino, who took over power in June 2010, stood up to China to distance himself from the corruption of his predecessor, Arroyo, and benefited from the growing anti-China sentiment among the population following the eruption of the JMSU-related political scandals in 2008.[110]

Another geopolitical factor that should not be ignored in this period was the 'Pivot to Asia' strategy developed by the Obama administration beginning in 2010. Impacted by the 2008 global financial crisis, the US economy entered a recession, leading to military spending cuts. The aim of the 'Pivot to Asia' strategy was to rebalance the US's foreign policy focus away from costly interventions in the Middle East to Asia, which was viewed as the prophesied centre of the 21st-century economy.[111] As an attempt to assert the US's leadership in Asia and to take advantages of the economic opportunities presented by

105 See *e.g.*, *ibid.*; Malaysia, Note Verbale No. HA/24/09 (20 May 2009); Malaysia, Note Verbale No. HA/41/09 (21 August 2009); Vietnam, Note Verbale No. 86/HC-2009 (8 May 2009), para.3; The Philippines, Note Verbale No. 000228 (5 April 2011).

106 M. Santos, PH wins arbitration case over South China Sea (12 July 2016), available at <https://globalnation.inquirer.net/140358/philippines-arbitration-decision-maritime-dispute-south-china-sea-arbitral-tribunal-unclos-itlos>.

107 CSIS, Case 3: Scarborough Shoal Standoff (2012), available at < https://amti.csis.org/counter-co-scarborough-standoff/ >. M. Green *et al.*, Counter-coercion Series: Scarborough Shoal Standoff (22 May 2017), available at <https://amti.csis.org/counter-co-scarborough-standoff/>.

108 Vu, n 71, 242.

109 Santamaria, n 84, 326.

110 *Ibid.*

111 J. Ford, The Pivot to Asia Was Obama's Biggest Mistake (21 January 2017), available at <https://thediplomat.com/2017/01/the-pivot-to-asia-was-obamas-biggest-mistake/>.

Asia's dynamic economic growth, the US had to counter-balance China's pervasive regional influence.[112] China overtook Japan as the world's second largest economy in 2010 and has become a leading market for all Asian countries. China's stunning economic growth in the 21st century has notably affected its military modernization and capacity-building, with its official military budget growing at an annual average of 8 per cent in inflation-adjusted terms during the past ten years from 2009 through 2018.[113] In light of this, the US assigned more military resources to Asia including sending its naval vessels to carry out the so-called Freedom of Navigation Programs (FONOPs) in the South China Sea on a routine basis.[114] US's military efforts in this region, to some extent, led to increased assertiveness shown by China with regard to the long-standing South China Sea territorial and maritime disputes, which undid the general tranquillity that existed before 2008.[115]

Apart from military efforts, another key element of the 'Pivot to Asia' strategy was the Trans-Pacific Partnership (TPP), a free trade agreement signed by the US and another 11 parties on 4 February 2016, which, in the view of many observers, would have served a geopolitical purpose to reduce the signatories' dependence on Chinese trade and bring them close to the US.[116] Brunei, Malaysia and the Philippines are parties to the TPP. Meanwhile, the US had generally improved its relations with all ASEAN countries under the Obama administration. An iconic event was that the US acceded to the Treaty of Amity and Cooperation in Southeast Asia in July 2009, which as seen as a symbol of upgrading the US's engagement in Southeast Asia.[117] The ASEAN States, in particular the Philippines, viewed the US's involvement in South China Sea issues as an opportunity to challenge China's claims respecting the region.[118]

---

112 R.C. De Castro, The Obama Administration's Strategic Pivot to Asia: From a Diplomatic to a Strategic Constrainment of an Emergent China?, 25(3) *Korea Journal of Defense Analysis* (2013), 332.

113 US Department of Defense, Annual Report to Congress: Military and Security Developments Involving the People's Republic of China 2019, 93–94.

114 K. Lee and K. Lee, US Freedom of Navigation Operations in South China Sea: An Ongoing Riddle between the United States and China, 29(3) *Korean Journal of Defense Analysis* (2017), 455–456.

115 Ford, n 111.

116 C.B. Roberts, ASEAN, the 'South China Sea' Arbitral Award, and the Code of Conduct: New Challenges, New Approaches, 10(2) *Asian Politics & Policy* (2018), 194. M. Green and M. Goodman, After TPP: The Geopolitics of Asia and the Pacific, 38(4) *The Washington Quarterly* (2015), 23.

117 M. Manyin *et al.*, U.S. Accession to the Association of Southeast Asian Nations' Treaty of Amity and Cooperation (TAC), CRS Report for Congress (13 July 2009), 1.

118 J. Santolan, Tensions escalate over the South China Sea (3 May 2011), available at <https://www.wsws.org/en/articles/2011/05/phil-m03.html>.

5.3.2.2 South China Sea Arbitration (2013–2016)

In January 2013, the Philippines initiated arbitration against China on the South China Sea issues under Articles 286 and 287 of UNCLOS and Article 1 of Annex VII of UNCLOS.[119] After an earlier award on jurisdiction and admissibility in 2015, the tribunal delivered a merits award on 12 July 2016,[120] which was described as 'a sweeping legal victory' for the Philippines against China.[121] China, on the other hand, has explicitly rejected the *South China Sea Arbitration* award as 'null and void'.[122]

The instigation of the *South China Sea arbitration* case indeed reflected the core foreign policy of the Aquino administration to form an outright alignment with the US and diplomatic confrontation with China.[123] During the Aquino administration, the prospect for joint development between China and the Philippines was poor. The Aquino administration had insisted that any prospective Chinese partner for development of Reed Bank in the South China Sea must recognize the Philippine sovereignty and sovereign rights, accept that all royalties going to the Philippines, and comply with the Philippine Constitution and Petroleum Act, which required that only companies with at least 60% of the capital owned by Philippine citizens could explore and exploit hydrocarbon resources within Philippine national territory.[124] These conditions, especially the recognition of the Philippine sovereignty and sovereign rights, were unacceptable for China. Responding to the hostility of the Aquino administration, China fought back by seizing control of the Scarborough Shoal, blocking the access of the Philippine supply ships to a garrison on Second Thomas Shoal, carrying out land reclamation activities and constructing artificial

---

119 For a detailed analysis of this case, please see chapter 3, section 3.3.2.2.

120 The South China Sea Arbitration, n 29.

121 See *e.g.*, R.C. De Castro, Taking the Cudgel for the 12 July 2016 UNCLOS Ruling? The Revival of the QUAD (20 September 2018), available at <https://www.jiia-jic.jp/en/policybrief/pdf/PB_DeCastro_Taking_the_Cudgel_for_the_12_July_2016_UNCLOS_Ruling.pdf>; C. Pichel Medina, Legal Victory for the Philippines against China: A Case Study (February 2017), available at <https://globalchallenges.ch/issue/1/legal-victory-for-the-philippines-against-china-a-case-study/>.

122 China, Statement on the Award of 12 July 2016 of the Arbitral Tribunal in the South China Sea Arbitration Established at the Request of the Republic of the Philippines (12 July 2016), available at <https://www.fmprc.gov.cn/nanhai/eng/snhwtlcwj_1/t1379492.htm>.

123 CIMSEC, Understanding the Philippines' South China Sea Policy (29 June 2018), available at <https://www.maritime-executive.com/editorials/understanding-the-philippines-south-china-sea-policy>.

124 T.J. Burgonio, Aquino open to joint oil dev't of Recto Bank, but ... (14 January 2013), available at <https://globalnation.inquirer.net/61547/aquino-open-to-joint-oil-devt-of-recto-bank-but>.

islands, which, according to the International Crisis Group, 'made joint development less palatable to the Philippine public and politically more perilous for leaders'.[125]

5.3.3 *New Momentum for Cooperation: 2016-Present*

The third period is the post-2016. In this period, two events have demonstrated signs of improvement of the relations between China and other disputant States. On the one hand, consultations between China and ASEAN on a potential South China Sea Code of Conduct have gained new momentum. The foreign ministers of China and the Philippines, on the other hand, signed a 'Memorandum of Understanding on Oil and Gas Development' (MoU) with respect to the South China Sea in November 2018.

5.3.3.1 Code of Conduct Negotiations (Since 2017)

In an 'unexpected twist', the relations between China and the ASEAN States have demonstrated signs of improvement following the release of the *South China Sea Arbitration* merits award.[126] The ASEAN forums, including the ASEAN Summits among the ASEAN leaders and the joint communiqués among the ASEAN foreign ministers, have not pushed strongly for the inclusion of the *South China Sea Arbitration* merits award in the organization's official documents.[127] Rather, in July 2016, China and ASEAN issued a joint statement in respect of the full and effective implementation of the 2002 DOC without referring to the decisions contained in the arbitral award to avoid direct conflicts.[128] The Philippine Foreign Affairs Secretary, Yasay, also called for 'restraint and sobriety' on the same day when the tribunal ruled in favor of the Philippines, clarifying that '[a]s the ruling will not address sovereignty and delimitation, it is possible that some time in the future, claimant countries might consider entering into arrangements such as joint exploration and utilization of resources in disputed areas that do not prejudice the parties' claims and delimitation of boundaries in accordance with UNCLOS'.[129]

---

125 International Crisis Group, n 82, 23–24.

126 L. Bautista, The Philippines and the Arbitral Tribunal's Award: A Sombre Victory and Uncertain Times Ahead, 38(3) *Contemporary Southeast Asia* (2016), 349.

127 *Ibid.*, 351. Roberts, n 116, 196–197.

128 ASEAN and China, Joint Statement of the Foreign Ministers on the Full and Effective Implementation of the Declaration on the Conduct of Parties in the South China Sea (25 July 2016).

129 Philstar.com, DFA calls for restraint, sobriety after tribunal favors Philippines (12 July 2016), available at <https://www.philstar.com/headlines/2016/07/12/1602130/dfa-calls-restraint-sobriety-after-tribunal-favors-philippines>.

Two major events have affected the dynamics of the South China Sea disputes since 2016, namely the inauguration of President Rodrigo Duterte in the Philippines on 30 June 2016, 12 days before the release of the *South China Sea Arbitration* merits award, and the inauguration of President Donald Trump in the US on 20 January 2017. First, the Duterte administration in the Philippines adopted a pro-China foreign policy, resulting from a lack of confidence in the US defense shield and the criticism by the west of his bloody war on drugs, as well as in exchange for increased trade, investment and ODA from China.[130] Second, the Trump administration abandoned the 'Pivot to Asia' strategy developed by the Obama administration. Trump signed a Presidential memorandum to withdraw the US from the TPP within three days of taking office.[131] When viewed in conjunction with Trump's assertiveness towards alliance commitments that requested the alliance partners to pay more for their security, countries relying on a military alliance with the US, including the ASEAN States, started to reconsider the value of the US security umbrella.[132]

Against this backdrop, consultations between China and ASEAN on a potential South China Sea Code of Conduct with legally binding force, a process which China had managed to draw out between 1992 and 2002, have gained new momentum since late 2016.[133] As a result, in August 2017, China and ASEAN adopted a bare-bones framework for the COC.[134] Subsequently, in August 2018, China and ASEAN announced the start of the negotiation for the COC based on a single draft negotiating text (SDNT).[135] Neither the COC framework nor the SDNT has been made available to the public. However, several

130 Santamaria, n 84, 326; Roberts, n 116, 194.

131 US, Presidential Memorandum Regarding Withdrawal of the United States from the Trans-Pacific Partnership Negotiations and Agreement, issued on 23 January 2017, available at <https://trumpwhitehouse.archives.gov/presidential-actions/presidential-memorandum-regarding-withdrawal-united-states-trans-pacific-partnership-negotiations-agreement/>.

132 Roberts, n 116, 194. J.M. Watts, ASEAN Tacks Away from Rocky South China Sea Issue: Final summit communiqué welcomes Beijing's cooperation on issues such as framework for maritime code of conduct (29 April 2017), available at <https://www.wsj.com/articles/asean-backs-off-confrontation-over-chinas-island-building-at-summit-1493524282>.

133 South China Sea Expert Working Group, A Blueprint for a South China Sea Code of Conduct (11 October 2018), available at <https://amti.csis.org/blueprint-for-south-china-sea-code-of-conduct/>.

134 Y. Lee, A South China Sea Code of Conduct: Is Real Progress Possible? (18 November 2017), available at <https://thediplomat.com/2017/11/a-south-china-sea-code-of-conduct-is-real-progress-possible/>.

135 C. Thayer, A Closer Look at the ASEAN-China Single Draft South China Sea Code of Conduct (3 August 2018), available at <https://thediplomat.com/2018/08/a-closer-look-at-the-asean-china-single-draft-south-china-sea-code-of-conduct/>.

observations can be drawn based on the unofficial briefings of the texts of these two documents.[136]

First, there is a possibility that the COC is designed to be a legally binding instrument. The SDNT, albeit not referring to the COC as a treaty under international law, does contain a proposal that the parties 'have consented to be bound by the present Code of Conduct'. Second, the SDNT does not clearly define the geographic scope where the COC is applicable. Vietnam proposed that 'the present Code of Conduct shall apply to all disputed features and overlapping maritime areas claimed under the 1982 UNCLOS in the South China Sea'. It remains to be seen whether this proposal will be accepted by other parties. Third, with respect to dispute settlement, the SDNT does not contain any specific reference to the dispute settlement procedures entailing binding decisions as set forth in Section 2 of Part XV of UNCLOS. Vietnam suggested that the parties settle their disputes 'through friendly negotiations, enquiry, mediation, conciliation and other means as may be agreed by the disputing Contracting Parties'. Indonesia, in contrast, proposed that the parties agreed to resort to the High Council of the Treaty of Amity and Cooperation in Southeast Asia or other appropriate international disputes settlement mechanism, at the consent of the parties concerned, to settle any dispute relating to incidents that may arise in the South China Sea. Fourth, as to the areas of cooperation, except for China, all the other parties basically proposed the same five areas of cooperation as set forth in Article 6 of the DOC, namely marine environmental protection, marine scientific research, safety of navigation and communication at sea, search and rescue operation, and combating transnational crime. In comparison, China adds a sixth area of cooperation, namely marine economy cooperation including oil and gas development.[137]

The negotiations on the COC are still in progress. It is beyond doubt that once adopted, the COC will be a critical component of a regime for managing the disputes in the South China Sea.[138] As stipulated in the COC framework, the COC is not itself a final resolution of the territorial dispute and maritime delimitation issues. Instead, it aims to provide general guidelines for the contracting parties to manage the tension surrounding the disputes and to remove the triggers for conflict. The COC will be without prejudice to the final

136 C. Thayer, ASEAN-China: Framework of a COC (6 August 2017), Thayer Consultancy Background Brief, available at <https://www.scribd.com/document/355938565/Thayer-ASEAN-China-Framework-of-a-COC-August-6-2017>. Thayer, n 135.

137 R. Amer and J. Li, From DOC to COC: A Regional Rules-based Order, in K. Zou (ed.), *Routledge Handbook of the South China Sea* (Routledge. 2021), 366.

138 South China Sea Expert Working Group, n 133.

settlement of disputes and have no impact on the parties' current legal positions toward the disputes.

Nevertheless, the COC has its limitations. Since the negotiating process involves not only the claimants respecting the Spratly Islands dispute but also other ASEAN members, the COC is not destined to be a suitable vehicle to negotiate the details of cooperative arrangements respecting matters such as resource and pollution management within the Spratly Islands area, in which the non-claimant ASEAN States have no direct stake. Thus, additional bilateral or multilateral negotiations among the claimants on specific cooperative arrangements will remain in need even if the COC is concluded.

5.3.3.2 Oil/Gas MoU (Since 2018)

During Duterte's State visit to China in October 2016, the Philippines and China issued a joint statement, establishing a bilateral dialogue mechanism to enhance understanding and broaden cooperation on matters including the South China Sea issues.[139] Duterte was open to the idea of entering into joint development of hydrocarbon resources with China in the South China Sea.[140] As a result of the friendly relations, the foreign ministers of China and the Philippines signed a 'Memorandum of Understanding on Oil and Gas Development' (MoU) with respect to the South China Sea on 20 November 2018.[141] The purpose of this MoU is to set up a mechanism for China and the Philippines to *negotiate* cooperative arrangements regarding the development of hydrocarbon operations in the South China Sea.[142]

To facilitate the negotiation process, the MoU establishes a two-tier structure, including an Inter-Governmental Joint Steering Committee and one or more Inter-Entrepreneurial Working Group.[143] The Committee, comprising an equal number of members nominated by the two governments including

---

139 China and the Philippines, Joint Statement (21 October 2016), available at <http://www.fmprc.gov.cn/mfa_eng/zxxx_662805/t1407682.shtml>.

140 Philippine Daily Inquirer, Joint exploration with China is co-ownership, says Duterte (1 March 2018), available at <https://globalnation.inquirer.net/164677/joint-exploration-china-co-ownership-says-duterte>.

141 C. Mendez and P. Romero, Philippines, China sign MOU on Joint Gas, Oil Development (21 November 2018), available at <https://www.philstar.com/headlines/2018/11/21/1870458/philippines-china-sign-mou-joint-gas-oil-developement>; J. Batongbacal, A Closer Look at China's Proposal for Joint Exploration with the Philippines (21 November 2018), available at <https://amti.csis.org/closer-look-chinas-proposal-joint-exploration-with-philippines/?from=groupmessage&isappinstalled=0>.

142 China and Philippines, Memorandum of Understanding on Cooperation on Oil and Gas Development (20 November 2018).

143 *Ibid.*, Article III(A).

their respective heads from foreign affairs ministries and energy ministries, will be responsible for functions including: negotiating and agreeing on the substantive cooperation arrangements; designating the maritime areas to which these arrangements will apply; and deciding the number of and responsible cooperation areas for Working Groups to be established.[144] Each Working Group, comprising representatives from enterprises authorized by the two governments, will take responsibility for negotiating and agreeing on inter-entrepreneurial technical and commercial arrangements that will apply in the applicable cooperation area.[145] China has authorized its State-owned oil company – CNOOC – as the Chinese enterprise for each Working Group.[146] The Philippines will authorize the enterprise(s) that has/have entered into a service contract with it with respect to the applicable working area or in the absence of such enterprise(s), its State-owned oil company – the PNOC-Exploration Corporation (PNOC-EC) – as the Philippine enterprise(s) for the relevant Working Group.[147] This MoU explicitly stipulates that it does not create any rights or obligations under international law or domestic law and shall be without prejudice to the respective positions of both parties.[148]

This MoU allows several observations. First, consisting of only six provisions, details remain highly sketchy. For example, this MoU has not precisely defined what areas will be considered relevant for joint development. In theory, the parties could include any areas in the South China Sea agreed by them, whether disputed or undisputed between them, as the MoU does not set parameters or restrictions.[149] In practice, however, cooperation without involving third parties that have claims to relevant areas would add complexity and even thwart the efforts of cooperation. Second, the two governments agreed to have a soft deadline, namely 12 months within which to agree on areas and substantive arrangements.[150] Yet, the non-binding character of the MoU makes the achievement of this aim without any guarantee. In fact, little progress has been made since the convening of the first meeting of the Inter-Governmental Joint Steering Committee on Cooperation on Oil and Gas Development in October 2019,[151] allegedly owing to the global COVID-19 outbreak in

144 *Ibid.*, Article III(A)&(B).
145 *Ibid.*, Article III(A)&(B).
146 *Ibid.*, Article III(C).
147 *Ibid.*
148 *Ibid.*, Article IV.
149 Batongbacal, n 141.
150 China and Philippines, n 142, Article III(D).
151 Ministry of Foreign Affairs of China, First Meeting of the China-Philippines Inter-Governmental Joint Steering Committee on Cooperation on Oil and Gas Development

2020.[152] Moreover, as a lesson learnt from the failure of the 2005 tripartite JMSU, any substantive arrangements relating to the joint development of hydrocarbon resources with the Philippines in the South China Sea would need to address the specific challenges and restrictions posed by the Philippine Constitution and legislation. The MoU has not touched upon this matter, which thus remains a problem that needs to be solved before substantive arrangements for cooperation can be successfully concluded.

5.4 Paradigm Shift from Balance of Power to Institutionalized Cooperation

The preceding analysis indicates that tensions in the South China Sea have ebbed and flowed in the past three decades. Though all the disputant States have agreed that contentious issues are not the totality of their foreign relations, and that they will all benefit from a peaceful atmosphere, the political will of these States to develop cooperative initiatives in relation to the Spratly Islands area tend to be heavily influenced by domestic politics. For instance, domestic politics did act as a spoiler for joint development in the Spratly Islands area between 2009 and 2016. The impasse on cooperation in that period largely resulted from the ASEAN countries' balance-of-power approach through forging military and economic reliance with the US to fight against China, used by political leaders as a tool to pander to nationalist sentiments within their domestic audience and to support their own political agendas. Another example is the Philippine foreign policy toward China, which, according to scholars, has come full circle in less than 15 years by going from bandwagoning with China under the Arroyo administration to balancing against it through an alliance with the US under the Aquino administration to bandwagoning again following the 2016 inauguration of Duterte.[153] With the decline of confidence in the US defense shield and economic alliance, the tide of domestic politics of

was held in Beijing (29 October 2019), available at <https://www.fmprc.gov.cn/mfa_eng/wjb_663304/zygy_663314/gyhd_663338/t1711668.shtml>.

152 L. Lectura, Covid-19 delays PHL-China talks on oil, gas deal (18 May 2020), available at <https://businessmirror.com.ph/2020/05/18/covid-19-delays-phl-china-talks-on-oil-gas-deal/>.

153 See *e.g.*, Santamaria, n 84, 326; A. Murphy, Great Power Rivalries, Domestic Politics and Southeast Asian Foreign Policy: Exploring the Linkages, 13(3) *Asian Security* (2017), 174–175.

the claimant ASEAN States has now turned in favor of cooperation with China in the Spratly Islands area.

5.4.1 *Balance of Power*

Power asymmetry in terms of military and economic resources exist among the claimant States, with China being the biggest power in the region. China's military expenditure in 2018 cost 239 billion US dollars, which was more than 19 times the combined military expenditure of Brunei, Malaysia, the Philippines and Vietnam in the same year.[154] China is also the only country among the claimants officially recognized as being in possession of nuclear weapons.[155] As to economic power, China's Gross Domestic Product (GDP) ranks second and represents 15% of the world economy, which is four times the total GDP of all ASEAN States.[156] The power differential between China and the other disputant States has prompted the latter to draw on external powers, particularly the US, to balance against China between 2009 and 2016. This strategy follows the balance-of-power theory, a classical theory in international relations used to explain the power dynamics in international politics.[157] According to this theory, a small power can adopt a balancing strategy against a great regional power by deriving relative power through forging an alliance or becoming dependent partners of other great powers, usually external to the region.[158] By engaging other powers outside of the system, weaker powers can affect the regional power equilibrium to effectively prevent a great regional power from abusing the power asymmetry to encroach their legitimate interests.[159]

The balance-of-power strategy, however, cannot lead to a resolution of the territorial and maritime disputes in the Spratly Islands area nor to the creation of a stable environment in which the development of marine natural resources can proceed. As exemplified in the period between 2009 and 2016,

---

154 Trading Economics, Military Expenditure – By Country (last updated in June 2019), available at <https://tradingeconomics.com/country-list/military-expenditure>.

155 See K. Davenport, Nuclear Weapons: Who Has What at a Glance (January 2018), available at <https://www.armscontrol.org/factsheets/Nuclearweaponswhohaswhat>.

156 The calculation is based on the data of GDP (current US$) in 2017 published by the World Bank. See World Bank, *Gross Domestic Product 2017*, available at <http://databank.worldbank.org/data/download/GDP.pdf>.

157 For discussions on the balance-of-power theory, see *e.g.*, W.H. Riker, *The Theory of Political Coalitions* (Yale University Press. 1962), 161; O. Niou *et al.*, *The Balance of Power: Stability in International Systems* (CUP. 1989), 21; M. Sheehan, *The Balance of Power: History & Theory* (Routledge. 1996).

158 R.C. De Castro, The Strategic Balance in East Asia and the Small Powers: The Case of the Philippines in the Face of the South China Sea Dispute, 31(1) *Pacific Focus* (2016), 129–130.

159 *Ibid.*, 130.

the engagement of the US to support the claimant ASEAN States on the South China Sea issues resulted in an impasse on cooperation. The maximum potential function of the balance-of-power strategy is to prevent or deter a great regional power from abusing its military and economic domination to exploit the interests of other weaker States. This power-based strategy, however, has two trade-offs. First, the balance of power does not necessarily prevent or deter wars, but rather, might ignite into a major systemic conflict by squarely putting small powers in the middle of a strategic standoff between two or more hegemonic powers.[160] Second, this strategy puts weaker powers and regionally hegemonic powers in a hostile relationship where cooperation in pursuit of shared prosperity has little chance to proceed. The balance of power, by its nature, remains within the paradigm described by Friedmann as diplomacy of 'coexistence', which refers to 'the conduct of international relations on the basis of national power'.[161] However, as Friedmann has rightly pointed out, the changing structure of international relations – especially the emergence of two destructive threats to humankind's survival caused by the advent of thermonuclear weapons and by the limits of natural resources of the Earth owing to the population explosion and the absence of coordinated conservation measures – underlines the need for more organized international collaboration as a practical way to give effect to coexistence.[162]

5.4.2 *Institutionalized Cooperation*

Tailored to the Spratly Islands setting, the coexistence between the claimants, roughly balanced through a strategic standoff between China and the US or any other external great powers, is not a viable means to sustain the peaceful relations among the claimants. Rather, institutionalized cooperation, a more active form of coexistence which promotes shared prosperity through more organized international collaboration, is more apt for the Spratly Islands setting. A paradigm shift from the balance of power to institutionalized cooperation is thus needed in the foreign policies that the disputant States apply respecting the Spratly Islands area. The following analysis focuses on the meaning of the concept of 'institutionalized cooperation', the preconditions to trigger its application, and the architecture composed of elements that are essential to the operation of this concept in practice.

---

160 De Castro, n 158, 128. Sheehan, n 157, 204. R.H. Wagner, Peace, War, and the Balance of Power, 88(3) *American Political Science Review* (1994). 593.

161 Friedmann, n 3, 14.

162 *Ibid.*, 365.

5.4.2.1 Meaning

'Cooperation', as discussed in section 5.2, has never been defined in any official international instruments but has a widely accepted definition as 'the voluntary co-ordinated action of two or more States which takes place under a legal regime and serves a specific objective'.[163] 'Institution' is an even fuzzier concept than 'cooperation', which are often discussed without being defined at all or after having been defined merely casually.[164] The vagueness of this term is showcased by scholarly literature. Numerous writings speak of treaties and organizations as institutions.[165] Bull describes 'the balance of power, international law, the diplomatic mechanism, the managerial system of greater powers, and war' as 'the institutions of international society'.[166] Greenwood also discusses 'war' as 'an institution of international law'.[167] Scholars such as Krasner and Sørensen write about sovereignty as an institution.[168]

It may help in sorting out some troubling confusions in these usages of the term 'institution' to refer to a statement made by Keohane, which, on the basis of the commonality shared by such usages, has coined the definition of institutions as 'persistent and connected sets of rules (formal or informal) that prescribe behavioural roles, constrain activity, and shape expectations'.[169] Keohane distinguishes two types of institutions, namely general institutions and specific institutions. General institutions refer to 'general pattern or categorization of activity' including 'norms that are applicable to a wide variety of situations' such as sovereignty, war, diplomacy and neutrality. Specific institutions are 'a particular human-constructed arrangement' that is established

---

163 Wolfrum, n 4, para.2.

164 R.O. Keohane, International Institutions: Two Approaches, 32(4) *International Studies Quarterly* (1988), 382.

165 See *e.g.*, C. Coglianese, Globalization and the Design of International Institutions, in J. Nye *et al.* (eds.), *Governance in a Globalizing World* (Brookings Institution Press. 2000), 297–318; B.A. Simmons and L.L. Martin, International Organizations and Institutions, in W. Carlsnaes *et al.* (eds.), *Handbook of International Relations* (Sage. 2002), 192–211; K. Conca *et al.*, Global Regime Formation or Complex Institution Building? The Principled Content of International River Agreements, 50(2) *International Studies Quarterly* (2006), 263–285; N. Chorev and S. Babb, The Crisis of Neoliberalism and the Future of International Institutions: A Comparison of the IMF and the WTO, 38(5) *Theory and Society* (2009), 459–484; R.W. Stone, *Controlling Institutions: International Organizations and the Global Economy* (CUP. 2011).

166 H. Bull, The Anarchical Society (Columbia University Press. 1977), 74.

167 C. Greenwood, The Concept of War in Modern International Law, 36(2) *ICLQ* (1987), 283.

168 See *e.g.*, S.D. Krasner, Sovereignty: An Institutional Perspective, 21(1) *Comparative Political Studies* (1988), 74; G. Sørensen, Sovereignty: Change and Continuity in a Fundamental Institution, 47(3) *Political Studies* (1999), 590–604.

169 Keohane, n 164, 383.

based on the decisions of particular individual actors, examples of which range from formal arrangements like international organizations and treaties to informal arrangements such as inter-State voluntary negotiations and consultations on certain international issues.[170]

'Institutionalized cooperation' discussed in the Spratly Islands setting belongs to a kind of specific institution, as it applies to the Spratly Islands area in particular, and its conclusion is at the disposal of the disputant States. In this context, 'institutionalized cooperation' can be defined as formal or informal cooperative arrangements established on a durable basis at the disposal of the States concerned with the aim of realizing common interests.[171] The relationship between 'cooperation' and 'institution' can be best described using Pinto's words that '[c]o-operation would seem to reach its most developed expression in the establishment by the parties of institutions through which regular contact could be maintained, co-operative action can be monitored and supervised and, perhaps, new co-operative initiatives proposed, adopted and implemented'.[172] Given the power differential between China and other disputant States, the purpose of institutionalized cooperation is to counterbalance the asymmetry of physical capacity through tempering the leading position of a big country like China by committing it to credible exercises of institutionalized restraints and to operate in compliance with agreed substantive norms, which, in turn, reduces fears from weaker States about the abuse of growing resource powers by that big power.

5.4.2.2 Preconditions

The presence of shared interests and the political will to cooperate are two cumulative prerequisites for institutionalized cooperation. In the context of the Spratly Islands area, it is beyond doubt that the disputant States have common interests in reducing the risk of conflicts and gaining economic benefits by entering into cooperation. However, the presence of shared interests alone cannot lead to actual cooperation. Another indispensable prerequisite to materialize cooperation is the political will of the disputant States to

170 *Ibid.*, 383–384.

171 T. Pedersen, Cooperative Hegemony: Power, Ideas and Institutions in Regional Integration, 28 *Review of International Studies* (2002), 677, 679. E. Goh, Institutions and the Great Power Bargain in East Asia: ASEAN's Limited 'Brokerage' Role, 11(3) *International Relations of the Asia-Pacific* (2011), 373.

172 M.C.W. Pinto, The Duty of Co-operation and the United Nations Convention on the Law of the Sea, in A. Bos and H. Siblesz (eds.), *Realism in Law-making: Essays on International Law in Honour of Willem Riphagen* (Martinus Nijhoff Publishers. 1986), 154.

cooperate. On the one hand, as concluded in section 5.3, the political will of the weaker powers in the Spratly Islands region tend to be heavily influenced by domestic politics, but the tide of domestic politics of these States has now turned in favor of cooperation with China. China, on the other hand, appears to have been embracing the policy of joint development with claimant ASEAN members since the 1970s.[173]

One may wonder why a great power such as China would need institutionalized cooperation, and some may be concerned that great powers might undermine international law through practical arrangements under the disguise of the duty to cooperate.[174] The traditional theory of hegemonic stability in the international relations discipline portrays regionally hegemonic powers as powerful States that are capable of imposing their will by unilateral means.[175] However, this portrait is no longer correct, as the exercise of military and economic advantages by a State to exploit the interests of another has been constrained by international law developed after WWII. On the one hand, Article 2(4) of the UN Charter has outlawed any offensive self-help by threats or use of armed force without a basis in Chapter VII of the UN Charter.[176] On the other hand, international trade law, particularly the WTO regime, aims at regulating the action of governments and companies to prevent the abuse of competitive edges that impedes fair competition and free trade.[177] As a result, according to international law as it stands currently, hegemons face legal constraints on their unilateral freedom of action. Consequently, for example, the prospect for China, even being a regionally hegemonic power, to succeed in exploiting hydrocarbon resources within the Spratly Islands area in a unilateral manner is very poor indeed, as the other disputant States would undoubtedly find some way to interfere with the exploitation activities. Hence, in order to achieve shared interests in the Spratly Islands area, China needs cooperation with other weaker disputant States just as the latter needs cooperation with China.

5.4.2.3 Architecture

Institutionalized cooperation comprises two phases, namely the formative phase and the operative phase. The formative phase is the process with the

173 Yahuda, n 74, 216. Kivimäki, n 74, 91.

174 S. Lee and L. Bautista, Semi-enclosed Seas Cooperation under UNCLOS, in K. Zou (ed.), *Routledge Handbook of the South China Sea* (Routledge. 2021), 332–333.

175 Pedersen, n 171, 679.

176 UN Charter, Article 2(4) & Chapter VII. B. Simma, NATO, the UN and the Use of Force: Legal Aspects, 10 *EJIL* (1999), 3–4.

177 WTO, *Understanding the WTO* (3rd ed. 2005), 12–13.

aim of agreeing on an arrangement for cooperation. Two factors play a critical role in the formative phase. First, as concluded in section 5.2, Articles 74(3) and 83(3) of UNCLOS oblige the disputant States to negotiate in good faith a provisional arrangement in respect of disputed marine areas in a period preceding delimitation. Second, some international organizations can play an important 'brokerage' role in terms of serving as an intermediary or providing fora for facilitating dialogues and building confidence among the disputant States.[178] As can be seen in section 5.3, ASEAN has helped to bring the disputant States to the negotiating table to discuss a common understanding of key strategic norms with regard to the South China Sea, which have been exemplified by the conclusion of the DOC and the ongoing negotiations on the COC. Yet, neither UNCLOS provisions nor the brokerage role of relevant international organizations can guarantee the eventual conclusion of an arrangement after negotiations. Whether a cooperative arrangement can be successfully concluded still depends on the presence of shared interests and the political will to cooperate.

As to the operative phase, the architecture of institutionalized cooperation captures two elements that are essential to the operation of this concept in practice, namely the substantive or normative element and the procedural or structural element. The substantive element refers to substantive norms including both rules and principles with binding force and other non-binding normative expectations of conduct, according to which marine natural resources and the environment should be utilized and conserved. The procedural element refers to cooperative institutions for maintaining order, resolving disputes and considering, applying or otherwise revisiting substantive norms.[179] Cooperative institutions can take diverse forms with varying degrees of institutionalization, from a simple legally binding instrument to regular intergovernmental meetings to permanent intergovernmental institutions without or even with independent legal personality under international law.

A further question is how to select the degree of institutionalization for a specific cooperative arrangement. First, one determinant is the degree of freedom of action that the parties intend to have by mutual consent. The lower the degree of States' freedom to act, the higher the degree of institutionalization. Second, another determinant is the level of complexity of regulatory problems that exist in substantive norms under current international law. The more

178 Goh, n 171, 374.

179 S. Huntington, *Political Order in Changing Societies* (Yale University Press. 1973), 8–9.

complex the regulatory problems, the more the achievement of a cooperative arrangement becomes dependent on the working of the cooperative institution. The underlying rationale is the complementary relationship between substantive norms and cooperative institutions in achieving the objective of realizing common interests through cooperation.[180] Pushing things to one extreme, if substantive norms under current international law are completely adequate in regulating every matter related to the operation of institutionalized cooperation, in theory, there would be no need to construct any cooperative institution to maintain order, resolve disputes or revise substantive norms. In another extreme, if there are no substantive norms at all, the successful operation of institutionalized cooperation would depend entirely on the working of the cooperative institution concerned. Yet, the real scenarios have always been somewhere between these two extremes. The Spratly Islands setting is not exceptional.

5.5 Conclusion

The duty to cooperate, as it currently stands in international law, sets out an obligation for the disputant countries to negotiate in good faith with a view to arriving at provisional arrangements in relation to the Spratly Islands area, leaving the content of these arrangements to be determined by these countries through mutual consent. The common interests in preventing and defusing tensions and conflicts and the efficient and sustainable utilisation of resources have resulted in a substantial motivation of these States to cooperate with each other. The political climate developed after the delivery of the *South China Sea Arbitration* award has gradually generated momentum for cooperation in this region. Furthermore, the power differential between China and the other disputant States calls for a paradigm shift from the balance of power to institutionalized cooperation, which promotes shared prosperity through more organized international collaboration. On this basis, the following

180 A similar position has been expressed by the ICJ in the *Pulp Mills on the River Uruguay* (*Argentina v. Uruguay*) judgment. In that case, the ICJ concluded that the 1975 Statute consisted of two categories of obligations, namely the substantive obligations that were frequently worded in broad terms and the procedural obligations that were narrower and more specific, which complemented each other perfectly, thereby enabling the parties to achieve the objective to achieve 'the optimum and rational utilization of the River Uruguay' by means of 'joint machinery' for cooperation set in Article 1 of this Statute. See Pulp Mills on the River Uruguay (Argentina v. Uruguay), Judgment of 20 April 2010 (ICJ), paras.75, 77.

chapters explore the implementation of institutionalized cooperation in the Spratly Islands setting concerning the management of hydrocarbon resources (chapter 6), fisheries resources (chapter 7), and marine pollution (chapter 8), respectively.

CHAPTER 6

Cooperation in Managing Hydrocarbon Resources

6.1 Introduction

States are sensitive to even the slightest possibility of loss or detriment of their claimed territorial sovereignty and sovereign rights. This sensitivity explains why sometimes it is so difficult, if not impossible, for States to reach delimitation boundary agreements for disputed areas. The situation of the Spratly Islands dispute is even more complicated since it involves multiple State parties and various offshore geographic features. It is thus reasonable to anticipate that the settlement of this dispute is unlikely in the short term. However, given that all the disputant States are developing countries with rapid economic growth, demands for energy are increasing. Hence, exploiting hydrocarbon resources in this region has become an issue of even greater urgency than the issue of boundary delimitation. Even if boundary delimitation agreements can be reached, cooperation in managing hydrocarbon resources may still be in need, as hydrocarbon deposits often straddle human-made boundaries.[1]

The abundant hydrocarbon reserves in the Spratly Islands area can tackle the disputant States' growing thirst for oil and gas to fuel their economic growth. The Spratly Islands area is estimated to have 2.5 billion barrels of oil, 25.5 trillion cubic feet of natural gas, and excellent potential for gas hydrate storage owing to its satisfactory conditions of temperature, pressure and organic sources to form and feed gas hydrate stability zone.[2] The first successful extraction of gas hydrates within the South China Sea was undertaken by China in non-disputed waters in 2017, which symbolized a breakthrough in energy technologies and might stimulate extraction attempts driven by huge business opportunities.[3]

1 K. Zou, Joint Development in the South China Sea: A New Approach, 21 *IJMCL* (2006), 89.

2 U.S. Energy Information Administration, *South China Sea* (7 February 2013), available at <https://www.eia.gov/beta/international/analysis_includes/regions_of_interest/South_China_Sea/south_china_sea.pdf>. N. Trung, The Gas Hydrate Potential in the South China Sea, 88–89 *Journal of Petroleum Science and Engineering* (2012), 46.

3 T. Paraskova, Energy Breakthrough? China Has Successfully Mined 'Fire Ice' From The Sea (18 May 2017), available at <http://oilprice.com/Energy/Natural-Gas/Energy-Breakthrough-China-Has-Successfully-Mined-Fire-Ice-From-The-Sea.html>.

 | DOI:10.1163/9789004504332_007

This chapter seeks to explore the implementation of institutionalized cooperation in the Spratly Islands setting in two dimensions, namely the substantive element and the procedural element, respectively (sections 6.2 and 6.3). The substantive element refers to substantive norms according to which hydrocarbon resources should be utilized and conserved. The procedural element refers to cooperative institutions for maintaining order, resolving disputes and considering, applying or otherwise revisiting substantive norms.[4]

6.2 Substantive Norms on Hydrocarbon Resources Management

To implement the substantive element of institutionalized cooperation in the Spratly Islands setting, this section explores the available legal framework that regulates offshore hydrocarbon activities and, on this basis, identifies regulatory limitations and proposes solutions to such limitations.

6.2.1 *Existing Regulatory Framework*

6.2.1.1 An Overview

Offshore drilling of hydrocarbon resources took off in the 1970s, owing to the desire of consumer States to reduce their dependence on the Persian Gulf States as well as advanced technologies making it possible to drill further from coastlines and at greater depths on a large scale.[5] As of today, a third of the oil consumed worldwide comes from offshore drilling, and it is common for oil rigs to drill at a depth of over two kilometres, whereas just after WWII, industries only drilled in around ten meters of water.[6] Offshore hydrocarbon activities within a State's national jurisdiction is usually perceived as commercial activities that are 'precisely determined by agreement among the parties concerned in the light of special circumstances'.[7] Thus, there has been a 'global inertia' to the development of unified international standards to prevent or regulate offshore hydrocarbon activities.[8]

4 S. Huntington, *Political Order in Changing Societies* (Yale University Press. 1973), 8–9.

5 J. Rochette, Towards an International Regulation of Offshore Oil Exploitation, Report of the experts workshop held at the Paris Oceanographic Institute on 30 March 2012, Working Papers No. 15/12, IDDRI, 5.

6 *Ibid.*

7 Third United Nations Conference on the Law of the Sea, Official Records, Vol. II (1973–1982), 275–276, para.32.

8 J. Harrison, *Saving the Oceans through Law: the International Legal Framework for the Protection of the Marine Environment* (OUP. 2017), 217.

Yet, catastrophic incidents associated with offshore hydrocarbon activities such as the 1979 Ixtoc blowout, one of the largest oil spills in history resulting from exploratory drilling of an oil well in the Gulf of Mexico, have raised concerns about the environmental impact of such activities. Awareness of the environmental risks posed by exploration and exploitation of offshore hydrocarbon has simultaneously increased. In particular, routine operations in connection with the offshore industry widely use chemicals and other polluting substances and generate waste cuttings and produced water (namely water produced as a by-product along with oil and gas), which can contaminate the surrounding marine environment without proper management.[9] As a response to such environmental concerns, the international legal framework prescribes environment-related duties associated with offshore hydrocarbon activities.

UNCLOS is the most important legal instrument in this regard. It confers coastal States with exclusive rights to explore and exploit living and non-living resources on the seabed and in the water column within its territorial sea, EEZ and continental shelf including the extended continental shelf beyond 200 M.[10] Alongside the allocation of rights to hydrocarbon resources, UNCLOS, in particular its Articles 194, 204, 205, 206 and 208, also sets out duties of the coastal State to manage these resources in a manner that respects the marine environment.

6.2.1.2 Articles 194, 204, 205 and 206 of UNCLOS: General Obligations

Article 194 of UNCLOS prescribes a general duty of States to take measures to prevent, reduce and control 'pollution from installations and devices used in exploration or exploitation of the natural resources of the seabed and subsoil'.[11] Article 204 stipulates that States shall endeavour to constantly monitor the risks or effects of pollution of the marine environment caused by any activities which they permit or in which they engage.[12] Article 205 obliges States to make reports of the results obtained pursuant to Article 204 available to all States.[13] Article 206 provides that States are obliged, 'as far as practicable', to conduct prior environmental impact assessment (EIA) to assess the potential effects of the planned activities under their jurisdiction or control on

9 *Ibid.*, 210. A. de Mestral, The Prevention of Pollution of the Marine Environment Arising from Offshore Mining and Drilling, 20 *Harvard International Law Journal* (1979), 474–475.

10 UNCLOS, Articles 2 (territorial sea), 56 (EEZ), and 77 (continental shelf).

11 UNCLOS, Article 194(3)(c).

12 UNCLOS, Article 204.

13 UNCLOS, Article 205.

the marine environment and to publish reports of the results of such assessments, provided that these States have reasonable grounds for believing that such planned activities may lead to 'substantial pollution of or significant and harmful changes to the marine environment'.[14]

6.2.1.3 Article 208 of UNCLOS: Rule of Reference

Article 208 sets out a legal framework to deal with pollution 'arising from' or 'in connection with' seabed activities within national jurisdiction. Though UNCLOS gives no definition of the term 'seabed activities', the term undoubtedly covers the exploration and exploitation of hydrocarbon resources from seabed areas. The use of the wording 'in connection with' further extends the applicable scope of Article 208 to cover associated activities, such as the storage of resources pending processing or shipment.[15]

As to its substantive content, Article 208 begins with an obligation of coastal States to adopt laws and regulations and to take other necessary measures to prevent, reduce and control this particular source of pollution.[16] It then continues with a rule of reference, stipulating that the laws, regulations and measures adopted by coastal States shall be no less effective than 'international rules, standards and recommended practices and procedures' established through competent international organizations or diplomatic conferences.[17] To that effect, the regulation promulgated by coastal States shall meet at least the international minimum requirements contained in relevant 'international rules, standards and recommended practices and procedures', regardless of whether such norms have binding force upon the States concerned.

A further question is how to identify relevant 'international rules, standards and recommended practices and procedures' stipulated in Article 208 of UNCLOS. The Division for Ocean Affairs and the Law of the Sea of the Offices of Legal Affairs (DOALOS), according to UNGA resolution 49/28 of 6 December 1994,[18] has prepared a matrix for identifying the obligations of States under UNCLOS in relation to international rules and standards beyond UNCLOS, which was published in 2004.[19] The 2004 DOALOS matrix, albeit

14 UNCLOS, Article 206.
15 Harrison, n 8, 212.
16 UNCLOS, Article 208(1) & (2).
17 UNCLOS, Article 208(3) & (5).
18 UN Doc.: A/RES/49/28, 78th Plenary Meeting (6 December 1994).
19 DOALOS, *The Law of the Sea: Obligations of States Parties under the United Nations Convention on the Law of the Sea and Complementary Instruments* (New York: United Nations. 2004), 3.

non-exhaustive, provides useful guidance. According to the DOALOS matrix, the 'international rules, standards and recommended practices and procedures' in relation to Article 208 of UNCLOS cover several IMO instruments, including an IMO treaty, namely the International Convention on Oil Pollution Preparedness, Response and Co-operation (OPRC) adopted in 1990, IMO Code for the Construction and Equipment of Mobile Offshore Drilling Units (MODU Code) adopted in 1989, and IMO resolutions A.671(16) and A.672(16).[20] Limited progress has been made since DOALOS published the matrix. The only new and relevant development is the IMO's adoption of the 2009 MODU Code, which supersedes the 1989 MODU Code.[21] Hence, the IMO instruments in relation to Article 208 of UNCLOS mainly consists of OPRC, the 2009 MODU Code and resolutions A.671(16) and A.672(16).

6.2.1.4 IMO Instruments in Relation to Article 208 of UNCLOS

This subsection gives an account of the substantive content of the IMO instruments that qualify as relevant 'international rules, standards and recommended practices and procedures' stipulated in Article 208 of UNCLOS.

First, a conference of leading industrial States held in 1989 called upon IMO to develop measures to prevent pollution from ships, prompted by the 1989 Exxon Valdez disaster where the tanker ran aground in Prince William Sound, Alaska, spilling 10 million gallons of oil.[22] IMO endorsed this call by working

20 *Ibid.*, 51. Notably, the matrix also mentions two other IMO instruments, namely MARPOL and a protocol to the OPRC relating to hazardous and noxious substances (OPRC PROT 2000). Yet, these two IMO instruments provide little regulation on offshore hydrocarbon activities. MARPOL, in general, excludes any 'release of harmful substances directly arising from the exploration, exploitation and associated offshore processing of sea-bed mineral resources' from its application scope. One exception is that MARPOL Annex I and V apply to the pollution by the oil and garbage discharge from offshore installations. Similar to MARPOL, OPRC PROT 2000 stipulates that the obligation of States to ensure platforms within their jurisdiction to have an approved emergency plan to incidents involving hazardous and noxious substances does not apply to offshore units such as 'Floating Production, Storage and Offloading Facilities and Floating Storage Units'. See MARPOL, Article 2(3)(b)(ii). Also see Resolution MEPC. 139(53), adopted on 22 July 2005, MEPC 53/24/Add.2, Annex 32, Guidelines for the Application of the Revised MARPOL Annex I Requirements to Floating Production, Storage and Offloading Facilities (FPSO s) and Floating Storage Units (FSU s), 4. MARPOL, Annex I, reg. 2 and 21, Annex V, reg. 4(1). OPRC PROT 2000, Article 3(1).

21 IMO Resolution A.1023(26), Code for the Construction and Equipment of Mobile Offshore Drilling Units (2 December 2009), para.1.

22 C. Brown, International Environmental Law in the Regulation of Offshore Installations and Seabed Activities: the Case for a South Pacific Regional Protocol, 17 *Australian Mining and Petroleum Law Journal* (1998), 122.

on a draft convention, with the aim of providing a global framework for international cooperation in combating major incidents or threats of marine pollution. The resultant convention, namely OPRC, was adopted in 1990. Pursuant to OPRC, States have a due diligence obligation to ensure that 'operators of offshore units under its jurisdiction have oil pollution emergency plans', mirroring the obligations that apply to ships.[23] OPRC defines 'offshore unit' as 'any fixed or floating offshore installation or structure engaged in gas or oil exploration, exploitation or production activities, or loading or unloading of oil'.[24]

Second, as a result of the rapidly evolving design technology of mobile offshore drilling units, the Marine Environment Protection Committee (MEPC) of IMO replaces the previous 1989 MODU Code by the 2009 MODU Code to regulate mobile offshore drilling units the keels of which are laid or which are at a similar stage of construction on or after 1 January 2012.[25] The purpose of the 2009 MODU Code is to recommend design criteria, construction standards and other safety measures for mobile offshore drilling units, with the aim of minimizing risks to such units, to the personnel on board and to the environment.[26] The criteria, standards and measures set in the 2009 MODU Code are intended to be international minimum requirements, and States may impose additional requirements regarding the operation of industrial systems not dealt with in this code.[27]

Third, IMO Assembly adopted resolution A.671(16) in 1989, providing recommended measures for coastal States to undertake in order to prevent infringement of safety zones around offshore installations and structures.[28] On the same day, IMO Assembly also adopted resolution A.672(16), which provides recommended guidelines and standards for coastal States to take into account when making decisions regarding the removal of offshore installations and structures on their continental shelf and EEZ.[29] The use of the wording 'should'

23 International Convention on Oil Pollution Preparedness, Response and Co-operation (OPRC), adopted 30 November 1990, entered into force 13 May 1995, 1891 *UNTS* 77, Article 3(2).

24 OPRC 1990, Article 2(4).

25 2009 MODU Code, Article 1.2.1.

26 2009 MODU Code, Article 1.1.

27 2009 MODU Code, Article 1.2.2.

28 IMO Resolution A.671(16), Safety Zones and Safety of Navigation around Offshore Installations and Structures (19 October 1989).

29 IMO Resolution A.672(16), IMO Guidelines and Standards for the Removal of Offshore Installations and Structures on the Continental Shelf and the Exclusive Economic Zone (19 October 1989).

in these two resolutions indicates that the measures, guidelines or standards as specified therein are merely recommendatory rather than obligatory.[30]

Tailored to the Spratly Islands setting, only China and Malaysia, among all the claimants, are parties to OPRC, and the provisions in both the 2009 MODU Code and resolutions A.671(16) and A.672(16) are merely recommendatory.[31] However, as guided by the DOALOS matrix, these instruments constitute 'international rules, standards and recommended practices and procedures' for the purposes of Article 208 of UNCLOS. Thus, they can be transformed, by virtue of the rule of reference contained in Article 208, into norms that require due respect from the disputant States.[32]

6.2.2 *Regulatory Limitations and Solutions*

The preceding analysis reveals two major limitations of the available regulatory framework on offshore hydrocarbon activities. First, there has been little regulation on offshore hydrocarbon activities except for the prescription of environment-related duties associated with such activities. Second, such environment-related duties have only touched upon a narrow range of environmental issues.[33] These duties are limited to two types. One type is directly set forth in Articles 194 and 204–206 of UNCLOS, including the general obligations: (1) to take measures to counteract pollution, (2) to conduct constant monitoring of the risks or effects of pollution, (3) to perform prior EIA on planned activities, and (4) to publish monitoring or EIA reports or results. The other type includes obligations to respect international minimum standards by virtue of the rule of reference contained in Article 208 of UNCLOS. Such obligations consist of: (1) the due diligence obligation of States to ensure offshore units within their jurisdiction to have an approved emergency plan to oil incidents under OPRC, (2) the duty to respect recommended design criteria, construction standards and other safety measures for mobile offshore drilling units set by the 2009 MODU Code, (3) the obligation to undertake recommended measures on safety zones around offshore installations and structures under IMO resolution A.671(16), and (4) the obligation to take into account recommended guidelines and standards regarding the removal of offshore

30 See *e.g.*, IMO Resolution A.671(16), Article 1; IMO A.672(16), Articles 2.2., 2.3 and 3.

31 The Status of OPRC, available at <https://treaties.un.org/Pages/showDetails.aspx?objid=080000028000aada6&clang=_en>.

32 W. van Reenen, Rules of Reference in the new Convention on the Law of the Sea, in particular in connection with the pollution of the sea by oil from tankers, 12 *Netherlands Yearbook of International Law* (1981), 17.

33 Harrison, n 8, 217.

installations and structures within their jurisdiction under IMO resolution A.672(16).

Two solutions can be proposed to remedy the above two regulatory limitations. The first solution is a remedy through IMO's making of new 'international rules, standards and recommended practices and procedures', which can be incorporated into the UNCLOS framework by virtue of the rule of reference contained in Article 208 of UNCLOS. Agenda 21 of the 1992 Rio Declaration on Environment and Development urged States to act 'within the framework of IMO' and other relevant international organizations as appropriate to assess the need for additional measures to address the degradation of the marine environment from offshore oil and gas platforms.[34] Little progress, however, has been made following the 1992 Rio Declaration. The problem, as rightly pointed out by some scholars, is that IMO, in general, is not considered to have the mandate to regulate the operational pollution directly arising from the exploration, exploitation and associated offshore processing of seabed mineral resources.[35] According to the IMO Convention, IMO was established to be a global standard-setting authority for the safety, security and environmental performance of international shipping.[36] Hence, the mandate of IMO relates more to shipping than to offshore hydrocarbon activities. The second solution is a remedy through a specific cooperative institution to be established based on mutual agreement of the disputant States. Whereas the function of the IMO framework is limited to the adoption of environment-related rules and standards, the intended cooperative institution can deal with a wider range of matters not limited to environmental concerns. To that effect, the IMO framework cannot be entirely in lieu of the role of the cooperative institution. In light of this, the following section discusses the viable cooperative institution for the Spratly Islands setting.

6.3 Cooperative Institution for Hydrocarbon Resources Management

This section aims to implement the procedural element of institutionalized cooperation in the Spratly Islands setting. Precedents in other sea regions may shed some light. Though such precedents appear to be 'naturally *sui generis*

34 Rio Declaration on Environment and Development, adopted in June 1992, Agenda 21, para.17.30(c).

35 See *e.g.*, Brown, n 22, 122; Harrison, n 8, 217.

36 Convention of the International Maritime Organization, adopted 6 March 1948, entered into force 17 March 1958, 289 *UNTS* 3, Article 1.

with their peculiar backgrounds and circumstances' and not suitable to be a model for all States, it is widely accepted that these precedents can, at least, be used for reference purposes, providing a checklist of issues and provisions to be addressed by the States concerned.[37] This section first analyses the salient features of three different types of management structures that have been adopted in precedents. Based on these salient features in combination with the unique characteristics of the Spratly Islands area, it then explores the most apt cooperative institution for this region.

6.3.1 *Typology of Management Structures in Precedents*

Owing to 'the absence of mutual trust or the predisposition to shelve maritime disputes', the number of cooperative hydrocarbon arrangements has not grown significantly since the Bahrain-Saudi Arabia arrangement, being the first one of this kind, was adopted about 60 years ago.[38] This section analyses the legal instruments of 19 precedents (Table 8),[39] after excluding a few precedents in which the fundamental instruments lack detailed contents and have never been implemented.[40] The common denominator of these precedents is the inclusion of a binding treaty that records the detailed rights and obligations of the State parties and establishes a management structure with respect to offshore hydrocarbon activities within a designated zone for cooperation. The fundamental difference among these precedents lies in varying degrees of

37 M. Miyoshi, *The Joint Development of Offshore Oil and Gas in Relation to Maritime Boundary Delimitation* (IBRU. 1999), 39. C.B. Okafor, Model Agreements for Joint Development: a Case Study, 25(1) *Journal of Energy & Natural Resources Law* (2007), 59, 102.

38 V. Becker-Weinberg, *Joint Development of Hydrocarbon Deposits in the Law of the Sea* (Springer. 2014), 141.

39 For literature regarding such precedents, see *e.g.*, H. Fox *et al.* (eds.), *Joint Development of Offshore Oil and Gas: A Model Agreement for States for Joint Development with Explanatory Commentary*, Vol. I (London: BIICL, 1989), 3–5 ('Table of Joint Development Agreements'); Becker-Weinberg, n 38; A.E. Bastida, *et al.*, Cross-Border Unitization and Joint Development Agreements: An International Law Perspective, 29 *Houston Journal of International Law* (2007), 355; .M. Ong, Joint Development of Common Offshore Oil and Gas Deposits: 'Mere' State Practice or Customary International Law?, 93 *AJIL* (1999), 771–804; Miyoshi, n 37.

40 See *e.g.*, Agreement between the Libyan Arab Socialist People's Jamahiriya and the Republic of Tunisia to Implement the Judgment of the International Court of Justice in the Tunisia/Libya Continental Shelf Case (8 August 1988), available at <http://www.un.org/depts/los/LEGISLATIONANDTREATIES/PDFFILES/TREATIES/LBY-TUN1988CS.PDF>; Japan-China Joint Press Statement: Cooperation between Japan and China in the East China Sea (18 June 2008), available at <http://www.mofa.go.jp/files/000091726.pdf >; Exchange of Letters between Malaysia and Brunei (16 March 2009), available at <https://www.kln.gov.my/archive/content.php?t=7&articleId=735675>.

institutionalization of their management structures. Three types of management structures are, according to the degree of institutionalization from the highest to the lowest, the joint authority structure, the joint venture structure, and the single State structure.

6.3.1.1 Joint Authority Structure

The joint authority structure comprises a legally binding agreement, which establishes one or more entity entrusted by the interested States with decision-making power and administrative functions.[41] The first example of this management structure is an arrangement adopted by Sudan and Saudi Arabia in 1974 through a bilateral treaty between them, with regard to a designated common zone in the Red Sea.[42] This arrangement confers both decision-making and administration power to one single entity, namely a Joint Commission comprising an equal number of representatives of each State. The Joint Commission enjoys fairly strong powers, including 'to survey, delimit and demarcate the boundaries of the Common Zone' and 'to consider and decide, in accordance with the conditions it prescribes, on the applications for licences and concessions concerning exploration and exploitation'.[43] As to the implementation, the Joint Commission was reported to have contracted an oil company – Preussag AG – to carry out exploratory work in the designated common zone.[44] However, little information can be found about whether this arrangement, established more than 40 years ago, is still in operation, since the Joint Commission has been criticized for not working in a transparent and publicly accountable manner.[45]

Except for the first example, all the subsequent examples adopting this management structure have incorporated the division between a decision-making

---

41 Ong, n 39, 791. R. Beckman and L. Bernard, Framework for the Joint Development of Hydrocarbon Resources (2010), 21.

42 Agreement between Saudi Arabia and Sudan relating to Joint Exploration and Exploitation of Red Sea Seabed and Subsoil Resources, adopted 16 May 1974, entered into force 26 August 1974, 952 *UNTS* 193.

43 *Ibid.*, Article VII.

44 C. Bertram *et al.*, Metalliferous Sediments in the Atlantis II Deep – Assessing the Geological and Economic Resource Potential and Legal Constraints, No. 1688 *Kiel Working Papers* (2011), sec. 4.4.

45 *Ibid.*, sec. 5. P. Park, What might Red Sea mining bring to Saudi Arabia and Sudan? (14 September 2012), available at <https://www.scidev.net/global/cooperation/feature/what-might-red-sea-mining-bring-to-saudi-arabia-and-sudan-.html>.

TABLE 8 Precedents of cooperative hydrocarbon arrangements

Management structures	Examples	Relevant documents
Joint authority structure (5)	Sudan-Saudi Arabia	1979 Agreement between Saudi Arabia and Sudan relating to Joint Exploration and Exploitation of Red Sea Seabed and Subsoil Resources
	Australia-Indonesia (area A)	1989 Treaty between Australia and the Republic of Indonesia on the Zone of Cooperation in an Area between the Indonesian Province of East Timor and Northern Australia
	Guinea-Bissau-Senegal	1993 Management and Cooperation Agreement between the Government of the Republic of Senegal and the Government of the Republic of Guinea-Bissau 1995 Protocol to the Agreement of 14 October 1993, concerning the Organization and Operation of the Management and Cooperation Agency
	Nigeria-São Tomé e Príncipe	2001 Treaty between the Federal Republic of Nigeria and the Democratic Republic of São Tomé e Príncipe on the Joint Development of Petroleum and other Resources, in respect of Areas of the Exclusive Economic Zone of the Two States
	Australia-East Timor	2002 Timor Sea Treaty between East Timor and Australia 2006 Treaty between Australia and the Democratic Republic of Timor-Leste on Certain Maritime Arrangements in the Timor Sea 2018 Treaty between Australia and the Democratic Republic of Timor-Leste Establishing their Maritime Boundaries in the Timor Sea

TABLE 8 Precedents of cooperative hydrocarbon arrangements (*cont.*)

Management structures	Examples	Relevant documents
Joint venture structure (11)	Kuwait-Saudi Arabia	1965 Agreement between the Kingdom of Saudi Arabia and the State of Kuwait on the Partition of the Neutral Zone
	Iran-United Arab Emirates	1971 Memorandum of Understanding between Iran and Sharjah
	Japan-South Korea	1974 Agreement concerning Joint Development of the Southern Part of the Continental Shelf Adjacent to Japan and South Korea
	France-Spain	1974 Convention between the Government of the French Republic and the Government of the Spanish State on the Delimitation of the Continental Shelves of the two States in the Bay of Biscay
	Norway-the UK	1976 Agreement relating to the Exploitation of the Frigg Field Reservoir and the Transmission of Gas therefrom to the United Kingdom
	Malaysia-Thailand	1979 Memorandum of Understanding between Malaysia and the Kingdom of Thailand on the Establishment of the Joint Authority for the Exploitation of the Resources of the Sea Bed in a Defined Area of the Continental Shelf of the Two Countries in the Gulf of Thailand
		1990 Agreement on the Constitution and Other Matters Relating to the Establishment of the Malaysia-Thailand Joint Authority
	Iceland-Norway	1981 Agreement between Norway and Iceland on the Continental Shelf between Iceland and Jan Mayen

	Malaysia-Vietnam	1992 Memorandum of Understanding between Malaysia and the Socialist Republic of Vietnam for the Exploration and Exploitation of Petroleum in a Defined Area of the Continental Shelf Involving the Two Countries
	Colombia-Jamaica	1993 Maritime Delimitation Treaty between Jamaica and the Republic of Colombia
	Argentina-the UK	1995 Joint Declaration: Cooperation over Offshore Activities in the South West Atlantic
	Barbados-Guyana	2004 Exclusive Economic Zone Co-operation Treaty between the State of Barbados and the Republic of Guyana concerning the exercise of jurisdiction in their exclusive economic zones in the area of bilateral overlap within each of their outer limits and beyond the outer limits of the exclusive economic zones of other States
Single state structure (3)	Saudi Arabia-Bahrain	1958 Bahrain-Saudi Arabia Frontier Agreement
	United Arab Emirates-Qatar	1969 Agreement concerning Settlement of Offshore Boundaries and Ownership of Islands between Qatar and the United Arab Emirates
	Australia-Indonesia (areas B & C)	1989 Treaty between Australia and the Republic of Indonesia on the Zone of Cooperation in an Area between the Indonesian Province of East Timor and Northern Australia

entity and an administrative entity.[46] The decision-making entity is normally composed of an equal number of ministers or persons of equivalent rank appointed by the respective heads of the States concerned, who meet regularly such as once a year or as often as may be required. It is responsible for deciding on important matters related to the joint development, *inter alia* the control in the appointment of rights-holders and operators. The administrative entity, usually controlled by equal representatives appointed by each interested State, is a permanent organ with a broad mandate and in charge of the daily management of activities within the designated zone. The administrative entity is obliged to report to and be supervised by the decision-making entity.

A representative example of adopting the joint authority structure is the Timor Sea arrangement. The first Timor Sea arrangement was detailed in a treaty concluded between Australia and Indonesia in 1989, which established a 'zone of cooperation' in the Timor Gap.[47] These two States used provisional delimitation lines to divide the 'zone of cooperation' into three areas: areas A, B and C.[48] Whereas areas B and C adopt the single State structure that is discussed in section 6.3.1.3, the management of area A follows the joint authority structure. The 1989 treaty prescribes a two-tier mechanism, including a Ministerial Council and a Joint Authority. On the one hand, the Ministerial Council, composed of an equal number of ministers designated by each contracting State

---

46 See *e.g.*, Treaty between the Federal Republic of Nigeria and the Democratic Republic of Sao Tome and Principe on the Joint Development of Petroleum and other Resources, in respect of Areas of the Exclusive Economic Zone of the Two States, adopted 21 February 2001, entered into force 16 January 2003, Articles 6 and 9 (A joint development zone established in this treaty is administrated by a Joint Development Authority that reports to a Joint Ministerial Council); Treaty between Australia and the Republic of Indonesia on the Zone of Cooperation in an Area between the Indonesian Province of East Timor and Northern Australia, adopted 11 December 1989, entered into force 9 February 1991, 1654 *UNTS* 105, Articles 5-6, 8; Management and Cooperation Agreement between the Government of the Republic of Senegal and the Government of the Republic of Guinea-Bissau, adopted 14 October 1993, entered into force 21 December 1995, 1903 *UNTS* 3, Article 5, and Protocol to the Agreement of 14 October 1993, concerning the Organization and Operation of the Management and Cooperation Agency, adopted 12 June 1995, entered into force 21 December 1995, 1903 *UNTS* 7 (This treaty sets up an international agency, consisting of a three-tiered structure, namely the High Authority, Secretary-General, and Enterprise, to manage the designated joint development zone. *Inter alia*, the High Authority and Secretary-General are decision-making entities, and the Enterprise is responsible for daily administration.); Timor Sea Treaty between East Timor and Australia, adopted 20 May 2002, entered into force 20 May 2002, 2258 *UNTS* 3, Article 6.

47 Treaty between Australia and the Republic of Indonesia on the Zone of Cooperation in an Area between the Indonesian Province of East Timor and Northern Australia, n 46.

48 *Ibid.*, Articles 3-4.

who shall meet annually or as often as may be required, directs and supervises the work of the Joint Authority by exercising its broad decision-making power on critical matters related to joint development, including especially the right to approve production sharing contracts which the Joint Authority may propose to enter into with corporations.[49] On the other hand, the Joint Authority, the executive board of which comprises an equal number of persons nominated by each Contracting State, can enter into production sharing contracts subject to the Ministerial Council's approval.[50] Apart from this function, the Joint Authority can also make decisions on its own for the purposes of day-to-day management, including dividing area A into several contract areas as necessary, establishing safety or restricted zones to ensure the safety of navigation and petroleum operations, and promulgating regulations related to petroleum operations such as matters on health, safety and environmental protection.[51] The 1989 treaty has proved to be successful in facilitating hydrocarbon operations within this area for a decade, which resulted in the first commercial production of petroleum in July 1998 in the Elang-Kakatua group of oilfields.[52] However, the unavoidable problem was that the Australia-Indonesia Agreement was found on Indonesia's illegal annexation of East Timor.[53] Subsequent to Indonesia's renunciation in 1999 of its claim to the territory of East Timor, this agreement was no longer in force as between Australia and Indonesia.[54]

A new Timor Sea arrangement was concluded between East Timor and Australia by entering into the Timor Sea Treaty in 2002, which designated a Joint Petroleum Development Area (JPDA) equivalent to area A of the previous

---

49 *Ibid.*, Article 5-6.

50 *Ibid.*, Article 8 (b).

51 *Ibid.*, Article 8(a), (i) and (j).

52 See *e.g.*, G. Triggs and D. Bialek, The New Timor Sea Treaty and Interim Arrangements for Joint Development of Petroleum Resources of the Timor Gap, 3(2) *MJIL* (2002), 327–328; G. Triggs, Legal and Commercial Risks of Investment in the Timor Gap, 1 *MJIL* (2000), 100.

53 It is noted that in 1991, Portugal instituted proceedings against Australia at the ICJ, submitting that Australia failed to observe the obligation to respect the duties and powers of Portugal as the Administering Power of East Timor and the right of the people of East Timor to self-determination by concluding the 1989 Australia-Indonesia Agreement. However, in 1995, the ICJ delivered its judgment, holding that it lacked jurisdiction over the submission. For more details, see East Timor (Portugal v. Australia), Judgment of 30 June 1995 (ICJ).

54 Conciliation between The Democratic Republic of Timor-Leste and The Commonwealth of Australia, Report and Recommendations of the Compulsory Conciliation Commission between Timor-Leste and Australia on the Timor Sea, 9 May 2018, para.33.

Australia-Indonesia arrangement.[55] Similar to the 1989 treaty, the Timor Sea Treaty adopts a joint authority structure for the management of JPDA. Yet, a noticeable difference is that the Timor Sea Treaty prescribes a three-tiered mechanism, comprising a Ministerial Council, a Joint Commission, and a Designated Authority.[56] Nonetheless, this three-tiered mechanism still follows a divide of decision-making and administrative entities, in the sense that the Ministerial Council and the Joint Commission are conferred with decision-making power, whereas the Designated Authority is in charge of day-to-day administrative functions. The Ministerial Council will only meet at the request of either Australia, East Timor or the Joint Commission.[57] In contrast, the Joint Commission, which shall meet annually or as may be required, acts as the main decision-maker, responsible for directing and supervising the work of the Designated Authority.[58] Moreover, while the Ministerial Council shall comprise an equal number of ministers from both countries, the Joint Commission shall consist of one more commissioner appointed by East Timor than by Australia.[59] To that effect, it would be reasonable to assume that Joint Commission acts on a majority vote, potentially to the advantage of East Timor, although the Timor Sea Treaty does not explicitly provide for voting procedures.[60] The Designated Authority is a permanent organ empowered to implement the day-to-day management of petroleum activities within the JPDA, including the establishment of safety or restricted zones, the issuance of regulations related to petroleum operations such as matters on health, safety and environmental protection, and other powers and functions as may be conferred on it by the Joint Commission.[61] A subsequent treaty concluded in 2006, namely the Treaty between Australia and the Democratic Republic of Timor-Leste on Certain Maritime Arrangements in the Timor Sea (CMATS), extended the life of the Timor Sea Treaty until 50 years after the entry into force of

55 Timor Sea Treaty between East Timor and Australia, n 46. For background information on the new Timor Sea arrangement, see Bastida *et al.*, n 39, 355, 411–413. G. Baldacchino, *Solution Protocols to Festering Island Disputes:'Win-Win'Solutions for the Diaoyu/Senkaku Islands* (Taylor & Francis. 2017), 125.

56 Timor Sea Treaty between East Timor and Australia, n 46, Article 6(a).

57 *Ibid.*, Article 6(d)(iii).

58 *Ibid.*, Article 6(c)(iv).

59 *Ibid.*, Article 6(c)(i) and (d)(i).

60 G. Triggs, The New Timor Sea Treaty between East Timor and Australia, 4(2) *Australian Journal of Asian Law* (2002), 195–196.

61 Timor Sea Treaty between East Timor and Australia, n 46, Annex C.

CMATS in 2007.[62] However, as a recent development, East Timor and Australia signed a treaty regarding the delimitation of their maritime boundaries in the Timor Sea in 2018, as guided by the 2018 compulsory conciliation report and recommendations.[63] When this treaty entered into force in August 2019, the Timor Sea Treaty and CMATS ceased to be in force. Having said that, the joint development has yielded considerable economic benefits for both countries. As of early 2017, Bayu-Undan, the largest petroleum development area within the JPDA, had generated approximately US$23.5 billion in upstream revenue for East Timor and US$2.4 billion in upstream revenue and extra downstream economic benefits for Australia.[64]

A cardinal feature of the joint authority structure is that both the decision-making process and the daily administration function are formalized through the introduction of specific institutions such as a Ministerial Council, Joint Commission, and Designated Authority. The high degree of institutionalization entails that States have less autonomy in the resource management process. This management structure has two advantages. First, the joint authority structure, by obtaining decision-making and administration power through an inter-State treaty, becomes, to some extent, immune to the influence of the changeable political will of the interested States. Yet, the reduction of the States' autonomy is not absolute. Indeed, the direct appointment of members of a decision-making entity by the interested States retains the necessary checks and control. Second, the joint authority structure possesses efficiency as a result of the formalized process, which spares the often lengthy and inefficient negotiations between the interested States. Whereas a designated entity can handle less important issues in relation to daily management in a timely manner, a decision-making entity consisting of representatives of the interested States can deal with important or complex matters according to its mandates as set forth in the inter-State treaty. However, the joint authority structure is not devoid of any weakness. First, the formalized entities can be bureaucratic and expensive, requiring the investment of a considerable amount of time and expense in their creation and operation.[65] Second, adopting this management

62 Treaty between Australia and the Democratic Republic of Timor-Leste on Certain Maritime Arrangements in the Timor Sea, adopted 12 January 2006, entered into force 23 February 2007, 2483 *UNTS* 359, Article 3.

63 Treaty between Australia and the Democratic Republic of Timor-Leste Establishing their Maritime Boundaries in the Timor Sea, adopted on 6 March 2018, entered into force 30 August 2019.

64 Conciliation between The Democratic Republic of Timor-Leste and The Commonwealth of Australia, n 54, para.40.

65 Okafor, n 37, 81.

structure requires a high level of trust between the States, as these States have relatively less direct control over the resource management process. Some States would take precautions so that their interests are not unduly infringed by the joint authority, which once established, is entitled to make decisions independent of their political will.

6.3.1.2 Joint Venture Structure

The joint venture structure also comprises a legally binding agreement entered into by the interested States to spell out the modality of cooperation. Distinct from the joint authority structure, the joint venture structure does not formalize or institutionalize the decision-making process, but instead, leaves the decision-making power directly to the States themselves. For instance, an agreement concluded between Malaysia and Thailand in 1990, concerning the establishment of a joint authority for the exploitation of the resources in a defined area of their disputed continental shelf in the Gulf of Thailand, provides that the permission of operations and conclusion of contracts relating to the exploration and exploitation of hydrocarbon resources in the defined area are subject to the approval of the governments of both States.[66] The approval procedures are meant to follow the domestic laws of the States concerned.

Despite this, the joint venture structure usually includes the establishment of an entity to carry out administrative functions. For example, the model agreement for joint development as proposed by the BIICL,[67] which comprises 25 articles with commentary, prescribes the establishment of a Joint Commission as the body to administer petroleum activities in a designated zone of cooperation.[68] The functions of the Joint Commission might include recommending a joint development plan relating to the petroleum activities and other wider or limited functions depending on the option of the parties.[69] According to the model agreement, the Joint Commission, normally composed of an equal number of representatives of each State party, should meet once annually or at any other time agreed by the States, and might have a permanent secretariat to carry out administrative work especially when the Joint Commission has a wider range of functions.[70]

66 Agreement on the Constitution and Other Matters Relating to the Establishment of the Malaysia-Thailand Joint Authority (30 May 1990), Article 7(2)(e).

67 Fox *et al.*, n 39. H. Fox *et al.* (eds.), *Joint Development of Offshore Oil and Gas: A Model Agreement for States for Joint Development with Explanatory Commentary*, Vol. II (London: BIICL, 1990).

68 Fox *et al.*, n 39, 309, citing Article 5(1) of the model agreement.

69 *Ibid.*

70 *Ibid.*, 310, citing Article 5(2), (5)&(6) of the model agreement.

In practice, most examples adopting the joint venture structure involve the creation of an administrative entity with a varying range of functions,[71] despite a few exceptions where the joint development arrangement is directly implemented by the States concerned or their appointed agents.[72] An example of an administrative entity with wider powers is the authority as set up in the joint development arrangement between Malaysia and Thailand regarding a defined area in the Gulf of Thailand, which can permit operations, conclude contracts subject to the ultimate approval of the governments of both States, and prepare the plan of operation and the working programme for the

71 See *e.g.*, Agreement between the Kingdom of Saudi Arabia and the State of Kuwait on the Partition of the Neutral Zone, adopted 7 July 1965, entered into force 10 July 1963, 1750 *UNTS* 39, Articles 17-19; Agreement concerning Joint Development of the Southern Part of the Continental Shelf Adjacent to Japan and South Korea (with map, appendix, agreed minutes and exchanges of notes), adopted 30 January 1974, entered into force 22 June 1978, 1225 *UNTS* 113, Article XXIV; Agreement relating to the Exploitation of the Frigg Field Reservoir and the Transmission of Gas therefrom to the United Kingdom (with annexes), adopted 10 May 1976, entered into force 22 July 1977, 1098 *UNTS* 3, Article 27; Memorandum of Understanding between Malaysia and the Kingdom of Thailand on the Establishment of the Joint Authority for the Exploitation of the Resources of the Sea Bed in a Defined Area of the Continental Shelf of the Two Countries in the Gulf of Thailand (21 February 1979), Article III(2), and Agreement on the Constitution and Other Matters Relating to the Establishment of the Malaysia-Thailand Joint Authority, n 66; Maritime Delimitation Treaty between Jamaica and the Republic of Colombia (with chart), adopted 12 November 1993, entered into force 14 March 1994, 1776 *UNTS* 17, Article 4; Joint Declaration between Argentina and the UK: Cooperation over Offshore Activities in the South West Atlantic (27 September 1995), Article 2; Exclusive Economic Zone Co-operation Treaty between the State of Barbados and the Republic of Guyana concerning the exercise of jurisdiction in their exclusive economic zones in the area of bilateral overlap within each of their outer limits and beyond the outer limits of the exclusive economic zones of other States (with annex and figure), adopted 2 December 2003, entered into force 5 May 2004, 2277 *UNTS* 201, Article 6.

72 See *e.g.*, Memorandum of Understanding between Iran and Sharjah (November 1971), para.4 (The joint development scheme in this arrangement is simple: a single oil company, Buttes Gas & Oil Company, is designated to operate the exploitation on behalf of these two governments, and this company directly pays half of the revenue generated from the exploitation to Iran and half to the United Arab Emirates.); Convention between the Government of the French Republic and the Government of the Spanish State on the Delimitation of the Continental Shelves of the two States in the Bay of Biscay, adopted 29 January 1974, entered into force 5 April 1975, 996 *UNTS* 344, Annex II, paras.2-4 (This arrangement provides that the oil companies designated by each State shall participate in the exploration and exploitation on the basis of equal partnership and proportional financing of operations.); Agreement between Norway and Iceland on the Continental Shelf between Iceland and Jan Mayen, adopted 22 October 1981, entered into force 2 June 1982, 2124 *UNTS* 247, Articles 3-4 (In the first exploration phase, the two States shall jointly carry out seismic and, if necessary, magnetic surveys. In the next phase, 'any exclusive

administration of the defined joint development area.[73] In contrast, the Joint Commission as set forth in a treaty between Japan and South Korea concerning the joint development of their disputed continental shelf in the East China Sea represents an example of an administrative entity with a narrower range of functions, which are limited to providing consultations, studying problems and receiving notices and reports.[74] Regardless of the range of functions, the resolutions made by these administrative entities are only recommendatory rather than obligatory.[75]

A cardinal feature of the joint venture structure is that the States concerned retain a high level of autonomy in deciding essential matters relating to resource management such as the right to directly designate the concessionaires and to approve operation contracts. However, a major drawback is that this management structure remains sensitive to the changes in the political will of the States at issue. This sensitivity can lead to another disadvantage that efficiency is not guaranteed. Whether the arrangement can proceed efficiently basically depends on whether the States concerned are willing to make concessions in good faith. A notable example is the Malaysia-Thailand joint development area, which was initially designated in 1979 for both parties to jointly exploit marine hydrocarbon resources in contested waters in the Gulf

exploration and production licences in respect of such special fields shall be based on joint venture contracts, unless the Parties agree on some other form of contract'.); Memorandum of Understanding between Malaysia and the Socialist Republic of Vietnam for the Exploration and Exploitation of Petroleum in a Defined Area of the Continental Shelf Involving the Two Countries (5 June 1992), Article 3(a)&(b) (Malaysia and Vietnam nominated their own national oil companies, PETRONAS and PetroVietnam, respectively, to undertake the exploration and exploitation of hydrocarbon resources on their respective behalves in the defined area. PETRONAS and PetroVietnam shall enter into a commercial arrangement between them, subject to the approval of their respective governments.).

73 Agreement on the Constitution and Other Matters Relating to the Establishment of the Malaysia-Thailand Joint Authority, n 66, Article 7(2)(d)&(e).

74 Agreement concerning Joint Development of the Southern Part of the Continental Shelf Adjacent to Japan and South Korea, n 71, Article XXV.

75 For relevant treaty provisions, see *e.g.*, Maritime delimitation treaty between Jamaica and the Republic of Colombia, n 71, Article 4(3); Agreement between the Kingdom of Saudi Arabia and the State of Kuwait on the Partition of the Neutral Zone, n 71, Article 19; Agreement concerning joint development of the southern part of the continental shelf adjacent to Japan and South Korea, n 71, Article XXV; Agreement relating to the exploitation of the Frigg Field Reservoir and the transmission of gas therefrom to the United Kingdom, n 71, Article 27; Joint Declaration: Cooperation over Offshore Activities in the South West Atlantic (1995), Article 4. Also see Ong, n 39, 790; Miyoshi, n 37, 42.

of Thailand.[76] The actual implementation of this arrangement was delayed for eleven years partly owing to several changes in the governments of both countries, which, according to Schofield, 'undermined the political will for joint development'.[77] Nevertheless, when these difficulties in domestic politics were overcome in 1990, this cooperative arrangement turned out to be a success.[78]

6.3.1.3 Single State Structure

The single State structure comprises a legally binding agreement entered into by the interested States pursuant to which a single State is responsible for managing hydrocarbon resources in a designated area on behalf of all States while other States share proceeds accrued from exploitation activities.[79] Only a few examples have adopted this management structure. The first example is an agreement concluded between Saudi Arabia and Bahrain in 1958, which devised a joint development area for equal revenue sharing in addition to boundary delimitation.[80] These two States agreed that Saudi Arabia enjoys exclusive rights to exploit oil resources in the oil field on the condition that it pays half of the net revenue generated from the exploitation to Bahrain.[81] Similar arrangements can be seen in the subsequent Agreement concerning Settlement of Offshore Boundaries and Ownership of Islands concluded between the United Arab Emirates and Qatar in 1969,[82] as well as the Treaty on the Zone of Cooperation concluded between Australia and Indonesia in 1989 insomuch as areas B and C are concerned.[83]

---

76 Memorandum of Understanding between Malaysia and the Kingdom of Thailand on the Establishment of the Joint Authority for the Exploitation of the Resources of the Sea Bed in a Defined Area of the Continental Shelf of the Two Countries in the Gulf of Thailand, n 71, Article III (2).

77 C.H. Schofield, Blurring the Lines: Maritime Joint Development and the Cooperative Management of Ocean Resources, 8(1) *Issues in Legal Scholarship* (2009), 16.

78 C. Santamaria, Sino – Philippine Joint Development in the South China Sea: Is Political Will Enough?, 10(2) *Asian Politics & Policy* (2018), 329.

79 Ong, n 39, 791.

80 Bahrain-Saudi Arabia Frontier Agreement, adopted and entered into force 22 February 1958, 1733 *UNTS* 3. Also see relevant background information in: Miyoshi, n 37, 27.

81 Bahrain-Saudi Arabia Frontier Agreement, n 80, Second Clause.

82 Agreement concerning Settlement of Offshore Boundaries and Ownership of Islands between Qatar and the United Arab Emirates, adopted and entered into force 20 March 1969, 2402 *UNTS* 49, Article 7. (The United Arab Emirates has the exclusive right to exploit the hydrocarbon resources in the above oil field through its concession with an oil company, Abu Dhabi Marine Areas (ADMA). All royalties, profits and other government fees due in respect of this oil field shall be equally divided between these two States.).

83 Treaty between Australia and the Republic of Indonesia on the Zone of Cooperation in an Area between the Indonesian Province of East Timor and Northern Australia, n 46, Article

The single State structure is straightforward in the sense that 'it requires the least amount of effort in the way of formal bilateral cooperation and legal and institutional harmonization'.[84] An interesting observation is that the parties to the arrangements adopting this management are all petroleum export countries. It is reasonable to expect that States with a high degree of petroleum import dependencies would prefer other management structures through which they can have direct participation in oil and gas extractions. Such preference is understandable since the priority of these States is to satisfy their domestic need for petroleum resources. Direct participation in exploitation is usually far more cost-effective than importing from other States. Hence, petroleum import States are less prone to select the single State model as the form of joint development, which dramatically curtails the application of this structure in practice.

6.3.2 *Application to the Spratly Islands Setting*

Based on the salient features of the three management structures in combination with the unique characteristics of the Spratly Islands area, this section explores the most viable cooperative institution for this region. The single State model can be first ruled out, as it is usually preferred by petroleum export countries, but in this case, both China and the Philippines have high energy import dependencies.[85] The joint authority structure has a higher degree of institutionalization than the joint venture structure. The former institutionalizes both the decision-making process and the daily administration functions through the introduction of specific institutions such as a Ministerial Council, Joint Commission, and Designated Authority, whereas the latter retains decision-making powers to the States concerned. The question is thus about the selection of the degree of institutionalization. As mentioned in section 5.3.4, two determinants play a critical role, namely the degree of freedom of action that the parties intend to have, and the level of complexity of regulatory problems in relation to substantive norms. The lower the degree of States' freedom to act, the higher the degree of institutionalization. The more complex the regulatory problems, the more the achievement of a cooperative arrangement becomes dependent on the working of the cooperative institution.

---

4. (In respect of areas B and C, each State unilaterally manages the hydrocarbon resources in one of the two areas adjacent to its territory and pays 10% of any revenue to the other.).

84 Ong, n 39, 788.

85 World Bank Group, Energy Imports Statistics (last updated on 24 April 2019), available at <http://data.worldbank.org/indicator/EG.IMP.CONS.ZS>.

First, tailored to the Spratly Islands setting, the disputant States would prefer a lower degree of freedom of one another to act and a resultant higher degree of institutionalization for cooperation. On the one hand, as a result of the power asymmetry in terms of military and economic resources between China and other claimant States, the latter would prefer to use stable and predictable institutionalized restraints to prevent China's potential abuse of its growing powers. Hence, the joint authority structure is a more apt option than the joint venture structure, as the former, by formalizing both the decision-making process and the exercise of administrative functions, possesses more stability and predictability and less vulnerability to the changeable political will of the claimants. China, on the other hand, would not reject this option because the reduction of a State's autonomy is not absolute. The direct appointment of members of a decision-making entity by the interested States retains the necessary checks and control. The checks and control are also attractive to weaker powers. It is important to note that all the claimant States have been colonized in the past, which cause these States and their nationals have a high degree of sensitivity to the risk of losing control over territorial sovereignty and sovereign rights.[86] When these countries restored their sovereignty after WWII, they became highly conscious of the new status and desirous of preserving it.[87] As rightly pointed out by Choon-Ho Park, '[o]nly within this context is it possible to appreciate their sensitivity to whatever affects their territorial integrity, a sensitivity that has yet to subside'.[88] The checks and control introduced through the decision-making entity can help reduce national sentiments in domestic politics of the claimant States.

Second, as concluded in section 6.2.2, the current international legal framework significantly falls short of regulating offshore hydrocarbon activities by only touching upon a narrow range of environmental issue associated with such activities. Given the inadequacy of existing substantive norms, the achievement of cooperation becomes reliant on the working of the cooperative institution. In this circumstance, a higher degree of institutionalization, instead of frequent resorts to redundant and lengthy negotiations directly between States as required by the joint venture structure, is more desirable owing to its efficiency in dealing with unpredictable matters that might occur from time to time during the normal course of administration. Moreover, reaching

---

86 C.H. Park, The South China Sea Disputes: Who Owns the Islands and the Natural Resources?, 5 *ODIL* (1978), 34.

87 *Ibid.*, 34–35.

88 *Ibid.*, 35.

resolutions by consensus can also enhance the efficiency of decision-making. It is not uncommon that examples adopting the joint authority structure have provided that a decision-making entity shall reach resolutions by consensus.[89] Distinct from other voting procedures such as unanimity and decision by majority, consensus is 'a procedure for adopting a decision or a statement without proceeding to a formal vote when there are no formal objections'.[90] Consensus reflects a high degree of compromise and allows a decision to pass even if that decision does not fully reflect the interests of each State involved, and a State may do so 'if its main interests are not at stake or if it is "compensated" in other decisions'.[91]

On the basis of the above two observations, the joint authority structure, which institutionalizes both the decision-making process and the exercise of administrative functions, is the most viable choice for the Spratly Islands setting. Apart from the level of institutionalization, there are five key provisions that the disputant States need to consider carefully in order to make the cooperative hydrocarbon arrangement function well: (1) the 'without prejudice' provision, (2) the designation of the cooperation zone, (3) the proceeds-sharing regime, (4) the dispute settlement regime, and (5) the participation of non-State actors, notably oil companies.

First, the 'without prejudice' provision frequently appears in cooperative hydrocarbon arrangements that do not include permanent boundaries.[92] Its purpose is to ensure the provisional nature of relevant arrangements. Nevertheless, as rightly pointed out by some scholars, inserting a 'without prejudice' provision is unnecessary if the States concerned are parties to UNCLOS, as a general 'without prejudice' provision has already been contained in UNCLOS.[93] Having said that, it is still recommended to write down the 'without

89 See *e.g.*, Treaty between the Federal Republic of Nigeria and the Democratic Republic of Sao Tome and Principe on the Joint Development of Petroleum and other Resources, in respect of Areas of the Exclusive Economic Zone of the Two States, n 46, Articles 7.4 and 10.5; Treaty between Australia and the Republic of Indonesia on the Zone of Cooperation in an Area between the Indonesian Province of East Timor and Northern Australia, n 46, Articles 5(5) and 7(4).

90 R. Wolfrum and J. Pichon, Consensus, *MPEPIL* (2010), para.3.

91 *Ibid.*, para.18.

92 The only exception is the 1993 Colombia – Jamaica arrangement. These two countries established a cooperation zone where they were unable to agree on delimitation. There was no 'without prejudice' article in the Maritime delimitation treaty between Jamaica and the Republic of Colombia of 12 November 1993. It is also interesting to note that this Treaty had no provision for its duration.

93 See *e.g.*, S.P. Kim, *Maritime Delimitation and Interim Arrangements in North East Asia* (Martinus Nijhoff Publishers. 2004), 53; Beckman and Bernard, n 41, 17.

prejudice' provision in the cooperative agreement, which may spare the disputant States and their nationals the wariness of losing control over sensitive issues including territorial sovereignty or sovereign rights.

Second, it is necessary to define the exact scope of the cooperation zone in the Spratly Islands area. In practice, the cooperation zone is usually decided based on geographical distributions of hydrocarbon deposits. Exploration is thus necessary in order to gather information in this regard. The 2005 tripartite JMSU was intended for collecting seismic survey data in part of the South China Sea but did not lead to conclusive results.[94] Therefore, the undertaking of joint surveys of the seabed and subsoil to collect data about the mineral resource potential of this region remains in need and could serve as the first step towards cooperation.[95] Moreover, the cooperation zone can be further divided into several subzones.[96] The unsuccessful practice of the tripartite JMSU, which involved seismic survey and research over a significant portion of the area, indicates that the selection of a vast sea area as the zone of cooperation tends to trigger national sentiments.[97] Hence, it is suggested to initiate the collaboration in exploiting hydrocarbon resources in a small subzone. Although all existing arrangements happen to be bilateral, in theory, it is possible to have multilateral arrangements.[98] Yet, considering that marine areas of bilateral and multilateral disputes co-exist in the Spratly Islands area, it is recommended to first experiment with the cooperative exploitation in the form of a bilateral arrangement since multilateral negotiations are usually more time-consuming than bilateral talks. If the pilot bilateral arrangement in a small subzone succeeds, it will help the disputant States build up trust and confidence, thereby increasing the chance of entering into more extensive cooperation. In this sense, the 2018 China-Philippines MoU, if implemented with caution, might serve as a good starting point.

Third, as to the 'proceeds-sharing' provision, some scholars opined that the allocation of shares in proceeds enjoyed by interested States must be closely related to the proportions of their claims, controls or influence over the cooperation zone.[99] Observations of the precedent arrangements show that in the

---

94 C. Santamaria, Sino-Philippine Joint Development in the South China Sea: Is Political Will Enough?, *Asian Politics & Policy* (2018), 330.
95 Becker-Weinberg, n 38, 163.
96 Agreement concerning joint development of the southern part of the continental shelf adjacent to Japan and South Korea, n 71, Articles V and VI. Miyoshi, n 37, 12.
97 Santamaria, n 94, 331.
98 Beckman and Bernard, n 41, 16. Miyoshi, n 37, 46.
99 See *e.g.*, Beckman and Bernard, n 41, 22; Zou, n 1, 108.

absence of a delimitation line, most precedents have the costs and profits shared equally between the State parties. This system of proceeds-sharing is arguably the most reasonable one. After all, pending delimitation, it is impossible to know for sure the proportions of shares that should be enjoyed by each disputant State. However, in the presence of gas resources in the cooperation zone, the economic benefits generated by gas resources exist not only in the production at the wellhead but also downstream. Thus, the production sharing basis may not be 50:50 provided that another State may enjoy more benefits generated downstream. For example, in the Australia-East Timor arrangement, the sharing basis is 90:10 between East Timor and Australia for the revenue achieved at the wellhead.[100] Even with the 90:10 sharing basis, Australia's ultimate benefits might exceed those of East Timor, taking into account downstream employment benefits and tax revenue from the liquefied natural gas facility and pipelines. Take the largest petroleum development in the area A – the Bayu-Undan field – for example. It has been reported that as of early 2017, the upstream revenue generated by Bayu-Undan was about US$23.5 billion for Timor-Leste and US$2.4 billion for Australia,[101] while the downstream economic benefits accrued to Australia, though debatable, might be not less than US$25 billion.[102] Tailored to the Spratly Islands setting, the most equitable regime of sharing proceeds is to share costs and proceeds equally between the disputant States. Since this region is abundant in hydrocarbon resources including gas resources, the balance between economic profits generated from both the wellhead and downstream must be taken into account in allocating the proceeds.

Fourth, most precedents contain provisions on inter-State dispute settlement. Some of them only provide for procedures that do not confer binding results, such as diplomatic channels and negotiation or consultation,[103]

---

100 Timor Sea Treaty between East Timor and Australia, n 46, Article 4.

101 Conciliation between The Democratic Republic of Timor-Leste and The Commonwealth of Australia, n 54, para.40.

102 The former Timor-Leste president Gusmão proposed that East Timor should give up 10% of the revenue share in return for a Timorese processing plant, which would bring about $25bn in downstream revenue. See H. Davidson and C. Knaus, Treaty confirms Australia profited from Timor-Leste oil and gas, rights groups say (7 March 2018), available at <https://www.theguardian.com/world/2018/mar/07/treaty-confirms-australia-profited-from-timor-leste-oil-and-gas-rights-groups-say>.

103 See *e.g.*, Memorandum of Understanding between Malaysia and the Kingdom of Thailand on the Establishment of the Joint Authority for the Exploitation of the Resources of the Sea Bed in a Defined Area of the Continental Shelf of the Two Countries in the Gulf of Thailand, n 71, Article VII; Agreement between Norway and Iceland on the continental

while others include submission to an arbitral tribunal or the ICJ that can deliver binding decisions.[104] Considering the defiance against adjudication of the claimants, especially China, as evidenced in 2002 DOC and the 2011 China-Vietnam Agreement to Guide Settlement of Maritime Issues,[105] it is prudent to say that the disputant States are more likely to adopt non-binding procedures such as diplomatic channels and negotiation or consultation as the dispute settlement regime for any inter-State dispute arising from the cooperative hydrocarbon arrangement concerning the Spratly Islands area.[106] Nevertheless, the disputant States may agree to submit the disputes between an oil company and a State (or its designated State-own oil company) to third-party dispute settlement regimes, such as the International Centre for Settlement of Investment Disputes (ICSID) or those provided in relevant

---

shelf between Iceland and Jan Mayen, n 72, Articles 7 and 9; Treaty between Australia and the Republic of Indonesia on the Zone of Cooperation in an Area between the Indonesian Province of East Timor and Northern Australia, n 46, Article 30; Memorandum of Understanding between Malaysia and the Socialist Republic of Vietnam for the Exploration and Exploitation of Petroleum in a Defined Area of the Continental Shelf Involving the Two Countries, n 72, Article 6; Treaty between the Federal Republic of Nigeria and the Democratic Republic of Sao Tome and Principe on the Joint Development of Petroleum and other Resources, in respect of Areas of the Exclusive Economic Zone of the Two States, n 46, Article 48; Exclusive Economic Zone Co-operation Treaty between the State of Barbados and the Republic of Guyana concerning the exercise of jurisdiction in their exclusive economic zones in the area of bilateral overlap within each of their outer limits and beyond the outer limits of the exclusive economic zones of other States, n 71, Article 10.

104 See *e.g.*, Agreement between the Kingdom of Saudi Arabia and the State of Kuwait on the Partition of the Neutral Zone, n 71, Article 22; Convention between the Government of the French Republic and the Government of the Spanish State on the Delimitation of the Continental Shelves of the two States in the Bay of Biscay, n 72, Article 5(3); Agreement concerning joint development of the southern part of the continental shelf adjacent to Japan and South Korea, n 71, Article XXVI(5); Agreement between Saudi Arabia and Sudan relating to Joint Exploration and Exploitation of Red Sea Seabed and Subsoil Resources (1974), Article XVI; Agreement relating to the exploitation of the Frigg Field Reservoir and the transmission of gas therefrom to the United Kingdom, n 71, Article 28(2); Management and Cooperation Agreement between the Government of the Republic of Senegal and the Government of the Republic of Guinea-Bissau, n 46, Article 9; Timor Sea Treaty between East Timor and Australia, n 46, Article 23(b).

105 ASEAN and China, Declaration on the Conduct of Parties in the South China Sea (2002), Article 4; China and Vietnam, Agreement to Guide Settlement of Maritime Issues (11 October 2011), Article 3.

106 Becker-Weinberg has observed that 'coastal States in the Asia-Pacific region have seemed to prefer bilateral negotiations to regional efforts or compulsory settlement of disputes regarding common mineral resources'. See Becker-Weinberg, n 38, 165.

bilateral investment treaties. For instance, the Chinese domestic legislation stipulates that any dispute arising between foreign oil companies and its State-owned oil company – CNOOC – which has exclusive and overall responsibility for the work of exploiting offshore petroleum resources owned by China, shall be first settled through friendly consultations, and that if consultations fail, the dispute may be submitted for mediation or arbitration.[107]

Fifth, another issue concerns the participation of non-State actors, notably oil companies, in the cooperative hydrocarbon arrangement. The actual exploration and exploitation activities are eventually carried out by oil companies. Many developing countries have established their State-owned enterprises for managing hydrocarbon resources since the 1960s owing to the pressure from the growing national sentiment of sovereignty over natural resources and the preference for autarkic policies.[108] The disputant States in this region are no exception. Each of them has its own State-owned oil company, which is endowed with exclusive rights relating to the exploration for and exploitation of marine natural resources within the jurisdiction of that State, including entering into operation contracts with other oil companies. Despite the existence of the State-owned oil companies, most developing countries remain reliant on foreign oil companies to provide both capital and technologies necessary for carrying out hydrocarbon operations, as such operations are an expensive business and require advanced technologies. Hence, a developing State usually enacts domestic laws to regulate the cooperation between its State-owned oil company and foreign oil companies. It has to be borne in mind that a State-owned oil company of one State is regarded as a foreign oil company according to another State's petroleum legislation.[109] Accordingly, oil companies can participate in the cooperative hydrocarbon arrangement by entering into operation contracts with the disputant States according to relevant provisions of the inter-State cooperation agreement or in the absence of such provisions, according to domestic petroleum legislation of the disputant States. Domestic legislation of the claimants, however,

107 China, Regulation of the People's Republic of China on the Exploitation of Offshore Petroleum Resources in Cooperation with Foreign Enterprises, issued 30 January 1982, entered into force 30 January 1982, amended 18 July 2013, Article 24.

108 D.N. Smith, Mineral Agreements in Developing Countries: Structures and Substance, 69 *AJIL* (1975), 562. J.R. O'Brien, *South China Sea Oil: Two Problems of Ownership and Development* (ISEAS. 1977), 57.

109 For example, when a State-owned oil company A of State B enters into cooperation with State C for operating in waters within State C's jurisdiction, company A is indeed treated as a foreign company pursuant to State C's legislation.

might pose legal challenges to the formulation of the cooperative hydrocarbon arrangement. As mentioned earlier, the 1987 Constitution of the Philippines stipulates that the concessionaire shall be a citizen of the Philippines, or an association of individuals, being either a partnership or a corporation duly organized and constituted under the laws of the Philippines, at least sixty per cent of the capital of which is and shall at all times be owned and held by citizens of the Philippines.[110] The 'sixty per cent' cap might make the cooperative hydrocarbon arrangement between the Philippines and other disputant States impossible, as the latter is unlikely to accept this constraint. Other similar legal challenges posed by domestic petroleum legislation may include the mandatory bidding procedure and assets/ data ownership restriction.[111] The disputant States must ensure that the cooperative hydrocarbon arrangement is ironclad to ward off potential legal challenges stemming from their domestic petroleum legislation. Therefore, the disputant States would need to be prepared to lift relevant restrictions respecting foreign investment in the development of marine natural resources in the Spratly Islands area through amendments to the constitution or laws concerned.[112]

6.4 Conclusion

The water that swallows up the boat can be the same that bears it.[113] Hydrocarbon resources, which have been the catalyst for stimulating international conflict in the Spratly Islands area since the 1970s, may offer an opportunity for building up cooperation between the disputant States. Nevertheless, the current international legal framework falls short of regulating offshore hydrocarbon activities by only touching upon a narrow range of environmental issues associated with such activities. Preceding arrangements in other sea

110 The Philippines, Constitution (1987), section 2. The Philippines, Petroleum Act, Republic Act 387 (1949), Article 31.

111 Regarding the mandatory bidding procedure, see *e.g.*, The Philippines, Oil and Exploitation and Development Act, Presidential Decree No. 87 (1972), sec. 5; Brunei, Petroleum Mining Act (2002), Article 4. Regarding the assets/data ownership restriction, see *e.g.*, China, Regulation on the Exploitation of Offshore Petroleum Resources in Cooperation with Foreign Enterprises (1982), Articles 20 and 21; Vietnam, Petroleum Law (1993), Articles 11-12.

112 A.J. Rabena, Philippines-China Joint Development Agreement in the South China Sea under Duterte, in H. Qi and S. Xue (eds.), *Cooperative Development in the South China Sea: Policies, Obstacles, and Prospects* (Routledge. 2021), 89–90.

113 See *Xunzi*, Vol. 31, para.10 [A book with an ancient Chinese collection of philosophical writings attributed to Xun Kuang], available at <https://ctext.org/xunzi/ai-gong/zh>.

regions can, however, shed light on the formulation of the cooperative hydrocarbon arrangement for the Spratly Islands area. Based on the salient features of these precedents in combination with the unique characteristics of this region, a cooperative institution consisting of a joint authority with the formalized decision-making process and administrative functions is the most apt choice.

This recommendation is a pragmatic approach towards deadlock situations as a result of complex territorial and maritime disputes associated with the demand of developing offshore hydrocarbon deposits without prejudice to respective sovereign claims of the disputant States.[114] The fact that this pragmatic approach will be the consequence of political and economic drives rather than a legal one would not diminish its role, as its outcome – a cooperative institution established on the basis of a legally binding agreement – would offer the indispensable legal assurance as required by the disputant States and oil companies to undertake the technically complex, time-consuming and highly costly offshore exploration and exploitation activities.

114 Becker-Weinberg, n 38, 164.

CHAPTER 7

Cooperation in Managing Fishery Resources

7.1 Introduction

Under the influence of alternating monsoons, the Spratly Islands area is a rich fishing ground with the cohabitation of various fish stocks and has remarkable ecological and environmental value, which is among the most biodiverse in the world.[1] As concluded in section 4.5, non-harmful fishing practices are, in general, permissible in the Spratly Islands area. Owing to the contested status of the region, the fishery resources therein are not subject to the exclusive jurisdiction of any claimant States, but instead, are used by all claimant States and their nationals. Fishery resources in the specific context of disputed marine areas can indeed be viewed as having the status of 'commons' because they are *de facto* shared by two or more States, although this point is less emphasized in literature than 'commons' that concern areas beyond national jurisdiction.[2] Moreover, the lack of effective fisheries management in this region has resulted in the 'tragedy of the commons' problem with certain species depleted or overfished.[3] Environmental stress is growing, and the stakes are high, as the risks include the loss of 'one of the Earth's great natural repositories for marine species' and 'a source of larvae for small-scale fisheries' throughout the region.[4] According to a study published in 2015, all the eleven species groups that contribute substantially to existing fisheries in the South China Sea are projected to experience decreases in biomass by up to 59% under the business-as-usual

1 The South China Sea Arbitration (The Philippines v. China), Award of 12 July 2016 (PCA), para.823. Y. Song, A Marine Biodiversity Project in the South China Sea: Joint Efforts Made in the South China Sea Workshop Process, 26 *IJMCL* (2011), 121.

2 Regarding natural resources in disputed marine areas as commons are in line with the views of Weeramantry and Schrijver. According to Weeramantry, '[n]atural resources are not individually, but collectively, owned, and a principle of their use is that they should be used for the maximum service of the people'. In a similar vein, Schrijver opined that resources shared by two or more States could be viewed as commons from a broad point of view. See Gabčíkovo-Nagymaros Project (Hungary/Slovakia), Separate Opinion of Vice-President Weeramantry dated 25 September 1997, 110; N. Schrijver, Managing the Global Commons: Common Good or Common Sink?, 37(7) *Third World Quarterly* (2016), 1253.

3 FAO Asia-Pacific Fishery Commission, *Regional Overview of Fisheries and Aquaculture in Asia and the Pacific* (2012), RAP Publication 2012/26, 17–18.

4 J.W. McManus, The Spratly Islands: A Marine Park? 23(3) *AMBIO: A Journal of the Human Environment* (1994), 181.

 DOI:10.1163/9789004504332_008

scenario by 2045 as a result of overfishing, ocean warming, acidification and changes in primary productivity, with serious food security implications.[5] Cooperation between and among the disputant States is needed to tackle the 'tragedy of the commons' problem.

This chapter aims to investigate the extent to which current international law can guide the disputant States to enter into cooperation in fisheries management in order to address the 'tragedy of the commons' problem in the Spratly Islands area. Building on the discussion on the 'tragedy of the commons' problem in the Spratly Islands setting (section 7.2), this chapter adds to existing research by analysing the dual aspects – substance and procedure – of international law and exploring their practical implications for fisheries management in the Spratly Islands area. As to the substantive aspect, this chapter conducts a holistic analysis of relevant substantive norms in international fisheries law, which includes UNCLOS and beyond, identifies regulatory limitations, and examines available legal mechanisms for remedying such limitations (section 7.3). With regard to the procedural aspect, this chapter analyses whether the existing cooperative mechanisms are viable to serve the functions of the intended cooperative institution (subsections 7.4.1–7.4.2). It also explores a suitable arrangement on the allocation of fisheries jurisdiction between or among the disputant States based on a careful examination of precedents that are implemented in other sea regions (subsections 7.4.3–7.4.4).

7.2 Tragedy of the Commons

Fishery resources in this region have dual properties, namely commodities and commons. On the one hand, fishery resources are of significant socio-economic importance to the claimant States as an essential source of food, employment, recreation, trade and economic well-being.[6] On the other hand, owing to the disputed status of the region, such fishery resources have the

5 U.R. Sumaila and W.L. Cheung, *Boom or Bust: The Future of Fish in the South China Sea* (2015), 22.

6 Fish is an important source of both protein and foreign currency for the disputant States. The net trade values of fish products in the five disputant States reached 12.4 billion US dollars in 2014. Fisheries in the South China Sea are estimated to create over 3 million jobs for the population of these disputant States. See T.N. Dang, Fisheries Co-operation in the South China Sea and the (Ir)relevance of the Sovereignty Question, 2 *Asian Journal of International Law* (2012), 63. FAO Asia-Pacific Fishery Commission, n 3, 27.

status of 'commons' in the sense that they are not subject to the exclusive jurisdiction of any claimant States, but instead, are used by all claimant States and their nationals.

The concept of 'commons' is defined as an arrangement under which 'property or resources [are] held in common and jointly exploited'.[7] It resembles '*res communes*' (common goods) used by Grotius in his seminal work *Mare Liberum* in 1609 to support his famous claim that 'the sea is common to all ... so infinite that it cannot be possessed and applied to all uses ... [including] navigation or fishing'.[8] In a system of commons, the 'tragedy of the commons' problem may occur as a result of mismanagement. The term 'tragedy of the commons', coined by Hardin in 1968, depicts a situation where individual users act independently to maximize their own self-interest and thus go contrary to the common good of all users by depleting or spoiling the shared resource.[9]

Fisheries in the Spratly Islands area suffer from the 'tragedy of the commons' problem. Due to the lack of effective fisheries management and improper fishing practices, certain stocks such as dermal, surimi and crustaceans species are depleted or overfished in this region.[10] The depletion or overfishing not only threats target species but also might alter ecosystem structures and the diversity of marine life.[11] Fishing may adversely impact a marine ecosystem in three main ways. First, by direct removal of target species, fishing can change the size structure of target populations and cause food-chain effects such as trophic cascades and altered predation pressure.[12] Second, fishing operations sometimes result in 'bycatch' of non-target species, thereby leading to overfishing and slowing efforts to rebuild fish stocks.[13] Third, fishing may cause physical damage to marine habitats mainly as a result of the use of bottom trawlers

7 N. Schrijver, *Development Without Destruction: The UN and Global Resource Management* (Indiana University Press. 2010), 6.

8 H. Grotius, The Free Sea (Indianapolis: Liberty Fund. 2004) [Web, translated by R. Hakluyt], 'chapter 5: That the sea or right of sailing on it is not proper to the Portugals by title of possession'. M.J., Schermaier, Res Communes Omnium: The History of an Idea from Greek Philosophy to Grotian Jurisprudence, 30 *Grotiana* (2009), 22.

9 H. Garrett, The Tragedy of the Commons, 162 *Science* (1968), 1244.

10 FAO Asia-Pacific Fishery Commission, n 3, 17–18.

11 J. Harrison, *Saving the Oceans through Law: the International Legal Framework for the Protection of the Marine Environment* (OUP. 2017), 166–167.

12 C.L.J. Frid, Ecosystem-based Management of Fisheries: Is Science Limiting?, 63 *ICES Journal of Marine Science* (2006), 1567.

13 NOAA Fisheries, Understanding Bycatch, available at <https://www.fisheries.noaa.gov/insight/understanding-bycatch>.

with part of the gear penetrating the ocean floor.[14] Restoring and preventing fish stocks from over-exploitation is a major challenge for fisheries management in modern times. The existence of territorial and maritime disputes in the Spratly Islands area adds more complexity to this challenge. Since none of the disputant States has exclusive jurisdiction to regulate fisheries in the contested area, effective fisheries management has to rely on their coordinated action.

One way to tackle the 'tragedy of the commons' problem is to turn the commons into private property, which amounts to making the disputed area undisputed by delimiting the maritime boundary.[15] However, this option is difficult, if not impossible, to be achieved, as the claimants are unlikely to abandon or compromise in their maritime claims or to submit this maritime dispute voluntarily to a third-party dispute settlement mechanism. An alternative is to keep the fishery resources therein as commons preceding delimitation and to allocate the rights and obligations regarding the utilization and conservation of such resources among the claimants based on agreed-upon rules and standards. In light of this, the next section examines substantive norms that apply to fisheries management within the Spratly Islands area.

7.3 Substantive Norms on Fisheries Management

7.3.1 *Scope of Examination*

This section examines the rights and obligations that current international law confers upon the claimants when managing fishery resources within the Spratly Islands area. The modern law of the sea broadly divides the ocean space into three categories, including: zones under territorial sovereignty, notably internal waters, the territorial sea and archipelagic waters; zones under sovereign rights, notably the EEZ and continental shelf; and high seas. The fisheries regulatory regimes vary in these maritime zones.[16] The scope of this section is limited in two aspects. First, since the Spratly Islands area is part of the South

14 E. Hey, A Healthy North Sea Ecosystem and A Healthy North Sea Fishery: Two Sides of the Same Regulation?, 23 *ODIL* (1992), 221.

15 Garrett, n 9, 1245.

16 Relevant literature includes: W.T. Burke, *The New International Law of Fisheries: UNCLOS 1982 and Beyond* (Clarendon Press. 1994); E. Hey, *Developments in International Fisheries Law* (Kluwer Law International. 1999); R.R. Churchill and V. Lowe, *The Law of the Sea* (MUP 3rd ed. 1999), 279–327; S.M. Kaye, *International Fisheries Management* (Kluwer Law International. 2001); Harrison, n 11, 166–208.

China Sea, a semi-enclosed sea primarily covered by the EEZs of surrounding countries as well as potential maritime areas (at least the territorial sea) generated around the islands therein, the analysis focuses on the fisheries regulatory framework governing areas within national jurisdiction, notably the territorial sea and EEZ. Second, for simplicity, the analysis only deals with fishery jurisdiction of the disputant States as coastal States. International instruments that deal with either fishing on high seas[17] or jurisdictional rights other than the coastal State jurisdiction[18] are thus excluded from the ambit of the discussion.

The relevant international instruments can be further divided into two groups, namely instruments with direct binding force upon the claimants and those without. (see Table 9) The former group includes UNCLOS, Convention

17 For international instruments that deal with fishing on high seas exclusively, see *e.g.*, UN Doc.: A/RES/46/215, Large-scale Pelagic Drift-net Fishing and Its Impact on the Living Marine Resources of the World's Oceans and Seas (20 December 1991) (This UNGA resolution calls for a driftnet fishing moratorium on the high seas of the world's oceans and seas by 31 December 1992.); Agreement to Promote Compliance with International Conservation and Management Measures by Fishing Vessels on the High Seas, adopted 24 November 1993, entered into force 24 April 2003, 2221 *UNTS* 91 (This FAO treaty mainly provides for the flag State responsibilities to ensure that fishing vessels do not engage in any activity that undermines the effectiveness of international conservation and management measures on the high seas.); FAO International Guidelines for the Management of Deep-sea Fisheries in the High Seas (2008) (The Guidelines aim to ensure the long-term conservation and sustainable use of deep-sea marine living resources with unique biological characteristics such as slow growth, long life expectancies and low natural mortality rates.).

18 For international instruments that deal with jurisdictional rights other than the coastal State jurisdiction, see *e.g.*, FAO International Plan of Action to Prevent, Deter and Eliminate Illegal, Unreported and Unregulated Fishing (2001) (This FAO instrument aims to eliminate IUU fishing by providing States with comprehensive, effective, and transparent measures by which to act. Apart from the flag State responsibilities and port State measures, it incorporates a new approach that calls for internationally agreed market-related measures to address IUU fishing, which include controls on the importation and exportation of fisheries goods, either processed or raw.); Agreement on Port State Measures to Prevent, Deter and Eliminate Illegal, Unreported and Unregulated Fishing, adopted 22 November 2009, entered into force 5 June 2016, *UNTS* Registration No. 54133 (This FAO agreement prescribes port State measures to tackle IUU fishing that have occurred in all types of marine areas, thereby ensuring the long-term conservation and sustainable use of living marine resources.); FAO Voluntary Guidelines for Flag State Performance (2013) (This FAO instrument aims to ensure the effective implementation of flag State responsibilities in deterring IUU fishing. It applies to fishing on the high seas and fishing within the national jurisdiction of a flag State or a coastal State upon their respective consent. A major contribution of this instrument is that it develops a set of performance assessment criteria to evaluate the performance of flag States, which may produce tangible results by identifying clear actions that need to be taken.).

on Biological Diversity (CBD), and Convention on International Trade in Endangered Species of Wild Fauna and Flora (CITES), to which all the claimants are parties.[19] The latter consists of UN Fish Stocks Agreement (UNFSA), FAO Code of Conduct for Responsible Fisheries (CCRF) and the 2030 UN Agenda for Sustainable Development. The instruments of the latter group, though without direct binding force upon the claimants, remain relevant because they may inform the interpretation and application of the instruments of the former group and thus influence the behaviour of the disputant States. Relevant provisions of these six instruments are analysed in turn as follows.

7.3.2 *UNCLOS: Providing an Overall Legal Framework for Fisheries Management*

UNCLOS provides for an overall international legal framework for fisheries management. This framework is organized in a piecemeal fashion, as the applicable law varies with different maritime zones. When it comes to the territorial sea, UNCLOS contains no provisions that directly concern the conservation and utilization of fisheries within this area, except for the obligations related to marine environment protection in Part XII. The underlying reason might be that the coastal State enjoys absolute sovereignty over natural resources within the territorial sea, which can only be derogated or altered by its own express consent.[20] By contrast, under UNCLOS, a coastal State is obliged to take proper conservation and management measures to ensure that living resources in the EEZ are not endangered by over-exploitation[21] and to maintain or restore populations of harvested species at levels capable of producing the maximum sustainable yield (MSY).[22] To achieve MSY, a coastal State shall determine the total allowable catch (TAC) of a harvested species.[23]

Notably, a State enjoys a wide margin of discretion in deciding a TAC best fitting the individual circumstances within its EEZ, as the MSY target can be departed from as a result of qualifications set by 'relevant environmental and

19 Chronological lists of ratifications of, accessions and successions to UNCLOS and the related Agreements, available at <http://www.un.org/depts/los/reference_files/chronological_lists_of_ratifications.htm>; List of Parties to CBD, available at <https://www.cbd.int/information/parties.shtml>; List of Parties to CITES, available at <https://www.cites.org/eng/disc/parties/chronolo.php>.

20 M. Tsamenyi and Q. Hanich, Fisheries Jurisdiction under the Law of the Sea Convention: Rights and Obligations in Maritime Zones under the Sovereignty of Coastal States, 27 *IJMCL* (2012), 785–786.

21 UNCLOS, Article 61(2).

22 *Ibid.*, Article 61(3).

23 *Ibid.*, Article 61(1).

TABLE 9 The status of fisheries-related instruments in relation to the disputant States

Disputant states	**UNCLOS (in force since 16 November 1994)**	**CBD (in force since 29 December 1993)**	**CITES (in force since 1 July 1975)**	**UNFSA (in force since 11 December 2001)**	**CCRF (not in force)**	**2030 Agenda (not in force)**
Brunei	5 November 1996	27 July 2008	2 August 1990	---	---	---
China	7 June 1996	29 December 1993	8 April 1981	---	---	---
Malaysia	14 October 1996	22 September 1994	18 January 1978	---	---	---
Philippines	8 May 1984	6 January 1994	16 November 1981	24 September 2014	---	---
Vietnam	25 July 1994	14 February 1995	22 April 1994	18 December 2018	---	---

Notes: Each of the dates in the table refers to a date of ratification/acceptance of or accession to a relevant instrument by the State concerned. The symbol '---' means that the relevant instrument has no direct binding force upon the State concerned.

economic factors'.[24] These factors include 'the economic needs of coastal fishing communities and the special requirements of developing States, and ... fishing patterns, the interdependence of stocks'.[25] The 'economic factors' may require the maximum economic yield instead of MSY. Meanwhile, taking account of the economic needs of coastal fishing communities means that certain social outcomes such as maximizing community employment, which lack a direct relation to the physical situation of fish stocks, might be prioritized in setting a TAC.[26] In light of this, some scholars have expressed the concern that the 'relevant environmental and economic factors' qualifications basically empowered States to set 'practically any size of allowable catch' legitimately.[27]

Furthermore, though UNCLOS obliges States to take measures necessary for the conservation and optimal utilization of fishery resources within their EEZ, it does not mandate the substantive content of the measures. Rather, UNCLOS only sets out the conservation objectives and principles, including the avoidance of over-exploitation,[28] the maintenance of MSY for optimal exploitation,[29] the protection and preservation of 'rare or fragile ecosystems as well as the habitat of depleted, threatened or endangered species and other forms of marine life',[30] and the prevention of serious threats to the reproduction capacity of associated and dependent species.[31] As a result, States have a wide margin of discretion in selecting the measures to attain conservation objectives, which may result in markedly varied practices.

Another point worth mentioning is that MSY mainly focuses on the reproduction capacity of target species and their associated and dependent species.[32] Scholars have, however, criticized the use of MSY as the target reference for its failure to take into account other ecosystem variables such as pollution, ocean warming and acidification.[33] In light of this, Harrison commented that an ecosystem approach to fisheries management is needed, whereby States

24 *Ibid.*, Article 61(3).
25 *Ibid.*
26 Kaye, n 16, 100.
27 Churchill and Lowe, n 16, 289.
28 UNCLOS, Article 61(2).
29 *Ibid.*, Article 61(3).
30 *Ibid.*, Article 194(5).
31 *Ibid.*, Articles 61(3) & (4).
32 *Ibid.*
33 See Hey, n 14, 224; J.R. Beddington *et al.*, Current Problems in the Management of Marine Fisheries, 316(5832) *Science* (2007), 1713; Harrison, n 11, 169; D. Liu, Difficulties and Solutions Relating to Environment Protection Cooperation in the South China Sea: A Critical Analysis of the South China Sea Arbitral Award (in Chinese), *Foreign Affairs Review* (2017), 122.

must adopt conservation and management measures that go beyond the sustainable development of individual species and consider broader impacts on the marine ecosystems.[34]

Last but not least, the obligations related to the protection and preservation of the marine environment under Part XII apply to all kinds of marine areas, including disputed marine areas.[35] Yet, this part contains very few provisions that prescribe a precise threshold for protective action in order to address the adverse effect of fishing on the marine environment. The one and only exception is Article 194(5), which requires that the conservation measures shall 'include those necessary to protect and preserve rare or fragile ecosystems as well as the habitat of depleted, threatened or endangered species and other forms of marine life'.[36] A plain reading of this provision appears to indicate that protective measures are required only when the ecosystems become 'rare or fragile' or the species become 'depleted, threatened or endangered'. As rightly noted by Hey, 'waiting for these effects to materialize and taking measures only in reaction to them seems to be out of step with contemporary developments in international environmental policy and law, which advocate a more precautionary approach'.[37] In light of this, a more liberal interpretation of Article 194(5) is indeed needed in order to integrate the precautionary approach into its application in practice.

7.3.3 *CBD: Promoting Conservation and Sustainable Use of Biodiversity*

The 1992 CBD, which, to date, has 196 parties, is one the key international instruments regarding sustainable development.[38] CBD is aimed at promoting conservation and sustainable use of biodiversity and fair and equitable sharing of the benefits arising from the use of genetic resources.[39] CBD has a broad ambit of application. It applies to terrestrial, marine and other aquatic ecosystems in areas within and beyond limits of national jurisdiction.[40]

---

34 Harrison, n 11, 186–187.

35 This position is confirmed in the *South China Sea Arbitration* merits award, in which the tribunal stated that 'the obligations in Part XII apply to all States with respect to the marine environment in all maritime areas, both inside the national jurisdiction of States and beyond it' and that 'questions of sovereignty are irrelevant to the application of Part XII'. See The South China Sea Arbitration, n 1, para.940.

36 UNCLOS, Article 194(5).

37 Hey, n 14, 223–224.

38 CBD, List of Parties, available at <https://www.cbd.int/information/parties.shtml>.

39 Convention on Biological Diversity, adopted 5 June 1992, entered into force 29 December 1993, 1760 *UNTS* 79, Article 1.

40 CBD, Article 4.

Differing from the traditional conservation efforts that focus on protecting individual species, CBD has incorporated an ecosystem approach that pays attention to not only the diversity within and between species but also the diversity of the ecosystem.[41] CBD also incorporates the precautionary approach, stating that lack of full scientific certainty should not be used as a reason for postponing measures to avoid or minimize a threat of significant reduction or loss of biological diversity.[42]

CBD outlines a legal framework providing for obligations that parties shall implement in their national laws and international relations. As a general principle, parties shall ensure that activities within their jurisdiction and control shall not cause damage to the environment of other States or areas beyond national jurisdiction.[43] Parties also have a general duty to cooperate with one another, as far as possible and appropriate, in respect of areas beyond national jurisdiction and on other matters of mutual interests.[44] Moreover, parties must develop national strategies, plans or programmes for the purposes of conservation and sustainable use of biodiversity and integrate such purposes into relevant sectoral or cross-sectoral plans, programmes and policies.[45] In particular, parties have to identify and monitor components of biodiversity important for conservation and sustainable use as well as processes and categories of activities that may have significant adverse impacts on biodiversity.[46]

7.3.4 *CITES: International Trade and Endangered Species*

The 1973 CITES, currently with 183 contracting parties,[47] is aimed at ensuring that international trade in specimens of wild animals and plants does not threaten their survival.[48] CITES has three appendices, and the export or import of any specimen of a species included in these three appendices shall require the prior grant and presentation of an export or import permit, which shall only be granted when certain conditions have been met.[49]

---

41 CBD, Article 2.

42 CBD, Preamble.

43 CBD, Article 3.

44 CBD, Article 5.

45 CBD, Article 6.

46 CBD, Article 7.

47 CITES, List of Contracting Parties, available at <https://www.cites.org/eng/disc/parties/chronolo.php>.

48 Convention on International Trade in Endangered Species of Wild Fauna and Flora, adopted 3 March 1973, entered into force 1 July 1975, 993 *UNTS* 243.

49 CITES, Articles III-V.

Appendix I are species that are threatened with extinction and subject to the strictest level of international controls on trade.[50] Appendix II are species that are not necessarily threatened with extinction, but may become so unless trade in specimens of such species is placed under strict regulation.[51] Appendix III are species that are identified by a party State as being subject to regulation within its jurisdiction and as needing the cooperation of other parties in the control of trade.[52] The Conference of Parties can amend Appendices I and II,[53] whereas any party may at any time add or remove species to or from Appendix III.[54] Certain species found in the Spratly Islands area are listed in Appendices I and II to CITES. For instance, sea turtles (*Cheloniidae*) are listed in Appendix I, whereas giant clams (*Tridacnidae*) and many of the corals are listed in Appendix II.[55]

In 1994, the 9th Conference of the Parties of CITES adopted a resolution endorsing the precautionary approach. By virtue of this approach, in cases of uncertainty, the contracting parties shall act in the best interest of the conservation of the species when considering proposals for amendment of Appendices I and II, and scientific uncertainty should not be used as a reason for failing to act.[56]

7.3.5 *UNFSA: Cooperation in Managing Straddling and Highly Migratory Fish Stocks*

UNCLOS, albeit containing a general obligation of States to cooperate in respect of straddling fish stocks and highly migratory species within and beyond EEZ s,[57] has limitations, including, *inter alia*, 'unreliable databases and lack of sufficient cooperation between States'.[58] Thus, by Resolution 47/192, the UN General Assembly convened a conference to negotiate a new international

50 CITES, Article II(1).

51 CITES, Article II(2).

52 CITES, Article II(3).

53 CITES, Article XV.

54 CITES, Article XVI.

55 The South China Sea Arbitration, n 1, paras.956-957.

56 CITES, Resolution Conf. 9.24 (Rev. CoP17), para.2.

57 UNCLOS, Articles 63-64. Straddling fish stocks migrate between the EEZ s of two or more coastal States or between the EEZ and an area beyond and adjacent to it, whereas highly migratory species travel long distances, often across different maritime zones and are listed in Annex I of UNCLOS.

58 UN Doc.: A/CONF.151/26 (Vol. II), Report on the United Nations Conference on Environment and Development, Agenda 21 (13 August 1992), Chapter 17: 'Protection of the Oceans, All Kinds of Seas, Including Enclosed and Semi-enclosed Seas, and Coastal Areas and the Protection, Rational Use and Development of Their Living Resources', para.17.45.

agreement to promote effective implementation of UNCLOS provisions in this regard.[59] The resultant agreement, namely UNFSA, was concluded in 1995.[60] Yet, among the claimants, only the Philippines and Vietnam are parties to UNFSA.[61]

As to its application scope, UNFSA regulates the conservation and management of straddling fish stocks and highly migratory fish stocks in the highs seas, except that Articles 6 and 7 regarding the application of the precautionary approach and compatibility of conservation and management measures also apply to 'areas under national jurisdiction'.[62] The term 'areas under national jurisdiction' is used in UNFSA without any definition or qualification. Despite some controversies,[63] it is widely acknowledged that a more convincing interpretation is that 'areas under national jurisdiction' is a reference to the EEZ and does not include zones under territorial sovereignty.[64] It is because UNFSA, by its nature, is an implementation agreement of UNCLOS and is designed to give effect to Articles 63 and 64 of UNCLOS, which explicitly prescribe their applicable scope to be the EEZ and areas beyond national jurisdiction.[65]

According to Article 6, which is considered 'one of the most innovative provisions of this instrument',[66] States are obliged to apply the precautionary approach in managing straddling fish stocks and highly migratory fish stocks both on the high seas and in the EEZ.[67] Accordingly, States shall take caution when information is uncertain, unreliable or inadequate and shall not use the absence of adequate scientific information as a reason for inaction.[68] Annex II of UNFSA has practical guidelines for the implementation of the precautionary

59 UN Doc.: A/RES/47/192, United Nations Conference on Straddling Fish Stocks and Highly Migratory Fish Stocks (22 December 1992).

60 United Nations Agreement for the Implementation of the Provisions of the United Nations Convention on the Law of the Sea of 10 December 1982 relating to the Conservation and Management of Straddling Fish Stocks and Highly Migratory Fish Stocks, adopted 4 August 1995, entered into force 11 December 2001, 2167 *UNTS* 3.

61 List of Parties to UNFSA, available at <https://treaties.un.org/Pages/ViewDetails.aspx?src=IND&mtdsg_no=XXI-7&chapter=21&clang=_en>.

62 UNFSA, Article 3(1).

63 For example, W.R. Edeson pointed out that the normal meaning of the term 'areas under national jurisdiction' was capable of embracing zones under territorial sovereignty. In his view, a narrow interpretation of this term as a reference to EEZ only might lead to a very limited application of the provisions of UNFSA. See W.R. Edeson, Legal Aspects of the Collection of Fisheries Data, *FAO Fisheries Circular No. 953* (1999), 1, fn.1.

64 For detailed analysis in this regard, see Tsamenyi and Hanich, n 20, 789–793.

65 UNFSA, Articles 2 and 4; UNCLOS, Articles 63-64.

66 F. Orrego Vicuña, *The Changing International Law of High Seas Fisheries* (CUP. 1999), 162.

67 UNFSA, Article 6(1).

68 UNFSA, Article 6(2).

approach.[69] Moreover, according to Article 7, States shall ensure that conservation and management measures established for the high seas and for areas under national jurisdiction are compatible in order to ensure that straddling fish stocks and highly migratory fish stocks are conserved and managed in their entirety.[70]

UNFSA designates regional fisheries management organizations (RFMOs) as mechanisms for international cooperation concerning straddling fish stocks and highly migratory fish stocks.[71] Only States which are members of relevant RFMOs, or agree to apply conservation and management measures established by such RFMOs, can access the fishery resources to which those measures apply.[72] Non-members are obliged to comply with conservation and management measures established by such RFMOs if their vessels fish in relevant areas.[73]

7.3.6 *CCRF: Setting out Key Approaches for Fisheries Management*

FAO is a competent international organization in the area of fisheries.[74] According to its constitution, the functions of FAO include collecting, analysing, interpreting and disseminating information relating to nutrition, food and agriculture including marine fishery resources, as well as recommending national and international action with respect to the management of natural resources.[75] FAO contributes to the implementation of UNCLOS at the international level by 'providing a forum for the development of instruments intended to implement the objectives of fisheries management' as set out in UNCLOS.[76]

CCRF, unanimously adopted in 1995 by the FAO Conference, is 'the most important FAO instrument in the field of fisheries'.[77] CCRF has a broad ambit of application, encompassing fishing within and beyond national jurisdiction and all aspects of fishing including capture, processing and trade.[78] In light of

69 UNFSA, Annex II.
70 UNFSA, Article 7.
71 UNFSA, Part III.
72 UNFSA, Article 8(4).
73 UNFSA, Article 17.
74 FAO, Fisheries, available at <http://www.fao.org/fisheries/en/>.
75 FAO Constitution (adopted 1945, amended 1965), Article I, reproduced in *Basic Texts of the Food and Agriculture Organization of the United Nations* (2017), Vol. I.
76 D. Freestone and A.G. Oude Elferink, Flexibility and Innovation in the Law of the Sea – Will the LOS Convention Amendment Procedures Ever Be Used?, in A.G. Oude Elferink (ed.), *Stability and Change in the Law of the Sea: The Role of the LOS Convention* (Martinus Nijhoff Publishers. 2005), 217.
77 J. Harrison, *Making the Law of the Sea: A Study in the Development of International Law* (CUP. 2011), 213.
78 CCRF, Article 1.3.

this, Moore commented that the most salient features of CCRF were its 'all-encompassing scope' and the 'systematic approach … to cover all aspects of fisheries management and development'.[79] Albeit without binding force, CCRF provides a 'frame of reference for the international community, as well as individual states, in drawing up legal instruments aimed at addressing all manner of fisheries issues'.[80]

Environmental concerns relating to fisheries are central to the concept of responsible fisheries underpinning CCRF.[81] Accordingly, CCRF sets out principles and international standards of behavior for responsible fisheries. The most important ones include approaches or principles[82] of precaution, ecosystem, and integrated management.[83] Although relevant principles or approaches might have been mentioned previously elsewhere, CCRF was the first international instrument that systematically interpreted and applied this cluster of principles or approaches in the specific context of fisheries management. It is due to such a close relationship between CCRF and such key principles or approaches that this chapter analyzes these principles or approaches under the umbrella of CCRF.

7.3.6.1 The Precautionary Approach

CCRF is one of the first international instruments that calls for the general application of the precautionary approach to fisheries management in order to address the potential adverse effects of fishing on the marine environment.[84] Yet, the precautionary approach made its debut in international law in 1987 at the Second International Conference on the Protection of North Sea, requiring action to control discharges of dangerous substances into the North Sea even before a causal link had been established by absolutely clear scientific

79 G. Moore, The Code of Conduct on Responsible Fisheries, in E. Hey (ed.), *Developments in International Fisheries Law* (Kluwer Law International. 1999), 89.

80 Harrison, n 77, 219.

81 Harrison, n 11, 179.

82 It is widely accepted in literature that the 'approaches' or 'principles' of precaution, ecosystem, and integrated management can be used interchangeably. For example, when referring to 'the precautionary principle' and 'the precautionary principle', Schrijver stated that these two terms shared the same key elements, namely 'scientific uncertainty and the anticipation of possible environmental damage'. See N. Schrijver, *The Evolution of Sustainable Development in International Law: Inception, Meaning and Status* (Martinus Nijhoff Publishers. 2008), 187. Also see J. Peel, Precaution: A Matter of Principle, Approach or Process?, 5(2) *MJIL* (2004), 500.

83 CCRF, Article 6.

84 CCRF, Article 6.5.

evidence.[85] The 1992 Rio Declaration on Environment and Development was one of the first international instruments that formulated the precautionary approach in the context of the general protection of the environment at the international level, providing that:

> In order to protect the environment, the precautionary approach shall be widely applied by States according to their capabilities. Where there are threats of serious or irreversible damage, lack of full scientific certainty shall not be used as a reason for postponing cost-effective measures to prevent environmental degradation.[86]

The above formulation of the precautionary approach has been replicated in most international instruments.[87] Despite its wide acceptance in international instruments, whether the precautionary approach has already become a recognized principle of general or customary international law is subject to dispute.[88] Applicants in many cases before the ICJ and ITLOS have argued for the binding force of the precautionary approach in general or customary international law.[89] Both the ICJ and ITLOS have been noticeably hesitant or reluctant

85 Second International Conference on the Protection of North Sea, Ministerial Declaration (1987), para.VII.

86 UN Doc.: A/CONF.151/26 (Vol. I), Rio Declaration on Environment and Development (12 August 1992), Principle 15.

87 See *e.g.*, CCRF, Article 6.5; CBD, Preamble; UNFSA, Article 6(2).

88 See N. Schrijver, The Status of the Precationary Principle in International Law and Its Application and Interpretation in International Litigation, in *Liber amicorum Jean-Pierre Cot: Le procès international* (Bruylant. 2009), 250; Schrijver, n 82, 194; Orrego Vicuña, n 66, 157.

89 For relevant ICJ cases, see *e.g.*, Request for an Examination of the Situation in Accordance with Paragraph 63 of the Court's Judgment of 20 December 1974 in the Nuclear Tests (New Zealand v. France) Case, Order of 22 September 1995 (ICJ), para.5 (New Zealand claimed that France was under an obligation to provide evidence that its nuclear tests would not result in the introduction of radioactive material into the environment before carrying out nuclear tests 'in accordance with the "precautionary principle" very widely accepted in contemporary international law'.); Whaling in the Antarctic (Australia v. Japan: New Zealand intervening), Memorial of Australia, 9 May 2011, para. 4.8.1 (Australia argued that there were a number of relevant rules of international law in force as between it and Japan, including the precautionary approach.). Besides, despite the discussion on the precautionary approach, *Pulp Mills on the River Uruguay* is not a relevant case here, because this case focuses on the interpretation of the precautionary approach stipulated in the 1975 Statute, rather than on the status of the precautionary approach in general or customary international law. See Pulp Mills on the River Uruguay (Argentina v. Uruguay), Judgment of 20 April 2010, paras.160-161, 164. The same applies to *Construction of a Road in Costa Rica along the San Juan River* (*Nicaragua v. Costa Rica*), where Nicaragua argued

to take a stand on this point.[90] The 2011 advisory opinion in *Responsibilities and obligations of States sponsoring persons and entities with respect to activities in the Area*, using Treves's words, 'has come the closest to acceptance of the customary nature of the [precautionary] approach'.[91] In that advisory opinion, the ITLOS concluded that the incorporation of the precautionary approach into a growing number of international instruments 'has initiated a trend towards making this approach part of customary international law'.[92] In other words, the ITLOS considered the precautionary approach to be an emerging norm of customary international law.[93]

CCRF has taken up the formulation of the precautionary approach as expressed in the 1992 Rio Declaration, stipulating that States and relevant RFMOs must take into account the best scientific evidence available and should not use the absence of adequate scientific information as a reason for

---

that Costa Rica failed to adopt and implement the precautionary approach to pollution problems as stipulated in Article 3 of the Regional Agreement on the Transboundary Movement of Hazardous Wastes. See Construction of a Road in Costa Rica along the San Juan River (Nicaragua v. Costa Rica), Judgment of 16 December 2015, para.218. For relevant ITLOS cases, see *e.g.*, Southern Bluefin Tuna Cases (New Zealand v. Japan; Australia v. Japan), Provisional Measures, Order of 27 August 1999 (ITLOS), paras.28-29 and 34 (New Zealand and Australia requested the arbitral tribunal to declare that Japan failed in its obligations under UNCLOS in respect of the conservation and management of SBT, 'having regard to the requirements of the precautionary principle' and to prescribe that 'the parties act consistently with the precautionary principle in fishing for SBT pending a final settlement of the dispute'.); The MOX Plant Case (Ireland v. United Kingdom), Provisional Measures, Order of 3 December 2001, para.71 (Ireland claimed that 'the precautionary principle places the burden on the United Kingdom to demonstrate that no harm would arise from discharges and other consequences of the operation of the MOX plant'.); Case concerning Land Reclamation by Singapore in and around the Straits of Johor (Malaysia v. Singapore), Provisional Measures, Order of 8 October 2003, para.74 (Malaysia argued that 'Singapore has placed itself in breach of its obligations under international law, specifically ... in relation to ... the precautionary principle, which under international law must direct any party in the application and implementation of those [UNCLOS] obligations'.).

90 A. Boyle and C. Chinkin, *The Making of International Law* (OUP. 2007), 223. T. Treves, Environmental Impact Assessment and the Precautionary Approach: Why Are International Courts and Tribunals Reluctant to Consider Them as General Principles of Law?, in M. Andenas *et al.* (eds.), *General Principles and the Coherence of International Law* (Brill|Nijhoff. 2019), 382, 385.

91 Treves, n 90, 382, 384.

92 Responsibilities and obligations of States sponsoring persons and entities with respect to activities in the Area (Request for Advisory Opinion submitted to the Seabed Disputes Chamber), Advisory Opinion of 1 February 2011 (ITLOS), para.135.

93 D. Bederman, Responsibilities and Obligations of States Sponsoring Persons and Entities with Respect to Activities in the Area, 105 *AJIL* (2011), 760.

postponing or failing to take measures to conserve target species, associated or dependent species and non-target species and their environment.[94]

Notably, scientific uncertainty is the key element relating to the implementation of the precautionary approach. The primary function of the precautionary approach is to address the question of how policymakers should act when confronted with a high level of scientific uncertainty. In the context of marine pollution caused by the introduction of harmful substances into the environment where the precautionary approach was first established, precautionary management results in the imposition of drastic measures, usually including a moratorium on the discharges of relevant substances. Yet, it needs to be noted that fisheries management has been widely recognized as a 'wicked' problem owing to the factual obstacles inherent in determining cause and effect in relation to the use of living resources.[95] To that effect, scientific uncertainty is normally the rule rather than the exception in the course of fisheries management.[96] Hence, a strict application of the precautionary approach to fisheries 'would have resulted in the impossibility of proceeding with any activity relating to marine fisheries'.[97] In light of this, it has been argued that precautionary management of fisheries differs from that of pollution in the sense that a fishing moratorium and other drastic measures are necessary only in extreme cases.[98] Accordingly, the precautionary approach to fisheries management has been devised as an expression that 'provides managers with the power to continue harvesting along with the flexibility to introduce stringent cutbacks or

---

94 *Ibid.*

95 R. Barnes, The Convention on the Law of the Sea: An Effective Framework for Domestic Fisheries Conservation?, in D. Freestone *et al.* (eds.), *The Law of the Sea: Progress and Prospects* (OUP. 2006), 242. S. Jentoft and R. Chuenpagdee, Fisheries and Coastal Governance as a Wicked Problem, 33 *Marine Policy* (2009), 553. A.S. Khan and B. Neis, The Rebuilding Imperative in Fisheries: Clumsy Solutions for a Wicked Problem?, 87 *Progress in Oceanography* (2010), 347.

96 Orrego Vicuña, n 66, 157.

97 *Ibid.*

98 See *e.g.*, UN Doc.: A/CONF.164/L.22, Comments on Precautionary Management of Fisheries, submitted by Sweden (22 July 1993), para.2 (Sweden made the following statement: 'Fisheries have to be managed in a cautious manner. There has been a misconception about such management and there is an impression that it would immediately mean the imposition of drastic measures. This is certainly not the case. A moratorium, for example, is necessary only in extreme cases'.); UN Doc.: A/CONF.164/L.41, The Precautionary Approach in Fishery Management, submitted by Ukraine (17 March 1994), para.1 (Ukraine stated that the 'extreme instance of the precautionary approach is the introduction of a moratorium of fishing'.).

prohibitions only when a threshold has been reached that would threaten a stock's sustainability'.[99]

FAO has begun an attempt to define precautionary measures to address the specific needs of fisheries management in CCRF. CCRF prescribes three key precautionary measures. First, States and relevant RFMO s must determine reference points for certain fish stocks as well as the action to be taken if these reference points are exceeded.[100] There are two types of reference points, namely target reference points and limit reference points. Target reference points refer to 'a state of a fishing and/or resource which is considered to be desirable and at which management action ... should aim'.[101] MSY is often used in this sense. Limit reference points refer to 'a state of a fishery and/or a resource which is considered to be undesirable and which management action should avoid'.[102] Measures should be taken to ensure that limit reference points will not be exceeded.[103] Second, in the event of new or exploratory fisheries, States must adopt cautious measures including catch limits and effort limits without delay, until there are sufficient data to allow assessment of the impact of the fisheries on the long-term sustainability of the stocks.[104] Third, in case of a natural phenomenon that has a significant adverse impact of the status of living aquatic resources, States must adopt measures on an emergency basis to ensure that fishing does not exacerbate such an adverse impact.[105]

7.3.6.2 The Ecosystem Approach

In addition to the precautionary approach, CCRF contains a call on States and users of living aquatic resources to conserve aquatic ecosystems.[106] The term 'ecosystem' is defined in the 1992 CBD as 'a dynamic complex of plant, animal and micro-organism, communities and their non-living environment interacting as a functional unit'.[107] Similarly, the ILC refers to 'ecosystem' as 'an

---

99 J.M. Macdonald, Appreciating the Precautionary Principle as an Ethical Evolution in Ocean Management, 26(3) *ODIL* (1995), 273.

100 CCRF, Article 7.5.3.

101 J.F. Caddy and R. Mahon, Reference Points for Fisheries Management, *FAO Fisheries Technical Paper* No. 347 (1995), section 2.3.

102 *Ibid.*

103 CCRF, Article 7.5.3(b).

104 CCRF, Article 7.5.4.

105 CCRF, Article 7.5.5.

106 CCRF, Article 6.1.

107 CBD, Article 2.

ecological unit consisting of living and non-living components that are interdependent and function as a community'.[108]

The concept of 'ecosystem' in international law, in fact, is borrowed from ecology science.[109] An ecological system is organized at four levels, from species to population to community and to ecosystem. A species is 'a group of organisms that can reproduce with one another in nature and produce fertile offspring'.[110] For example, giant clam is a species found in the Spratly Islands area. A population is a group of 'organisms of the same species that live in a particular geographic area at the same time, with the capability of interbreeding'.[111] For example, all the giant clams within the Spratly Islands area can be called a population. A community is a group of different species that 'live together and interact with each other within an environment or habitat'.[112] All fishery resources within the Spratly Islands area belong to one community. An ecosystem is 'a single environment and every living (biotic) organism and non-living (abiotic) factor that is contained within it or characterizes it'.[113] Apart from biotic components including fishery resources, an ecosystem also includes abiotic components such as climate, pollution and temperature.[114]

The regulatory framework under UNCLOS mainly conserves fishery resources at population and community levels by using MSY as the target reference point to preserve the reproduction capacity of target species and their associated and dependent species. Conservation at the ecosystem level is really marginal in UNCLOS, which is basically limited to the protection of 'rare or fragile ecosystems as well as the habitat of depleted, threatened or endangered species and other forms of marine life'.[115] The main reason might be that although our scientific understanding of the ecosystem has greatly improved during recent decades, scientific uncertainty about the structure and functioning of the

108 UN Doc.: A/CN.4/SER.A/1994/Add.l (Part 2), Yearbook of the International Law Commission 1994, Vol. 2, Part 2, 118.

109 A.J. Willis, The Ecosystem: an Evolving Concept Viewed Historically, 11 *Functional Ecology* (1997), 268–271.

110 Nature Education, Definition of 'Species', available at <https://www.nature.com/scitable/definition/species-312>.

111 Biology Dictionary, Definition of 'Population', available at <https://biologydictionary.net/population/>.

112 Biology Dictionary, Definition of 'Community', available at <https://biologydictionary.net/community/ >.

113 Biology Dictionary, Definition of 'Ecosystem', available at <https://biologydictionary.net/ecosystem/ >.

114 Biology Dictionary, Definition of 'Abiotic Factors', available at <https://biologydictionary.net/abiotic-factors/ >.

115 UNCLOS, Article 194(5).

ecosystem remains a major challenge to integrating more ecosystem variables into the fisheries regulatory framework.[116]

To implement its general call on States and users of living aquatic resources to conserve aquatic ecosystems,[117] CCRF first requires States to assign priority to undertake research and data collection in order to improve scientific understanding of fisheries including their interaction with the ecosystem.[118] Second, being aware of the transboundary nature of many aquatic ecosystems, CCRF encourages States to enter into bilateral and multilateral cooperation in research.[119] Third, selective and environmentally safe fishing gear and practices should be further developed and applied in order to maintain biodiversity and to conserve aquatic ecosystems.[120]

7.3.6.3 The Integrated Management Approach

CCRF is perhaps the first international instrument that incorporates the integrated management approach into fisheries management. Yet, if we broaden the context to the ocean, UNCLOS, earlier than CCRF, has illustrated the spirit of integrated management related to the ocean, with its preamble stating that 'the problems of ocean space are closely interrelated and need to be considered as a whole'.[121] However, owing to its modest location within the preamble, this call for integration does not amount to a legal requirement to adopt an integrated approach. Indeed, despite a few exceptions,[122] the resource management framework outlined in UNCLOS, which varies with different maritime zones, follows more a piecemeal than an integrated approach. It is apparent that this inherently fragmented approach to resource management is contributing to the degradation of the marine environment.[123]

---

116 J. Rice, Managing Fisheries Well: Delivering the Promises of an Ecosystem Approach, 12(2) *Fish And Fisheries* (2011), 217–220. Frid, n 12, 1570. S.M. Garcia *et al.*, The Ecosystem Approach to Fisheries. Issues, Terminology, Principles, Institutional Foundations, Implementation and Outlook, *FAO Fisheries Technical Paper No. 443* (2003), 8.

117 CCRF, Article 6.1.

118 CCRF, Article 6.4.

119 CCRF, Article 6.4.

120 CCRF, Article 6.6.

121 UNCLOS, Preamble.

122 See *e.g.*, UNCLOS, Articles 63-64 & 66-67 (regarding cross-jurisdictional regulation of fisheries), 123 (regarding cooperation between States bordering enclosed or semi-enclosed seas), 195 (regarding the obligation of States not to transfer pollution from one area to another).

123 K.N. Scott, Integrated Oceans Management: A New Frontier in Marine Environmental Protection, in D.R. Rothwell et al. (eds.), *The Oxford Handbook of the Law of the Sea* (OUP. 2015), 464.

The notion of integration in relation to ocean governance has also received attention beyond UNCLOS. The need for an integrated approach to marine and coastal area management and development was recalled in Chapter 17 of Agenda 21, adopted at the Rio Conference on Environment and Development in 1992.[124] Yet, similar to UNCLOS, this instrument does not establish specific requirements for integration.

Barnes conceptualizes the integrated approach relating to ocean management in six dimensions: normative, spatial, sectoral, disciplinary, temporal and user integration.[125] First, normative integration pertains to the interaction between legal norms. Second, spatial integration requires the facilitation of governance across different maritime zones. Third, sectoral integration refers to the coordination of discrete activities and the consideration of the cumulative impacts of such activities. Fourth, disciplinary integration requires interdisciplinary knowledge to be applied to ocean governance. Fifth, temporal integration is concerned with the interaction between ocean-related activities over time. Sixth, user integration calls for capacity building to structure different stakeholders' inputs into the ocean governance.

Tailored to the Spratly Islands setting, spatial integration is the most relevant one among other dimensions.[126] The zone-based approach set out in the modern international law of the sea, according to which a sovereign State governs the ocean by dividing them on the basis of the distance from its coast, tends to neglect the fluid and dynamic nature of the ocean and marine natural resources therein.[127] Spatial integration remedies this regulatory limitation by harmonizing the management measures across different jurisdictional zones.

CCRF incorporates the integrated management approach into fisheries. It underlines the need of States to cooperate to ensure effective conservation and management of living aquatic resources 'throughout their range of distribution, taking into account the need for compatible measures in areas within and beyond national jurisdiction'.[128] CCRF further prescribes two procedures for the implementation of spatial integration. First, States and relevant RFMO s

124 UN Doc.: A/CONF.151/26 (Vol. II), Report on the United Nations Conference on Environment and Development (13 August 1992), Agenda 21, Chapter 17, para.17.1.

125 R. Barnes, The Law of the Sea Convention and the Integrated Regulation of the Oceans, 27 *IJMCL* (2012), 860.

126 See E. Hey, The Fisheries Provisions of the LOS Convention, in E. Hey (ed.), *Developments in International Fisheries Law* (Kluwer Law International. 1999), 20. Kaye, n 16, 90.

127 Y. Tanaka, *The International Law of the Sea* (CUP 3rd ed. 2019), 4. Y. Tanaka, Zonal and Integrated Management Approaches to Ocean Governance: Reflections on a Dual Approach in International Law of the Sea, 19 *IJMCL* (2004), 484.

128 CCRF, Article 6.12.

should determine, on the basis of the best scientific evidence, the entire area of distribution of fish stock, including the area through which it migrates during its life cycle, and carry out fisheries management of the whole stock unit over its entire area of distribution.[129] Second, for the effective conservation and management of transboundary fish stocks, straddling fish stocks, highly migratory fish stocks and high seas fish stocks throughout their range, States and relevant RFMOs must ensure the compatibility between the conservation and management measures established for such stocks according to their respective competences.[130]

7.3.7 *2030 Agenda for Sustainable Development: Towards Measurable Implementation of the Sustainable Development Principle*

The 2030 Agenda for Sustainable Development, adopted by the UN General Assembly in 2015, prescribes 17 Sustainable Development Goals (SDGs) and 169 targets to guide the implementation of the sustainable development principle[131] and sets out a global indicator framework to measure the implementation progress.[132]

The modern concept of sustainable development is derived from the *Our Common Future* report published by the Brundtland Commission in 1987 which defines sustainable development as developments 'meeting the needs of the present without compromising the ability of future generations to meet their own needs'.[133] This definition focuses merely on the temporal dimension of the concept. Yet, over time, the concept of sustainable development has been broadened in ambit and deepened in content.[134]

On the one hand, the applicable ambit of sustainable development has expanded from the rational and prudent use of natural resources to the general need to protect the nature, environment and the ecological system of the Earth that are vital for humankind.[135] The ICJ, on the other hand, considered in its 1997 judgment in *Gabčíkovo-Nagymaros Project* that the 'need to reconcile economic development with protection of the environment' was 'aptly expressed

129 CCRF, Article 7.3.1.
130 CCRF, Article 7.3.2.
131 UN Doc.: A/RES/70/1, Transforming Our World: the 2030 Agenda for Sustainable Development (25 September 2015).
132 UN Doc.: A/RES/71/313, Work of the Statistical Commission pertaining to the 2030 Agenda for Sustainable Development (10 July 2017).
133 UN Doc.: A/RES/42/187, Report of the World Commission on Environment and Development (11 December 1987).
134 Schrijver, n 7, 9.
135 *Ibid.*, 10.

in the concept of sustainable development'.[136] In so doing, apart from the intergeneration dimension, another dimension – integration – is added to the concept of sustainable development, which expressed the need to strike a delicate balance between the concerns of economic growth and environmental demands.[137] In the 2010 *Pulp Mills* judgment, the ICJ cited its previous findings in *Gabčíkovo-Nagymaros Project* with endorsement and took a step further to ascertain that Article 27 of the Statute of the River Uruguay reflected 'the need to strike a balance between the use of the waters and the protection of the river consistent with the objective of sustainable development'.[138] Barral commented on this case that 'sustainable development is now more than just a concept; it is an objective, and an objective with which specific state conduct (that defined in Article 27) must be consistent'.[139]

The expanded concept of sustainable development has, however, raised a concern that sustainable development becomes an all-encompassing concept, if not a *mantra*, including everything regarded as good for the Earth.[140] An accurate and continuous reconsideration of the exact legal substance and implication of this concept is thus needed. The 2030 Agenda for Sustainable Development plays a critical role in this regard by translating this concept into concrete and practical goals and targets. *Inter alia*, SDG 14, composed of ten targets, focuses on the sustainable use and conservation of the ocean.[141]

Targets 14.2, 14.4, 14.6 and 14.B are of particular relevance to fisheries management. First, Target 14.2 requires the sustainable management and protection of marine and coastal ecosystems to avoid significant adverse impacts.[142] Second, Target 14.4 aims to eliminate overfishing, illegal, unreported and unregulated (IUU) fishing and destructive fishing practices by 2020, in order to restore fish stocks at least to levels that can produce MSY as determined by their biological characteristics.[143] Third, Target 14.6 intends to prohibit fisheries subsidies

136 Gabčíkovo-Nagymaros Project (Hungary/Slovakia), Judgment of 25 September 1997 (ICJ), para.140.

137 Schrijver, n 7, 10.

138 Pulp Mills on the River Uruguay, n 89, para.177.

139 V. Barral, Sustainable Development in International Law: Nature and Operation of an Evolutive Legal Norm, 23(2) *EJIL* (2012), 387.

140 Schrijver, n 82, 24. M. Fitzmaurice, Conclusions: General Principles and Developing Areas of International Law, in M. Andenas *et al.* (eds.), *General Principles and the Coherence of International Law* (Brill|Nijhoff. 2019), 445 ('the sustainable development principle was subject to many views negating any legal content').

141 UN Doc.: A/RES/70/1, Transforming Our World: the 2030 Agenda for Sustainable Development (25 September 2015), 23.

142 *Ibid.*

143 *Ibid.*, 24.

that contribute to overcapacity, overfishing or IUU fishing by 2020.[144] Fourth, Target 14.B calls for the provision of access for small-scale artisanal fishers to marine resources and markets.[145] These four targets help specify and delineate the concept of sustainable development in the area of fisheries management.

Last but not least, despite the wide dissemination in international law, it must be conceded that the principle of sustainable development, using Schrijver's words, 'finds itself, for the moment, more in the area of progressive development than in that of codification of international law'.[146] It is widely acknowledged by scholars that the principle of sustainable development has not yet enjoyed a status of customary international law, largely owing to its flexible formulations making it difficult, if not impossible, to ascertain the evidence of *opinio juris* and State practice of an obligation to develop sustainably.[147]

7.3.8 *Evaluation: Regulatory Limitations and Remedy Mechanisms*

7.3.8.1 Regulatory Limitations

7.3.8.1.1 *International Instruments with Direct Binding Force upon the Claimants*

The regulatory framework regarding how the claimants shall utilize and conserve fishery resources within the Spratly Islands area according to UNCLOS, CBD and CITES has three major limitations. The first limitation is that the fisheries management framework, in general, follows a piecemeal fashion. Different from the EEZ, UNCLOS contains very few provisions concerning the utilization and conservation of fishery resources within the territorial sea. CBD

144 *Ibid.*

145 *Ibid.*

146 Schrijver, n 82, 231.

147 See *e.g.*, *ibid.*; A. Boyle and D. Freestone, Introduction, in A. Boyle and D. Freestone (eds.), *International Law and Sustainable Development: Past Achievements and Future Challenges* (OUP. 1999), 7 (Boyle and Freestone stated that 'there remain fundamental uncertainties about the nature of sustainable development ... which have a direct bearing on the question whether sustainable development is in any sense a legal principle'.); V. Lowe, Sustainable Development and Unsustainable Arguments, in A. Boyle and D. Freestone (eds.), *International Law and Sustainable Development: Past Achievements and Future Challenges* (OUP. 1999), 24 (Lowe stated that there was 'a lack of clear evidence that the authors [of international instruments that refer to sustainable development] regarded the concept as having the force of a rule or principle of customary international law'.). For an opposite view, see *e.g.*, Barral, n 139, 388. (Barral argued that 'sustainable development, as an objective, already constitutes a principle of customary law, even if this principle is a very general one, with a high degree of abstraction and which requires case by case substantiation'. Yet, she admitted that '[a]cademic objection to the existence of a general rule of customary international law relating to sustainable development has been fierce'.).

and CITES, though applicable to different marine areas with equal treatment, are related to limited facets of fisheries management, namely biodiversity and trades. The second limitation is that insofar as the claimants are concerned, their obligation to adopt a precautionary approach is limited to the conservation of marine biodiversity under CBD and to the protection of endangered species under CITES. These claimants do not have a general legal obligation to apply a precautionary approach when utilizing and conserving the fishery resources within the Spratly Islands area. The third limitation is that the current fisheries management framework mainly aims at protecting fish stocks for future exploitation and does not go beyond the development of individual species to consider broader impacts of fishing on the marine ecosystems.

7.3.8.1.2 *International Instruments without Direct Binding Force upon the Claimants*

To address the above regulatory limitations, as rightly pointed out by Hey, it 'would not require the adoption of new legal instruments ... but rather the adoption of a new philosophy in the implementation of existing instruments'.[148] The above three limitations can be tackled by incorporating the approaches or principles of integrated management, precaution, ecosystem and sustainable development into the implementation of the existing conservation obligations under UNCLOS, CBD and CITES. International instruments without direct binding force upon the claimants, namely UNFSA, CCRF, and UN SDG s, can provide useful guidance in this regard.

First, UNFSA, albeit not applicable to zones under territorial sovereignty, requires the adoption of a precautionary approach for the management of straddling fish stocks and highly migratory fish stocks and aims to ensure that such stocks are managed in their entirety by making the management measures compatible across the high seas and EEZ s. Second, CCRF encourages the incorporation of the approaches of integrated management, precaution and ecosystem into fisheries management. Third, the 2030 Agenda for Sustainable Development help specify four targets to guide the implementation of the sustainable development principle in the area of fisheries management. Notably, as to the relationship between CCRF and UNFSA, CCRF takes up the precautionary approach and the compatibility requirement as provided in UNFSA,[149] and goes a step further to expand their application to all aspects of fisheries management. Hence, for simplicity, when considering the guidance role of

148 Hey, n 14, 217.
149 CCRF, Articles 6.5, 6.12, 7.31, 7.32.

instruments without direct binding force, the analysis can focus on CCRF and the 2030 Agenda for Sustainable Development only.

A problem that remains unsolved is how, or through what legal mechanisms, the substantive content of CCRF and the 2030 Agenda for Sustainable Development can be incorporated into the fisheries management process in the Spratly Islands setting. Sections 7.2.8.2 and 7.3.8.3 address this problem. In general, there are two available legal mechanisms that can establish linkages between different sets of norms. One is the rule of reference under Article 61(3) of UNCLOS, and the other is the systemic interpretation through Article 31(3)(c) of VCLT.

7.3.8.2 Rule of Reference under Article 61(3) of UNCLOS

Article 61(3) of UNCLOS contains a rule of reference that requires States to take into account 'generally recommended international minimum standards' when taking conservation and management measures within the EEZ.[150] In 2004, DOALOS published a matrix for identifying the obligations of States under UNCLOS in relation to other international rules and standards beyond UNCLOS.[151] According to the DOALOS matrix, instruments that fit within the confinements of Article 61(3) include UNFSA, CBD and CCRF.[152] Yet, the DOALOS matrix is non-exhaustive. Whether the 2030 Agenda for Sustainable Development can amount to 'generally recommended international minimum standards' under Article 61(3) warrants further investigation. Article 61(3) contains two elements that need to be examined further in order to answer this question. First, what are 'generally recommended'? And second, what are 'international minimum standards'?

7.3.8.2.1 *'Generally Recommended'*

It is difficult to pinpoint an exact threshold according to which the acceptance of relevant international standards can be deemed 'generally recommended'.[153] Yet, it is prudent to argue that the approaches or principles of precaution, ecosystem and integrated management as identified in CCRF and the principle

150 UNCLOS, Article 61(3).

151 DOALOS, *The Law of the Sea: Obligations of States Parties under the United Nations Convention on the Law of the Sea and Complementary Instruments* (New York: United Nations. 2004).

152 *Ibid.*, 46, 63.

153 B.H. Oxman, The Duty to Respect Generally Accepted International Standards, 24 *NYUJ Int'l L. & Pol.* (1991), 155–158.

of sustainable development as expressed in the 2030 Agenda for Sustainable Development are widely accepted by States.[154]

For instance, an FAO Ministerial Meeting on Fisheries, held in 1999, adopted a Declaration on the Implementation of the Code of Conduct in which States committed themselves to implement CCRF as a matter of priority and to call upon all users of fishery resources to apply CCRF.[155] UN General Assembly has also recognized that CCRF sets out 'principles and global standards of behaviour for responsible practices for conservation of fishery resources and the management and development of fisheries'[156] and urged States and relevant RFMOs to implement and promote the application of CCRF within their areas of competence.[157]

Much the same could be said of the sustainable development principle. To support the implementation of SDG 14, the global UN Ocean Conference, held in 2017, adopted a political declaration titled 'Our Ocean, Our Future: Call for Action', in which States and other stakeholders unanimously affirmed their 'strong commitment to conserve and sustainably use our oceans, seas and marine resources for sustainable development'.[158] As a follow-up of the 2017 Ocean Conference, the UN launched nine thematic multi-stakeholder Communities of Ocean Action (COAs) in the same year to facilitate collaboration and networking amongst actors in support of SDG 14. One of these COAs is the COA on Sustainable Fisheries. This COA has received more than 500 voluntary commitments made by various stakeholders, including commitments concerning sustainable seafood, strengthening of RFMOs, community empowerment, and market access for small-scale fishers.[159]

7.3.8.2.2 *'International Minimum Standards'*

A cardinal feature of 'international minimum standards' is that such standards do not necessarily bind upon States, as one significant virtue of the duty to take into account such standards is to emphasize the nature of the general recommendation of a standard after promulgation, without regard to whether its initial adoption creates a legal obligation or not.[160]

---

154 Harrison, n 77, 219–220.

155 The Rome Declaration on the Implementation of the Code of Conduct for Responsible Fisheries, adopted by the FAO Ministerial Meeting on Fisheries, 10–11 March 1999.

156 UN Doc.: A/RES/63/112 (24 February 2009), preamble, 2; UN Doc.: A/RES/60/31 (10 March 2006), preamble, 2.

157 UN Doc.: A/RES/63/112, n 156,, para.39; UN Doc.: A/RES/60/31, n 156, para.30.

158 UN Doc.: A/RES/71/312, Our Ocean, Our Future: Call for Action (6 July 2017), para.1.

159 Communities of Ocean Action on Sustainable Fisheries, available at <https://oceanconference.un.org/commitments/?community=5>.

160 Oxman, n 153, 110.

Furthermore, it is essential to have in mind that the main purpose of the duty to respect 'international minimum standards' is to unify practices regarding fisheries management. Thus, as rightly pointed out by Oxman, to be regarded as a standard, a provision should inform the content of the action that States or relevant actors are required to take.[161] Myriad clauses that only confer an obligation of conduct or an exhortation to act such as 'States shall/should endeavour to' or 'States shall/should make effort to' would not constitute 'international rules and standards', as such clauses do not lead to uniform practices even by States legally bound by them.[162]

As can be seen in sections 7.3.6 and 7.3.7, CCRF and the 2030 Agenda for Sustainable Development do prescribe action or measures to be taken for the implementation of relevant approaches or principles. Hence, it is prudent to argue that the relevant approaches or principles as set out in these two instruments can qualify as 'international minimum standards' for the purpose of Article 61(3).

The preceding analysis concludes that the approaches or principles of precaution, ecosystem and integrated management as identified in CCRF and the principle of sustainable development as expressed in the 2030 Agenda for Sustainable Development can amount to 'generally recommended international minimum standards' under Article 61(3). It follows that State parties to UNCLOS shall take into account these approaches or principles when adopting and implementing fisheries management measures.

7.3.8.3 Systemic Interpretation through Article 31(3)(c) of VCLT

Article 31(3)(c) of VCLT enables systemic integration of different sources of international law within the international legal system.[163] It requires the interpretation of a treaty to take into account material sources external to the treaty itself.[164] Such external material sources are termed 'relevant rules of international law applicable in the relations between the parties' in Article 31(3)(c).[165]

There is little doubt that treaty-based rules, customary international law, and general principles of law as listed in Article 38(1) of the ICJ Statute are

161 *Ibid.*, 148.
162 *Ibid.*
163 UN Doc. A/CN.4/L.702, Fragmentation of International Law: Difficulties Arising from the Diversification and Expansion of International Law, Report of the Study Group of the International Law Commission (18 July 2006), para.18.
164 C. McLachlan, The Principle of Systemic Integration and Article 31(3)(C) of the Vienna Convention, 54(2) *ICLQ* (2005), 310.
165 VCLT, Article 31(3)(c).

of relevance to the interpretation of a treaty pursuant to Article 31(3)(c) of VCLT.[166] The ICJ judgment in *Case concerning Oil Platforms* (*Iran v United States*) represents a bold application of Article 31(3)(c) of VCLT by making reference to another treaty and customary international law when interpreting a treaty provision. In that case, the ICJ was called upon to decide whether Iran's alleged actions to imperil neutral commercial shipping in the Iran-Iraq war and the US Navy's subsequent destruction of three Iranian oil platforms in the Persian Gulf constituted breaches of the 1955 Treaty of Amity, Economic Relations and Consular Rights between the US and Iran.[167] For this purpose, the ICJ paid particular attention to whether these alleged actions fell inside the scope of Article XX, paragraph 1(d) of the Treaty that explicitly permitted the application of measures 'necessary to protect [the party's] essential security interests'.[168] The ICJ, based upon Article 31(3)(c) of VCLT, held that Article XX, paragraph 1(d) was not intended to 'operate wholly independently of the relevant rules of international law on the use of force'.[169] Consequently, the ICJ concluded that actions in violation of international law applicable to the use of force, namely the UN Charter and relevant customary international law, should not be interpreted to fit in with Article XX, paragraph 1(d) of the Treaty.[170] In a similar vein, the European Court of Human Rights (ECtHR) jurisprudence (e.g. *Al-Adsani v. UK*, *Fogarty v. UK*, and *McElhinney v. Ireland*) also resorted to Article 31(3)(c) of VCLT and concluded that the interpretation of Article 6(1) of the European Convention on Human Rights concerning the right of access to court in civil claims must take into account other relevant rules of international law of which this provision forms part, including those regarding the grant of State immunity that reflect 'generally recognised rules of public international law' or 'limitations generally accepted by the community of nations'.[171]

---

166 See *e.g.*, UN Doc. A/CN.4/L.702, n 163, paras.19-20; UN Doc. A/61/10, Report of the International Law Commission, 58th session, 1 May – 9 June and 3 July – 11 August 2006, 413, paras.18-21.

167 Oil Platforms (Islamic Republic of Iran v. United States of America), Judgment of 6 November 2003, para.18.

168 *Ibid.*, para.32.

169 *Ibid.*, para.41.

170 *Ibid.*, para.42.

171 See Al-Adsani v. the United Kingdom, Application No. 35763/97, Judgment of 21 November 2001, para.56; Fogarty v. the United Kingdom, Application No. 37112/97, Judgment of 21 November 2001, para.36; McElhinney v Ireland, Application No. 31253/96, Judgment of 21 November 2001, para.37.

However, it is much more difficult to argue with absolute certainty that norms without binding force upon the parties to the treaty that needs to be interpreted can fit within the confinements of Article 31(3)(c). For example, Villiger argued in his commentary to VCLT that the term 'applicable' in Article 31(3)(c) 'leaves no room for doubt: non-binding rules cannot be relied upon'.[172] One exception, if any, might be soft-law principles established in international environmental law. Both international jurisprudence and some legal commentators appear to recognize the relevance of such soft-law principles to Article 31(3)(c).

The ICJ and ITLOS have, in a few recorded instances, stated their endorsement, either implicitly or explicitly, in this regard. The ICJ stated in its 1999 judgment in *Gabčíkovo-Nagymaros Project* that the concept of sustainable development, which expressed the 'need to reconcile economic development with protection of the environment', must be taken into consideration and given proper weight 'not only when States contemplate new activities but also when continuing with activities begun in the past'.[173] Accordingly, the ICJ concluded that the interpretation of the treaty concerned (the 1977 Treaty concerning the construction and operation of the Gabcikovo-Nugymaros Systenz of Locks) should take account of the norms of international environmental law including sustainable development.[174] Lowe commented on this case that sustainable development acted as 'a meta-principle, acting upon other rules and principles – a legal concept exercising a kind of interstitial normativity, pushing and pulling the boundaries of true primary rules when they threaten to overlap or conflict with each other'.[175] In a similar vein, the ICJ stated in its 2010 *Pulp Mills* judgment that 'a precautionary approach may be relevant in the interpretation and application of the provisions of the [1975 Statute of the River Uruguay]'.[176] These two ICJ judgments, albeit without direct reference to Article 31(3)(c) of VCLT, endorse the relevance of soft-law principles established in international environmental law in treaty interpretation.

The ITLOS appears to have expressed its endorsement more explicitly than the ICJ. In its 2011 advisory opinion in *Responsibilities and obligations of States sponsoring persons and entities with respect to activities in the Area*, the ITLOS cited the ICJ's statement on the relevance of the precautionary approach to

172 M. Villiger, *Commentary on the 1969 Vienna Convention on the Law of Treaties* (Martinus Nijhoff Publishers. 2009), 433.

173 Gabčíkovo-Nagymaros Project, n 136, para.140.

174 *Ibid.*, para.141.

175 Lowe, n 147, 31.

176 Pulp Mills on the River Uruguay, n 89, para.164.

treaty interpretation in the *Pulp Mill* judgment.[177] The ITLOS considered that the ICJ's statement could be read in light of Article 31(3)(c) of VCLT, 'according to which the interpretation of a treaty should take into account not only the context but "any relevant rules of international law applicable in the relations between the parties" '.[178] By virtue of this statement, the ITLOS inferred that the precautionary approach could amount to 'relevant rules of international law applicable in the relations between the parties' under Article 31(3)(c) of VCLT to inform treaty interpretation.[179]

Scholars have also acknowledged the importance of soft-law principles established in international environmental law that 'derives principally from the influence they may exert on the interpretation, application and development of other rules of law'.[180] To decide cases, international courts and tribunals can apply general principles as identified in Article 38(1) of the ICJ Statute.[181] Article 38(1) only refers to 'general principles of law recognized by civilized nations' as derived from national legal systems. Yet, for the sake of doctrinal rigour, it has been argued that Article 38(1) also encapsulates 'general principles derived from international law' or 'soft-law general principles'.[182] To exert influence on the development of international law, such soft-law general principles do not need to mature into rules of customary international law to have legal effect, nor do they have to be incorporated in treaties.[183] Boyle and Chinkin opined that Article 31(3)(c) of VCLT appears to include a reference to such soft-law general principles 'as an aid to treaty interpretation'.[184] In their view, what gives such soft-law general principles their authority and legitimacy is simply the endorsement of States.[185]

As can be seen in section 7.3.8.2, the approaches or principles of precaution, ecosystem and integrated management as identified in CCRF and the principle of sustainable development as expressed in the 2030 Agenda for Sustainable

177 Responsibilities and obligations of States sponsoring persons and entities with respect to activities in the Area, n 92.
178 *Ibid.*, para.135.
179 R. Virzo, The 'General Rule of Interpretation' in the International Jurisprudence Relating to the United Nations Convention on the Law of the Sea, in A. Del Vecchio and Roberto Virzo (eds.), *Interpretations of the United Nations Convention on the Law of the Sea by International Courts and Tribunals* (Springer. 2019), 28.
180 Boyle and Chinkin, n 90, 223.
181 ICJ Statute, Article 38(1).
182 Harrison, n 77, 219.
183 Boyle and Chinkin, n 90, 223.
184 *Ibid.*
185 *Ibid.*, 224.

Development are widely endorsed by States.[186] It follows that such approaches or principles should not be ignored by States when taking fisheries management measures. They can, arguably, constitute 'relevant rules of international law applicable in the relations between the parties' under Article 31(3)(c) of VCLT and thus inform the interpretation and application of other primary norms of international law with direct binding force upon the claimants, notably UNCLOS, CBD and CITES. This position is tenable because no genuine conflicts exist between these soft-law general principles and those treaty provisions in UNCLOS, CBD and CITES, as required by Article 31(3)(c) of VCLT.[187]

Admittedly, the above conclusion rests on the premise that norms without binding force, especially soft-law principles established in international environmental law, can fit within the confinements of Article 31(3)(c) to inform the interpretation of other hard norms. This premise is not necessarily the strongest one, but as rightly pointed out by some scholars, it is definitely a pragmatic one, because it would be much easier to explain the use of relevant soft-law principles such as the precautionary approach by national and international courts and by international organizations, if they are viewed simply as a general principle of law under Article 38 of the ICJ Statute.[188]

7.3.8.4 Application to the Spratly Islands Setting

Effective management is needed in the Spratly Islands area in order to solve the 'tragedy of the commons' problem. The regulatory framework under UNCLOS, CBD and CITES with direct binding force leaves the claimants with a wide margin of discretion in taking management measures. Yet, through either the rule of reference contained in Article 61(3) of UNCLOS or the systemic interpretation through Article 31(3)(c) of VCLT, the approaches or principles of precaution, ecosystem, integrated management and sustainable development as identified in CCRF and the 2030 Agenda for Sustainable Development can guide the fisheries management process in the following aspects.

First, in implementing the precautionary approach, the disputant States should determine stock reference points as targets or limits as well as the action to be taken if these reference points are exceeded. Moreover, the disputant States must adopt cautious measures without delay in case of new or exploratory fisheries or measures on an emergency basis in the event of a natural phenomenon that adversely impacts fisheries.

186 Harrison, n 77, 219–220.

187 Mclachlan, n 164, 318.

188 P. Birnie *et al.*, *International Law and the Environment* (OUP 3rd edition. 2009), 162–163. Treves, n 90, 385–386.

Second, following the ecosystem approach, the disputant States should enter into cooperation in research and data collection as issues of priority, in order to improve scientific understanding of fisheries including their interaction with the ecosystem within the Spratly Islands area. The disputant States could further adopt selective and environmentally safe fishing gear and practices to maintain biodiversity and to conserve aquatic ecosystems in this region.

Third, pursuant to the integrated management approach, the disputant States should determine the entire area of distribution of fish stock based on the best scientific evidence. Furthermore, the disputant States must cooperate to ensure that the compatibility between the conservation and management measures established for the same fish stock. It follows that the disputant States are recommended not to use jurisdictional zones as the frame of reference when taking conservation and management measures for fish stocks in the Spratly Islands area but to regard this region as an integrated whole for the purpose of fisheries management.

Fourth, the operation of the sustainable development principle in the area of fisheries management requires the elimination of overfishing, IUU fishing and destructive fishing practices, the prohibition of fisheries subsidies that contribute to overcapacity, overfishing or IUU fishing, and the provision of access for small-scale artisanal fishers to marine resources and markets.

Last but not least, the implementation of the above four approaches or principles in the Spratly Islands area highly relies on the accuracy and adequacy of fisheries data. For example, the decision-making in relation to stock reference points, measures for ecosystem conservation, areas of distribution of fish stocks as well as the status of fisheries capacity all need to be based on scientific data. To this effect, cooperation in gathering and sharing fisheries data is at the forefront of cooperation priorities to be taken by the disputant States.

7.4 Cooperative Institution for Fisheries Management

Articles 74(3) and 83(3) of UNCLOS oblige the disputant States to negotiate in good faith a provisional arrangement on fisheries management with respect to the Spratly Islands area.[189] Article 123 of UNCLOS prescribes a similar obligation, requiring that in semi-closed seas, States shall 'endeavour ... to coordinate the management ... of the living resources'.[190] Yet, the use of the wording

189 UNCLOS, Articles 74(3) and 83(3).
190 UNCLOS, Article 123(a).

'endeavour to' in Article 123 indicates that the duty to cooperate under this provision also amounts to an obligation of conduct rather than an obligation of result to enter into cooperation eventually.[191] Hence, the outcome of the negotiation or the selection of cooperative institutions are not mandated by current international law but are left to be determined by the disputant States. In light of this, this section aims to figure out a cooperative institution that suits the Spratly Islands setting. For this purpose, this section first analyses the basic requirements of the intended cooperative institution (subsection 7.4.1). It continues to discuss whether the existing cooperative mechanisms are viable to serve the functions of the intended cooperative institution (subsection 7.4.2). It also explores a suitable arrangement on the allocation of fisheries jurisdiction between or among the disputant States based on a careful examination of precedents that are implemented in other sea regions (subsections 7.4.3–7.4.4).

7.4.1 *Basic Requirements of Intended Cooperative Institution*

It is important to realize that concrete measures, including the setting of the TAC or the determination of MSY, play a crucial role in achieving the conservation and management objectives. These measures must be capable of being adapted to changing situations. Hence, it is infeasible to 'freeze' all concrete measures in one single legal instrument. A certain degree of institutionalization is needed in order to carry out two main functions, including: (1) adopting, considering and revising the concrete measures from time to time; and (2) conducting constant surveillance and monitoring of the implementation of the measures adopted. For these purposes, the intended cooperative institution needs to fulfil two basic requirements. First, the cooperative institution should be *intergovernmental* that can provide a formal forum for the disputant States to negotiate and make decisions on fisheries management according to any new and changed situations. Second, the cooperative institution must comprise some *permanent* mechanisms to be responsible for constantly evaluating and monitoring the implementation of the concrete measures.

7.4.2 *Evaluation of Existing Cooperative Mechanisms*

Some scholars suggested making use of the existing cooperative mechanisms to serve the functions of the intended cooperative institution.[192] Relevant

---

191 J. Symonides, The Legal Status of the Enclosed and Semi-Enclosed Seas, 27 *German YB Int'l L.* (1984), 315, 327. The South China Sea Arbitration, n 1, paras.906 and 984.

192 See *e.g.*, S. Kao *et al.*, Regional Cooperation in the South China Sea: Analysis of Existing Practices and Prospects, 43 *ODIL* (2012), 286–290; D. Wang, From Dangerous Ground to

mechanisms consist of Workshop on Managing Potential Conflicts in the South China Sea (Workshop-SCS), Southeast Asian Fisheries Development Center (SEAFDEC), Asia-Pacific Fishery Commission (APFIC), and the ASEAN+ mechanism.[193]

First, since its establishment in 1990, Workshop-SCS, as a mechanism specifically aimed at addressing the South China Sea issues, facilitates dialogues and negotiations among experts, scholars and government officials from the disputant States who participate in workshops in their personal capacity.[194] However, this informal and non-governmental cooperative mechanism is not a viable option, as it lacks the capacity to adopt measures for the disputant States to observe and implement.

Second, SEAFDEC is an autonomous intergovernmental body established by the ASEAN States in 1967, aimed to 'promote and facilitate concerted actions among the Member Countries to ensure the sustainability of fisheries and aquaculture in Southeast Asia'.[195] SEAFDEC is an advisory regional fisheries body that can only make non-binding recommendations to its member States and does not have a defined geographical area of competence.[196] Arguably, the SEAFDEC is not a viable mechanism for the disputant States to cooperate in fisheries management respecting the Spratly Islands area. On the one hand, the functions of SEAFDEC are largely limited to providing fisheries-related training and research for the member States.[197] SEAFDEC does not have the power to adopt concrete measures for the actual management of living resources. On the other hand, the membership to SEAFDEC is only open to the ASEAN States and Japan.[198] Thus, China cannot become a member of SEAFDEC. Moreover, the fact that Japan has one vote in the supreme and decision-making organ of

---

Safe Playground: A Revisit to Fishery Co-operation in the South China Sea, 34 *Chinese (Taiwan) Yearbook of International Law and Affairs* (2016), 33–37; Liu, n 33, 122–123.

193 One scholar also mentioned Western Pacific Fisheries Consultative Committee (WPFCC) as an option. However, WPFCC, which aimed to coordinate cooperative efforts in fisheries development and management between ASEAN countries and the Pacific Island Nations, ceased to exist on 31 December 1996. See Liu, n 33, 123.

194 Z. Gao, Review and Prospect of the Security Cooperation Mechanisms in the South China Sea (in Chinese), 1 *Boundary and Ocean Studies* (2016), 6–7.

195 Resolution on the Future of SEAFDEC (15 November 2017), available at <http://www.seafdec.org/strategies/>.

196 FAO, Regional Fishery Bodies Summary Descriptions: Southeast Asian Fisheries Development Center (SEAFDEC), available at <http://www.fao.org/fishery/rfb/seafdec/en>.

197 Agreement Establishing the Southeast Asian Fisheries Development Center, adopted and entered into force 28 December 1967, 651 *UNTS* 20, Article 2.

198 *Ibid.*, Article 3.

SEAFDEC also makes it impossible for China to agree on the use of SEAFDEC as a cooperative institution to manage fisheries respecting the Spratly Islands area.[199]

Third, APFIC is a regional fisheries body established by FAO in 1948 at the request of its members, who share 'mutual interest in the development and proper utilization of the living aquatic resources of the Asia-Pacific area and desiring to further the attainment of these ends through international cooperation'.[200] The area of competence of APFIC covers the Spratly Islands area.[201] APFIC has a wide range of functions and responsibilities in relation to fisheries management, including conducting a continuous review of the state of fishery resources and formulating or recommending measures to conserve and manage fishery resources.[202] Decisions of APFIC are taken by a majority of the votes cast where each member State has one vote.[203] Yet, APFIC is not a viable mechanism to deal with fisheries management respecting the Spratly Islands area. Firstly, APFIC does not have the power to adopt binding management measures for fisheries.[204] Secondly, aside from the disputant States, the current members to APFIC include other States such as the US, Australia, Japan, Republic of Korea and France. Thus, it is unlikely that the disputant States, especially China, would agree to use APFIC as the cooperative mechanism for fisheries management, as the use of this mechanism would amount to letting non-disputant States including those not bordering the South China Sea have decision-making power on matters related to the contested region.

Fourth, some scholars advocated a regional cooperation approach through the ASEAN+ mechanism, or in other words, through the cooperation between ASEAN as a whole and China.[205] Given the disproportionate power structure in the region with China being the greatest power, this approach might gain the support from the disputant States that are members to ASEAN because it could 'lock China into a network of constraining multilateral arrangements'.[206]

---

199 *Ibid.*, Articles 6-7.

200 Agreement for the Establishment of the Indo-Pacific Fisheries Council (later became the Asia-Pacific Fishery Commission), adopted 15–29 November 1948, entered into force 9 November 1948, 120 *UNTS* 59, Preamble.

201 *Ibid.*, Article VI.

202 *Ibid.*, Article IV.

203 *Ibid.*, Article II.

204 E. Meltzer and S. Fuller, *The Quest for Sustainable International Fisheries* (NRC Research Press. 2009), 57.

205 D. Denoon and S.J. Brams, Fair Division: A New Approach to the Spratly Islands Controversy, 2 *International Negotiation* (1997), 303.

206 M. Leifer, Truth about the Balance of Power, in D. da Cunha (ed.), *The Evolving Pacific Power Structure* (Singapore: Institute of Southeast Asian Studies. 1996), 51.

However, as rightly pointed out by Gao, this approach is problematic because some of the ASEAN States, including Laos and Myanmar, are not coastal States bordering the South China Sea.[207] Thus, similar to APFIC, the ASEAN+ mechanism is probably unacceptable to States bordering the South China Sea, as it confers decision-making power to States without any stake in fishery resources therein.

The preceding analysis concludes that the existing cooperative mechanisms are not viable to serve the functions of the intended cooperative institution.[208] Nevertheless, these mechanisms may still play an important brokerage role in bringing the disputant States to the negotiating table to negotiate a common understanding of key strategic norms with regard to fisheries management. Furthermore, the disputant States have to establish a new cooperative institution for fisheries management. First, such a cooperative institution may take the form of a joint commission that is intergovernmental and permanent. In practice, it is common to establish a joint commission to manage fishery resources in overlapping zones where no boundary has (yet) been agreed.[209] Second, participants to the cooperative institution are not necessarily limited to the disputant States alone. Indonesia, Singapore, Thailand and Cambodia, which are bordering the South China Sea, must be encouraged to participate in the cooperative institution to the extent that the best scientific evidence shows that fisheries management respecting the Spratly Islands area and other sea areas of the South China Sea are interconnected.

7.4.3 *Typology of Precedents*

As concluded in section 7.4.2, the disputant States have to establish a new cooperative institution for fisheries management because of the infeasibility of the existing cooperative mechanisms to serve the functions of the intended

207 Gao, n 194, 7.

208 Wang held the same opinion, commenting that the 'current organizations and arrangements in the South China Sea are not sufficient to deal effectively with the management and conservation of the region's fishery resources'. See K. Wang, Fishery Disputes and Regional Cooperation, in C.J. Jenner (ed.), *The South China Sea A Crucible of Regional Cooperation or Conflict-making Sovereignty Claims?* (CUP. 2016), 286–291.

209 See *e.g.*, Agreement between Norway and the Soviet Union on a Temporary Practical Arrangement for Fishing in an Adjacent Area in the Barents Sea, with Attached Protocol, adopted 11 January 1978, entered into force 27 April 1978, reproduced in: T. Henriksen and G. Ulfstein, Maritime Delimitation in the Arctic: The Barents Sea Treaty, 42 *ODIL* (2011), 10; Agreement on Fishery Co-operation in the Beibu Gulf between the Government of the People's Republic of China and the Government of the Socialist Republic of Vietnam, adopted 25 December 2000, entered into force 30 June 2004, reproduced in: H.T. Nguyen, Maritime Delimitation and Fishery Cooperation in the Tonkin Gulf, 36 *ODIL* (2005), 35–44.

cooperative institution. The allocation of fisheries jurisdiction between or among the disputant State respecting the Spratly Islands area is a core element of such a new cooperative institution, and a careful examination of precedents that are implemented in other sea regions would help. The precedents of cooperative fisheries arrangements, diverse as they are, can be broadly divided into four models, namely 'provisional fisheries boundary', 'white zone', 'grey zone' and 'light grey zone'.[210] Most existing precedents were concluded before the 21st century, largely because following the adoption of UNFSA in 1995, inter-State fisheries cooperation is usually carried out through RFMO s. These models share one common denominator, notably the 'without prejudice' clause, the effect of which is to ensure the provisional nature of the fisheries arrangement and to prevent any impact on the maritime claims of the disputant States. Each of these models corresponds to a specific type of arrangement on the allocation of fisheries jurisdiction between the disputant States, which is analysed in turn as follows.

7.4.3.1 Provisional Fisheries Boundary

The 'provisional fisheries boundary' model, as its name indicates, involves the establishment of a provisional fisheries boundary in contested marine areas.[211] This model allocates fishery jurisdiction between the States concerned in an area-based approach. Each State has exclusive surveillance and enforcement jurisdiction over fisheries on one side of the provisional boundary. A notable example is a fisheries agreement concluded between Australia and Indonesia in 1981, stipulating that each State is obliged refrain from taking enforcement action and prevent its nationals from fishing beyond a well-defined provisional line in the Timor Sea.[212] Another example is an agreement entered into by Japan and Korea in 1998, according to which fishers were required to obtain permits from the responsible State before fishing in relevant areas of their alleged EEZ that was subject to that State's jurisdiction based on the provisionally delimited boundary.[213]

---

210 For discussions about this categorization, see *e.g.*, Dang, n 6, 77; R.R. Churchill, Fisheries Issues in Maritime Boundary Delimitation, 17 *Marine Policy* (1993), 45–51.

211 Dang, n 6, 78.

212 Memorandum of Understanding between the Government of Australia and Government of the Republic of Indonesia Concerning the Implementation of a Provisional Fisheries Surveillance and Enforcement Arrangement, adopted 29 October 1981, entered into force 1 February 1982, reproduced in: J.I. Charney and L.M. Alexander (eds.), *International Maritime Boundaries* Vol. 2 (Martinus Nijhoff Publishers. 1993), 1238–1239.

213 Agreement on Fisheries between the Republic of Korea and Japan, adopted 28 November 1998, entered into force 22 January 1999, reproduced in: S.P. Kim, *Maritime Delimitation*

7.4.3.2 White Zone

The 'white zone' model comprises an arrangement based on which the disputant States agree to refrain from extending their fisheries jurisdiction to a precisely defined area.[214] This model amounts to treating the contested marine areas as high seas. The most representative example is an agreement concluded between the USSR and Sweden in 1977, according to which both States abstained from extending their fisheries jurisdiction into a potentially disputed area of some 13,000 km^2 in the Baltic Sea.[215] Pending delimitation, the above area disputed between the USSR and Sweden was regarded as high seas and subject to the regulation by an RFMO, namely the International Baltic Sea Fisheries Commission.[216]

7.4.3.3 Grey Zone

The 'grey zone' model consists of an arrangement that accords the disputant States with fisheries jurisdiction in a precisely defined area.[217] The term 'grey zone' originated from the Grey Zone Agreement between Norway and the USSR in 1978, according to which these two States set up a joint commission to determine the TAC for various fish stocks and to allocate the quota of catch roughly equally between them in respect of a well-defined area of some 67,500 km^2 in the Barents Sea.[218] The fisheries agreement relating to Tonkin Gulf between China and Vietnam in 2000 also adopted this model.[219] This agreement clearly defined the 'Common Fishery Zone' of about 33,500 km^2 as the zone for fisheries cooperation, covering most of the fishing grounds of high productivity in Tonkin Gulf.[220] This agreement indeed established a two-tier structure for

and Interim Arrangements in North East Asia (Martinus Nijhoff Publishers. 2004), 'Appendix 2', 327.

214 Dang, n 6, 79.

215 Agreement between the USSR and Sweden on Mutual Relations in the Field of Fisheries, adopted 22 December 1977, entered into force 24 January 1980, 1260 *UNTS* 220. [This Agreement is in Russian and Swedish. English version is not publicly available.] Also see Churchill, n 210, 49.

216 Churchill, n 210, 49.

217 Churchill, n 210, 45. Dang, n 6, 79.

218 Agreement between Norway and the Soviet Union on a Temporary Practical Arrangement for Fishing in an Adjacent Area in the Barents Sea, n 209, reproduced in: Henriksen and Ulfstein, n 209, 10.

219 Agreement on Fishery Co-operation in the Beibu Gulf between the Government of the People's Republic of China and the Government of the Socialist Republic of Vietnam, n 209.

220 Nguyen, n 209, 30. It is notable that this agreement differs from other agreements mentioned above in the sense that it applies the 'grey zone' model in a delimited marine area.

fisheries management. On the one hand, China and Vietnam established a Joint Fishery Committee.[221] The functions of the Joint Fishery Committee comprise the adoption of regulations and measures on the management of fishery resources in the Common Fishery Zone, including setting the quantity of vessels allowed to fish therein in the current year.[222] On the other hand, to implement the regulations and measures adopted by the Joint Fishery Committee, China and Vietnam shall carry out the licensing system for fishing conducted by their vessels in the Common Fishery Zone.[223] The implementation system basically rests on the exercise of flag State enforcement jurisdiction. Yet, this agreement also provides that the competent authorities of China and Vietnam may coordinate to conduct joint monitoring and inspection and to handle any breach of the fisheries regulations laid down by the Joint Fishery Committee when necessary.[224]

7.4.3.4 Light Grey Zone

Similar to the 'grey zone' model, the 'light grey zone' model also includes the allocation of fisheries jurisdiction between the disputant States. As Churchill pointed out: 'like the colours themselves, the distinction between these two types of agreement is not always clear-cut and they may shade into one another'.[225] Having said that, this model does differ from the 'grey zone' model in two aspects: first, the area of application in this model is not precisely defined but encompasses an area much larger than the contested area; and second, the model usually aims to regulate individual fish species, especially straddling and highly migratory fish stocks, rather than to create an overall management framework for all fish stocks.[226] Since fish stocks know no artificial boundaries, it is understandable why this model does not intend to define the area of application clearly. Two examples adopt this model. One example is a fisheries protocol signed by Canada and the US in 1979 stipulating that the International Halibut Commission was responsible for regulating the fishing for halibut in the whole area of US's and Canadian fisheries jurisdiction in

221 Agreement on Fishery Co-operation in the Beibu Gulf between the Government of the People's Republic of China and the Government of the Socialist Republic of Vietnam, n 209, Article 13(1).
222 *Ibid.*, Articles 13(2) and 7(1).
223 *Ibid.*, Article 7.
224 *Ibid.*, Article 9(3).
225 Churchill, n 210, 47.
226 Churchill, n 210, 47. Dang, n 6, 79.

the North Pacific.[227] Another is the agreement between Denmark, Iceland and Norway in 1989 according to which these three States would jointly determine the TAC for capelin stocks in the waters between Greenland, Iceland and Jan Mayen.[228]

7.4.4 *Application to the Spratly Islands Setting*

Due to the complexity of the territorial and maritime disputes, reaching provisional boundaries is difficult, if not impossible, in the Spratly Islands area in the foreseeable future. Thus, the 'provisional fisheries boundary' model can be ruled out.[229] The 'white zone' model is also infeasible for this region. As rightly pointed out by some scholars, overfishing is likely to occur in the white zone in the absence of effective management undertaken by a competent RFMO.[230] Owing to this limitation, even the USSR and Sweden, which adopted the 'white zone' model in 1977 for their disputed marine area in the Baltic Sea, switched to the 'grey zone' model in 1992.[231] Tailored to the Spratly Islands setting, there is not an RFMO that can adopt binding conservation and management measures for this region. Moreover, considering that the Spratly Islands area has already been subject to depletion or overfishing caused by excessive fishing efforts, regulations and proactive exercises of jurisdiction are very much needed in this region.

Both the 'grey zone' and the 'light grey zone' models involve the allocation of fisheries jurisdiction between the disputant States, thus placing the contested marine areas under regulation. Dang held that the 'grey zone' model was more suitable for the South China Sea than the 'light grey zone' model since the latter would be less effective in mitigating friction involving fishing incidents due to the lack of a well-defined area of application.[232] However, the utilization of the 'grey zone' and the 'light grey zone' models in combination is most apt for the Spratly Islands setting, considering that this region consists of highly

---

227 Protocol Amending the Convention for the Preservation of the Halibut Fishery of the North Pacific Ocean and the Bering Sea, adopted 29 March 1979, entered into force 15 October 1980, 1273 *UNTS* 270.

228 Agreement between Denmark, Iceland and Norway concerning Capelin Stocks in the Waters between Greenland, Iceland and Jan Mayen, adopted 12 June 1989, entered into force 1 July 1989, 1548 *UNTS* 165.

229 Dang, n 6, 78–79, 84.

230 Dang, n 6, 82. Churchill, n 210, 49.

231 Agreement between the Government of the Kingdom of Sweden and the Government of the Russian Federation in the Fields of Fisheries, adopted 11 December 1992, entered into force 10 August 1993, 1823 *UNTS* 103.

232 Dang, n 6, 84.

migratory or transboundary stocks as well as other fish species.[233] The 'grey zone' model can be used to provide an overall regulatory framework on all fish stocks in a well-defined area, whereas the 'light grey zone' model is suitable for managing individual fish stocks such as straddling and highly migratory fish stocks. Accordingly, similar to the arrangement as stipulated in the Tonkin Gulf agreement between China and Vietnam, the disputant States can jointly establish a joint commission to adopt fisheries management measures including the setting of the TAC, and exercise the flag State enforcement jurisdiction to implement such measures against their vessels that fish within the Spratly Islands area.[234] The disputant States may coordinate to conduct joint monitoring and inspection and to handle any breach of the fisheries regulations laid down by the joint commission when necessary.[235] There might be some concern that this type of cooperative fisheries arrangement would 'complicate law enforcement' and 'implementation would be particularly challenging for countries with relatively limited maritime law enforcement capabilities', thus 'creating loopholes for fishermen in the region to more easily engage in illegal fishing'.[236] This concern, to some extent, could be addressed by strengthening capacity building cooperation among the disputant States to improve fisheries-related law enforcement performance in the region, which could open up more opportunities for confidence building.

Several technical or operational recommendations can be drawn from the precedents in other sea regions. First, the fisheries agreement between Australia and Indonesia in 1981 stipulated that the fisheries arrangement would not affect the traditional fishing rights enjoyed by Indonesians over the areas on the Australian side of the provisional line with the aim of protecting the livelihoods of the artisanal fishers.[237] Considering that some of the fishing activities carried out in the Spratly Islands area are likely to be of a traditional or artisanal nature, the disputant States are recommended to make an analogical arrangement to allow the traditional fishing rights enjoyed by the artisanal

233 *Ibid.*, 62–63. E. Franckx, Fisheries in the South China Sea: A Centrifugal or Centripetal Force?, 11 *CJIL* (2012), 741.

234 Agreement on Fishery Co-operation in the Beibu Gulf between the Government of the People's Republic of China and the Government of the Socialist Republic of Vietnam, n 209, Article 7.

235 *Ibid.*, Article 9(3).

236 A. Hsiao, Opportunities for Fisheries Enforcement Cooperation in the South China Sea, 121 *Marine Policy* (2020), 8.

237 Memorandum of Understanding between the Government of Australia and Government of the Republic of Indonesia Concerning the Implementation of a Provisional Fisheries Surveillance and Enforcement Arrangement, n 212, Article 15.

fishers to remain unaffected by the new fisheries arrangement. Second, apart from the area for joint fisheries jurisdiction, the Tonkin Gulf agreement between China and Vietnam set up two additional precisely defined zones, namely a zone for transitional periods and a buffer zone for small fishing boats, as opposed to large and commercial fishing vessels. The zone for transitional periods, which would last for four years, is aimed to prepare the fishers from these two States to adapt their fishing practice to the new arrangement.[238] The buffer zone is intended for avoiding disputes caused by illegal entry by mistake of small fishing boats of one party to the territorial sea of the other.[239] In the buffer zone, the party shall refrain from detaining or using force against the vessels in question but is entitled to send a warning or take necessary enforcement measures to order the vessels to leave.[240] The disputant States may also consider establishing a zone for transitional periods and a buffer zone for small fishing boats in the Spratly Islands area.

7.5 Conclusion

The importance of conserving and utilizing fishery resources in a sustainable and responsible manner has been regularly emphasized in international law.[241] Effective fisheries management is especially needed in the Spratly Islands area, owing to the 'tragedy of the commons' problem therein with certain species depleted or overfished. However, the fisheries regulatory framework that binds upon the disputant States has three major limitations, namely a piecemeal management approach, the lack of a general obligation to apply the precautionary approach to all aspects of fisheries, and inadequate ecosystem concerns. To remedy these regulatory limitations, instead of adopting new legal instruments, what the disputant States need to do is to incorporate the approaches or principles of precaution, ecosystem, integrated management and sustainable development – as contained in UNFSA, CCRF and the 2030 Agenda for Sustainable Development – into the fisheries management process. Such approaches or principles can be taken into account via either the rule of reference contained in Article 61(3) of UNCLOS or the systemic interpretation

238 Agreement on Fishery Co-operation in the Beibu Gulf between the Government of the People's Republic of China and the Government of the Socialist Republic of Vietnam, n 209, Article 11.

239 *Ibid.*, Article 12.

240 *Ibid.*

241 Harrison, n 77, 234.

through Article 31(3)(c) of VCLT, so as to inform the interpretation and application of existing legal obligations contained in instruments that bind upon the States concerned, including UNCLOS, CBD and CITES. In particular, cooperation in gathering and sharing fisheries data is at the forefront of cooperation priorities to be taken by the disputant States.

Another regulatory limitation concerns the procedural aspect of a cooperative arrangement. The selection of cooperative institutions is not mandated under international law but is left to be determined by the disputant States. 'Freezing' all the concrete measures in one single legal instrument is infeasible, as the concrete measures need to be able to adapt to changing situations. Instead, a certain degree of institutionalization is needed in order to adopt, consider and revise the concrete measures from time to time and to conduct constant surveillance and monitoring of the implementation of the measures adopted. However, the existing cooperative mechanisms, including Workshop-SCS, SEAFDEC, APFIC and the ASEAN+ mechanism, are not viable to serve the functions of the intended cooperative institution. Thus, the disputant States are recommended to establish a new cooperative institution, for example, a joint commission that is intergovernmental and permanent, to undertake the fisheries management functions and responsibilities. The non-disputant States that are bordering the South China Sea are also encouraged to participate in the cooperative fisheries mechanism to the extent that the best scientific evidence shows that fisheries management respecting the Spratly Islands area and other sea areas of the South China Sea are interconnected. When it comes to the allocation of jurisdictional rights between the disputant States, it is suggested that the utilization of the 'grey zone' and the 'light grey zone' models in combination is most apt for the Spratly Islands setting. The 'grey zone' model can be used to provide an overall regulatory framework on all fish stocks in a well-defined area, and the 'light grey zone' model is suitable for managing individual fish stocks such as straddling and highly migratory fish stocks. Accordingly, the joint commission established by the disputant States can adopt fisheries management measures including the setting of the TAC, whereas the disputant States exercise the flag State enforcement jurisdiction to implement such measures against their vessels that fish within the Spratly Islands area. The disputant States may coordinate to conduct joint monitoring and inspection and to handle any breach of the fisheries regulations laid down by the joint commission when necessary.

By sidestepping the issue of territorial and maritime disputes and focusing on the common interest of the conservation and utilization of fishery resources, cooperation in fisheries management is a feasible and desired way forward in the Spratly Islands setting and might have a 'spill-over effect' in other areas of cooperation such as military cooperation, joint development of hydrocarbon resources and marine scientific research.[242] Meanwhile, it has to be admitted that the next step remains entirely reliant on the disputant States' political will and determination to pursue cooperation in this matter.[243] To attract the disputant States to cooperate in promoting the stability and economic development of the region, the recommendations proposed in this chapter advocate a blueprint of joint cooperation that is undertaken at a relatively low level of efforts or changes by making use of the existing international instruments or available cooperative mechanisms as much as possible.

242 K.-H. Wang, Bridge over Troubled Waters: Fisheries Cooperation as a Resolution to the South China Sea Conflicts, 14 *The Pacific Review* (2001), 542, 547. Franckx, n 233, 746. Liu, n 33, 135.

243 Wang, n 242, 547.

CHAPTER 8

Cooperation in Managing Pollution

8.1 Introduction

The Spratly Islands area is highly vulnerable to marine pollution owing to the small volume of waters and the absence of currents to change the waters in this semi-closed sea, which lowers the capacity for absorption.[1] Similar to fishery resources, the marine environment in this region also has the status of 'commons' in the sense of being 'held in common and jointly exploited' by the disputant States and their nationals.[2] The difference is that fishing is taking something out of the commons, while pollution is putting something in. Mismanagement of pollution in this region would lead to the 'tragedy of the commons' problem.[3] In fact, as indicated by scientific statistics, the South China Sea where the Spratly Islands area is located is becoming 'a sink for regional environmental pollution'.[4]

Public concern about marine environmental protection, nevertheless, did not always exist in history. There had been little concern until the 1960s when oil spill accidents, the blow-out of oil wells and the discovery of Dichloro-Diphenyl-Trichloroethane (DDT) in marine animals alerted people to the growing problem of marine pollution.[5] International law has responded to this problem by developing a legal regime governing the prevention and control of marine pollution. From then on, pollution could no longer be treated as an implicit freedom of the seas.[6] That being said, a State is unlikely to voluntarily accept stricter anti-pollution standards unless other States do the same, as

1 Third United Nations Conference on the Law of the Sea, Official Records, Vol. II (1973–1982), 273, para.6. Also see UN Doc.: A/CONF.62/C.2/SR.38, Summary Records of Meetings of the Second Committee 38th Meeting (10 December 1982).

2 N. Schrijver, *Development Without Destruction: The UN and Global Resource Management* (Indiana University Press. 2010), 6. Also see N. Schrijver, Managing the Global Commons: Common Good or Common Sink?, 37(7) *Third World Quarterly* (2016), 1253.

3 H. Garrett, The Tragedy of the Commons, 162 *Science* (1968), 1244.

4 See *e.g.*, R. Jennings, South China Sea Succumbing to Pollution Due to Political Impasse (12 September 2017), available at < https://www.voanews.com/a/south-china-sea-pollution/4025014.html >; D. Rosenberg, Environmental Pollution Around the South China Sea: Developing a Regional Response, 21(1) *Contemporary Southeast Asia* (1999), 119.

5 R.R. Churchill and V. Lowe, *The Law of the Sea* (MUP 3rd ed. 1999), 328. Y. Tanaka, *The International Law of the Sea* (CUP 3rd ed. 2019), 323.

6 P. Birnie *et al.*, *International Law and the Environment* (OUP. 2009), 383.

 | DOI:10.1163/9789004504332_009

the adoption of stricter anti-pollution standards will lead to higher costs for shipping and other industries, and any State will not like to have their industries lose the competitive edge.[7] Hence, tackling marine pollution cannot rely exclusively on self-regulation based on the principle of reciprocity, but instead, depends highly on international cooperation.[8]

This chapter aims to evaluate the extent to which international law as it currently stands can promote the cooperation between or among the disputant States in combating marine pollution within the Spratly Islands area. Similar to chapters 6 and 7, this chapter adds to existing research by analysing the dual aspects – substance and procedure – of international law and exploring their practical implications for pollution management in the Spratly Islands area. The substantive aspect refers to substantive norms, including anti-pollution rules and standards that apply to the Spratly Islands area. The procedural aspect refers to cooperative institutions and procedures for the actual implementation and enforcement of relevant anti-pollution rules and standards in the Spratly Islands setting. As to the structure, this chapter begins with the introduction to four main sources of marine pollution and their relevance to the Spratly Islands area (section 8.2). It then conducts a holistic analysis of relevant substantive norms in international anti-pollution law, which includes UNCLOS and beyond (section 8.3). This chapter also explores a suitable cooperative institution to better implement and enforce relevant anti-pollution rules and standards in the Spratly Islands setting (section 8.4).

The scope of this chapter is defined by three dimensions. First, this chapter focuses on the legal frameworks regulating marine pollution from shipping and dumping with respect to the Spratly Islands area, while pollution caused by seabed and land-based activities is excluded from the ambit of discussion owing to the reasons explained in section 8.2. Second, this chapter focuses on the role of the disputant States as flag and coastal States in combating pollution from shipping and dumping. In theory, the disputant States may act as flag, coastal and port States when combating pollution in the Spratly Islands area. A flag State is a State under whose laws a vessel is registered or licensed. A coastal State is a State that has maritime entitlements over the sea areas where a vessel stays or navigates. A port State is a State that owns or controls the port where a vessel enters.[9] At the moment, the offshore features that are

7 Churchill and Lowe, n 5, 338.

8 Tanaka, n 5, 324.

9 A port State's legislative and enforcement competence applies to pollution discharge violations within its territorial sea or EEZ and may also act as an agent to ensure prosecution against violations on high seas or within the jurisdictional zones of other States when

disputed in this region do not have ports where foreign ships can access.[10] All the relevant ports in this region are located on the mainland territory of the claimants. Thus, in theory, there is no overlapping jurisdiction over these ports. Third, as indicated in chapter 3, the disputant States may claim the marine areas within the Spratly Islands area to be their territorial sea, contiguous zones and EEZ. However, this chapter only centres on marine areas to be claimed as the territorial sea and EEZ. It is because a State's jurisdiction to a contiguous zone does not include the prevention and control of marine pollution, but instead, are limited to preventing or punishing infringements occurring within its territory or territorial sea of its customs, fiscal, immigration or sanitary laws and regulations.[11]

8.2 Sources of Marine Pollution

It may be useful to look at what is precisely meant by marine pollution in international law. Article 1(1)(4) of UNCLOS has defined the term 'pollution' as:

> the introduction by man, directly or indirectly, of substances or energy into the marine environment, including estuaries, which results or is likely to result in such deleterious effects as harm to living resources and marine life, hazards to human health, hindrance to marine activities, including fishing and other legitimate uses of the sea, impairment of quality for use of sea water and reduction of amenities.[12]

As this definition indicates, international law does not prevent all kinds of substances from entering into the ocean but only forbids those that result in or are likely to result in deleterious effects such as 'harm to living resources and marine life, hazards to human health, hindrance to marine activities'. There are four main sources of marine pollution, namely shipping, dumping, seabed activities and land-based activities.[13] These sources of pollution as well as their relevance to the Spratly Islands area is introduced below.

---

requested to do so by costal or flag States. See UNCLOS, Articles 220(1), 211(3). Also see A. Boyle, Marine Pollution under the Law of the Sea Convention, 79 *AJIL* (1985), 365.

10 Ports.com, South China Sea Ports Map, available at <http://ports.com/sea/south-china-sea/map/>.

11 UNCLOS, Article 33.

12 UNCLOS, Article 1(1)(4).

13 UNCLOS, Articles 210-212.

8.2.1 *Pollution from Shipping*

Over 90 per cent of the world trade is carried by around 90,000 ships across the ocean.[14] Article 211 of UNCLOS obliges States to prevent, reduce and control pollution of the marine environment from ships.[15] Pollution from shipping mainly results from their cargoes and operation. One the one hand, cargoes, by far, constitute the greatest amount of pollution from ships.[16] Oil and other noxious cargos such as chemicals, liquid gas and radioactive substances enter the ocean due to accidents including collisions and explosions, as happened in cases like the *Sanchi* oil tanker collision and the *Torrey Canyon* oil spill.[17] On the other hand, the operation of ships causes pollution in several ways. First, emissions of greenhouse gas (GHG) into the atmosphere during shipping will eventually return to the seas, which might lead to ocean acidification.[18] Second, ships might take seawaters onboard to serve as ballast water that is later pumped out to the ocean again, which may adversely impact the marine environment by introducing invasive aquatic species.[19] Third, garbage from ships, especially plastic, can be just as harmful to marine life as oil or other noxious chemicals.[20] Fourth, ships driven by oil-burning diesel engines may discharge some oil with their bilge water.[21] Fifth, fishing vessels may pollute the marine environment by engaging in destructive fishing practices through the use of underwater explosives and other harmful substances.[22]

Tailored to the Spratly Islands setting, a frequently reported type of ship-source pollution is destructive fishing practices. To boost yields, some fishers used explosives and cyanide to kill or injure target species in this region.[23]

---

14 OCEANA, Shipping Pollution, available at <https://eu.oceana.org/en/shipping-pollution-1#>.

15 UNCLOS, Article 211.

16 Churchill and Lowe, n 5, 329.

17 ITOPF, Oil Tanker Spill Statistics 2018 (January 2019), available at <https://www.itopf.org/fileadmin/data/Documents/Company_Lit/Oil_Spill_Stats_2019.pdf>.

18 IMO, Greenhouse Gas Emissions, available at <http://www.imo.org/en/OurWork/Environment/PollutionPrevention/AirPollution/Pages/GHG-Emissions.aspx>.

19 B. Werschkun *et al.*, Emerging Risks from Ballast Water Treatment: The Run-up to the International Ballast Water Management Convention, 112 *Chemosphere* 112 (2014), 257.

20 IMO, Prevention of Pollution by Garbage from Ships, available at <http://www.imo.org/en/OurWork/Environment/PollutionPrevention/Garbage/Pages/Default.aspx>.

21 M.A. Sayed, Ship Bilge Water Degrading Marine Environment (29 January 2011), available at <https://www.thedailystar.net/news-detail-171896>.

22 S.B. Saila, Modelling the Effects of Destructive Fishing Practices on Tropical Coral Reefs, 94 *Marine Ecology Progress Series* (1993), 51.

23 R. Bale, One of the World's Biggest Fisheries Is on the Verge of Collapse (29 August 2016), available at <https://www.nationalgeographic.com/animals/article/wildlife-south-china-sea-overfishing-threatens-collapse>.

Dynamite and cyanide are substances introduced by human that 'result in such deleterious effects as harm to living resources and marine life', as 'explosives shatter coral and cyanide can kill or injure non-target species'.[24] Accordingly, the use of both dynamite and cyanide in fisheries have been considered by the *South China Sea Arbitration* tribunal to be pollution of the marine environment within the meaning of UNCLOS.[25] Moreover, oil spill incidents are likely to take place in the Spratly Islands area because a majority of the global crude oil and liquefied natural gas passes through this region by shipping.[26]

8.2.2 *Pollution from Dumping*

According to Article 210 of UNCLOS, States shall adopt laws and regulations as well as take other necessary measures to prevent, reduce and control pollution from dumping.[27] UNCLOS has defined 'dumping' as 'any deliberate disposal at sea of wastes or other matter from vessels, aircraft, platforms or other man-made structures at sea' or 'any deliberate disposal at sea of vessels, aircraft, platforms or other manmade structures at sea'.[28] As this definition suggests, ocean dumping shall be done deliberately and be for the purpose of disposal of matter at sea. It includes neither the disposal of matter at sea incidental to or derived from the normal operations of relevant structures nor the placement of matter for a purpose other than the mere disposal thereof.[29] Though waste is frequently dumped into the ocean from ships, international law treats dumping as a source of pollution separate from shipping, because dumping, unlike other pollution from ships, is not only deliberate and the *raison d'être* of a particular voyage but also is usually an extension of pollution from land in the sense that the waste comes from land territory.[30] Yet, dumping obviously differs from the pollution from land-based activities because it takes place at sea, which is jurisdictionally different from land territory.[31]

Tailored to the Spratly Islands setting, dumping of wastes or other matter by vessels in transit is very likely to occur in this region owing to its busy shipping

---

24 The South China Sea Arbitration (The Philippines v. China), Award of 12 July 2016 (PCA), para.970.

25 *Ibid.*

26 Rosenberg, n 4, 121. U.S. Energy Information Administration, *South China Sea* (7 February 2013), available at <https://www.eia.gov/beta/international/analysis_includes/regions_of_interest/South_China_Sea/south_china_sea.pdf>.

27 UNCLOS, Article 210.

28 UNCLOS, Article 1(5)(a).

29 UNCLOS, Article 1(5)(b).

30 Churchill and Lowe, n 5, 330.

31 *Ibid.*

lanes.[32] The fact that incidents of dumping in this region have been rarely detected might largely result from the absence of an effective surveillance and response mechanism to detect and combat pollution therein. Another point worth clarifying is that land reclamation activities in the construction of artificial islands, which transform low-tide elevations or submerged features to be above high tide all the time, have usually involved the dumping of massive amounts of filling materials such as sands on top of such offshore features.[33] However, such activities do not constitute ocean dumping because the purpose of such activities is to place the filling material thereof for construction's sake rather than the mere disposal of those materials at sea.[34] Nevertheless, the dumping of unwanted materials, such as industrial debris, produced in the course of constructing artificial islands would undoubtedly fall within the ambit of dumping.[35]

8.2.3 *Pollution from Seabed Activities*

Article 194 of UNCLOS oblige States to take measures to minimize 'pollution from installations and devices used in exploration or exploitation of the natural resources of the seabed and subsoil'.[36] This obligation is further developed by Article 208, which obliges coastal States to adopt laws and regulations and other necessary measures to prevent, reduce and control 'pollution of the marine environment arising from or in connection with seabed activities subject to their jurisdiction and from artificial islands, installations and structures under their jurisdiction'.[37] Though UNCLOS does not define the term 'seabed activities', this term certainly covers the exploration and exploitation of

---

32 Rosenberg, n 4, 121, 124.

33 See *e.g.*, N. Davison, China defends construction on disputed Spratly Islands (10 April 2015), available at <https://www.telegraph.co.uk/news/worldnews/asia/china/11528435/China-defends-construction-on-disputed-Spratly-Islands.html>; J. Batongbacal, Environmental Aggression in the South China Sea (7 May 2015), available at <https://amti.csis.org/environmental-aggression-in-the-south-china-sea/>.

34 When addressing the adverse impact on the marine environment caused by land reclamation activities in the construction of artificial islands on certain maritime features in the Spratly Islands area, the *South Sea Arbitration* tribunal did not mention 'pollution', but instead referred to 'severe, irreparable harm to the coral reef ecosystem'. See The South China Sea Arbitration, n 24, para.1203(B)(13)(a)&(16)(b).

35 R. Warner, Stemming the Black Tide: Cooperation on Oil Pollution Preparedness and Response in the South China Sea and East Asian Seas, 18 *Journal of International Wildlife Law & Policy* (2015), 189.

36 UNCLOS, Article 194(3)(c).

37 UNCLOS, Article 208(1).

hydrocarbon deposits from seabed areas.[38] The pollution from seabed activities may result from blow-outs of oil from the seabed, the breaking of pipelines, or the oily and chemical waste from drilling.[39]

Tailored to the Spratly Islands setting, chapter 4 concludes that unilateral seabed activities such as exploitation and explanatory drilling of hydrocarbon deposits in disputed marine areas are generally forbidden under international law. Chapter 6 indicates that the disputant States must enter into cooperative arrangements for managing hydrocarbon resources in the Spratly Islands area. In practice, as most precedents that are implemented in other sea regions suggest, the detailed rights and obligations of the States concerned with regard to the prevention and control of pollution originating from seabed activities are usually recorded in specific legal instruments that establish relevant cooperative arrangements.[40] Moreover, the substantive norms regulating pollution from seabed activities, especially activities related to hydrocarbon resources, have already been analysed in chapter 6. Therefore, pollution from seabed activities is excluded from the ambit of discussion in this chapter.

8.2.4 *Pollution from Land-Based Activities*

Article 207 of UNCLOS obliges States to prevent, reduce and control pollution of the marine environment from activities carried out on land territory.[41] The land-based sources of pollution include sewage, industrial wastes, agricultural chemicals such as fertilizers and pesticides, or other harmful substances discharged into the ocean from 'rivers, estuaries, pipelines and outfall structures'.[42] Land-based activities are 'the most "national" source of marine

38 J. Harrison, *Saving the Oceans through Law: the International Legal Framework for the Protection of the Marine Environment* (OUP. 2017), 212.

39 Churchill and Lowe, n 5, 330.

40 See *e.g.*, Treaty between Australia and the Republic of Indonesia on the Zone of Cooperation in an Area between the Indonesian Province of East Timor and Northern Australia, adopted 11 December 1989, entered into force 9 February 1991, 1654 *UNTS* 105, Articles 18 and 19; Timor Sea Treaty between East Timor and Australia, adopted 20 May 2002, entered into force 20 May 2002, 2258 *UNTS* 3, Article 10; Exclusive Economic Zone Co-operation Treaty between the State of Barbados and the Republic of Guyana concerning the exercise of jurisdiction in their exclusive economic zones in the area of bilateral overlap within each of their outer limits and beyond the outer limits of the exclusive economic zones of other States (with annex and figure), adopted 2 December 2003, entered into force 5 May 2004, 2277 *UNTS* 201, Article 8.

41 UNCLOS, Article 211.

42 UNCLOS, Article 211(1).

pollution', as only the State that owns the land territory has the right to regulate the pollution caused by those activities.[43]

Tailored to the Spratly Islands setting, land-based activities constitute a significant source of pollution. Statistics indicated that approximately 70% of contaminants entering the South China Sea were derived from coastal rivers.[44] Notably, between 1996 and 2009, there was a cooperative initiative aimed to reverse environmental degradation trends among seven States bordering the South China Sea (including those not parties to the Spratly Islands disputes),[45] which was facilitated by the UN Environment Programme (UNEP) and funded by the Global Environment Facility (GEF).[46] ('the UNEP/GEF-SCS Project') Vietnam, Malaysia, the Philippines, Indonesia, Thailand and Cambodia had endorsed this project since the very beginning because of their shared preference of a multilateral approach towards China on issues relating to the South China Sea.[47] By contrast, China was hesitant to participate in this project owing to its reluctance to internationalize issues related to the South China Sea and the fear of losing its dominance if it was forced to negotiate with multiple States.[48] In particular, China was reluctant to incorporate the disputed marine areas in this region into the implementation ambit of this project.[49] UNEP compromised and agreed to focus only on land-based sources of pollution as a concession to China. Finally, China approved this project in 2000 and became one of the seven States to join this project. When the UNEP/GEF-SCS Project was finished in 2009, the application of the agreed standards to data collected from the various sites had resulted in a comparative analysis of the regional importance of different contaminants, based on which national action plans to tackle land-based pollution were adopted.[50]

---

43 Churchill and Lowe, n 5, 379.

44 UNEP, Land-based Pollution in the South China Sea, *UNEP/GEF/SCS Technical Publication* No. 10 (2007), 2.

45 Seven out of the nine countries bordering the South China Sea approved this project. Brunei and Singapore did not participate in this project because they were not eligible for GEF funding support. See S. Chen, Environmental Cooperation in the South China Sea: Factors, Actors and Mechanisms, 85 *OCM* (2013), 132.

46 For more information about the UNEP/GEF-SCS Project, see *e.g.*, V. Tuan and J. Pernetta, The UNEP/GEF South China Sea Project: Lessons Learnt in Regional Cooperation, 53 *OCM* (2010), 589–596; J.C. Pernetta and Y. Jiang, Managing Multi-lateral, Intergovernmental Projects and Programmes: the Case of the UNEP/GEF South China Sea Project, 85 *OCM* (2013), 141–152.

47 Chen, n 45, 134.

48 *Ibid.*, 135.

49 *Ibid.*, 136.

50 UNEP/GEF, Terminal Report of the UNEP/GEF South China Sea Project (25 February 2009), 22–23.

Considering that pollution from land-based activities, indeed, mainly relates to the mainland territory of the claimants rather than to disputed marine areas in the Spratly Islands area, no overlapping jurisdiction exists between the claimants because each claimant has absolute control over respective activities that occur on its land territory. Therefore, pollution from land-based activities is excluded from the ambit of discussion in this chapter.

8.3 Substantive Norms on Pollution Management

8.3.1 *A Fundamental Problem in Relation to Pollution Management*

Pollution in the Spratly Islands area may have detrimental effects on the global ocean.[51] Thus, the benefits of compliance with environmental restraints are widely dispersed. Yet, the immediate self-interest of the disputant States might not suffice to ensure compliance with all inconvenient or expensive environmental restraints.[52] Therefore, to avoid the 'tragedy of the commons' problem,[53] it is necessary to bring anti-pollution regulation adopted and implemented by the disputant States respecting the Spratly Islands area under universal restraints to prevent the 'undesirable proliferation of national standards'.[54]

As summarized by Oxman, universal restraints have four objectives that an international regulatory regime needs to fulfil, notably universality, precision, adaptability and legal obligation.[55] The first objective is the universal enforcement of environmental standards, which means that States or other actors concerned are all obliged to conform to relevant standards.[56] Second, environmental restraints should be detailed and precise to ensure uniform application.[57] Third, environmental standards must respond in a timely manner to the growing scientific knowledge about the natural environment and the advances in economic, political and social sciences concerning the strategies to further environmental goals.[58] Fourth, there ought to be an obligation to observe and

51 B.H. Oxman, The Duty to Respect Generally Accepted International Standards, 24 *NYUJ Int'l L. & Pol.* (1991), 109–110.
52 *Ibid.*, 112.
53 Garrett, n 3, 1244.
54 C. Redgwell, Mind the Gap in the GAIRS: The Role of Other Instruments in LOSC Regime Implementation in the Offshore Energy Sector, in N. Bankes and S. Trevisanut (eds.), *Energy from the Sea: An International Law Perspective on Ocean Energy* (Brill|Nijhoff. 2015), 57.
55 Oxman, n 51, 110–113.
56 *Ibid.*, 141–143.
57 *Ibid.*, 143.
58 *Ibid.*

enforce relevant environmental standards, which provides a legal guarantee for universal compliance.[59] These four objectives are indispensable for materializing an effective regulatory regime for environmental protection.

Unfortunately, traditional means for imposing legal obligations on a consensual basis are unfitting to achieve universal restraints. On the one hand, 'freezing' detailed technical international standards in a treaty is unrealistic. First, participants may lack the specific technical expertise to negotiate precise standards or prefer to minimize the time or potential for disagreement involved in technical matters.[60] Second, precise articulation in a treaty may also risk omission and insufficient adaptability to changes and new information. On the other hand, it might be difficult to assert that certain environmental regulatory measures are declaratory of customary international law when adopted, as most of such measures mainly aim to provide new and updated detailed regulatory guidance for restraining the specific conduct of actors concerned, most of them being private actors.[61] A fundamental regulatory problem thus arises as to how to think outside the consensual basis of international law and contemplate an international regulatory framework that is best suited to further the above four objectives.

8.3.2 *Rules of Reference in UNCLOS*

8.3.2.1 Relevant UNCLOS Provisions

In response to the above regulatory problem, UNCLOS does not itself prescribe pollution-related standards, but rather provides that under certain circumstances, 'generally accepted international rules and standards' or 'applicable international rules and standards' external to UNCLOS are the criteria for evaluating whether domestic legislation conforms to the pollution obligations as outlined in UNCLOS.[62] First, with respect to pollution from shipping, Article 211(2) stipulates that the laws and regulations adopted by flag States for the prevention, reduction and control of pollution from vessels flying their flag or of their registry shall 'at least have the same effect' as that of 'generally accepted international rules and standards' established through the competent international organization or general diplomatic conference.[63] Similarly, according to Article 211(5), the coastal State is obliged to adopt anti-pollution laws and

59 *Ibid.*, 144.
60 *Ibid.*, 140.
61 *Ibid.*, 118.
62 T. Treves, The Law of the Sea' System' of Institutions, 2 *Max Planck Yearbook of United Nations Law* (1998), 327.
63 UNCLOS, Article 211(2).

regulations in respect of the EEZ 'conforming to and giving effect to' the 'generally accepted international rules and standards'.[64] In the territorial sea, Article 21(2) stipulates that a coastal State is free to adopt laws and regulations relating to marine pollution for foreign vessels to observe provided that such legislation shall not apply to the design, construction, manning or equipment of ships unless 'giving effect to' 'generally accepted international rules or standards'.[65] Second, as regards pollution from dumping, Article 216 sets forth that States shall enforce 'applicable international rules and standards' established through competent international organizations or diplomatic conferences.[66]

Each of these provisions contains a rule of reference that entails a general legal duty to respect and apply specific international rules and standards that come to be 'generally accepted' or 'applicable'. By becoming parties to UNCLOS, States accept to be bound by rules or standards adopted by competent international organizations or diplomatic conferences that they may not participate in or may not have concurred to adopt.[67] This regulatory regime emphasizes the fact of general acceptance or applicability of a rule or standard after promulgation, irrespective of whether its initial adoption by an international organization or conference creates a legal obligation.[68] As commented by Redgwell, generally accepted international rules and standards play an essential role in 'facilitating, strengthening and updating the LOSC [i.e., UNCLOS] in the light of legal and technical developments', which leads to 'a process of normative reinforcement rather than normative conflict'.[69] Tanaka also considered the legal technique of rules of reference 'a useful tool to take the new demands of the international community into account in the interpretation and application of existing rules and standards', contributing to maintaining 'uniformity of national and international regulation with regards to marine environmental protection'.[70]

The utility and efficiency of these rules of reference highly depend on the interpretation of 'generally accepted international rules and standards' and 'applicable international rules and standards', given the ambiguity surrounding these norm, which might introduce unwelcome uncertainties.[71]

---

64 UNCLOS, Article 211(5).
65 UNCLOS, Article 21(2).
66 UNCLOS, Article 216.
67 Treves, n 62, 327.
68 Oxman, n 51, 110.
69 Redgwell, n 54, 40.
70 Y. Tanaka, *The South China Sea Arbitration: Toward an International Legal Order in the Oceans* (Hart Publishing. 2019), 150.
71 Redgwell, n 69, 47.

A restrictive interpretation of the above phrases, with only a few international rules and standards falling within the scope, might prejudice the adaptability of the regulatory regime.[72] A liberal interpretation, in contrast, might compel States to attempt to restrain the emergence or content of new international rules or standards, thus rendering this regulatory regime superfluous.[73] Thus, to ensure the utility, too strict or too liberal an interpretation must be avoided. With this in mind, the following subsections explore a proper interpretation of the phrases 'generally', 'accepted', 'applicable' and 'international rules and standards', respectively.

8.3.2.2 'Generally': How Much Acceptance Is Required?

The term 'generally' indeed answers the question of how much acceptance of relevant international norms is required in order for the duty to respect such norms to arise. The duty to respect generally accepted international rules and standards was first articulated by the ILC in its work on the international law of the sea in the 1950s, which subsequently became the basis for UNCLOS I as well as for UNCLOS III.

The ILC put this duty in Article 34 of Articles concerning the Law of the Sea in its 1956 Report that in issuing regulations to ensure safety at sea for ships under its jurisdiction, 'each State is required to observe internationally accepted standards'.[74] Notably, a previous draft of this provision contained an expression 'the vessels forming the greater part of the tonnage of sea-going ships' to serve as a criterion to assess whether relevant standards were internationally accepted.[75] The reason was that 'in the matter of safety of human life at sea, the interest of each State may be judged by the number of persons on board its ships'.[76] Certain members of the ILC had a different opinion, proposing to use 'the majority of maritime States' or 'the majority of vessels' as the criterion.[77] They opined that the size of a vessel was irrelevant, as a small vessel could also do a considerable amount of damage.[78] Due to the controversy, at its

---

72 Oxman, n 51, 159.

73 *Ibid.*, 134.

74 UN Doc.: A/CN.4/104, Report of the International Law Commission on the Work of its Eighth Session, *Official Records of the General Assembly, Eleventh Session, Supplement No. 9, (A/3159)* (4 July 1956), 260.

75 UN Doc.: A/CN.4/94, Report of the International Law Commission Covering the Work of its Seventh Session, *Official Records of the General Assembly, Tenth Session, Supplement No. 9., (A/2934)* (2 May-8 July 1955), 23, Article 9.

76 *Ibid.*, 24.

77 *Ibid.*

78 *Ibid.*

eighth session in 1956, the majority of the ILC decided to delete the explicit reference to a requisite majority and preferred a more general expression, namely 'internationally accepted standards'.[79] This general expression was intended to cover regulations that were a product of international cooperation, without necessarily having been confirmed in formal treaties.[80] However, what constituted 'internationally accepted standards' remained unclarified.

At UNCLOS I (1958), the UK proposed to delete the above draft Article 34 because it was concerned with a possible duty to apply 'internationally accepted standards' including standards for labour conditions at sea as laid down in conventions and recommendations adopted by the ILO.[81] The British proposal received objections from several participants including France, the Netherlands, the US and the Soviet Union.[82] Under pressure, the British delegation redrafted the text of the proposal, requesting to substitute the phrase 'generally accepted international standards' for 'internationally accepted standards' and to explicitly exclude 'applicable international labour instruments' from 'generally accepted international standards'.[83] This proposal ultimately became Article 10 of the Convention on the High Seas.[84]

UNCLOS III (1973–1982) significantly broadened the contexts in which the duty to respect generally accepted international standards applied. This duty was no longer limited to safety at sea but also applied to marine pollution from ships and dumping.[85] During a decade of negotiations on UNCLOS, none of the participating States ever expressed objections to the 'generally accepted' criterion.[86] It was probably because the duty to comply with generally accepted

79 UN Doc.: A/CN.4/104, n 74, 260.

80 *Ibid.*

81 UN Doc.: A/CONF.13/C.2/L.49, United Kingdom of Great Britain and Northern Ireland: proposal relating to Article 34, *United Nations Conference on the Law of the Sea* (24 February to 27 April 1958), 129. Also see Oxman, n 51, 128.

82 Oxman, n 51, 129.

83 UN Doc.: A/CONF.13/C.2/L.114, Netherlands and United Kingdom of Great Britain and Northern Ireland: proposal, *United Nations Conference on the Law of the Sea* (24 February to 27 April 1958), 148. Also see Oxman, n 51, 129, fn. 56.

84 Convention on the High Seas, adopted 29 April 1958, entered into force 30 September 1962, 450 *UNTS* 11, Article 10. ('1. Every State shall take such measures for ships under its flag as are necessary to ensure safety at sea with regard, inter alia, to: (a) The use of signals, the maintenance of communications and the prevention of collisions; (b) The manning of ships and labour conditions for crews taking into account the *applicable international labour instruments*; (c) The construction, equipment and seaworthiness of ships. 2. In taking such measures each State is required to conform to *generally accepted international standards* and to take any steps which may be necessary to ensure their observance. [emphasis added]').

85 UNCLOS, Articles 94, 211(2)&(5), 210(6) and 216.

86 Oxman, n 51, 156.

standards was designed to serve as a positive alternative to unilateral or absolute coastal State competence to prescribe and enforce safety or pollution regulations for foreign vessels navigating off the coast. As rightly pointed out by Oxman, this alternative would have been undermined if UNCLOS drafters had sought to restrict or even discuss the scope of the duty.[87] In his view, why the threshold required by the 'generally accepted' criterion was left unclarified in UNCLOS is because 'it is better to allow coastal states some flexibility in determining which international standards are generally accepted than to risk collapse of the rule that coastal state competence is generally limited to enforcing international standards'.[88]

8.3.2.3 'Accepted' or 'Applicable': Where to Find Acceptance?

A further question of relevance is where to find acceptance. There are three possible sources to determine whether an international rule or standard has been accepted. They include: (1) 'the practice of governments, reflected in ratification of treaties, national laws and regulations, and authoritative statements of policy', (2) 'events at the organization or conference that adopted the standard', and (3) 'the practice of individuals and companies whose activities are the object of a particular standard'.[89] These sources may be accorded different weights in determining the existence or extent of acceptance.

First, the adoption and enforcement of international rules or standards by States are critical or fundamental factors to measure acceptance. Relevant action may include promulgating national legislation and regulation, issuing authoritative policies, and ratifying a treaty containing relevant rules or standards. Only *de facto* or substantive adoption and application, instead of mere formal or rhetorical adoption, can be determinative. It would be unfair to characterize States that fail to adopt relevant safety or environmental standards as 'free rider' when many others, though adopting relevant standards formally, are in fact not conforming to those standards.[90]

Second, events at the organization or conference that adopt relevant rules or standards can be an indicator of acceptance. Yet, caution should be taken not to accord significant effect to votes in organizations or at conferences on determining whether States accept new rules or standards or not. The adaptability of the duty to respect generally accepted international rules and standards

87 *Ibid.*
88 *Ibid.*
89 *Ibid.*, 149.
90 *Ibid.*, 152–153.

requires that such rules or standards can respond timely to changing scientific insights and technological or economic possibilities.[91] According significant effect to votes would curtail the flexibility of delegations at organizations or conferences and compel States to refrain from voting in favour of any instruments even those concerning only a nonbinding resolution or the text of a treaty subject to ratification.[92] More important than the formal acceptance by votes in organizations or at conferences is the substantive acceptance demonstrated through actual conduct of the State concerned.

Third, being the ultimate goal of regulation, the behaviour of individuals and companies is a relevant factor in assessing acceptance. Nevertheless, the mere non-compliance by individuals and companies with specific standards will not necessarily suggest the non-acceptance of such standards by national governments. Instead, States may identify such non-compliance as a violation of certain standards and take law enforcement measures against such violation. In these circumstances, these States should be regarded as accepting relevant standards *de facto*, irrespective of whether they have affirmatively adopted such standards. Similarly, acceptance can also be demonstrated when nationals are voluntarily and uniformly implementing relevant standards with the express or tacit approval of their national governments.

Furthermore, in contrast with Article 211 using 'generally accepted international rules and standards' to regulate pollution from shipping, Article 216 uses the phrase 'applicable international rules and standards' for pollution from dumping.[93] One may question whether the use of a different qualifying word 'applicable' suggests that the underlying idea is not precisely the same as that using 'generally accepted'. However, as rightly noted by Oxman, for UNCLOS, which is a huge convention 'drafted and negotiated by so many different people in disparate groups over many years', it cannot be assumed that 'the use of different words … necessarily represents an intentional decision to convey a different meaning'.[94] In fact, in drafting UNCLOS, it was not uncommon that delegates remained silent about imperfect texts that emerged from informal negotiations and consultations 'for fear of upsetting those or other parts of the package on which a consensus was beginning to emerge'.[95] Hence, the term 'applicable' should be interpreted in much the same way as one would interpret 'generally accepted'.[96] It is implausible to assume that flag or coastal

91 *Ibid.*, 151.
92 *Ibid.*, 151–152.
93 UNCLOS, Article 216.
94 Oxman, n 51, 132, fn. 74.
95 *Ibid.*
96 *Ibid.*, 135.

States are significantly more (or less) willing to be obliged to observe environmental restraints regarding ocean dumping than those regarding vessel-source pollution.[97]

8.3.2.4 'International Rules and Standards': Accepting What?

The term 'international' can be easily interpreted to include instruments that have been adopted at the international or global level by a relevant international organization or at an international conference.[98] Yet, norms recorded in instruments adopted at the regional level might become 'international' provided that such norms are replicated across a number of regions.[99] Moreover, a plain reading of the words 'rules' and 'standards' suggests that the former refers to a form of potentially binding obligation, while the latter intends to cover non-binding instruments such as resolutions adopted by international organizations.[100] As Redgwell rightly observed, such 'rules' and 'standards' are norms either referred to in a binding instrument to which the State concerned is not a party or expressed in non-binding form.[101]

However, international rules and standards must not be interpreted in a way to encompass any provisions contained in any international instruments.[102] As mentioned earlier, too liberal an interpretation might compel States to attempt to restrain the emergence or content of new international rules or standards, thus rendering this duty superfluous.[103] Hence, in interpreting 'international rules and standards', it is essential to have in mind that the main purpose of the duty is to establish uniform practices. It means that the duty requires States to achieve specific results, notably uniform practices regarding certain environmental standards. This duty thus amounts to an obligation of result. Therefore, myriad clauses that only confer an obligation of conduct or an exhortation to act such as 'States shall/should endeavour to' or 'States shall/should make an

97 *Ibid.*, 133.
98 Harrison, n 38, 215.
99 *Ibid.*
100 Boyle, n 9, 356.
101 Redgwell, n 54, 50.
102 One scholar suggested interpreting 'international rules' as rules that are adopted by a diplomatic conference or authorized international body and are ratified by a sufficient number of States to enter into force. This interpretation is too liberal and would include many instruments to fall within the scope of the duty. See M.A. Stephenson, Vessel-Source Pollution under the Law of the Sea Convention-An Analysis of the Prescriptive Standards, 17 *U. Queensland LJ* (1992), 117, 125.
103 Oxman, n 51, 134.

effort to' do not constitute 'international rules and standards', as such clauses do not lead to uniform practices even by States legally bound by them.[104]

8.3.3 *Generally Accepted International Rules and Standards beyond UNCLOS*

Although UNCLOS does not itself prescribe pollution-related standards, the rules of reference contained in Articles 21(2) and 211(2) & (5) of UNCLOS together with those norms they refer to help close gaps in regulating pollution from shipping or dumping at sea. However, one obstacle to identifying generally accepted international rules and standards beyond UNCLOS is that the requisite threshold for acceptance to be 'general' remains unclarified. As rightly noted by Boyle, a significant level of discretion remained with sovereign States in 'defining the acceptable content of pollution obligations and their limits'.[105] The matrix published by DOALOS in 2004, which is aimed at identifying the obligations of States under UNCLOS relating to other international rules and standards beyond UNCLOS, provides useful guidance.[106] According to the DOALOS matrix, international instruments that fit within the confinements of Articles 21(2) and 211(2) & (5) of UNCLOS in relation to pollution from shipping are mainly IMO instruments, especially the International Convention for the Prevention of Pollution from Ships (MARPOL).[107] International instruments that fall within the ambit of Article 216 in relation to pollution from dumping include the London Convention and London Protocol.[108]

8.3.3.1 IMO Instruments in Relation to Pollution from Shipping

IMO was established to be a global standard-setting authority for the safety, security and environmental performance of international shipping.[109] According to the IMO Convention, the mandate of IMO includes 'the prevention and control of marine pollution from ships'.[110] Among all the IMO instruments, MARPOL, adopted in 1973 and further amended by the Protocol of 1978, is the most important treaty to deal with all forms of marine pollution caused

104 *Ibid.*, 148.

105 Boyle, n 9, 357.

106 DOALOS, *The Law of the Sea: Obligations of States Parties under the United Nations Convention on the Law of the Sea and Complementary Instruments* (New York: United Nations. 2004).

107 *Ibid.*, 42, 52, 66.

108 *Ibid.*, 53.

109 Convention of the International Maritime Organization, adopted 6 March 1948, entered into force 17 March 1958, 289 *UNTS* 3, Article 1.

110 Convention of the International Maritime Organization, n 109, Article 1(a).

by the deliberate, negligent or accidental release of oil and other harmful substances from ships.[111] Several other IMO instruments are also of relevance to shipping-source pollution, such as the 1974 International Convention for the Safety of Life at Sea (SOLAS) as well as the 1981 Code of Safety for Nuclear Merchant Ships (CODES).

MARPOL has six annexes setting out detailed pollution standards for six kinds of substances, including oil (Annex I), noxious liquid substances in bulk (Annex II), harmful substances carried by sea in packaged form (Annex III), sewage (Annex IV), garbage (Annex V) and air pollution (Annex VI).[112] Whereas accepting Annexes I and II is compulsory for all contracting parties to MARPOL, a State may opt not to accept one or the other annexes at the time of becoming a party to MARPOL.[113] As of 17 June 2021, 160 States, representing 99% of the gross tonnages of the world's merchant vessels, are parties to MARPOL and Annexes I and II.[114] For Annexes III, IV, and V, there are 150, 146, and 155 State parties, representing 98%, 96%, and 98% of the gross tonnages of the world's merchant fleet, respectively.[115]

Annex I of MARPOL details discharge requirements for the prevention of marine pollution caused by oil and oily materials evicted from the machinery spaces of all ships and the cargo areas of oil tankers. First, ships of 400 gross tonnages and above are obliged to limit their discharges into the sea of oil or oily mixtures when they are proceeding *en route*.[116] Second, in terms of oil tankers, any discharge into the sea of oil or oily mixtures from the cargo area of an oil tanker shall normally be limited when proceeding *en route*.[117] Third, ships are required to adopt certain technologies and equipment. For example, in order to prevent pollution arising from cleaning the cargo areas of the tanks, oil tankers of 150 gross tonnages and above shall be equipped with an

---

111 International Convention for the Prevention of Pollution from Ships, adopted 2 November 1973, 1340 *UNTS* 184; Amended by Protocol of 1978 Relating to the International Convention for the Prevention of Pollution from Ships, adopted 17 February 1978, entered into force 2 October 1983, 1340 *UNTS* 61. Notably, as the 1973 Convention had not yet entered into force, the 1978 Protocol absorbed the parent Convention.

112 IMO, Information about MARPOL, available at <http://www.imo.org/en/about/conventions/listofconventions/pages/international-convention-for-the-prevention-of-pollution-from-ships-(marpol).aspx>.

113 MARPOL, Article 14.

114 IMO, Status of Treaties (as of 17 June 2021), available at <https://www.imo.org/en/About/Conventions/Pages/StatusOfConventions.aspx>.

115 *Ibid.*

116 MARPOL Annex I: Regulations for the Prevention of Pollution by Oil, adopted 2 November 1973, entered into force 2 October 1983, Regulation 15.2.

117 MARPOL Annex I, Regulation 34.

oil discharge monitoring and control system and effective oil/water interface detectors,[118] and crude oil tankers of no less than 20,000 tonnes deadweight delivered after 1 June 1982 shall be fitted with a cargo tank cleaning system using crude oil washing rather than water washing.[119] Fourth, State parties shall provide reception facilities in their ports which ships can use to discharge their oily residues.[120]

MARPOL Annex II prohibits discharges into the sea of residues containing noxious liquid substances unless discharges are made in full compliance with the applicable operational requirements detailed in this annex.[121] MARPOL Annex III lays down detailed standards concerning packing, marking, labelling, documentation, stowage, quantity limitations and exceptions in order to prevent marine pollution caused by harmful substances carried by sea in packaged form.[122] MARPOL Annex IV prohibits discharges of sewage into the sea within 3 M from the nearest land unless the ship has in operation an approved sewage treatment plant.[123] A ship is permitted to discharge sewage between 3 and 12 M from the nearest land provided that such sewage had been comminuted and disinfected before discharge.[124] Sewage that is not comminuted or disinfected must be discharged at a distance of more than 12 M from the nearest land.[125] MARPOL Annex V sets forth the minimum distances from the land and the manner in which different types of garbage may be disposed of into the sea.[126] Disposal of all forms of plastics is prohibited in all sea areas.[127] MARPOL Annex VI lays down the prevention of deliberate emissions of ozone-depleting substances and limits on sulphur oxide and nitrogen oxide emissions from ship exhausts.[128] Moreover, mandatory measures to reduce GHG emissions were introduced in 2011 by adding a new chapter to Annex VI on 'Regulations

118 MARPOL Annex I, Regulations 31–32.
119 MARPOL Annex I, Regulation 33.
120 MARPOL Annex I, Regulation 38.
121 MARPOL Annex II: Regulations for the Control of Pollution by Noxious Liquid Substances in Bulk, adopted 2 November 1973, entered into force 2 October 1983, Regulation 13.
122 MARPOL Annex III: Prevention of Pollution by Harmful Substances Carried by Sea in Packaged Form, entered into force 1 July 1992, Regulations 2–7.
123 MARPOL Annex IV: Prevention of Pollution by Sewage from Ships, adopted 2 November 1973, entered into force 27 September 2003, Regulation 11.
124 *Ibid.*
125 *Ibid.*
126 MARPOL Annex V: Prevention of Pollution by Garbage from Ships, adopted 2 November 1973, entered into force 31 December 1988.
127 MARPOL Annex V, Regulation 5.
128 MARPOL Annex VI: Prevention of Air Pollution from Ships, adopted 26 September 1997, entered into force 19 May 2005.

on energy efficiency for ships'.[129] For substances regulated by Annexes II, IV, V and VI, States that are parties to these Annexes shall undertake to ensure the provision of reception facilities where ships can discharge their residues that contain these substances.[130]

Notably, according to the Guidelines for the Designation of Special Areas under MARPOL 73/78, States can submit a proposal to IMO for the designation of certain marine areas to be 'special areas', under Annexes I, II, IV, and V to MARPOL.[131] Special areas are sea areas adopting special mandatory methods to prevent pollution by substances such as oil, noxious liquid substances, sewage and garbage, due to recognized technical reasons relating to: (1) oceanographical conditions; (2) ecological conditions; and (3) vessel traffic characteristics.[132] Under MARPOL, special areas are provided with a higher level of protection than other sea areas. For example, no discharges of oil or oily mixtures and garbage are permitted from any ship in special areas.[133] Another parallel concept is Particularly Sensitive Sea Areas (PSSAs). PSSAs are defined as sea areas requiring special protection through action by IMO, due to their recognized (1) ecological, (2) socio-economic, or (3) scientific attributes, which may be vulnerable to damage by international shipping activities.[134] States can submit a proposal to IMO for the designation of certain marine areas to be PSSAS, pursuant to the procedures as outlined in the Guidelines for the Identification and Designation of Particularly Sensitive Sea Areas.[135] Importantly, although IMO is the only international body responsible for designating areas as special areas and PSSAs, designations of these two types of areas are separate processes that adhere to different criteria and procedures. For example, a major difference is that the associated protective measures for PSSAs are not limited to restrictions on discharges of substances such as oil, noxious liquid substances, sewage and garbage as required in special areas. Rather, IMO can adopt any necessary associated protective measures for PSSAs, even including navigation restrictions through traffic separation schemes, as in the case of the Baltic Sea Area PSSA.[136] A comparison of the lists of current special areas and

---

129 Resolution MEPC.203(62): Amendments to MARPOL Annex VI (15 July 2011).

130 MARPOL Annex II, Regulation 18; MARPOL Annex IV, Regulation 12; MARPOL Annex V, Regulation 7; MARPOL Annex VI, Regulation 17.

131 IMO, A 28/Res.1087 (21 February 2014).

132 IMO, MEPC.1/Circ.778/Rev.3 (2 July 2018), para.1.

133 See *e.g.*, MARPOL Annex I, Regulation 15.3–6; Annex V, Regulation 5.

134 IMO, MEPC.1/Circ.778/Rev.3 (2 July 2018), para.5.

135 IMO, A 24/Res.982 (6 February 2006).

136 A. Prylipko, *PSSA in the Baltic Sea: Protection on Paper or Potential Progress?* (WMU. 2014), 7.

PSSAs suggests that a certain marine area can be designated as a special area and PSSA at the same time.[137]

Apart from MARPOL, several other IMO instruments are also relevant to shipping-source pollution. First, chapter VII of the 1974 SOLAS contains provisions regulating the packing, marking, labelling, placarding, documentation and stowage of dangerous goods, which would assist in decreasing the risk of marine pollution caused by the carriage of such dangerous goods by shipping.[138] Second, chapter VIII of the 1974 SOLAS and the 1981 CODES aims to decrease the risk of accidental or deliberate marine pollution resulting from the operation of nuclear ships.[139] Third, the 1997 IMO resolution A.868(20) on ballast water guidelines and the subsequent International Convention for the Control and Management of Ships' Ballast Water and Sediments (BWM) adopted in 2004, establish standards and procedures for the management and control of ships' ballast water and sediments, in order to minimize the transfer and spread of harmful aquatic organisms from one region to another.[140] Fourth, the 2001 International Convention on the Control of Harmful Anti-fouling Systems on Ships (AFS) prohibits the use of harmful organotins in anti-fouling paints on ships and establishes a mechanism to prevent the potential future use of other harmful substances in anti-fouling systems.[141]

---

137 For examples, the Baltic Sea area is designated as a special area and a PSSA. For the list of current special areas, see IMO, Special Areas under MARPOL, available at <http://www.imo.org/en/OurWork/Environment/SpecialAreasUnderMARPOL/Pages/Default.aspx>. For the list of current PSSAs, see IMO, Particularly Sensitive Sea Areas, available at <http://www.imo.org/en/OurWork/Environment/PSSAs/Pages/Default.aspx>.

138 International Convention for the Safety of Life at Sea, adopted 1 November 1974, entered into force 25 May 1980, 1184 *UNTS* 277, chapter VII. Similarly, Convention on the Control of Transboundary Movements of Hazardous Wastes and their Disposal (Basel Convention), adopted in 1989 under the auspices of UNEP, also provides that hazardous wastes and other wastes shall be 'packaged, labelled, and transported in conformity with generally accepted and recognized international rules and standards' in order to reduce potential marine pollution during transportation including shipping. See Convention on the Control of Transboundary Movements of Hazardous Wastes and their Disposal, adopted 22 March 1989, entered into force 5 May 1992, 1673 *UNTS* 57, Article 4(7)(b).

139 SOLAS, chapter VIII; IMO Resolution A.491(XII), Code of Safety for Nuclear Merchant Ships (19 November 1981).

140 IMO Resolution A.868(20), Guidelines for the Control and Management of Ships' Ballast Water to Minimize the Transfer of Harmful Aquatic Organisms and Pathogens (27 November 1997); International Convention for the Control and Management of Ships' Ballast Water and Sediments, adopted 13 February 2004, entered into force 8 September 2017.

141 International Convention on the Control of Harmful Anti-fouling Systems on Ships, adopted 5 October 2001, entered into force 17 September 2008.

8.3.3.2 London Convention and Protocol in Relation to Pollution from Dumping

London Convention was concluded in 1972 to regulate pollution from dumping.[142] London Convention defines dumping as 'any deliberate disposal at sea of wastes or other matter from vessels, aircraft, platforms or other man-made structures at sea' and 'any deliberate disposal at sea of vessels, aircraft, platforms or other man-made structures at sea'.[143] This definition has later been followed by UNCLOS.[144] London Convention adopts a 'black- and grey-list' approach to regulate the disposal of wastes at sea based on the assimilative capability of the seas. Dumping of the blacklist items is completely prohibited,[145] while dumping of the grey-listed materials requires a prior special permit.[146] All other waters or matter can be dumped at sea provided that a prior general permit has been obtained.[147] As of 17 June 2021, 87 States, representing 58% of the gross tonnages of the world's merchant vessels, are parties to London Convention.[148]

London Protocol was adopted in 1996 in order to modernize London Convention and eventually replace it.[149] Article 23 of London Protocol provides that this protocol will supersede London Convention as between contracting parties to both London Convention and Protocol.[150] London Protocol adopts a more restrictive, holistic and modernized approach towards dumping at sea. Two salient features are worth noting. First, London Protocol adopts a 'reverse list' approach, which means that all dumping is prohibited unless explicitly permitted.[151] The substances on the reverse list include dredged materials, sewage sludge, fish waste or material resulting from industrial fish processing operations, vessels and platforms or other man-made structures at sea, inert, inorganic geological material, organic material of natural origin, bulky items primarily comprising iron, steel, concrete and similarly non-harmful materials,

---

142 Convention on the Prevention of Marine Pollution by Dumping of Wastes and Other Matter, adopted 29 December 1972, entered into force 30 August 1975, 1046 *UNTS* 120.

143 London Convention, Article III(1)(a).

144 UNCLOS, Article 1(5)(a).

145 London Convention, Article IV(1)(a) & Annex I.

146 London Convention, Article IV(1)(b) & Annex II.

147 London Convention, Article IV(1)(c).

148 IMO, n 114.

149 IMO, Convention on the Prevention of Marine Pollution by Dumping of Wastes and Other Matter, available at <http://www.imo.org/en/OurWork/Environment/LCLP/Pages/default.aspx>.

150 Protocol to the Convention on the Prevention of Marine Pollution by Dumping of Wastes and Other Matter 1972, adopted 11 July 1996, entered into force 24 March 2006, Article 23.

151 London Protocol, Article 4.

and carbon dioxide streams from carbon dioxide capture processes for sequestration.[152] Second, the precautionary approach is incorporated into London Protocol. State parties are obliged to take appropriate preventative measures 'when there is reason to believe that wastes or other matter introduced into the marine environment are likely to cause harm even when there is no conclusive evidence to prove a causal relationship between inputs and their effects'.[153] As of 17 June 2021, 53 States are parties to London Protocol, representing 40% of the gross tonnages of the world's merchant vessels.[154]

8.3.4 *Application to the Spratly Islands Setting*

First, Table 10 indicates that all the disputant States are parties to MARPOL, MARPOL Annexes I, II, III and V, as well as SOLAS. Hence, the disputant States shall comply with regulations as set forth in these instruments in relation to pollution caused by discharges of harmful substances from ships. Given the fragile environment and high ecological value of the Spratly Islands area, the disputant States may consider submitting a joint proposal to IMO, to designate the whole or part of the Spratly Islands area as a special area under MARPOL, or as a PSSA, whereby stricter pollution standards shall be adopted and enforced. In so doing, restrictions on discharges of certain harmful substances as required in special areas, as well as associated protective measures adopted by IMO for the PSSA would apply in the Spratly Islands area.

Second, not all the disputant States have ratified or are bound by other international instruments such as MARPOL Annexes IV and VI, BWM, AFS, CODES, IMO resolution A.868(20), London Convention and London Protocol. Yet, according to Articles 21(2), 211(2) & (5) and 216 of UNCLOS, the disputant States shall respect environmental norms adopted by competent international organizations or diplomatic conferences insomuch as they are generally accepted, irrespective of whether these States have concurred in adopting such norms.[155] As guided by the DOALOS matrix, the above instruments fit within the confinements of Articles 21(2), 211(2) & (5) and 216, and their provisions thus amount to generally accepted or applicable international rules and standards to the extent that they set out standards to unify practices.

Third, aside from existing instruments, IMO can also guide the regulation of vessel-source pollution within the Spratly Islands area through the promulgation of new international instruments in relation to 'the prevention and

152 London Protocol, Annex 1.
153 London Protocol, Article 3(1).
154 IMO, n 114.
155 Treves, n 62, 327.

TABLE 10 The status of anti-pollution instruments in relation to the disputant States

Disputant states	UNCLOS	Generally accepted international rules and standards beyond UNCLOS											
		Pollution from shipping										Pollution from dumping	
		MARPOL, Annexes I, II	*MARPOL Annex III*	*MARPOL Annex IV*	*MARPOL Annex V*	*MARPOL Annex VI*	*SOLAS*	*BWM*	*AFS*	*CODES*	*A.868(20)*	*London convention*	*London protocol*
Brunei	5 Nov 1996	23 Jan1987	25 Jul 2016	---	25 Jul 2016	---	23 Jan 1987	---	---	---	---	---	---
China	7 Jun 1996	2 Oct 1983	13 Dec 1994	2 Feb 2007	21 Feb 1989	23 Aug 2006	25 May 1980	22 Jan 2019	7 Jun 2011	---	---	14 Dec 1985	29 Oct 2006
Malaysia	14 Oct 1996	1 May 1997	27 Dec 2010	27 Dec 2010	1 May 1997	27 Dec 2010	19 Jan 1984	8 Sep 2017	27 Dec 2010	---	---	---	---
Philippines	8 May 1984	15 Sep 2001	15 Sep 2001	27 Sep 2003	15 Sep 2001	24 Jul 2018	15 Mar 1982	6 Sep 2018	6 Sep 2018	---	---	30 Aug 1975	8 Jun 2012
Vietnam	25 Jul 1994	29 Aug 1991	19 Mar 2015	19 Mar 2015	19 Mar 2015	19 Mar 2015	18 Mar 1991	---	27 Feb 2016	---	---	---	---

Notes: (1) Each of the dates in the table refers to a date of ratification/acceptance of or accession to a relevant instrument by the State concerned. The symbol '---' means that the relevant instrument has no direct binding force upon the State concerned. (2) The status of each instrument: UNCLOS, in force since 16 November 1994; MARPOL, Annexes I, II, in force since 2 October 1983; MARPOL Annex III, in force since 1 July 1992; MARPOL Annex IV, in force since 27 September 2003; MARPOL Annex V, in force since 31 December 1988; MARPOL Annex VI, in force since 19 May 2005; SOLAS, in force since 25 May 1980; BWM in force since 8 September 2017; AFS, in force since 17 September 2008; CODES and IMO resolution A.868(20), not in force; London Convention, in force since 30 August 1975; London Protocol, in force since 24 March 2006. (3) Sources: UNCLOS, List of Parties, available at < https://www.un.org/depts/los/reference_files/chronological_lists_of_ratifications.htm >; IMO, Status of Treaties (as of 17 June 2021), available at < https://www.imo.org/en/About/Conventions/Pages/StatusOfConventions.aspx >.

control of marine pollution from ships' according to its mandates.[156] Such new IMO instruments would fall within the ambit of Articles 21(2) and 211(2) & (5) of UNCLOS to be obligatory for the disputant States to observe, insofar as relevant environmental standards as outlined in such instruments become generally accepted. To that effect, the IMO mandate on standard-setting for vessel-source pollution, in combination with the rules of reference under UNCLOS, creates a dynamic regulatory framework to guide the regulation of vessel-source pollution within the Spratly Islands area.

8.4 Cooperative Institution for Pollution Regulation

This section aims to figure out a suitable cooperative institution to better implement and enforce anti-pollution rules and standards in the Spratly Islands setting. For this purpose, this section examines the juridical allocation of prescriptive jurisdiction and enforcement jurisdiction among the disputant States under current international law and identifies relevant regulatory limitations (subsections 8.4.1–8.4.2). It further proposes solutions to remedy such limitations (subsection 8.4.3).

8.4.1 *Juridical Allocation of Prescriptive Jurisdiction*

Prescriptive jurisdiction refers to a State's competence to promulgate legislation for ships or individuals to comply with. The claimants, when acting as flag States, can undoubtedly promulgate anti-pollution legislation to be applied to ships under their registry. However, when acting as coastal States, none of the claimants is entitled to have exclusive rights to combat pollution from foreign ships within the Spratly Islands area. Thus, when a foreign vessel, which is not under the registry of any claimants, is suspected of discharging pollutants during its navigation through this region, one may wonder which claimant's anti-pollution legislation should apply. In case these States promulgate different anti-pollution standards, it would be difficult to explain why vessels must comply with standards enacted by some States but not others. This section analyses whether the existing regulatory framework adequately addresses this problem of concurrent prescriptive jurisdiction between or among the disputant States acting as coastal States.

156 Convention of the International Maritime Organization, n 109, Article 1(a).

8.4.1.1 Prescriptive Jurisdiction in Relation to Pollution from Shipping

In respect of the EEZ, a coastal State can enact pollution regulations for foreign vessels provided that these regulations 'conform to and give effect to' generally accepted international rules and standards.[157] In exceptional circumstances, if a coastal State considers the foregoing rules inadequate to provide sufficient protection due to the special circumstances of the sea areas concerned, it may choose to adopt international rules and standards or navigational practices that are made applicable by IMO for special areas, or it may adopt additional laws and regulations of its own.[158] Since such extra legislation amounts to posing an additional limitation on the freedom of navigation enjoyed by foreign vessels in the EEZ, strict procedural requirements are provided. According to Article 211(6)(a) of UNCLOS, a coastal State proposing additional legislation is required to consult with 'any other States concerned' through IMO and to obtain the approval from IMO.[159]

Article 211(6)(a) does not explain what constitutes 'other States concerned'. Yet, it is not unreasonable to assume that other disputant States belong to 'other States concerned'. Accordingly, before a disputant State adopts stricter pollution standards within its alleged EEZ, that State shall consult with the other disputant States through IMO. This procedural requirement indeed provides a channel for the disputant States to negotiate with one another, thereby, to some extent, solving the problem of concurrent prescriptive jurisdiction relating to pollution from shipping. As rightly pointed out by Dux, the consultation procedure is of significance because 'it not only heightens the acceptance and thereby the effectiveness of the measures in question but also provides a helpful means of arriving at a solution satisfactory for all the stakeholders involved'.[160]

Article 211(6)(a) is, however, not flawless. The brevity of Article 211(6)(a) makes it unclear as to whether the outcome of the consultation with 'other States concerned' has any bearing on either the opportunity of the coastal State to direct a communication to IMO or the final decision made by IMO after receiving such communication. The answer is in the negative. First, decisions of IMO are usually made by consensus. Therefore, the outcome of the consultation would only make a material difference in case any of the 'other

157 UNCLOS, Article 211(5).
158 UNCLOS, Article 211(6).
159 UNCLOS, Article 211(6)(a).
160 T. Dux, *Specially Protected Marine Areas in the Exclusive Economic Zone (EEZ): The Regime for the Protection of Specific Areas of the EEZ for Environmental Reasons Under International Law* (Lit. 2011), 196.

States concerned' is not represented at IMO where decisions are made.[161] This exceptional scenario does not apply here, as all the disputant States are members to IMO.[162] Second, the practices of IMO respecting PSSAs has shown that the designation of an area does not depend on the procedural question of consultation but merely on the satisfaction of the substantive conditions.[163] Though the concept of PSSAs is not exactly the same as the one envisaged under Article 211(6)(a),[164] it is arguable that the practices of the former can equally apply to the latter, as Article 211(6)(a) also stipulates that what IMO needs to determine is whether the oceanographical and ecological conditions in the marine area concerned meet the substantive requirements as outlined in this provision.[165]

Tailored to the Spratly Islands setting, the procedural requirements, namely to consult with 'any other States concerned' through IMO and to obtain the approval from IMO, significantly limit the disputant States' discretion in promulgating stricter rules or standards that apply in the alleged EEZ. As rightly pointed out by Boyle, the power to enact stricter rules or standards rests primarily with the States that make up IMO, and thus, international regulations adopted through that institution are not merely of the interests of particular coastal States but instead are an expression of compromise and common interest among the various groups represented at IMO.[166]

Furthermore, distinct from the EEZ where a coastal State has less discretion over the pollution standards that it may apply, a coastal State is free to promulgate anti-pollution rules and standards to be applied to its claimed territorial sea, except about those relating to the design, construction, manning or equipment of foreign ships.[167] Therefore, in terms of areas subject to claims of the territorial sea, the problem of concurrent prescriptive jurisdiction in relation to pollution from shipping is more likely to arise between or among the disputant States.

161 *Ibid.*

162 IMO, *Member States*, available at <http://www.imo.org/en/About/Membership/Pages/MemberStates.aspx>.

163 Dux, n 160, 196.

164 For a detailed comparison between PSSAs and the special areas under Article 211(6)(a), see M.J. Kachel, *Particularly Sensitive Sea Areas: The IMO's Role in Protecting Vulnerable Marine Areas* (Springer. 2008), 253.

165 UNCLOS, Article 211(6)(a).

166 Boyle, n 9, 362.

167 UNCLOS, Article 21(2).

8.4.1.2 Prescriptive Jurisdiction in Relation to Pollution from Dumping

A coastal State enjoys prescriptive jurisdiction against dumping within its territorial sea and EEZ.[168] Two compulsory conditions are posed upon such legislation by coastal States: first, such legislation shall ensure that any dumping is carried out with the permission of the competent authorities of States (the 'compulsory permission' requirement);[169] and second, such legislation shall be 'no less effective' than applicable international rules and standards.[170] The phrase 'no less effective' indicates that the applicable international rules and standards represent the minimum standards for the coastal State to observe. Coastal States may set forth stricter constraints if they so choose.

The contested status of the Spratly Islands area gives rise to a question as to from which disputant State a dumping actor needs to request compulsory permission. It can be imagined that none of the disputant States would let go of this regulatory power because it is likely to be perceived as an opportunity to demonstrate and increase the prominence of their claims in the region. On the one hand, requiring ocean dumping actors to obtain compulsory permissions from all the disputant States would cause undue burden to these actors. On the other hand, obtaining compulsory permissions from one disputant State alone is also unfitting for protecting the marine environment in this region. It is because dumping actors would incline to obtain permission from the disputant State that promulgates the least strict environmental constraints. Consequently, it would be difficult for some disputant States to enforce stricter constraints which they believe are necessary owing to the special circumstances of the region. In light of this, a viable solution is that all the disputant States cooperate to establish a coordinating entity to grant compulsory permission for dumping activities and to unify dumping-related standards respecting the Spratly Islands area.

8.4.1.3 Analysis of Regulatory Limitations

Tailored to the Spratly Islands setting, the current regulatory framework can solve the concurrent prescriptive jurisdiction problem relating to pollution from shipping within the EEZ, by obliging the States concerned to consult with one another through IMO before they can promulgate stricter environmental restraints than international standards against foreign vessels. However, this regulatory framework is apparently not without its limitations. First, it provides inadequate guidance for unifying the legislation practices of the

168 UNCLOS, Article 210(5).
169 UNCLOS, Article 210(3).
170 UNCLOS, Article 210(6).

disputant States against pollution from shipping in respect of contested areas involving territorial sea claims. Second, in a similar vein, this regulatory framework falls short of unifying the legislation practices of the disputant States against dumping within the Spratly Islands area.

8.4.2 *Juridical Allocation of Enforcement Jurisdiction*

Enforcement jurisdiction refers to a State's competence to enforce its legislation.[171] Applicable enforcement measures may include requesting necessary information, physical inspection and instituting proceedings including detention or arrest of the vessel and judicial trials.

8.4.2.1 Enforcement Jurisdiction in Relation to Pollution from Shipping

In the Spratly Islands area, when a disputant State acts as a *flag* State, it is obliged to effectively enforce legislation against its vessels irrespective of where a violation occurs.[172] In general, a flag State shall prohibit its vessels from sailing unless they observe the requirements of relevant international rules and standards, ensure that these vessels carry on board certificates, periodically inspect these certificates, and immediately investigate violations alleged to have been committed by its vessels.[173] When a violation occurs, a flag State is obliged to 'provide for immediate investigation and where appropriate institute proceedings in respect of the alleged violation irrespective of where the violation occurred or where the pollution caused by such violation has occurred or has been spotted'.[174] It follows that a flag State is entitled to institute judicial proceedings against a violation regardless of where they occur. Yet, UNCLOS contains no provision to explicitly grant flag States the right to arrest their vessels in the EEZ of another State. It is arguable that flag States are allowed to do so,[175] as flag States can arrest their vessels on high seas,[176] and the regime of high seas shall equally apply to EEZ s and certainly with respect to the enforcement of anti-pollution legislation unless specifically provided otherwise.[177]

When a disputant State acts as a *coastal* State, it is entitled to enforce any violation of its national anti-pollution legislation or applicable international

171 Churchill and Lowe, n 5, 344.
172 UNCLOS, Article 217(1).
173 UNCLOS, Article 217(2)-(6).
174 UNCLOS, Article 217(4).
175 Churchill and Lowe, n 5, 348–349.
176 UNCLOS, Article 92.
177 UNCLOS, Article 58(2).

rules and standards relating to pollution from vessels when such a violation has occurred within its alleged territorial sea or EEZ.[178] Where there are clear grounds for believing that a vessel (national or foreign) navigating in the territorial sea has committed violations during its passage therein, a coastal State can undertake a physical inspection of the vessel and institute other proceedings where the evidence so warrants.[179] By contrast, the power of a coastal State in respect of its EEZ is graduated according to the degree of harm threatened.[180] First, where there are clear grounds for believing that a vessel navigating in the territorial sea or the EEZ has committed violations in the EEZ, the coastal State can request the vessel to provide necessary information in relation to 'its identity and port of registry, its last and its next port of call and other relevant information required to establish whether a violation has occurred'.[181] Second, if the vessel has refused to provide necessary information or has provided manifestly incorrect information, a coastal State is entitled to undertake a physical inspection of the vessel, provided that there are clear grounds for believing that the alleged violation has resulted in 'a substantial discharge causing or threatening significant pollution of the marine environment'.[182] Third, if there is clear objective evidence that the alleged violation has resulted in 'a discharge causing major damage or threat of major damage to the coastline or related interests of the coastal State, or to any resources of its territorial sea or exclusive economic zone', the coastal State is entitled to institute proceedings including detention of the vessel.[183]

8.4.2.2 Enforcement Jurisdiction in Relation to Pollution from Dumping

Article 216 outlines the legal framework of enforcement jurisdiction relating to pollution from dumping.[184] Accordingly, a coastal State enjoys enforcement jurisdiction with regard to dumping within its territorial sea and EEZ,[185] and a flag State can enforce against vessels flying its flag or of its registry.[186] However, the brevity of this provision may bring some unclarities, if not controversies. Neither UNCLOS nor London Convention or London Protocol specifies the exact geographical extent of the flag State's enforcement jurisdiction. Thus, it

178 UNCLOS, Article 220(1).
179 UNCLOS, Article 220(2).
180 Boyle, n 9, 364.
181 UNCLOS, Article 220(3).
182 UNCLOS, Article 220(5).
183 UNCLOS, Article 220(6).
184 UNCLOS, Article 216(1).
185 UNCLOS, Article 216(1)(a).
186 UNCLOS, Article 216(1)(b).

remains disputable as to whether a flag State can arrest a vessel flying its flag alleged to have committed illegal dumping when the latter is navigating in the EEZ of another State.

According to the UNCLOS commentary, a comparison between UNCLOS provisions regulating pollution from shipping (Articles 217 and 220) and those regulating pollution from dumping (Article 216) suggests that the latter basically 'adds little to what already appears in article 217 as regards the primary enforcement obligations of the flag State and in article 220 as regards the enforcement powers of coastal States'.[187] Therefore, it is arguable that provisions regulating pollution from shipping should apply equally to pollution from dumping in the absence of explicit provisions relating to the latter. Thus, by analogy to the provisions regulating pollution from shipping, a flag State is allowed to exercise its enforcement jurisdiction against dumping violations alleged to have been committed by its vessels irrespective of where they occur and to arrest its vessels in the EEZ of another State.

8.4.2.3 Analysis of Regulatory Limitations

The existence of a dispute over a particular marine area adds complexity to enforcement at sea. The Spratly Islands area is no exception. The disputant States, acting as either flag or coastal States, are prone to have the concurrent enforcement jurisdiction problem. To better illustrate this point, an imaginary case is presented. Assume that States A, B, C all claim a particular marine area to be their territorial sea or EEZ. A merchant vessel flying the flag of State A is navigating in this area, and this vessel is alleged to have committed violations of international anti-pollution rules or standards relating to pollution from shipping or dumping. Concurrent enforcement jurisdiction may, therefore, occur between or among States A, B and C. There are two types of concurrent enforcement jurisdiction. One is between a flag State and a coastal State (for example, between States A and B, or between States A and C). The other is between a coastal State and another coastal State (for example, between States B and C).

First, UNCLOS contains provisions addressing the problem of concurrent enforcement jurisdiction that exists between a flag State and a coastal State. According to Article 228(1), when a coastal State is instituting proceedings to impose penalties over a *foreign* vessel that is alleged to have committed violations of anti-pollution legislation *beyond the territorial sea* of that State, the

187 M.H. Nordquist *et al.* (eds.), *United Nations Convention on the Law of the Sea, 1982: A Commentary. Vol. 4: Articles 192 to 278, Final Act, Annex VI* (Nijhoff. 1991), 239.

flag State of this vessel has the right to request the coastal State to suspend relevant proceedings and take the proceedings itself to impose penalties in respect of corresponding charges, except in the events of major damage to the coastal State or the flag State's repeated disregard of its enforcement duty.[188] Therefore, within the EEZ, a flag State enjoys primary enforcement jurisdiction in relation to the institution of penal proceedings against vessels flying its flag or of its registry.[189]

Second, it is worth noting that in the 2015 *Arctic Sunrise Arbitration* merits award, the tribunal supported the exclusive jurisdiction of a flag State over its ships in the EEZ of another State based on a combined reading of Articles 92(1) and 58(2) of UNCLOS.[190] On this basis, the tribunal further concluded that within the EEZ, 'a coastal State may only exercise jurisdiction, including law enforcement measures, over a ship, with the prior consent of the flag State'.[191] However, as the tribunal admitted, there are exceptions to this principle.[192] In the tribunal's view, aside from the coastal State's right of visit on suspicion of piracy and right of hot pursuit, such exceptions also include the coastal State's enforcement jurisdiction in relation to the reduction and control of marine pollution under Article 220 of UNCLOS.[193] Therefore, in case of combating marine pollution in the EEZ, the flag State jurisdiction does not necessarily prevail over the coastal State jurisdiction, except in respect of the institution of penal proceedings against its national vessels according to Article 228(1) of UNCLOS.

Third, the flag State pre-emption does not apply to coastal State proceedings for territorial sea offenses, either. In other words, a flag State does not necessarily enjoy priority to institute penal proceedings for pollution discharge violations that occur within another State's territorial sea. Rather, Article 228(2) of UNCLOS sets forth that '[p]roceedings to impose penalties on foreign vessels ... shall not be taken by any State in the event of proceedings having been instituted by another State'.[194] Therefore, once a disputant State, acting

188 UNCLOS, Article 228(1).

189 Boyle, n 9, 362.

190 Article 92(1) provides for the exclusive jurisdiction of a State over ships flying its flag in the high seas. Article 58(2) stipulates that Article 92 equally applies to the EEZ insofar as it is not incompatible with the EEZ regime as outlined in UNCLOS. Accordingly, the exclusive jurisdiction of a State over ships flying its flag also applies to the EEZ. See Arctic Sunrise Arbitration (Netherlands v. Russia), Award on the Merits of 14 August 2015 (PCA), para.231.

191 *Ibid.*

192 *Ibid.*

193 *Ibid.*, paras. 286, 290.

194 UNCLOS, Article 228(2).

as a flag or coastal State, has instituted proceedings to impose penalties against violations committed in its alleged territorial sea, the other disputant States shall not institute proceedings against the same offenses. The prioritization of one State's enforcement jurisdiction to institute penal proceedings is aimed to avoid double or multiple jurisdiction jeopardy.[195]

Fourth, apart from Article 228(1) and (2), UNCLOS contains no provisions that directly coordinate other types of concurrent enforcement jurisdiction, including those relating to physical inspection, detention and the initiation of civil proceedings. For instance, Article 226(2) simply provides that States are obliged to develop procedures to avoid unnecessary physical inspection of vessels at sea.[196] Similarly, Article 229 stipulates that nothing in UNCLOS affects the institution of civil proceedings regarding any claim of loss or damage caused by marine pollution.[197] These provisions do not give an effective restraint on or offer adequate practical guidance to the disputant States in the exercise of their enforcement jurisdiction over contested marine areas.

Tailored to the Spratly Islands setting, only in two scenarios, there are provisions that clearly allocate enforcement jurisdiction. First, a disputant State enjoys primary enforcement jurisdiction in relation to the institution of penal proceedings against vessels flying its flag or of its registry navigating in an area which is alleged to be its EEZ. Second, once a disputant State, acting as a flag or coastal State, has instituted proceedings to impose penalties against vessels (national or foreign) that have committed violations in its alleged territorial sea, the other disputant States shall not institute proceedings against the same offenses. Thus, it can be concluded that the existing regulatory framework is limited when it comes to the coordination of conflicting enforcement jurisdiction except about the institution of penal proceedings between or among the disputant States against pollution violation occurring within the Spratly Islands area.

The existence of concurrent enforcement jurisdiction is understandable if seen against the development of the legal framework governing enforcement jurisdiction at sea. Before the adoption of UNCLOS, enforcement powers over vessels for pollution at sea rested primarily with flag States except that coastal States could arrest and prosecute for violations committed in the territorial sea.[198] However, it was generally accepted that relying on flag State enforcement alone would not suffice to minimize marine pollution. Due

195 Nordquist *et al.*, n 187, 350.
196 UNCLOS, Article 226(2).
197 UNCLOS, Article 229.
198 Boyle, n 9, 362–363.

to this concern, UNCLOS revised the jurisdictional framework by enhancing the enforcement power of coastal States to the EEZ to supplement the flag State jurisdiction. To this extent, it is fair to say that concurrent enforcement jurisdiction was intended by UNCLOS drafters for strengthening and making 'more effective machinery for enforcing pollution laws'.[199] This is the bright side of concurrent enforcement jurisdiction. However, it also has a dark side that has been termed by scholars as 'creeping jurisdiction'[200] or 'jurisdictional uncertainty'.[201] Owing to the inconvenience and costly expenses, a coastal State might be lax in inspecting and prosecuting pollution discharge violations occurring within undisputed waters in its territorial sea or EEZ. Thus, concurrent enforcement jurisdiction is usually unproblematic in respect of undisputed waters. However, the dark side of concurrent enforcement jurisdiction would be significantly amplified in contested marine areas such as those in the Spratly Islands area, as the disputant States are usually proactive in enforcing their anti-pollution legislation over the contested areas, seeking to demonstrate and strengthen their maritime claims over the region.

8.4.3 *Solutions to Remedy Regulatory Limitations*

The preceding analysis demonstrates that to remedy existing regulatory limitations, cooperative arrangements are needed in two situations: first, to unify the legislation practices of the disputant States against pollution from shipping in respect of contested areas involving territorial sea claims and against ocean dumping in the whole Spratly Islands area; and second, to coordinate the concurrent enforcement jurisdiction except about the institution of penal proceedings. Notably, Article 197 of UNCLOS imposes on States a general obligation to cooperate in formulating and elaborating international rules and standards consistent with UNCLOS for protecting the marine environment.[202] However, this obligation focuses on the establishment of minimum environmental restraints for States to observe but offers no guidance about how to reconcile concurrent prescriptive jurisdiction caused by conflicting national legislation as long as such legislation is not inconsistent with international environmental restraints. In a similar vein, Articles 74(3), 83(3) and 123 of UNCLOS oblige the disputant States to negotiate with a view to reaching cooperative pollution arrangements but does not mandate the outcome of the

199 *Ibid.*, 365.

200 D.P. O'Connell, *The International Law of the Sea. Vol. II* (Clarendon Press. 1984), 733.

201 I.A. Shearer, Problems of Jurisdiction and Law Enforcement Against Delinquent Vessels, 35 *ICLQ* (1986), 322.

202 UNCLOS, Article 197.

negotiation or the substantive content of such arrangements.[203] Therefore, it is entirely up to the disputant States to decide how to unify their anti-pollution legislation and enforcement practices within the Spratly Islands area. In light of this, below are several observations on tentative solutions to remedy the limitations that exist in the current regulatory framework.

First, it is necessary for the disputant States not to use jurisdictional zones as the frame of reference when promulgating anti-pollution legislation and enforce such legislation in the Spratly Islands area. Rather, the disputant States are recommended to adopt an integrated management approach to tackle pollution in this region. As indicated in chapter 3, it is not uncommon that a disputant State claims a particular marine area within the Spratly Islands area to be within its territorial sea, while the others claim the same area to be their EEZ. UNCLOS prescribes different regulatory frameworks for the territorial sea and EEZ. Consequently, the piecemeal fashion and zonal approach of pollution regulation as outlined in UNCLOS are prone to lead to jurisdictional uncertainties. This regulatory problem can be remedied by incorporating an integrated management approach to combat marine pollution across the whole Spratly Islands area, without regard to the nature and types of maritime claims. Promulgating consistent and uniform anti-pollution legislation across the whole region can also promote the efficient implementation of such legislation.

Second, the key to harmonizing concurrent prescriptive jurisdiction is to unify substantive environmental standards adopted in the national legislation promulgated unilaterally by each disputant State. As mentioned earlier, substantive environmental standards require adaptability, or in other words, timely response to changing scientific insights and technological or economic possibilities. Therefore, it is infeasible to 'freeze' uniform environmental rules or standards in a legally binding instrument. A more viable solution is to make use of a dynamic mechanism through which the substantive content of national anti-pollution legislation can be unified and at the same time adapted to changing contexts. Accordingly, the disputant States are recommended to convene regular ministerial meetings or even to jointly establish a permanent and intergovernmental commission to discuss and promulgate 'common environmental rules and standards' consistent with UNCLOS to be applied to the Spratly Islands area. The non-disputant States that are bordering the South China Sea are encouraged to participate in such decision-making mechanisms to the extent that the best scientific evidence shows that pollution

203 UNCLOS, Articles 74(3), 83(3) and 123.

management respecting the Spratly Islands area and other sea areas of the South China Sea are interconnected.

Third, the solution to the concurrent enforcement jurisdiction problem is to allocate the jurisdiction in a predictable manner. What matters more here is not adaptability but precision and predictability. Accordingly, it is recommended to 'freeze' the legal framework regarding the allocation of enforcement jurisdiction in a legally binding instrument. A further question is how to allocate enforcement jurisdiction effectively. Precedents in other sea regions may provide useful guidance. For example, for surveillance of pollution discharge violations as an aid to detect and combat pollution, the North Sea area is divided into zones of responsibility.[204] Some of these zones are under surveillance of a single State, and others are jointly controlled by two State parties, which is also called zones of joint responsibility.[205] A contracting State party, in whose responsible zone the presence of oil and other harmful substances causing a grave and imminent danger to the coast or related interest of one or more parties occur, is obliged to make necessary assessment of the situation, keep the substances under observation and immediately inform other contracting parties about the situation and the action to be taken.[206] The division of the zones of responsibility does not precisely align with maritime boundaries of contracting parties. The parties agree that the division of these zones of responsibility shall not be invoked as an argument in any matter relating to sovereignty or jurisdiction.[207] The zones of responsibility are divided merely for the immediate detection of pollution discharge violations. Contracting parties do not necessarily enjoy other enforcement jurisdictional rights in these zones. By analogy, the Spratly Islands area is partly subjected to bilateral disputes and partly to multilateral disputes. Accordingly, the disputant States might divide the whole region into several zones of joint responsibility for surveillance of pollution discharge violations. For example, the marine area around Reed Bank is in dispute between China and the Philippines and thus can be established as a zone of joint responsibility where both countries

---

204 Agreement for Cooperation in dealing with Pollution of the North Sea by Oil and Other Harmful Substances, adopted 13 September 1983, entered into force 1 September 1989, 1605 *UNTS* 34, Article 6.

205 The contracting parties have adopted a decision to modify the zones of responsibility to align them with Exclusive Economic Zones in 2001. Nevertheless, this process is still ongoing. See History and Key Milestones, available at <https://www.bonnagreement.org/about/history>.

206 Agreement for Cooperation in dealing with Pollution of the North Sea by Oil and Other Harmful Substances, n 204, Article 6.

207 *Ibid.*, Article 8(2).

are obliged to inform each other of their observations regarding any pollution offence. For enforcement purposes, the disputant States, which have claims over the contested areas, are recommended to jointly develop and establish guidelines and contingency plans for the practical, operational and technical aspects of joint or coordinated enforcement actions within their zones of joint responsibility.

Fourth, some international organizations, such as ASEAN and UNEP, can play a critical 'brokerage' role in terms of serving as an intermediary or providing fora for facilitating dialogue and building confidence among the disputant States to solve the concurrent prescription and enforcement jurisdiction problems. For example, as can be seen in section 5.3, ASEAN has helped to bring the disputant States to the negotiating table to negotiate a common understanding of key strategic norms with regard to the South China Sea, which has been exemplified by the conclusion of the DOC and the ongoing negotiations on the COC.[208] Similarly, as mentioned in section 8.2.4, UNEP has facilitated and implemented a cooperative initiative – the UNEP/GEF-SCS Project – aimed to reverse environmental degradation trends among seven States bordering the South China Sea, including those not parties to the Spratly Islands disputes.[209]

8.5 Conclusion

Pollution is no longer an explicit freedom at sea in modern days, not even in contested waters where none of the disputant States can claim exclusive jurisdiction. The prevention and control of pollution in the Spratly Islands area are beneficial for the conservation of marine biodiversity within and beyond the region. Moreover, the 'neutral' nature of environmental problems and the shared benefits of compliance with environmental restraints has made marine environmental cooperation a less sensitive issue in the view of the disputant States and thus a relatively easy subject area for initiating substantive inter-State cooperation.[210] Thus, pollution management cooperation might be a good starting point for building trust and confidence between the disputant States.

208 E. Goh, Institutions and the Great Power Bargain in East Asia: ASEAN's Limited 'Brokerage' Role, 11(3) *International Relations of the Asia-Pacific* (2011), 374.

209 For more information about the UNEP/GEF-SCS Project, see *e.g.*, Tuan and Pernetta, n 46, 589–596; Pernetta and Jiang, n 46, 141–152.

210 Chen, n 45, 139.

The process of promoting environmental cooperation is indeed about achieving changes in our perception of the environment and its resources, 'the role that science, technology and economic aspects can play in determining the manner in which we use the environment and its resources', as well as 'our ethical perceptions – both in terms of inter- and intra-generational equity'.[211] In this process of change, international law has a role to play. This statement undoubtedly applies to the Spratly Islands area, where international law can guide the disputant States to cooperate in minimizing marine pollution. After evaluating the current pollution regulatory framework, it can be concluded that this framework adequately addresses issues, including:

(1) deterring unilateral anti-pollution legislation and closing gaps between international rules or standards and national legislation that apply to the Spratly Islands area;
(2) eliminating the risk of concurrent prescriptive jurisdiction relating to pollution from shipping within the EEZ by obliging the disputant States to consult with each other through IMO before they can promulgate stricter environmental restraints than international standards against foreign vessels; and
(3) coordinating the conflicting enforcement jurisdiction about the institution of penal proceedings by giving the flag State primary jurisdiction against offenses within the EEZ or by giving pre-emption to the disputant State that first institutes the proceedings against violations within other contested areas.

However, regulatory limitations and uncertainties do remain in some parts of the existing regulatory framework, resulting in unsatisfactory and ineffective results in dealing with matters such as:

(1) unifying the legislation practices of the disputant States against pollution from shipping in respect of contested areas involving territorial sea claims;
(2) unifying the legislation practices of the disputant States against ocean dumping in the Spratly Islands area; and
(3) coordinating conflicting enforcement jurisdiction except about the institution of penal proceedings between the disputant States against violations occurring within the contested marine areas.

---

211 E. Hey, The International Regime for the Protection of the North Sea: From Functional Approaches to a More Integrated Approach, 17 *IJMCL* (2002), 348–349.

Four observations are put forward on tentative solutions to remedy the limitations that exist in the current regulatory framework. First, to ensure efficient implementation of anti-pollution legislation, the disputant States could adopt an integrated management approach to enact consistent and uniform anti-pollution legislation across the whole Spratly Islands area without regard to the nature and types of maritime claims. Second, to remedy the concurrent prescriptive jurisdiction problem, the disputant States could jointly establish a dynamic mechanism – for example, regular ministerial meetings or a permanent and intergovernmental commission – through which the substantive content of national anti-pollution legislation can be unified and at the same time adapted to changing contexts. Third, when it comes to the problem of concurrent enforcement jurisdiction, the disputant States could 'freeze' the allocation of enforcement jurisdiction in a static and legally binding instrument. Fourth, some international organizations, such as ASEAN and UNEP, can play an important 'brokerage' role in terms of serving as an intermediary or providing fora for facilitating dialogue and building confidence among the disputant States to solve the concurrent prescription and enforcement jurisdiction problems.

CHAPTER 9

Conclusion

This book seeks to address the question of to what extent international law provides a normative framework for the management of the Spratly Islands area preceding delimitation. For this purpose, the preceding chapters have analysed the existing legal regulatory frameworks and their potential for providing an adequate normative framework for the disputant States on their coexistence and cooperation in the Spratly Islands area, especially concerning the following four aspects: (1) addressing the underlying territorial dispute, (2) identifying the disputed marine areas, (3) regulating unilateral conduct, and (4) promoting cooperation in resource and pollution management in respect of the Spratly Islands area. This chapter summaries the responses to the above question (sections 9.1–9.4). It then reflects on the functions and limitations of international law in managing the Spratly Islands area (section 9.5).

9.1 Underlying Territorial Dispute and Law of Territory

The territorial dispute is the most fundamental dispute, as a State can only claim maritime entitlements over specific areas when it enjoys territorial sovereignty over certain land areas according to the legal principle of '*la terre domine la mer*'.[1] All the disputant States put forward multiple legal bases for their territorial claims, including historic title, *effectivités*, treaty title, cession, and discovery of *terra nullius*.[2] Chapter 2 addresses whether the legal arguments put forward by the disputant States for claiming territorial sovereignty over the Spratly Islands are substantiated under international law.

This chapter applies the dichotomy of titles and *effectivités* as the analytical framework, which is a well-accepted pattern of analysis in cases involving territorial disputes.[3] The titles/*effectivités* dichotomy is built upon the special nexuses

1 North Sea Continental Shelf (Federal Republic of Germany/Denmark), Judgment of 20 February 1969 (ICJ), para.96. C. van Bijnkershoek, *De Dominio Maris Dissertatio* (OUP 2nd ed. 1744) (translated by R. Van Deman Magoffin), 43.

2 See chapter 2, section 2.3.

3 See *e.g.*, Frontier Dispute (Burkina Faso/Republic of Mali), Judgment of 22 December 1986 (ICJ), para.63; Territorial Dispute (Libyan Arab Jamahiriya/Chad), Judgment of 3 February 1994 (ICJ), paras.75-76; Land and Maritime Boundary between Cameroon and Nigeria (Cameroon v. Nigeria: Equatorial Guinea intervening), Judgment of 10 October 2002 (ICJ),

 DOI:10.1163/9789004504332_010

between these two concepts.[4] First, a legal title always prevails over *effectivités*. Where *effectivités* correspond to the title to territory, *effectivités* are confirmatory of that title. In contrast, *effectivités* contradictory to an existing title are unlawful, which have been called '*effectivités* contra legem' in the *Cameroon/Nigeria* judgment.[5] Second, in the absence of a title, the role of *effectivités* becomes significant and can be constitutive of a title. In this circumstance, *effectivités* become a 'law-establishing mechanism'.[6] Third, where a legal title, or more precisely, the evidence of a legal title, is obscure or equivocal, *effectivités* can play a probative or interpretative role in clarifying the extent of that title.[7]

The settlement of territorial sovereignty dispute can never lead to a win-win situation for all the disputant States, as 'only one of two conflicting interests is to prevail, because sovereignty can be attributed to but one of the Parties'.[8] Moreover, modern international law rejects the applicability of *terra nullius* and tends to attribute a certain territory to a country whenever possible: 'in many cases the tribunal [that deals with a territorial dispute] has been satisfied with very little in the way of the actual exercise of sovereign rights, provided that the other State could not make out a superior claim'.[9] The rejection of *terra nullius* is necessary for attaining a stable territorial order and thus worth supporting, despite its side effect that picking the best argument out of a mediocre bunch might sometimes be difficult and thus has little chance to enjoy unanimous support.

A careful analysis in this book suggests that China's territorial claim based on historic title, among all the claims advanced by the disputant States, is the

---

para.68; Sovereignty over Pulau Ligitan and Pulau Sipadan (Indonesia/Malaysia), Judgment of 17 December 2002 (ICJ), para.126; Frontier Dispute (Benin/Niger), Judgment of 12 July 2005 (ICJ), para.77; Territorial and Maritime Dispute between Nicaragua and Honduras in the Caribbean Sea (Nicaragua v. Honduras), Judgment of 8 October 2007 (ICJ), para.152; Territorial and Maritime Dispute (Nicaragua v. Colombia), Judgment of 19 November 2012 (ICJ), para.66; Arbitration between the Republic of Croatia and the Republic of Slovenia, Final Award of 29 June 2017 (PCA), para.340.

4 Frontier Dispute, n 3, para.63. M.G. Kohen, Titles and Effectivités in Territorial Disputes, in M.G. Kohen and M. Hébié (eds.), *Research Handbook on Territorial Disputes in International Law* (Edward Elgar Publishing. 2018), 164.

5 Land and Maritime Boundary between Cameroon and Nigeria, n 3, para.223.

6 M.N. Shaw, *International Law* (CUP. 8th ed. 2017), 382.

7 M.G. Kohen, Titles and Effectivités in Territorial Disputes, in M.G. Kohen and M. Hébié (eds.), *Research Handbook on Territorial Disputes in International Law* (Edward Elgar Publishing. 2018), 164.

8 Island of Palmas (The United States of America v. The Netherlands), Award of 4 April 1928 (PCA), 870.

9 Legal Status of Eastern Greenland (Denmark v. Norway), Judgment of 5 April 1933, PCIJ Series A/B No. 53, 46.

most plausible one when evaluated in terms of the law of territory.[10] First, the activities taken by the disputant States respecting the Spratly Islands fail to amount to *effectivités* in the present case.[11] Second, there is no sufficient evidence to show that the 1887 China-France Treaty or the 1951 Treaty of Peace with Japan has a bearing on the disposition of the Spratly Islands.[12] Third, due to the presence of a pre-existing title enjoyed by China prior to the French occupation and the lack of agreement of cession between France and Vietnam, Vietnam's claim of a territorial title to the islands in the Spratly Islands by right of cession is untenable.[13] Fourth, China and the Philippines' territorial claims based on discovery of *terra nullius* are unsubstantiated under international law, because of either the lack of an affirmation of sovereignty or the inapplicability of discovery after the middle of the 16th century.[14]

Nevertheless, owing to various factors such as China's resistance to any recourse to third-party settlement as well as the foreseeable difficulties in negotiations for claimant States to compromise their territorial interests, there appears to be little possibility of resolving this territorial dispute by either judicial or diplomatic methods in the foreseeable future.[15] Thus, the settlement of this territorial dispute cannot be counted on as the only method to maintain the peaceful coexistence of the disputant States in the region. Alternative solutions are needed in order to coordinate the conduct of the claimants and to make efficient uses of marine natural resources therein in the absence of delimitation.

9.2 Identifying Disputed Marine Areas in Light of Complex Maritime Claims

Identifying the seaward limit of the disputed marine areas in the Spratly Islands area is necessary before applying relevant international obligations preceding delimitation, such as Articles 74(3) and 83(3) of UNCLOS, to the disputant

10 See chapter 2, sections 2.4–2.9.
11 See chapter 2, section 2.5.
12 See chapter 2, section 2.6.
13 See chapter 2, section 2.7.
14 See chapter 2, section 2.8.
15 See H. Park, The South China Sea Disputes: Who Owns the Islands and the Natural Resources?, 5 *ODIL* (1978), 34; B.K. Murphy, Dangerous Ground: The Spratly Islands and International Law, 1 *OCLJ* (1995), 189; U. Hideshi, The Problems in the South China Sea, *Review of Island Studies* (2013), 2–3; S. Wu, China's Maritime Law Enforcement Practice in the South China Sea: Challenges and Prospects, in M.H. Nordquist, *et al.* (eds.), *Legal Order in the World's Oceans: UN Convention on the Law of the Sea* (Brill|Nijhoff, 2017), 451.

States. Nevertheless, the presence of ambiguity and alleged excessiveness associated with maritime claims put forward by the disputant States add difficulties to the identification process. There are two competing approaches in identifying disputed marine areas in the Spratly Islands setting: (1) the areas of overlapping claims approach taking into account all claims, and (2) an alternative approach excluding unreasonable claims.

First, the geographical extent of disputed marine areas identified according to the areas of overlapping claims approach must take into account all claims advanced by the disputant States. Such claims would result in two categories of disputed marine areas as specified in section 3.3.1.1: (1) areas of overlapping claims related to the same type of maritime zone, and (2) areas of overlapping claims related to different types of maritime zones.[16] Accordingly, the extent of disputed marine areas basically covers the whole of the Spratly Islands area.[17]

Second, the key to the alternative approach is defining and excluding 'unreasonable claims'. The test of plausibility, which is widely recognized and used as a criterion for the indication of provisional measures in international jurisprudence which requires that the rights a party seeks to protect are plausible,[18] can be a good criterion for filtering out unreasonable claims.[19] On this basis, it is sufficient for a disputant State's rights over the area in dispute to be considered as plausible and thus reasonable, provided that such rights constitute a possible interpretation and application of relevant international law such as UNCLOS provisions.[20] Notably, the *South China Sea Arbitration* award entails that China's maritime claims, including those based on the U-shaped line and entitlements to the EEZ and continental shelf generated by the islands in the

16 See chapter 3, section 3.3.1.1.

17 See chapter 3, section 3.3.1.2 and Map 2.

18 See *e.g.*, Questions relating to the Obligation to Prosecute or Extradite (Belgium v. Senegal), Order of 28 May 2009 (Request for the indication of provisional measures) (ICJ), para.57; Certain Activities carried out by Nicaragua in the Border Area (Costa Rica v. Nicaragua), Provisional Measures Order of 8 March 2011 (ICJ), paras.53, 57; Request for Interpretation of the Judgment of 15 June 1962 in the Case concerning the Temple of Preah Vihear (Cambodia v. Thailand) (Cambodia v. Thailand), Order of 18 July 2011 (Request for the Indication of Provisional Measures) (ICJ), para.33; Dispute Concerning Delimitation of the Maritime Boundary between Ghana and Côte d'Ivoire in the Atlantic Ocean (Ghana/Côte d'Ivoire), Order of 25 April 2015, Request for the prescription of provisional measures (ITLOS), para.58.

19 S.D. Murphy, Obligations of States in Disputed Areas of the Continental Shelf, in T. Heider (ed.), *New Knowledge and Changing Circumstances in the Law of the Sea* (Brill. 2020), 185–186.

20 See chapter 3, section 3.3.2.1.

Spratly Islands area, cannot be a possible interpretation and application of UNCLOS.[21] According to this award, these maritime claims would be deemed implausible and thus unreasonable. Thus, taking into full account the impact of the *South China Sea Arbitration* award, the extent of disputed marine areas according to the alternative approach must reflect the following categories of disputed marine areas, including: (1) the territorial sea generated around the disputed islands; (2) the contiguous zone generated around the disputed islands; (3) the overlaps between the contiguous zone generated around the disputed islands and the EEZ generated by the mainland territories of Brunei, Malaysia, the Philippines and Vietnam; (4) the overlaps between an EEZ derived from a mainland territory and a continental shelf based upon another mainland territory; and (5) the potential disputed areas of the extended continental shelf.[22] Accordingly, the size of disputed marine area according to the alternative approach is smaller than that according to the areas of overlapping claims approach.[23] Moreover, it is difficult to know exactly how large or small the high seas remain in the Spratly Islands area. Nevertheless, this region, as part of a semi-enclosed sea primarily covered by the EEZs of surrounding countries, only has a part remaining susceptible to the status of high seas (which approximates the orange zone indicated in Map 3). This remaining part is further covered by the territorial sea and contiguous zone generated around the disputed islands.

Neither the areas of overlapping claims approach taking into account all claims nor the alternative approach excluding unreasonable claims would obtain unanimous support from these States.[24] On the one hand, a considerable drawback of the areas of overlapping claims approach is that States with a stronger claim would be reluctant to accept this approach. On the other hand, excluding unreasonable claims probably would not prevent States from undertaking unilateral conduct in areas over which they assert such unreasonable claims. The main difference between these two approaches is that the former encompasses a larger disputed marine area than the latter. A larger disputed marine area is, arguably, more apt for attaining the peaceful coexistence of the claimants in the region, as it imposes constraints on unilateral State conduct in broader areas prior to delimitation. Following this approach, the geographical extent of disputed marine areas basically amounts to the entire Spratly Islands

21 The South China Sea Arbitration (The Philippines v. China), Award of 12 July 2016 (PCA), paras.278 and 646.

22 See chapter 3, section 3.3.2.4.

23 See a comparison of Maps 2 and 3, or Table 7.

24 See chapter 3, section 3.3.

area. Accordingly, the disputant States shall observe specific international obligations as outlined in chapter 4 when behaving unilaterally in this region.

9.3 Permissible Scope for Unilateralism: Hydrocarbon-Related, Fisheries-Related and Law Enforcement Conduct

The UNCLOS regulatory framework is inadequate in determining the permissible scope for unilateralism under international law within the disputed marine areas in the Spratly Islands area, owing to the limited applicable scope and vagueness in the substantive content of relevant provisions, especially Articles 15, 74(3) and 83(3).[25] To remedy the limitation in applicable scope, it is recommended to implement Articles 74(3) and 83(3) of UNCLOS as a unified regulatory standard across the Spratly Islands area, regardless of the different categories of disputed marine areas. To remedy the vagueness in the substantive content of Articles 74(3) and 83(3), their interpretation and application to the Spratly Islands setting can take into account other UNCLOS provisions, especially Part XII concerning environmental protection, and relevant general principles in customary international law, pursuant to the interpretation rules of Article 31(2) and (3)(c) of VCLT. Accordingly, the permissible scope for different types of unilateral acts in the Spratly Islands setting has been clarified as follows.

First, the obligation 'not to jeopardize or hamper delimitation' under Articles 74(3) and 83(3) of UNCLOS reflects a delicate balance between ensuring a party's ability to pursue economic development and preventing irreparable harm to another party's rights and is thus not meant to suspend all economic activities.[26] A review of relevant international jurisprudence suggests that the 'permanent physical change to the marine environment' test is the review standard for assessing the lawfulness of the unilateral hydrocarbon-related conduct that occurs within the Spratly Islands area preceding delimitation.[27] Accordingly, extracting oil or gas reserves, including exploitation and exploratory drilling, is prohibited, as such extraction activities would cause permanent physical change to the marine environment. By contrast, seismic surveys, to the extent of not causing irreversible harm to marine life, are permissible provided that the information related to marine natural resources collected through seismic

25 See chapter 4, section 4.2.
26 UNCLOS, Articles 74(3) and 83(3).
27 Guyana v. Suriname, Arbitral Award dated 17 September 2007 (PCA), para.470. Aegean Sea Continental Shelf (Greece v. Turkey), Order of 11 September 1976, Request for the Indication of Interim Measures of Protection (ICJ), para.30.

surveys is communicated and made available to other disputant States.[28] The mere issuance or declaration of oil blocks without further action is unlikely to cause a permanent physical change to the marine environment directly and thus is permissible under international law. This conclusion is also an inevitable result if seismic surveys are deemed lawful within contested waters, as in regular practice, States would need to designate oil lease blocks and grant concessions before seismic surveys can actually take place.

Second, under a general constraint set by a due diligence obligation in relation to environmental protection under Part XII of UNCLOS, the disputant States shall not engage in direct exploitation of depleted, threatened or endangered species or any activities that may indirectly destroy the habitats of such species.[29] Moreover, as a result of the *mutatis mutandis* application of the 'permanent physical change to the marine environment' test, harmful fishing practices, such as degrading habitats of important species and destroying the structure of seabed and subsoils by using explosives, are prohibited within the Spratly Islands area.[30] For non-harmful fishing, international jurisprudence indicates that they are generally permissible to the extent of not exceeding the current annual catch within the Spratly Islands area, unless the scientific evidence suggests otherwise.[31] Last but not least, traditional or artisanal fishing practices, if any, remain permissible across the whole Spratly Islands area.[32]

Third, the obligation 'not to jeopardize or hamper delimitation' under Articles 74(3) and 83(3) of UNCLOS also curtails how the disputant States can respond to another State's unilateral resources-related conduct. It is prudent to argue that there should be a *de minimis* threshold for a forcible act taken within a disputed marine area to be qualified as a threat or use of force under Article 2(4) of the UN Charter.[33] Thus, forcible acts taken by disputant States against a foreign vessel navigating within the Spratly Islands area falling below the *de minimis* threshold of the Article 2(4) prohibition are not generally prohibited and should, in principle, be seen as police enforcement. These forcible

---

28 See chapter 4, section 4.4.

29 UNCLOS, Part XII, especially Article 194.

30 See chapter 4, section 4.5.3.

31 Fisheries Jurisdiction (United Kingdom of Great Britain and Northern Ireland v. Iceland), Order of 17 August 1972, Provisional Measures (ICJ), para.26. Fisheries Jurisdiction (Federal Republic of Germany v. Iceland) – Provisional Measures, Order of 17 August 1972 (ICJ), para.27. Southern Bluefin Tuna Cases (New Zealand v. Japan; Australia v. Japan), Order of 27 August 1999, Provisional Measures (ITLOS), paras.81, 90(1)(c).

32 See chapter 4, sections 4.5.5–4.5.6.

33 See chapter 4, section 4.6.2.

acts, albeit likely to have the risk of intensifying conflicts, could be essential to the protection of the legitimate interests of disputant States in those areas, especially when the rescue through the compulsory dispute settlement mechanism as outlined in UNCLOS is unavailable in certain circumstances. Most law enforcement measures that have occurred in this region are taken unilaterally by coast guard administrations of the disputant States, and are thus less likely to trigger the application of Article 2(4).[34] Moreover, according to the principles applicable to law enforcement measures in general, a disputant State cannot take unilateral enforcement actions to halt another disputant State's fishing or seismic surveys, unless this State has a reasonable belief that the latter breaches its obligations under international law such as the obligation to protect and preserve the marine environment.[35]

9.4 Cooperation in Resource and Pollution Management: Substantive Norms and Cooperative Institutions

Chapters 5–8 deal with the cooperative management of hydrocarbon resources, fisheries and pollution. It is noted that the political climate developed after the delivery of the *South China Sea Arbitration* award has gradually generated momentum for cooperation in this region.[36] Meanwhile, the coexistence between the claimant States, roughly balanced through a strategic standoff between China and the US or any other external great powers, is not a viable means to sustain a peaceful environment for development in the Spratly Islands area. Rather, institutionalized cooperation, a more active form of coexistence which promotes shared prosperity through more organized international collaboration, is more apt for the Spratly Islands setting. Given the power differential between China and other disputant States, the purpose of institutionalized cooperation is to counterbalance the asymmetry of physical capacity through tempering the leading position of a big country like China by committing it to credible exercises of institutionalized restraints and to operate in compliance with agreed substantive norms, which, in turn, reduces fears from weaker States about the abuse of growing resource powers by that big power. A paradigm shift from the balance of power to institutionalized

34 See chapter 4, sections 4.6.1, 4.6.2 and 4.6.4.
35 See chapter 4, sections 4.6.1, 4.6.3 and 4.6.4.
36 See chapter 5, section 5.3.3.

cooperation is thus needed in the foreign policies that the disputant States apply respecting the Spratly Islands area.[37]

International law provides limited guidance in regulating resource and pollution management. First, international law falls short of regulating offshore hydrocarbon activities by only touching upon a narrow range of environmental issue associated with such activities.[38] Second, the fisheries regulatory framework incumbent on the disputant States is characterized by and suffering from a piecemeal management approach, the lack of a general obligation to apply the precautionary approach to all aspects of fisheries, and inadequate ecosystem concerns.[39] Third, most instruments in relation to pollution from shipping and dumping are not ratified by or do not bind upon all the disputant States, such as BWM, AFS, CODES, IMO resolution A.868(20), London Convention and London Protocol.[40]

International law, nevertheless, contains certain adaptive mechanisms that can interpret, apply or develop relevant substantive norms according to changing contexts, without reliance on the political will of individual States. One of such mechanisms is through the rules of reference as outlined in UNCLOS. The rules of reference entail a general legal duty to respect and apply specific international rules and standards adopted by competent international organizations or diplomatic conferences that come to be 'generally accepted' or 'applicable'.[41] The rules of reference contained in UNCLOS include: (1) Article 208 in relation to hydrocarbon resource management, (2) Article 61(3) in relation to fisheries, and (3) Articles 21(2), 211(2) & (5) and 216 in relation to pollution.[42] Another adaptive mechanism is through systemic integration under Article 31(3)(c) of VCLT. For example, as concluded in chapter 7, by virtue of Article 31(3)(c), the approaches or principles of precaution, ecosystem, integrated management and sustainable development as identified in CCRF and the 2030 Agenda for Sustainable Development can guide the fisheries management process, through informing the interpretation and application of other primary norms of international law with direct binding force upon the claimant States, notably those in UNCLOS, CBD and CITES.[43]

---

37 See chapter 5, section 5.4.

38 See chapter 6, section 6.2.

39 See chapter 7, section 7.3.

40 See chapter 8, section 8.3.

41 T. Treves, The Law of the Sea' System' of Institutions, 2 *Max Planck Yearbook of United Nations Law* (1998), 327.

42 See chapter 6, sections 6.2.1.3 and 6.2.1.4; chapter 7, section 7.3.8.2; chapter 8, sections 8.3.2 and 8.3.3.

43 See chapter 7, section 7.3.8.3.

Turning to cooperative institutions, international law obliges the disputant States to negotiate with a view to reaching cooperative arrangements, but does not prescribe the outcome of the negotiation or the substantive content of such arrangements.[44] Therefore, the selection of cooperative institutions is entirely up to the disputant States. A comparison of the analyses in chapters 6–8 suggests that cooperative arrangements for the resource and pollution management require varying degrees of institutionalization, from a simple legally binding instrument to regular intergovernmental meetings to permanent intergovernmental institutions. The more complex the regulatory problems, the more the achievement of a cooperative arrangement becomes dependent on the working of the cooperative institution.[45]

First, compared with the management of fisheries and pollution that have the status of commons, hydrocarbon resources management has received relatively less available guidance under international law.[46] The inertia to develop unified international standards is probably because offshore hydrocarbon activities in a specific location are often perceived as commercial activities in the hands of a limited number of countries, and their management is often 'precisely determined by agreement among the parties concerned in the light of special circumstances'.[47] Thus, the disputant States are recommended to adopt a cooperative institution with a high degree of institutionalization, namely a joint authority with the formalized decision-making process and administrative functions.[48]

Second, the disputant States are recommended to establish a joint commission to adopt fisheries management measures including the setting of the TAC, and exercise the flag State enforcement jurisdiction to implement such measures against their vessels that fish within the Spratly Islands area.[49]

Third, as to pollution management, hosting regular ministerial meetings or establishing an intergovernmental commission to unify the content of their national anti-pollution legislation respecting the Spratly Islands area would suffice to remedy the problem of concurrent prescriptive jurisdiction.[50] To remedy the problem of concurrent enforcement jurisdiction, the disputant

---

44 UNCLOS, Articles 74(3), 83(3) and 123.
45 See chapter 5, section 5.4.
46 See chapter 6, section 6.2; chapter 7, section 7.3; chapter 8, section 8.3.
47 Third United Nations Conference on the Law of the Sea, Official Records, Vol. II (1973–1982), 275–276, para.32.
48 See chapter 6, section 6.3.2.
49 See chapter 7, section 7.4.4.
50 See chapter 8, sections 8.4.1 and 8.4.3.

States are recommended to enter into a legally binding agreement that specifies the allocation of enforcement jurisdiction among the States concerned.[51]

Overall, cooperation is and will continue to be the key element to the management of the Spratly Islands area, although it will be the consequence of political and economic drives rather than a legal one. As mentioned in the introductory chapter, this book seeks to provide legal solutions to the problems arising from the absence of maritime boundaries in the Spratly Islands area. For this purpose, it has delved into a broad historical trajectory of international law, from the customary rule of discovery of *terra nullius* relating to territorial acquisition developed in the 15th century, to the law of the sea conventions relating to the allocation of maritime entitlements adopted in the 20th century, and further to the 2030 Agenda for Sustainable Development in the 21st century. The main findings as concluded in sections 9.1–9.4 reveal that international law does, on the one hand, provide useful guidance in addressing the underlying territorial dispute, identifying the disputed marine areas, regulating unilateral conduct, and promoting cooperation in resource and pollution management respecting the Spratly Islands area, but on the other hand, has its limitations.

The most significant limitation is that international law cannot and does not provide for the compulsory settlement of the complex territorial and maritime disputes respecting the Spratly Islands area, and that it does not mandate the outcome, modalities, scope or locations in respect of cooperation but leaves it to be agreed upon by the parties concerned prior to actual implementation. Thus, the peaceful coexistence of the disputant States and sustainable development of the region remain reliant on whether the disputant States are willing to make concessions in good faith and facilitate collaboration. It is beyond doubt that proactive cooperation in broader areas and at a greater depth between or among the disputant States will benefit the development of the region from a long-term perspective. In light of this, the recommendations proposed in this book advocate a blueprint of joint cooperation that can be undertaken at a relatively low level of efforts or changes by making use of international instruments or cooperative institutions that are available under current international law as much as possible. The fact that cooperation will be the consequence of political and economic drives rather than a legal one would not diminish its role, as its outcomes – cooperative institutions established on the basis of legally binding agreements – would offer the

51 See chapter 8, sections 8.4.2 and 8.4.3.

indispensable legal assurance as required by the disputant States and other stakeholders concerned.

It should also be noted that the varying cooperative institutions proposed for resource and pollution management in chapters 6–8 do not amount to the endorsement of a piecemeal approach to the management of the Spratly Islands area. Rather, it is recommended to incorporate such cooperative institutions into an overall institution, where the Arctic and Antarctica models can provide prominent solutions for negotiation. An analogy can be made to the Arctic Council,[52] which establishes, oversees and coordinates the work of subordinate working groups for collaboration on specific topics.[53] To that effect, the cooperative institutions for resource and pollution management in the Spratly Islands can be incorporated as separate working groups, subordinate to the minister-level meeting of claimant States with decision-making and negotiations functions and senior officials appointed by claimant States in charge of daily operation (Figure 1). A secretariat can be established to provide administrative support to senior officials and working groups, and other countries, non-State actors and other stakeholders (e.g. Taiwan) can be involved as observers to primarily contribute through their consultation rights in connection with negotiation and decisions and also through their engagement at the level of working groups.[54] In contrast to the model of the Arctic Council being a soft-law regime and an advisory body that lacks the power to create legally binding documents,[55] an alternative is to use a binding treaty system in the Spratly Islands similar to the Antarctica model, which includes the 1959 Antarctica treaty as the core together with other multilateral or bilateral legal instruments.[56] The proposed treaty system can consist of a core treaty providing a comprehensive framework for cooperation, together with protocols to the core treaty or other separate treaties with a focus on resources and pollution management (Figure 2). In a similar vein, observers can be engaged in the treaty system to provide information or advice.

52 Z. Gao, Review and Prospect of the Security Cooperation Mechanisms in the South China Sea (in Chinese), 1 *Boundary and Ocean Studies* (2016), 8.

53 Declaration on the Establishment of the Arctic Council, adopted 19 September 1996, Article 1.

54 Arctic Council Secretariat, *The Arctic Council: A Quick Guide* (2nd ed. 2020). T. Barry *et al.*, The Arctic Council: An Agent of Change?, 63 *Global Environmental Change* (2020), 3.

55 E. Lennon, A Tale of Two Poles: A Comparative Look at The Legal Regimes in The Arctic And The Antarctic, 8(3) *Sustainable Development Law & Policy* (2008), 33.

56 A.H. McCarthy, Antarctica: The Final Frontier for Marine Biological Invasions, 25 *Global Change Biology* (2019), 2233–2234.

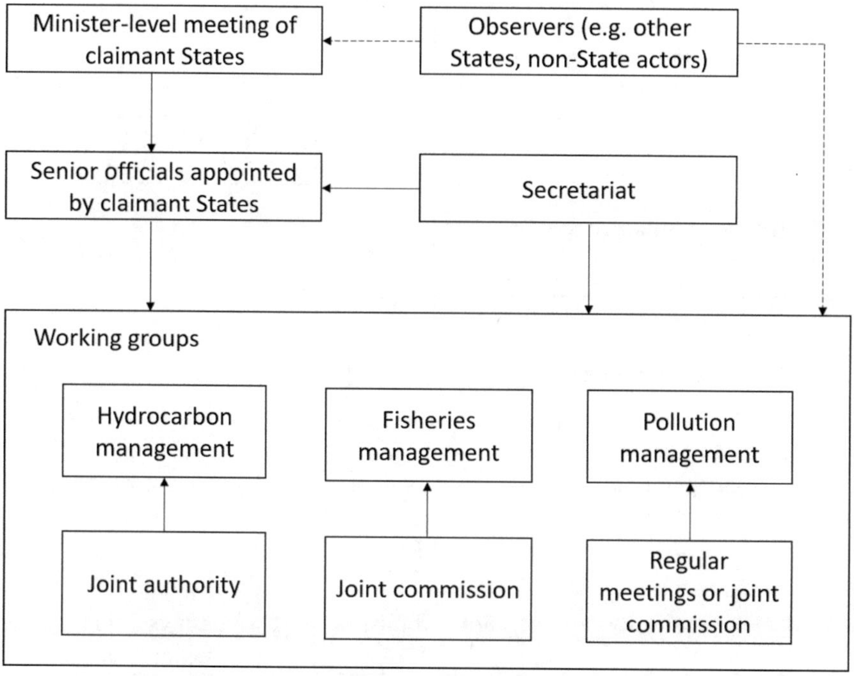

FIGURE 1 The proposed structure to integrate resources and pollution management in the Spratly Islands area according to the Arctic model

9.5 Reflections on Functions and Limitations of International Law

Lastly, the author would like to reflect on the functions and limitations of international law in the management of the Spratly Islands area prior to delimitation.

First, the functions of international law in managing the Spratly Islands area can be achieved through the interaction between its substantive and procedural elements. The substantive element denotes norms including both principles and rules with binding force and other non-binding normative expectations of conduct, according to which marine natural resources and pollution should be managed. The procedural element refers to institutions and mechanisms for maintaining order, resolving disputes and considering, applying or otherwise revisiting substantive norms.[57] Such institutions and

57 S. Huntington, *Political Order in Changing Societies* (Yale University Press. 1973), 8–9.

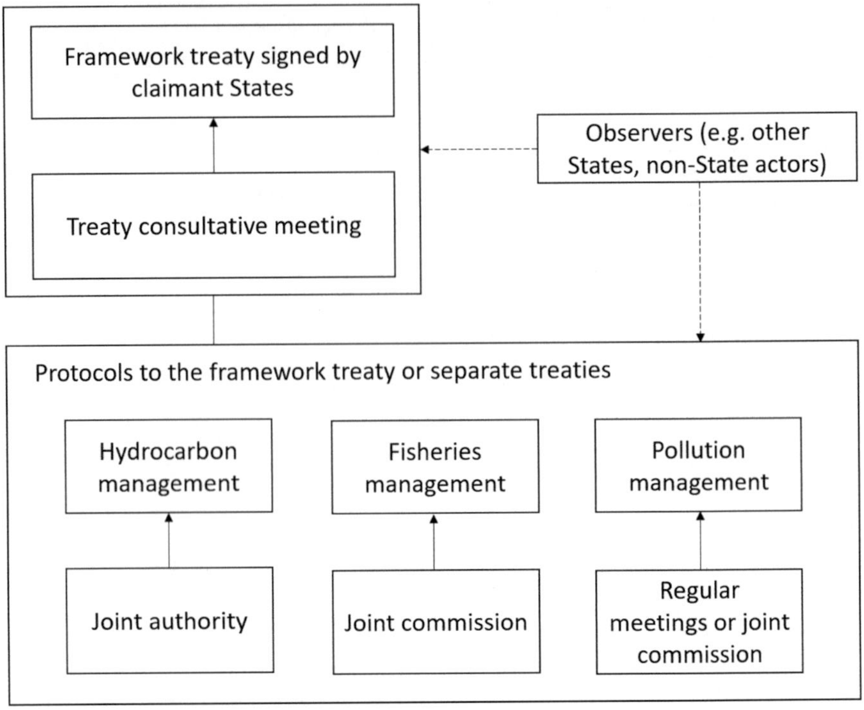

FIGURE 2 The proposed structure to integrate resources and pollution management in the Spratly Islands area according to the Antarctica model

mechanisms can take diverse forms with varying degrees of institutionalization, from a simple legally binding instrument to regular intergovernmental meetings to permanent intergovernmental institutions. The substance-procedure duality is hardly a novelty in international law.[58] More than 60 years ago, Kelsen already recognized this duality 'in deriving the law's validity from a dynamic and a static principle – the former relating to the processes whereby law establishes competences, the latter relating to the ascertainment of existing law' content'.[59] In the 2010 *Pulp Mills* Judgment, the ICJ also confirmed the complementary relationship between substantive norms and cooperative

58 M. Koskenniemi, *From Apology to Utopia: The Structure of International Legal Argument* (CUP. 2007), 20.

59 *Ibid.*, 20, fn.9. See H. Kelsen, *Principles of International Law* (Rinehart. 1952), 409–411.

institutions in achieving the objective of realizing common interests through cooperation.[60]

The substance-procedure duality is playing an increasingly important role in the management of the Spratly Islands area, owing to the recent changes in the structure of the international relations between the disputant States. As pointed out in chapter 5, the power differential between China and the other disputant States prompted the latter to draw on external powers, particularly the US, to balance against China between 2009 and 2016.[61] The balance of power, by its nature, remains within the paradigm described by Friedmann as diplomacy of 'coexistence', which refers to 'the conduct of international relations on the basis of national power'.[62] However, with the decline of confidence in the US defense shield and economic alliance since 2017, the tide of domestic politics of the claimant ASEAN States has now turned in favor of cooperation with China for joint development of hydrocarbon resources in the Spratly Islands area.[63] This change calls for a paradigm shift from the balance of power to institutionalized cooperation, which promotes shared prosperity through more organized international collaboration.[64] Thus, the law of cooperation, which seeks to pursue the realization of common interests shared by sovereign States through cooperation,[65] will play a cardinal role in the Spratly Islands setting.

Unlike the law of existence which mainly consists of prohibitive rules to restrain States from conducting activities that could aggravate the dispute and finally lead to armed conflicts,[66] the law of cooperation relies not only on substantive norms but also on institutions. The relationship between 'cooperation' and 'institution' can be best described using Pinto's words that '[c]o-operation would seem to reach its most developed expression in the establishment by the parties of institutions through which regular contact could be maintained, co-operative action can be monitored and supervised and, perhaps,

60 Pulp Mills on the River Uruguay (Argentina v. Uruguay), Judgment of 20 April 2010 (ICJ), paras.75, 77.

61 For discussions on the balance-of-power theory, see *e.g.*, W.H. Riker, *The Theory of Political Coalitions* (Yale University Press. 1962), 161; O. Niou *et al.*, *The Balance of Power: Stability in International Systems* (CUP. 1989), 21; M. Sheehan, *The Balance of Power: History & Theory* (Routledge. 1996).

62 W. Friedmann, *The Changing Structure of International Law* (Columbia University Press. 1964), 14.

63 See chapter 5, section 5.3.3.

64 See chapter 5, section 5.4.

65 Friedmann, n 62, 58–59.

66 *Ibid.*, 89.

new co-operative initiatives proposed, adopted and implemented'.[67] This observation applies to the Spratly Islands setting. Given the power differential between China and other disputant States, institutionalized cooperation can counterbalance the asymmetry of physical capacity through tempering the leading position of a big country like China by committing it to credible exercises of institutionalized restraints and to operate in compliance with agreed substantive norms, which, in turn, reduces fears from weaker States about the abuse of growing resource powers by that big power.

Second, as concluded in chapters 2–7, the role of international law in managing the Spratly Islands area is subject to limitations resulting from the classic 'territoriality' model of jurisdiction. The essence of the successful management of the Spratly Islands area preceding delimitation is to allocate jurisdictional rights and duties respecting the disputed islands and waters in a way that is acceptable to all the disputant States. Both the law of territory and the law of the sea, two main bodies of international law discussed in this book, are primarily constructed on the basis of the territoriality principle, which is the 'most basic principle of jurisdiction in international law' and characterized by exclusiveness in the sense that for a particular territory, only one State can hold a territorial title.[68] Under the territoriality principle, the factual links between particular conduct and a given spatial location, or between the effects of that conduct and a given spatial location, determine a sovereign State's jurisdiction or authority over the conduct.[69] The territoriality principle captures the triangular relationship of three elements: spatial location (land or sea), sovereignty, and jurisdiction.[70] Sovereignty is defined by reference to a particular spatial extent. Jurisdiction is 'an aspect of sovereignty', coextensive with and limited by sovereignty.[71]

The 'territoriality' model of jurisdiction is self-evident in the law of territory in the sense that a sovereign independent State 'should possess jurisdiction

67 M.C.W. Pinto, The Duty of Co-operation and the United Nations Convention on the Law of the Sea, in A. Bos and H. Siblesz (eds.), *Realism in Law-making: Essays on International Law in Honour of Willem Riphagen* (Martinus Nijhoff Publishers. 1986), 154.

68 C. Ryngaert, *Jurisdiction in International Law* (OUP 2nd ed. 2015), 49.

69 H.L. Buxbaum, Territory, Territoriality, and the Resolution of Jurisdictional Conflict, 57 *American Journal of Comparative Law* (2009), 632. G. Kegel and I. Seidl-Hohenveldern, On the Territoriality Principle in Public International Law, 5(2) *Hastings International and Comparative Law Review* (1982), 249.

70 Buxbaum, n 69, 632.

71 F.A. Mann, *The Doctrine of Jurisdiction in International Law* (Brill|Nijhoff. 1964) (Collected Courses of the Hague Academy of International Law, Volume 111), 30, quoted in: Buxbaum, n 69, 632.

over all persons and things within its territorial limits and in all cases, civil and criminal, arising within these limits'.[72] The territoriality principle has also shaped the law of the sea in two significant ways. On the one hand, the sea is closely tied to the land according to the legal principle of '*la terre domine la mer*', whereby a State can only claim maritime entitlements over specific marine areas when it enjoys territorial sovereignty over certain land territories.[73] On the other hand, the modern international law of the sea uses the zone-based approach as a predominant tool to manage the ocean, according to which the jurisdictional rights and obligations of a sovereign State over a specific marine area are determined based on the distance of that area from its coast.[74] As commented by Mann, the territoriality principle 'seems to establish a satisfactory regime for the whole world' by dividing the world into 'compartments within each of which a sovereign State has jurisdiction'.[75]

However, in the Spratly Islands setting, the classical 'territoriality' model of jurisdiction, which relies on spatial connections in determining the scope of a sovereign State's regulatory power, has been called into question. The limitations of the law of territory and the law of the sea in untangling the overlapping jurisdictions alleged by the disputant States are largely due to the uncertainty and indeterminacy of the spatial extent of the sovereignty resulting from the underlying territorial and maritime disputes in this region. Such limitations require us to think outside the box and to break the constraints posed by the strict application of the classical 'territoriality' model of jurisdiction, which Berman has criticized for amounting to 'motionless demarcations frozen in time and space'.[76] Rather, as suggested by Ong, where a maritime boundary has been delimited or where it is absent are two different phases on the 'time-space continuum'.[77] Accordingly, two alternative approaches have been proposed in the preceding chapters. Firstly, in terms of breaking the constraints on 'space', the disputant States are recommended to move away from the use of jurisdictional zones as the frame of reference when managing the resources and pollution in Spratly Islands area but to regard this region as an integrated

---

72 This statement is made by Lord Macmillan, quoted in: Buxbaum, n 69, 632.

73 North Sea Continental Shelf, n 1, para.96. Van Bijnkershoek, n 1, 43.

74 Y. Tanaka, *The International Law of the Sea* (CUP 3rd ed. 2019), 4. Y. Tanaka, Zonal and Integrated Management Approaches to Ocean Governance: Reflections on a Dual Approach in International Law of the Sea, 19 *IJMCL* (2004), 484.

75 Mann, n 71, 30, quoted in: Buxbaum, n 69, 632.

76 P.S. Berman, The Globalization of Jurisdiction, 151(2) *University of Pennsylvania Law Review* (2002), 322.

77 D. Ong, Joint Development of Common Offshore Oil and Gas Deposits: 'Mere' State Practice or Customary International Law?, 93(4) *AJIL* (1999), 783.

whole for the purpose of management.[78] Secondly, in terms of breaking the constraints on 'time', built on Ong's 'time-space continuum', van Logchem argued that 'it seems more prudent to approach the period before and after delimitation in terms of degrees rather than absolutes', since these two phases fall on the same continuum after all.[79] Agreeing with Ong and van Logchem, this book suggests that certain rules and principles that apply to undisputed marine areas can, arguably, apply with equal force to disputed marine areas.[80]

In short, this book seeks to provide a balanced perspective on the functions and limitations of international law in the management of the Spratly Islands area prior to delimitation. Criticizing the limitations of international law without appreciating its functions would amount to throwing out the baby with the bathwater. The implementation of the remedies to limitations, indeed, is reliant on the functions of international law through the adoption or revision of substantive norms via certain cooperative institutions to be established based on the agreement of the disputant States. The dynamics of international law functioning through the substance-procedure duality will continue to play an important role in the management of the Spratly Islands area.

78 See *e.g.*, chapter 4, section 4.2.4.1 (regulating unilateral State conduct); chapter 7, section 7.3.8.4 (promoting cooperation in fisheries management); chapter 8, section 8.5.3 (promoting cooperation in pollution management).

79 Y. van Logchem, *Disputed Maritime Areas: The Rights and Obligations of States under International Law* (PhD Dissertation, Utrecht University, defended on 8 January 2019), 317.

80 See *e.g.*, chapter 4, section 4.3 (general principles), section 4.6.2 (principle of prohibition of threat or use of force), section 4.6.3 (principles applicable to law enforcement measures in general); chapter 6, section 6.2.1 (Articles 194, 204, 205, 206 and 208 of UNCLOS); chapter 7, section 7.3 (substantive norms on fisheries management); chapter 8, section 8.4 (substantive norms on pollution management), section 8.5.1 (juridical allocation of prescriptive jurisdiction), section 8.5.2 (juridical allocation of enforcement jurisdiction).

Selected Bibliography

Official Documents and Reports

UN Documents and Resolutions

UN Doc.: A/6230, Report of the 1966 Special Committee on Principles of International law concerning Friendly Relations and Co-operation among States (27 June 1966).

UN Doc.: A/6799, Report of the 1966 Special Committee on Principles of International law concerning Friendly Relations and Co-operation among States (26 September 1967).

UN Doc.: A/CONF.13/C.1/SR.56-60, Summary Records of the 60th Meeting of 22 April 1958.

UN Doc.: A/CONF.13/C.2/L.49, United Kingdom of Great Britain and Northern Ireland: Proposal relating to Article 34, United Nations Conference on the Law of the Sea (24 February to 27 April 1958).

UN Doc.: A/CONF.13/C.2/L.114, Netherlands and United Kingdom of Great Britain and Northern Ireland: Proposal, United Nations Conference on the Law of the Sea (24 February to 27 April 1958).

UN Doc.: A/CONF.62/29, Organization of the second session of the Conference and allocation of items: decisions taken by the Conference at its 15th meeting on 21 June 1974, UNCLOS III (1974).

UN Doc.: A/CONF.62/C.2/L.43, Ireland: draft article on delimitation of areas of continental shelf between neighbouring States (6 August 1974).

UN Doc.: A/CONF.62/L.8/Rev.1, Working Paper of the Second Committee: Main Trends (17 October 1974), UNCLOS III, Official Records, Vol. 3.

UN Doc.: A/CONF.62/RCNG/2, Reports of the Committees and Negotiating Groups on negotiations at the resumed seventh session contained in a single document both for the purposes of record and for the convenience of delegations (1978).

UN Doc.: A/CONF.62/61, Report of the General Committee on the organization of the work of the seventh session (11 April 1978).

UN Doc.: A/CONF.62/SR.108, Summary Records of 108th Plenary Meeting (15 September 1978).

UN Doc.: A/CONF.62/SR.126, Summary Records of 126th Plenary Meeting (2 April 1980).

UN Doc.: A/CONF.62/SR.162, Summary Records of 162nd plenary Meeting (31 March 1982).

UN Doc.: A/CONF.62/C.2/SR.38, Summary Records of Meetings of the Second Committee 38th Meeting (10 December 1982).

UN Doc.: A/CONF.144/28/REV.1, Basic Principles on the Use of Force and Firearms by Law Enforcement Officials, adopted by the Eighth United Nations Congress on the Prevention of Crime and the Treatment of Offenders (27 August to 7 September 1990).

UN Doc.: A/CONF.151/26 (Vol. I), Rio Declaration on Environment and Development (12 August 1992).

UN Doc.: A/CONF.151/26 (Vol. II), Report on the United Nations Conference on Environment and Development, Agenda 21 (13 August 1992).

UN Doc.: A/CONF.164/L.22, Comments on Precautionary Management of Fisheries, submitted by Sweden (22 July 1993).

UN Doc.: A/CONF.164/L.41, The Precautionary Approach in Fishery Management, submitted by Ukraine (17 March 1994).

UN Doc.: A/RES/2625(XXV), Declaration on Principles of International Law concerning Friendly Relations and Co-operation among States (24 October 1970).

UN Doc.: A/RES/34/169, Commentary on Article 3, Code of Conduct for Law Enforcement Officials (17 December 1979).

UN Doc.: A/RES/37/10, Peaceful Settlement of Disputes between States (15 November 1982).

UN Doc.: A/RES/42/187, Report of the World Commission on Environment and Development (11 December 1987).

UN Doc.: A/RES/46/215, Large-scale Pelagic Drift-net Fishing and Its Impact on the Living Marine Resources of the World's Oceans and Seas (20 December 1991).

UN Doc.: A/RES/47/192, United Nations Conference on Straddling Fish Stocks and Highly Migratory Fish Stocks (22 December 1992).

UN Doc.: A/RES/56/83, ILC Articles on Responsibility of States for Internationally Wrongful Acts (28 January 2002).

UN Doc.: A/RES/70/1, Transforming Our World: the 2030 Agenda for Sustainable Development (25 September 2015).

UN Doc.: A/RES/71/312, Our Ocean, Our Future: Call for Action (6 July 2017).

UN Doc.: A/RES/71/313, Work of the Statistical Commission pertaining to the 2030 Agenda for Sustainable Development (10 July 2017).

Inter-state Non-binding Instruments

China and Malaysia, Joint Statement on the Framework for Future Bilateral Cooperation (31 May 1999).

China and Malaysia, Joint Statement (29 May 2004).

China and Malaysia, Joint Statement on the 40th Anniversary of the Establishment of Diplomatic Relations (1 June 2014).

China and Malaysia, Joint Statement (3 November 2016).

China and Philippines, Agreed Minutes on the First Philippines-China Bilateral Consultations on the South China Sea Issue (10 August 1995).

China and Philippines, Joint Statement: Philippine-China Experts Group Meeting on Confidence Building Measures (23 March 1999).

China and Philippines, Joint Statement: Framework of Bilateral Cooperation in the Twenty-First Century (16 May 2000).

China and Philippines, Joint Statement: 3rd Philippines-China Experts' Group Meeting on Confidence-Building Measures (4 April 2001).

China and Philippines, Joint Press Statement on the State Visit of H.E. President Gloria Macapagal-Arroyo to the People's Republic of China, 1-3 September 2004 (3 September 2004).

China and Philippines, Joint Statement (1 September 2011).

China and Philippines, Joint Statement (21 October 2016).

China and Philippines, Memorandum of Understanding on Cooperation on Oil and Gas Development (20 November 2018).

China and Vietnam, Agreement on Basic Principles Guiding Resolution of Maritime Issues (11 October 2011).

China and Vietnam, Joint Statement (15 October 2013).

CLCS Submissions and Related Note Verbales

Brunei, Preliminary Submission concerning the Outer Limits of its Continental Shelf (12 May 2009).

China, Note Verbale No. CML/17/2009 (7 May 2009).

China, Note Verbale No. CML/8/2011 (14 April 2011).

China, Note Verbale No. CML/42/2020 (17 April 2020).

China, Submission on the Outer Limits of the Continental Shelf in Part of the East China Sea (14 December 2012).

Malaysia and Vietnam, Joint Submission to the CLCS pursuant to Article 76, paragraph 8 of the United Nations Convention on the Law of the Sea 1982 in respect of the southern part of the South China Sea (7 May 2009).

Malaysia, Note Verbale No. HA/24/09 (20 May 2009).

Malaysia, Note Verbale No. HA/41/09 (21 August 2009).

Malaysia, Partial Submission to the Commission on the Limits of the Continental Shelf pursuant to Article 76, paragraph 8 of the United Nations Convention on the Law of the Sea 1982 in the South China Sea (12 December 2019).

Philippines, A Partial Submission of Data and Information on the Outer Limits of the Continental Shelf in Benham Rise Region (8 April 2009).

Philippines, Note Verbale No. 000819 (4 August 2009).

Philippines, Note Verbale No. 000228 (5 April 2011).

Vietnam, Outer Limits of the Continental Shelf beyond 200 nautical miles in respect of the North Area (VNM-N) (7 May 2009).

Vietnam, Note Verbale No. 86/HC-2009 (8 May 2009).

Vietnam, Note Verbale No. 22/HC-2020 (30 March 2020).

National Legislation and Official Documents

Brunei, Declaration on the Exclusive Economic Zone (1993).

China, Regulations on the Organization of the Office of the Chief Executive of the Hainan Special District (6 June 1949).

China, Declaration on China's Territorial Sea (1958).

China, Regulation on the Exploitation of Offshore Petroleum Resources in Cooperation with Foreign Enterprises (issued 30 January 1982, entered into force 30 January 1982, amended 18 July 2013).

China, Law on the Territorial Sea and the Contiguous Zone (25 February 1992).

China, Law on the Exclusive Economic Zone and the Continental Shelf (26 June 1998).

China, Announcement on the 2012 Summer Ban on Marine Fishing in the South China Sea Maritime Space (10 May 2012).

China, Statement on the Territorial Sea Baselines for Diaoyu Dao and Its Affiliated Islands (10 September 2012).

China, White Paper: China Adheres to the Position of Settling Through Negotiation the Relevant Disputes Between China and the Philippines in the South China Sea (13 July 2016).

Malaysia, Continental Shelf Act (1966).

Malaysia, Proclamation of the Economic Zone (1978).

Malaysia, Exclusive Economic Zone Act (1984).

Malaysia, Declaration upon the Ratification of UNCLOS (14 October 1996).

Philippines, Petroleum Act, Republic Act 387 (1949).

Philippines, Presidential Proclamation No. 370 Declaring as Subject to the Jurisdiction and Control of the Republic of the Philippines all Mineral and other Natural Resources in the Continental Shelf (1968).

Philippines, Presidential Decree No. 1596 (11 June 1978).

Philippines, Presidential Decree No. 1599 establishing an Exclusive Economic Zone and for other purposes (11 June 1978).

Philippines, Constitution (1987).

Philippines, Republic Act No. 9522 (10 March 2009).

Vietnam, White Paper on Hoang Sa (Paracel) and Truong Sa (Spratly) Islands (1975).

Vietnam, Statement on the Territorial Sea, the Contiguous Zone, the Exclusive Economic Zone and the Continental Shelf (12 May 1977).

Vietnam, Petroleum Law (issued 6 July 1993, entered into force 1 September 1993).

Vietnam, the Law of the Sea of Viet Nam (21 June 2012).

Other Documents, Resolutions and Reports

Arctic Council Secretariat, *The Arctic Council: A Quick Guide* (2nd ed. 2020).

ASEAN and China, Declaration on the Conduct of Parties in the South China Sea (2002).

ASEAN and China, Joint Statement of the Foreign Ministers of ASEAN Member States and China on the Full and Effective Implementation of the Declaration on the Conduct of Parties in the South China Sea (25 July 2016).

BIICL, *Report on the Obligations of States under Articles 74(3) and 83(3) of UNCLOS in respect of Undelimited Maritime Areas* (2016).

BIICL, *Report on the Use of Force in relation to Sovereignty Disputes over Land Territory* (2018).

Lord Collins of Mapesbury (Rapporteur), Provisional Measures, 78 *Annuaire de l'Institut de Droit international* (2017).

FAO, *A Fishery Manager's Guidebook* (2009).

FAO, Code of Conduct on Responsible Fisheries (1995).

FAO, *Securing Sustainable Small-scale Fisheries: Sharing Good Practices from around the World* (2019), FAO Fisheries and Aquaculture Technical Paper 644.

FAO Asia-Pacific Fishery Commission, *Regional Overview of Fisheries and Aquaculture in Asia and the Pacific* (2012), RAP Publication 2012/26.

IMO Resolution A.491(XII), Code of Safety for Nuclear Merchant Ships (19 November 1981).

IMO Resolution A.671(16), Safety Zones and Safety of Navigation around Offshore Installations and Structures (19 October 1989).

IMO Resolution A.672(16), IMO Guidelines and Standards for the Removal of Offshore Installations and Structures on the Continental Shelf and the Exclusive Economic Zone (19 October 1989).

IMO Resolution A.868(20), Guidelines for the Control and Management of Ships' Ballast Water to Minimize the Transfer of Harmful Aquatic Organisms and Pathogens (27 November 1997).

IMO Resolution A.1023(26), Code for the Construction and Equipment of Mobile Offshore Drilling Units (2 December 2009).

OES, Straight Baselines: The Faeroes, *Limits in the Seas* (12 March 1970).

OES, Straight Baselines: Svalbard, *Limits in the Seas* (6 March 1972).

OES, Straight Baselines: Ecuador, *Limits in the Seas* (23 May 1972).

OES, Straight Baselines Claim: China, *Limits in the Seas* (9 July 1996).

OES, China: Maritime Claims in the South China Sea, *Limits in the Seas* (5 December 2014).

UNDOALOS, The Law of the Sea: Obligations of States Parties under the United Nations Convention on the Law of the Sea and Complementary Instruments (2004).

UNEP, Land-based Pollution in the South China Sea, *UNEP/GEF/SCS Technical Publication No. 10* (2007).

Books

Andenas, M., *et al.* (eds.), *General Principles and the Coherence of International Law* (Brill|Nijhoff. 2019).

Bankes, N., and Trevisanut, S. (eds.), *Energy from the Sea: An International Law Perspective on Ocean Energy* (Brill|Nijhoff. 2015).

Becker-Weinberg, V., *Joint Development of Hydrocarbon Deposits in the Law of the Sea* (Springer. 2014).

Beckman, R., *et al.* (eds.), *Beyond Territorial Disputes in the South China Sea Legal Frameworks for the Joint Development of Hydrocarbon Resources* (Edward Elgar Publishing. 2013).

Birnie, P., *et al.*, *International Law and the Environment* (OUP. 2009).

Boyle, A. and Chinkin, C., *The Making of International Law* (OUP. 2007).

Burke, W.T., *The New International Law of Fisheries: UNCLOS 1982 and Beyond* (Clarendon Press. 1994).

Charney, J.I., and Alexander, L.M. (eds.), *International Maritime Boundaries* Vol. 2 (Martinus Nijhoff Publishers. 1993).

Chemillier-Gendreau, M., *Sovereignty Over the Paracel and Spratley Islands* (Springer. 2000).

Churchill, R.R. and Lowe, A.V, *The Law of the Sea* (MUP 3rd ed. 1999).

Corten, O., *The Law against War: the Prohibition on the Use of Force in Contemporary International Law* (Bloomsbury Publishing. 2010).

Crawford, J., *Brownlie's Principles of Public International Law* (OUP 9th ed. 2019).

De Visscher, Charles, *Theory and Reality in Public International Law* (Princeton University Press. 1957).

Dux, T. *Specially Protected Marine Areas in the Exclusive Economic Zone (EEZ): The Regime for the Protection of Specific Areas of the EEZ for Environmental Reasons Under International Law* (LIT Verlag Münster. 2011).

Dworkin, R., *Law's Empire* (Harvard University Press. 1986).

Dzurek, D.J., *The Spratly Islands Dispute: Who's on First?* (IBRU. 1996).

Fox, H., *et al.* (eds.), *Joint Development of Offshore Oil and Gas: A Model Agreement for States for Joint Development with Explanatory Commentary*, Vol. I (London: BIICL, 1989).

Fox, H., *et al.* (eds.), *Joint Development of Offshore Oil and Gas: A Model Agreement for States for Joint Development with Explanatory Commentary*, Vol. II (London: BIICL, 1990).

Friedmann, W., *The Changing Structure of International Law* (Columbia University Press. 1964).

Gerstl, A., and Strašáková, M., (eds.), *Unresolved Border, Land and Maritime Disputes in Southeast Asia: Bi- and Multilateral Conflict Resolution Approaches and ASEAN's Centrality* (Brill. 2017).

Guangdong Province Geographic Names Committee, *The Collection of the Geographic Names of the Islands in South China Sea* (*Nan Hai Zhu Dao Di Ming Zi Liao Hui Bian*) (in Chinese) (Guangdong Province Map Publishing House. 1987).

Haller-Trost, R., *The Brunei-Malaysia Dispute over Territorial and Maritime Claims in International Law* (IBRU. 1994).

Haller-Trost, R., *The Spratly Islands: A Study on the Limitations of International Law* (University of Kent, Centre of South-East Asian Studies. 1990).

Han, Z., *The Collection of the Historical Materials of the Islands in South China Sea* (*Wo Guo Nan Hai Zhu Dao Shi Liao Hui Bian*) (in Chinese) (Eastern Publishing House. 1988).

Hancox, D., *Secret Hydrographic Surveys in the Spratly Islands* (ASEAN Academic Press. 1999).

Harrison, J., *Making the Law of the Sea: A Study in the Development of International Law* (CUP. 2011).

Harrison, J., *Saving the Oceans through Law: the International Legal Framework for the Protection of the Marine Environment* (OUP. 2017).

Heinzig, D., *Disputed Islands in the South China Sea: Paracels, Spratlys, Pratas, Macclesfield Bank* (Otto Harrassowitz. 1976).

Hey, E. (ed.), *Developments in International Fisheries Law* (Kluwer Law International. 1999).

Hodgkin, H.T., *China in the Family of Nations* (George Allen & Unwin. 1923).

Hsü, I.C.Y., *China's Entrance into the Family of Nations: the Diplomatic Phase 1858–1880* (Harvard University Press. 1960).

Huntington, S., *Political Order in Changing Societies* (Yale University Press. 1973).

Jayakumar, S., *et al.* (eds.), *The South China Sea Arbitration: The Legal Dimension* (Edward Elgar Publishing. 2018).

Jenner, C.J. (ed.), *The South China Sea A Crucible of Regional Cooperation or Conflict-making Sovereignty Claims?* (CUP. 2016).

Jennings, R.Y., *The Acquisition of Territory in International Law* (MUP. 1963).

Kachel, M.J., *Particularly Sensitive Sea Areas: The IMO's Role in Protecting Vulnerable Marine Areas* (Springer. 2008).

Kaye, S.M., *International Fisheries Management* (Kluwer Law International. 2001).

Kim, S.P., *Maritime Delimitation and Interim Arrangements in North East Asia* (Martinus Nijhoff Publishers. 2004).

Kivimäki, T., *War or Peace in the South China Sea?* (NIAS. 2002).

Kohen, M.G. and Hébié, M., (eds.), *Research Handbook on Territorial Disputes in International Law* (Edward Elgar Publishing. 2018).

Kopela, S., *Dependent Archipelagos in the Law of the Sea* (Martinus Nijhoff Publishers. 2013).

Merkouris, P., *Article 31(3)(c) VCLT and the Principle of Systemic Integration: Normative Shadows in Plato's Cave* (Brill. 2015).

Merrills, J.G., *International Dispute Settlement* (CUP 6th ed. 2017).

Miller, R.J. and Ruru, J., *Discovering Indigenous Lands: The Doctrine of Discovery in the English Colonies* (Oxford Scholarship Online. 2010).

Miyoshi, M., *The Joint Development of Offshore Oil and Gas in Relation to Maritime Boundary Delimitation* (IBRU. 1999).

Nandan, S.N. and Rosenne, S. (eds.), *United Nations Convention on the Law of the Sea, 1982: A Commentary. Vol. 3: Articles 86 to 132 and Documentary Annexes* (Nijhoff. 1995).

Nordquist, M.H., *et al.* (eds.), *Legal Order in the World's Oceans: UN Convention on the Law of the Sea* (Brill|Nijhoff, 2017).

Nordquist, M.H., *et al., Recent Developments in the Law of the Sea and China* (Martinus Nijhoff Publishers. 2006).

Nordquist, M.H., *et al.* (eds.), *United Nations Convention on the Law of the Sea, 1982: A Commentary. Vol. 2: Articles 1 to 85, Annexes I and II, Final Act, Annex II* (Nijhoff. 1993).

Nordquist, M.H., *et al.* (eds.), *United Nations Convention on the Law of the Sea, 1982: A Commentary. Vol. 4: Articles 192 to 278, Final Act, Annex VI* (Nijhoff. 1991).

O'Brien, J.R., *South China Sea Oil: Two Problems of Ownership and Development* (ISEAS. 1977).

O'Connell, D.P., *The International Law of the Sea. Vol. II* (Clarendon Press. 1984).

Odgaard, L., *Maritime Security Between China and Southeast Asia: Conflict and Cooperation in the Making of Regional Order* (Ashgate. 2002).

Orrego Vicuña, F., *The Changing International Law of High Seas Fisheries* (CUP. 1999).

Oude Elferink, A.G., *et al.* (eds.), *Maritime Boundary Delimitation: The Case Law: Is it Consistent and Predictable?* (CUP. 2018).

Oude Elferink, A.G. (ed.), *Stability and Change in the Law of the Sea: The Role of the LOS Convention* (Martinus Nijhoff Publishers. 2005).

Qi, H., and Xue, S. (eds.), *Cooperative Development in the South China Sea: Policies, Obstacles, and Prospects* (Routledge. 2021).

Rothwell, D.R., and Letts, D. (eds.), *Law of the Sea in South East Asia: Environmental, Navigational and Security Challenges* (Routledge. 2019).

Samuels, M., *Contest for the South China Sea* (Taylor & Francis. 1982).

Schrijver, N., *Development Without Destruction: The UN and Global Resource Management* (Indiana University Press. 2010).

Schrijver, N., *Sovereignty over Natural Resources: Balancing Rights and Duties* (CUP. 1997).

Schrijver, N., *The Evolution of Sustainable Development in International Law: Inception, Meaning and Status* (Martinus Nijhoff Publishers. 2008).

Shaw, M.N., *International Law* (CUP. 8th ed. 2017).

Storey, I., and Lin, C.Y., (eds.), *The South China Sea Dispute: Navigating Diplomatic and Strategic Tensions* (Singapore: ISEAS Yusof Ishak Institute. 2016).

Sumaila, U.R., and Cheung, W.L., *Boom or Bust: The Future of Fish in the South China Sea* (2015).

Tanaka, Y., *The International Law of the Sea* (CUP 3rd ed. 2019).

Tanaka, Y., *The South China Sea Arbitration: Toward an International Legal Order in the Oceans* (Hart Publishing. 2019).

Tseng, H., *Rethinking South China Sea Disputes: The Untold Dimensions and Great Expectations* (Routledge. 2016).

Van Genugten, W.J.M., *et al.*, *Discover International Law: With Special Attention for the Hague, City of Peace and Justice* (Wolf Legal Publishers. 2017).

Van Logchem, Y. *Disputed Maritime Areas: The Rights and Obligations of States under International Law* (PhD Dissertation, Utrecht University, defended on 8 January 2019).

Whiteman, Marjorie Millace, *Digest of International Law, Vol. 3* (Department of State Publications. 1964).

Wu, S., and Nong, H. (eds.), *Recent Developments in the South China Sea Dispute: the Prospect of a Joint Development Regime* (Routledge. 2014).

Yahuda, M., *The International Politics of the Asia Pacific* (Routledge. 2011).

Zhang, Y., *China Politics and Geography Study on Oceans* (Science Publishing House. 2004).

Zou, K. (ed.), *Routledge Handbook of the South China Sea* (Routledge. 2021).

Zou, K., and Wu, S., (eds.), *Non-Traditional Security Issues and the South China Sea: Shaping a New Framework for Cooperation* (Routledge. 2014).

Zhou, W. and Tang, L., *Hainan Tianshu-Hainan Fishermen's Cultural Explanation of 'Geng Lu Bu'* (in Chinese) (Kunlun Publisher. 2015).

Book Chapters

Amer, R., and Li, J., From DOC to COC: A Regional Rules-based Order, in K. Zou (ed.), *Routledge Handbook of the South China Sea* (Routledge. 2021).

Barnes, R., The Convention on the Law of the Sea: An Effective Framework for Domestic Fisheries Conservation?, in D. Freestone *et al.* (eds.), *The Law of the Sea: Progress and Prospects* (OUP. 2006).

Dang, V.H., Biodiversity and Conservation, in K. Zou (ed.), *Routledge Handbook of the South China Sea* (Routledge. 2021).

Davenport, T., The Exploration and Exploitation of Hydrocarbon Resources in Areas of Overlapping Claims, in R. Beckman, *et al.* (eds.), *Beyond Territorial Disputes in the South China Sea Legal Frameworks for the Joint Development of Hydrocarbon Resources* (Edward Elgar Publishing. 2013).

Delbrück, J., The International Obligation to Cooperate–An Empty Shell or a Hard Law Principle of International Law? –A Critical Look at A Much Debated Paradigm of Modern International Law, in H. Hestermeyer and R. Wolfrum (eds.), *Coexistence, Cooperation and Solidarity: Liber Amicorum Rüdiger Wolfrum* (Brill. 2012).

Distefano, G., The Time Factor and Territorial Disputes, in M.G. Kohen and M. Hébié (eds.), *Research Handbook on Territorial Disputes in International Law* (Edward Elgar Publishing. 2018).

Diver, C.S., Regulatory Precision, in K. Hawkins and J. Thomas (eds.), *Making Regulatory Policy* (University of Pittsburgh Press. 1989).

Fitzmaurice, M., Conclusions: General Principles and Developing Areas of International Law, in M. Andenas *et al.* (eds.), *General Principles and the Coherence of International Law* (Brill|Nijhoff. 2019).

Freestone, D., and Oude Elferink, A.G., Flexibility and Innovation in the Law of the Sea – Will the LOS Convention Amendment Procedures Ever Be Used?, in A.G. Oude Elferink (ed.), *Stability and Change in the Law of the Sea: The Role of the LOS Convention* (Martinus Nijhoff Publishers. 2005).

Guilfoyle, D., The High Seas, in D.R. Rothwell *et al.* (eds.), *The Oxford Handbook of the Law of the Sea* (OUP. 2015).

Hébié, M., The Acquisition of Original Titles of Territorial Sovereignty in the Law and Practice of European Colonial Expansion, in M.G. Kohen and M. Hébié (eds.), *Research Handbook on Territorial Disputes in International Law* (Edward Elgar Publishing. 2018).

Hey, E., The Fisheries Provisions of the LOS Convention, in E. Hey (ed.), *Developments in International Fisheries Law* (Kluwer Law International. 1999).

Klein, N., Provisional Measures and Provisional Arrangements, in A.G. Oude Elferink, *et al.* (eds.), *Maritime Boundary Delimitation: The Case Law: Is it Consistent and Predictable?* (CUP. 2018).

Kohen, M.G., Titles and Effectivités in Territorial Disputes, in M.G. Kohen and M. Hébié (eds.), *Research Handbook on Territorial Disputes in International Law* (Edward Elgar Publishing. 2018).

Lee, S., and Bautista, L., Semi-enclosed Seas Cooperation under UNCLOS, in K. Zou (ed.), *Routledge Handbook of the South China Sea* (Routledge. 2021).

Leifer, M., Truth about the Balance of Power, in D. da Cunha (ed.), *The Evolving Pacific Power Structure* (Singapore: Institute of Southeast Asian Studies. 1996).

Letts, D., and Rothwell, D.R., Challenges for the law of the sea in South East Asia: resolving current controversies and addressing horizon threats, in D.R. Rothwell and D. Letts (eds.), *Law of the Sea in South East Asia: Environmental, Navigational and Security Challenges* (Routledge. 2019).

Liu, F.-K., Mainland China-Taiwan Interplay in the South China Sea, in K. Zou (ed.), *Routledge Handbook of the South China Sea* (Routledge. 2021).

Lowe, V., Sustainable Development and Unsustainable Arguments, in A. Boyle and D. Freestone (eds.), *International Law and Sustainable Development: Past Achievements and Future Challenges* (OUP. 1999).

Ma, X., The Spratly Islands and Territorial Rights, in M. Kocsis (ed.), *Global Encyclopedia of Territorial Rights* (Springer Nature. 2020).

McDorman, T.L., The Territorial Sovereignty Disputes in the South China Sea, in K. Zou (ed.), *Routledge Handbook of the South China Sea* (Routledge. 2021).

Merrills, J.G., The Principle of Peaceful Settlement of Disputes, in M. Akehurst, *et al.* (eds.), *The United Nations and the Principles of International Law: Essays in Memory of Michael Akehurst* (Routledge. 1994).

Moore, G., The Code of Conduct on Responsible Fisheries, in E. Hey (ed.), *Developments in International Fisheries Law* (Kluwer Law International. 1999).

Murphy, S.D., Obligations of States in Disputed Areas of the Continental Shelf, in T. Heider (ed.), *New Knowledge and Changing Circumstances in the Law of the Sea* (Brill. 2020).

O'Connell, M.E., The Prohibition on the Use of Force, in N.D. White and C. Henderson (eds.), *Research Handbook on International Conflict and Security Law: Jus ad Bellum, Jus in Bello and Jus post Bellum* (Edward Elgar Publishing. 2013).

N.B. O'Sullivan, The Case Law's Handling of Issues Concerning Third States, in A.G. Oude Elferink, T. Henriksen and S.V. Busch (eds.), *Maritime Boundary Delimitation: The Case Law: Is it Consistent and Predictable?* (CUP. 2018).

Ohnesorge, H.W., A Sea of Troubles: International Law and the Spitsbergen Plus Approach to Conflict Management in the South China Sea, in E. Fels and T.-M. Vu (eds.), *Power Politics in Asia's Contested Waters: Territorial Disputes in the South China Sea* (Springer. 2016).

Oral, N., The South China Sea Arbitral Award, Part XII of UNCLOS, and the Protection and Preservation of the Marine Environment, in S. Jayakumar, *et al.* (eds.), *The South China Sea Arbitration: The Legal Dimension* (Edward Elgar Publishing. 2018).

Pinto, M.C.W., The Duty of Co-operation and the United Nations Convention on the Law of the Sea, in A. Bos and H. Siblesz (eds.), *Realism in Law-making: Essays on International Law in Honour of Willem Riphagen* (Martinus Nijhoff Publishers. 1986).

Rabena, A.J., Philippines-China Joint Development Agreement in the South China Sea under Duterte, in H. Qi and S. Xue (eds.), *Cooperative Development in the South China Sea: Policies, Obstacles, and Prospects* (Routledge. 2021).

Redgwell, C., Mind the Gap in the GAIRS: The Role of Other Instruments in LOSC Regime Implementation in the Offshore Energy Sector, in N. Bankes and S. Trevisanut (eds.), *Energy from the Sea: An International Law Perspective on Ocean Energy* (Brill|Nijhoff. 2015).

Schofield, C., Untangling A Complex Web: Understanding Competing Maritime Claims in the South China Sea, in I. Storey and C.Y. Lin (eds.), *The South China Sea Dispute: Navigating Diplomatic and Strategic Tensions* (Singapore: ISEAS Yusof Ishak Institute. 2016).

Schrijver, N., Law of the Sea, in W.J.M. van Genugten, *et al.* (eds.), *Discover International Law: With Special Attention for the Hague, City of Peace and Justice* (Wolf Legal Publishers. 2017).

Scott, K.N., Integrated Oceans Management: A New Frontier in Marine Environmental Protection, in D.R. Rothwell *et al.* (eds.), *The Oxford Handbook of the Law of the Sea* (OUP. 2015).

Storey, I., Brunei's Contested Sea Border with China, in B. Elleman, *et al.* (eds.), *Beijing's Power and China's Borders: Twenty Neighbors in Asia* (Taylor and Francis. 2014).

Treves, T., Environmental Impact Assessment and the Precautionary Approach: Why Are International Courts and Tribunals Reluctant to Consider Them as General Principles of Law?, in M. Andenas *et al.* (eds.), *General Principles and the Coherence of International Law* (Brill|Nijhoff. 2019).

Treves, T., Historical Development of the Law of the Sea, in D.R. Rothwell *et al.* (eds.), *The Oxford Handbook of the Law of the Sea* (OUP. 2015).

Van Logchem, Y., The Scope for Unilateralism in Disputed Maritime Areas, in C. Schofield, *et al.* (eds.), *The Limits of Maritime Jurisdiction* (Brill. 2014).

Virzo, R., The 'General Rule of Interpretation' in the International Jurisprudence Relating to the United Nations Convention on the Law of the Sea, in A. Del Vecchio and Roberto Virzo (eds.), *Interpretations of the United Nations Convention on the Law of the Sea by International Courts and Tribunals* (Springer. 2019).

Vu, T., The Logic of Strategic Restraint and Prospects for Joint Development in the South China Sea, in A. Gerstl and M. Strašáková (eds.), *Unresolved Border, Land and Maritime Disputes in Southeast Asia: Bi- and Multilateral Conflict Resolution Approaches and ASEAN's Centrality* (Brill. 2017).

Wang, K., Fishery Disputes and Regional Cooperation, in C.J. Jenner (ed.), *The South China Sea A Crucible of Regional Cooperation or Conflict-making Sovereignty Claims?* (CUP. 2016).

White, G., The Principle of Good Faith, in M. Akehurst, *et al.* (eds.), *The United Nations and the Principles of International Law: Essays in Memory of Michael Akehurst* (Routledge. 1994).

Wu, S., China's Maritime Law Enforcement Practice in the South China Sea: Challenges and Prospects, in M.H. Nordquist, *et al.* (eds.), *Legal Order in the World's Oceans: UN Convention on the Law of the Sea* (Brill|Nijhoff, 2017).

Xue, G., The South China Sea: Competing Claims and Conflict Situations, in C. Schofield, *et al.* (eds.), *The Limits of Maritime Jurisdiction* (Brill. 2014).

Zou, K., Realizing Sustainability in the South China Sea, in K. Zou and S. Wu (eds.), *Non-Traditional Security Issues and the South China Sea: Shaping a New Framework for Cooperation* (Routledge. 2014).

Journal Articles

Barry, T., *et al.*, The Arctic Council: An Agent of Change?, 63 *Global Environmental Change* (2020).

Beddington, J.R., *et al.*, Current Problems in the Management of Marine Fisheries, 316(5832) *Science* (2007).

Bertram, C., *et al.*, Metalliferous Sediments in the Atlantis II Deep – Assessing the Geological and Economic Resource Potential and Legal Constraints, No. 1688 *Kiel Working Papers* (2011).

Buzan, B., Negotiating by Consensus: Developments in Technique at the United Nations Conference on the Law of the Sea, 75(2) *AJIL* (1981).

Abramson, S.F. and Carter, D.B., The Historical Origins of Territorial Disputes, 110 *American Political Science Review* (2016).

Barnes, R., The Convention on the Law of the Sea: An Effective Framework for Domestic Fisheries Conservation?, *The Law of the Sea: Progress and Prospects* (2006).

Barnes, R., The Law of the Sea Convention and the Integrated Regulation of the Oceans, 27 *IJMCL* (2012).

Bastida, A.E., *et al.*, Cross-Border Unitization and Joint Development Agreements: An International Law Perspective, 29 *Houston Journal of International Law* (2007).

Beckman, R. and Bernard, L., Framework for the Joint Development of Hydrocarbon Resources, *Centre for International Law, National University of Singapore* (2010).

Bennett, M., The People's Republic of China and the Use of International Law in the Spratly Islands Dispute, 28 *Stan. J. Int'l L.* (1991).

Bowett, D.W., The Dubai/Sharjah Boundary Arbitration of 1981, 65 *BYIL* (1994).

Boyle, A., Marine Pollution under the Law of the Sea Convention, 79 *AJIL* (1985).

Carty, A. and Lone, F.N., Some New Haven International Law Reflections on China, India and Their Various Territorial Disputes, 19 *Asia Pacific Law Review* (2011).

Chen, S., Environmental Cooperation in the South China Sea: Factors, Actors and Mechanisms, 85 *OCM* (2013).

Churchill, R.R., Fisheries Issues in Maritime Boundary Delimitation, 17 *Marine Policy* (1993).

Churchill, R.R., The Greenland-Jan Mayen Case and its Significance for the International Law of Maritime Boundary Delimitation, 9 *IJMCL* (1994).

Cordner, L.G., The Spratly Islands Dispute and the Law of the Sea, 25 *ODIL* (1994).

Dan, L., Difficulties and Solutions Relating to Environment Protection Cooperation in the South China Sea: A Critical Analysis of the South China Sea Arbitral Award (in Chinese), *Foreign Affairs Review* (2017).

Dang, T.N., Fisheries Co-operation in the South China Sea and the (Ir)relevance of the Sovereignty Question, 2 *Asian Journal of International Law* (2012).

Denoon, D.B.H. and Brams, S.J., Fair Division: A New Approach to the Spratly Islands Controversy, 2 *International Negotiation* (1997).

Distefano, G., The Conceptualization (Construction) of Territorial Title in the Light of the International Court of Justice Case Law, 19 *LJIL* (2006).

Dupuy, P.M., International Law: Torn between Coexistence, Cooperation and Globalization. General Conclusions, 9 *EJIL* (1998).

Dutton, P., Three Disputes and Three Objectives – China and the South China Sea, 64(4) *Naval War College Review* (2011).

Fitzmaurice, G., The Law and Procedure of the International Court of Justice, 1951–54, 31 *BYIL* (1954).

Franckx, E., Fisheries in the South China Sea: A Centrifugal or Centripetal Force?, 11 *CJIL* (2012).

French, D., In the Matter of the South China Sea Arbitration: Republic of Philippines v People's Republic of China, Arbitral Tribunal Constituted under Annex VII to the 1982 United Nations Law of the Sea Convention, Case No. 2013-19, Award of 12 July 2016, 19(1) *Environment Law Review* (2017).

Fry, J.D. and Loja, M.H., The Roots of Historic Title: Non-Western Pre-Colonial Normative Systems and Legal Resolution of Territorial Disputes, 27 *LJIL* (2014).

Gao, Z., Review and Prospect of the Security Cooperation Mechanisms in the South China Sea (in Chinese), 1 *Boundary and Ocean Studies* (2016).

Garrett, H., The Tragedy of the Commons, 162 *Science* (1968).

Gioia, A., Historic Titles, *MPEPIL* (2013).

Hasan, M., and Jian, H., Spratly Islands Dispute in the South China Sea: Potential Solutions, 12(1) *Journal of East Asia and International Law* (2019).

Henriksen, T. and Ulfstein, G., Maritime Delimitation in the Arctic: The Barents Sea Treaty, 42 *ODIL* (2011).

Hey, E., A Healthy North Sea Ecosystem and A Healthy North Sea Fishery: Two Sides of the Same Regulation?, 23 *ODIL* (1992).

Hey, E., The International Regime for the Protection of the North Sea: From Functional Approaches to a More Integrated Approach, 17 *IJMCL* (2002).

Hsiao, A., Opportunities for Fisheries Enforcement Cooperation in the South China Sea, 121 *Marine Policy* (2020).

Jensen, Ø., The Svalbard Treaty and Norwegian Sovereignty, 11 *Arctic Review on Law and Politics* (2020).

Jentoft, S. and Chuenpagdee, R., Fisheries and Coastal Governance as a Wicked Problem, 33 *Marine Policy* (2009).

Johnson, D.H.N., Consolidation as a Root of Title in International Law, 13 *Cambridge Law Journal* (1955).

Kao, S., *et al.*, Regional Cooperation in the South China Sea: Analysis of Existing Practices and Prospects, 43 *ODIL* (2012).

Khan, A.S. and Neis, B., The Rebuilding Imperative in Fisheries: Clumsy Solutions for a Wicked Problem?, 87 *Progress in Oceanography* (2010).

Kohen, M.G. and Hébié, M., Territory, Acquisition, *MPEPIL* (2011).

Kohen, M.G. and Hébié, M., Territory, Discovery, *MPEPIL* (2011).

Koo, M.G., Scramble for the Rocks: The Disputes over the Dokdo /Takeshima, Senkaku /Diaoyu, and Paracel and Spratly Islands, *ProQuest Dissertations Publishing* (2005).

Kwiatkowska, B., The Eritrea-Yemen Arbitration: Landmark Progress in the Acquisition of Territorial Sovereignty and Equitable Maritime Boundary Delimitation, 32 *ODIL* (2001).

Lagoni, R., Interim Measures pending Maritime Delimitation Agreements, 78 *AJIL* (1984).

Lennon, E., A Tale of Two Poles: A Comparative Look at The Legal Regimes in The Arctic And The Antarctic, 8(3) *Sustainable Development Law & Policy* (2008).

Lin, C., Taiwan's South China Sea Policy, 37 *Asian Survey* (1997).

Linebaugh, C., Joint Development in a Semi-Enclosed Sea: China's Duty to Cooperate in Developing the Natural Resources of the South China Sea, 52 *Columbia Journal of Transnational Law* (2014).

Li, J., *et al.*, Hydrocarbon Resources within the U-Shaped Line in the Southern China Sea: Distribution Characteristics and Development Status, 1 *China Oceans Law Review* (2013).

Loja, M.H., The Spratly Islands as a Single Unit Under International Law: A Commentary on the Final Award in Philippines/China Arbitration, 47 *ODIL* (2016).

Lucy, R. and Kenneth, W., Marine Entitlements in the South China Sea: The Arbitration Between the Philippines and China, 110 *AJIL* (2016).

Ma, X., Historic Title over Land and Maritime Territory, 4 *Journal of Territorial and Maritime Studies* (2017).

Ma, X., International Jurisprudence Concerning the Group or Unity Principle in Territorial Allocation, 18(1) *CJIL* (2019).

McCarthy, A.H., Antarctica: The Final Frontier for Marine Biological Invasions, 25 *Global Change Biology* (2019).

Milano, E. and Papanicolopulu, I., State Responsibility in Disputed Areas on Land and at Sea, 71 *Zeitschrift* (2011).

Murphy, B.K., Dangerous ground: The Spratly Islands and International Law, 1 *OCLJ* (1995).

Ong, D.M., Joint Development of Common Offshore Oil and Gas Deposits: 'Mere' State Practice or Customary International Law?, 93 *AJIL* (1999).

Oude Elferink, A.G., Does Undisputed Title to a Maritime Zone Always Exclude its Delimitation: The Grey Area Issue, 3 *IJMCL* (1998).

Oude Elferink, A.G., The Islands in the South China Sea: How Does Their Presence Limit the Extent of the High Sea and Area and the Maritime Zones of the Mainland Coasts, 32(2) *ODIL* (2001).

Oxman, B.H., The Duty to Respect Generally Accepted International Standards, 24 *NYUJ Int'l L. & Pol.* (1991).

Park, C.H., The South China Sea Disputes: Who Owns the Islands and the Natural Resources?, 5 *ODIL* (1978).

Pernetta, J.C. and Jiang, Y., Managing Multi-lateral, Intergovernmental Projects and Programmes: the Case of the UNEP/GEF South China Sea Project, 85 *OCM* (2013).

Perrez, F.X., The Efficiency of Cooperation: A Functional Analysis of Sovereignty, 15 *Arizona Journal of International and Comparative Law* (1998).

Roach, J. Ashley, Malaysia and Brunei: An Analysis of their Claims in the South China Sea, *Center for Naval Analyses Occasional Paper* (2014).

Roach, J.A., Offshore Archipelagos Enclosed by Straight Baselines: An Excessive Claim?, *ODIL* (2018).

Roberts, A., Traditional and Modern Approaches to Customary International Law: A Reconciliation, 95(4) *AJIL* (2001).

Ruys, T., The Meaning of 'Force' and the Boundaries of the Jus Ad Bellum: Are 'Minimal' Uses of Force Excluded from UN Charter Article 2(4)?, 108 *AJIL* (2014).

Scholfield, C., Blurring the Lines: Maritime Joint Development and the Cooperative Management of Ocean Resources, 7 *Issues Legal Scholarship* (2008).

Schrijver, N., Managing the Global Commons: Common Good or Common Sink?, 37(7) *Third World Quarterly* (2016).

Schrijver, N., The Changing Nature of State Sovereignty, 70 *BYIL* (1999).

Schrijver, N. and Prislan, V., Cases Concerning Sovereignty over Islands before the International Court of Justice and the Dokdo/Takeshima Issue, 46 *ODIL* (2015).

Schwarzenberger, G., Title to Territory: Response to a Challenge, 51 *AJIL* (1957).

Shearer, I.A., Problems of Jurisdiction and Law Enforcement Against Delinquent Vessels, 35 *ICLQ* (1986).

Smith, D.N., Mineral Agreements in Developing Countries: Structures and Substance, 69 *AJIL* (1975).

Song, Y.-H., The South China Sea Workshop Process and Taiwan's Participation, 41 *ODIL* (2010).

Song, Y.-H. and Tonnesson, S., The Impact of the Law of the Sea Convention on Conflict and Conflict Management in the South China Sea, 44 *ODIL* (2013).

Stephenson, M.A., Vessel-Source Pollution under the Law of the Sea Convention-An Analysis of the Prescriptive Standards, 17 *University of Queensland Law Journal* (1992).

Stevenson, J.R. and Oxman, B.H., The Third United Nations Conference on the Law of the Sea: The 1974 Caracas Session, 69(1) *AJIL* (1975).

Stevenson, J.R. and Oxman, B.H., The Third United Nations Conference on the Law of the Sea: The 1975 Geneva Session, 69(4) *AJIL* (1975).

Symonides, J., The Legal Status of the Enclosed and Semi-Enclosed Seas, 27 *German YB Int'l L.* (1984).

Tanaka, Y., Zonal and Integrated Management Approaches to Ocean Governance: Reflections on a Dual Approach in International Law of the Sea, 19 *IJMCL* (2004).

Thao, N., Maritime Delimitation and Fishery Cooperation in the Tonkin Gulf, 36 *ODIL* (2005).

Thao, N. and Amer, R., A New Legal Arrangement for the South China Sea?, 40 *ODIL* (2009).

Treves, T., The Law of the Sea' System' of Institutions, 2 *Max Planck Yearbook of United Nations Law* (1998).

Triggs, G., Legal and Commercial Risks of Investment in the Timor Gap, 1 *MJIL* (2000).

Triggs, G. and Bialek, D., The New Timor Sea Treaty and Interim Arrangements for Joint Development of Petroleum Resources of the Timor Gap, 3(2) *MJIL* (2002).

Trung, N., The Gas Hydrate Potential in the South China Sea, 88–89 *Journal of Petroleum Science and Engineering* (2012).

Tsamenyi, M. and Hanich, Q., Fisheries Jurisdiction under the Law of the Sea Convention: Rights and Obligations in Maritime Zones under the Sovereignty of Coastal States, 27 *IJMCL* (2012).

Tseng, H. and Ou, C., The Evolution and Trend of the Traditional Fishing Rights, 53(5–6) *OCM* (2010).

Tuan, V. and Pernetta, J., The UNEP/GEF South China Sea Project: Lessons Learnt in Regional Cooperation, 53 *OCM* (2010).

Udoinyang, I. and Igboekwe, M.U., The Impacts of Seismic Activities on Marine Life and its Environment, 2 *International Archive of Applied Sciences and Technology* (2011).

Usuki, E., China's Three Distinctive Assertions under the 'Nine-dash-line' Claims and the Annex VII Arbitral Tribunal's Interpretation of Article 121 Regarding an Island and Rocks under the 1982 UN Convention on the Law of the Sea, 21 *Asian Yearbook of International Law* (2015).

Valero, G., Spratly Archipelago Dispute: Is the Question of Sovereignty Still Relevant?, 18 *Marine Policy* (1994).

Van Heydte, F.A.F., Discovery, Symbolic Annexation and Virtual Effectiveness in International Law, 29 *AJIL* (1935).

Wang, D., From Dangerous Ground to Safe Playground: A Revisit to Fishery Co-operation in the South China Sea, 34 *Chinese (Taiwan) Yearbook of International Law and Affairs* (2016).

Wang, K.-H., Bridge over Troubled Waters: Fisheries Cooperation as a Resolution to the South China Sea Conflicts, 14 *The Pacific Review* (2001).

Wang, K.-H., The ROC's Maritime Claims and Practices with Special Reference to the South China Sea, 41 *ODIL* (2010).

Warner, R., Stemming the Black Tide: Cooperation on Oil Pollution Preparedness and Response in the South China Sea and East Asian Seas, 18 *Journal of International Wildlife Law & Policy* (2015).

Whiting, D., The Spratly Islands Dispute and the Law of the Sea, 26 *Denver Journal of International Law and Policy* (1998).

Whomersley, C., The Award on the Merits in the Case Brought by the Philippines against China Relating to the South China Sea: A Critique, 16 *CJIL* (2017).

Wolfrum, R., Cooperation, International Law of, *MPEPIL* (2010).

Wolfrum, R. and Pichon, J., Consensus, *MPEPIL* (2010).

Womack, B., The Spratlys: From Dangerous Ground to Apple of Discord, 33 *Contemporary Southeast Asia: A Journal of International and Strategic Affairs* (2011).

Xiao, F., and Liu, Z., Clan, Market, Bandits and Dan Min: Clan Groups and Society in the Pearl River Delta Since the Ming Dynasty (in Chinese), 3 *Journal of Chinese Social and Economic History* (2004).

Yang, P., Ocean Governance during the Qing Dynasty: The Evolution of Fisheries Tax Regulations in the Southeast Coast (in Chinese), 55(3) *Journal of Sun Yat-Sen University (Social Science Edition)* (2015).

Young, M. A. and Sullivan, S.R., Evolution through the Duty to Cooperate: Implications of the Whaling Case at the International Court of Justice, 16 *MJIL* (2015).

Zhang, H., Fisheries Cooperation in the South China Sea: Evaluating the Options, 89 *Marine Policy* (2018).

Zhao, B., The Curious Case of Ghana/Côte d'Ivoire: A Consistent Approach to Hydrocarbon Activities in the Disputed Area?, *Asian Journal of International Law* (2019).

Zou, K., Joint Development in the South China Sea: A New Approach, 21 *IJMCL* (2006).

Index